A Factious People

POLITICS AND SOCIETY IN COLONIAL NEW YORK

A FACTIOUS PEOPLE

POLITICS AND SOCIETY
IN COLONIAL NEW YORK

Patricia U. Bonomi

COLUMBIA UNIVERSITY PRESS
New York and London   *1971*

Copyright © 1971 Columbia University Press
ISBN: 0-231-03509-8
Library of Congress Catalog Card Number: 74-156803
Printed in the United States of America

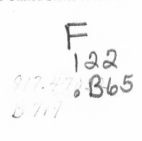

For Jack, Kathy, and John

PREFACE

THE WRITTEN HISTORY of colonial New York is at present not in an orderly state. Its condition hardly encourages anyone either to take up with confidence a study of some particular aspect of it or, in a more general way, to try fitting New York and its affairs into the larger story of colonial America. There are two major reasons for this. One is that there have been very few efforts to fashion an overall view of early New York life. The principal exception, the work of Carl Becker,[1] is being slowly buried under a growing accumulation of criticism, but no one as yet has taken the next step and produced a new synthesis that can replace the pattern of Becker's picture. The other problem has to do with the inordinately fragmented nature of recent work. There have been a number of good doctoral dissertations treating certain aspects of New York colonial history, but most of these have never been published. Instead, cullings from them are scattered through more than half a dozen scholarly journals, and though this is better than nothing, it does little to remedy the general disjointedness of the literature. Some specialized studies of great merit have recently been published; most notable among these is Stanley Katz's monograph on the Anglo-American aspects of New York politics. There have been a few recent biographies, some interesting volumes on the Beekmans and their mercantile activities, and some older and still useful studies of labor, land patterns, and New York City merchants. Each of these works sheds light on some otherwise dark corner of New York colonial life, but taken all together

[1] Carl Lotus Becker, *The History of Political Parties in the Province of New York, 1760–1776* (Madison, Wis., 1909, 1960). See also Chap. I below.

they form a whole which seems somehow less, not more, than the sum of its parts.[2]

The present study had its genesis in a conventional effort to carve out a restricted and "manageable" area of early New York history for a doctoral dissertation. But I wanted the principal focus to be on politics, and I very quickly discovered that there was no generally recognized context in which such a limited study might fit and thus no agreed-upon standards that could be counted on to guarantee it against triviality. The logic behind New York provincial politics, whatever it might be, seemed so shrouded by an intricate web of factional divisions, competing interests, and shifting patterns of leadership as to be virtually indiscernible. I could not hope to fit a particular piece of the picture into place if the picture itself were veiled in obscurity, and I did not feel that there was much point in studying political events in isolation. From this came my decision to survey instead the overall setting—social, economic, cultural, and geographic—within which New York politics evolved.

Chronologically the study covers the period from the aftermath of Leisler's Rebellion up to, but short of, the Revolution. "Short of," in order that political events might be seen consistently through the eyes of New Yorkers simply as provincials rather than as revolutionaries—which few knew they would become until the moment was virtually upon them. To assume that these people spent the last seventy years of their colonial history getting ready for their revolution—and that all else should be put down to aimless factionalism—did not seem the only available principle for finding unity in these events. The accumulation of political experience, the forming of political habits, the coming to act upon certain kinds of reflexes—in trivial matters as well as large ones, and in behalf of "selfish" interest as well as those of grave public import—promised at least something in the way of an alternative.

The present effort, then, is a survey and an exploratory one. It is not itself a "history" in any comprehensive sense; rather it reflects an effort to grasp in an intelligible way the main features of New York's early political life. The approach is topical; each chapter is built around some problem area in New York's provincial history and historiography. It is hoped that the drawing together of a variety of scat-

[2] For a note on the recent literature, see Bibliography, p. 317.

tered materials in one book will provide something of benefit to future work on these same subjects.

I wish to acknowledge my debt to a number of institutions that made available their extensive collections of early New York manuscripts. Foremost among them is the New-York Historical Society, whose curator of manuscripts, Mr. Arthur J. Breton, was ever alert to material which bore on my interests. The helpfulness and courtesy of Miss Judith Hale, Mr. Thomas Dunnings, and other staff members is also appreciated. My gratitude goes also to Miss Patricia E. Smith, Librarian, and Professor Jacob Judd, Consultant, at Sleepy Hollow Restorations, Irvington, New York; the New York Public Library, Rare Book and Manuscript Rooms; the Museum of the City of New York; Rutgers University Library, Special Collections Division; the New Jersey Historical Society; Columbia University Libraries, Special Collections; the New York State Library at Albany; the Municipal Archives and Records Center, New York City; and the Houghton Library of Harvard University. I also wish to thank the staff of the Warner Library, Tarrytown, New York, for their many services.

Prior to a final revision, the manuscript was carefully read and critically appraised by Stanley N. Katz and Alden Vaughan. It is better than it would have been as a result. The dependable support of Richard B. Morris, who encouraged the project at every point, and approved the latitude necessary for it to have been carried out in its present form, is warmly appreciated. It has been a pleasure to work with him.

PATRICIA UPDEGRAFF BONOMI

CONTENTS

ABBREVIATIONS

AHR	*American Historical Review*
CU	Columbia University
DAB	*Dictionary of American Biography*
DCHS	Dutchess County Historical Society
MCNY	Museum of the City of New York
MVHR	*Mississippi Valley Historical Review*
NJHS	New Jersey Historical Society
N.Y. Col. Docs.	*Documents Relative to the Colonial History of the State of New York.*
N.Y. Doc. Hist.	*Documentary History of the State of New York*
NYH	*New York History*
NYHS	New-York Historical Society
NYHS *Colls.*	New-York Historical Society, *Collections*
NYPL	New York Public Library
PRO	Public Record Office
PSQ	*Political Science Quarterly*
SHR	Sleepy Hollow Restorations
WMQ	*William and Mary Quarterly*

A Factious People

POLITICS AND SOCIETY IN COLONIAL NEW YORK

I

SOME PROBLEMS IN COLONIAL NEW YORK HISTORY

IF ONE WERE TO SKETCH the "character" of the modern State of New York, certain outstanding qualities would come immediately to mind. The people of New York are drawn from a remarkably rich mixture of races, religions, and cultures. The State's economy is a varied one, encompassing the Wall Street financial community, industrial and commercial centers, and important farming and dairy enterprises. Strong sectional feelings are reflected in an upstate-downstate rivalry that has had both political and economic consequences. All of these find expression in New York's politics, which are known to be raucous and schismatic, if always colorful. The modern observer is likely to associate these characteristics with the twentieth or, at the earliest, with the nineteenth century. But one need only go back to the colonial beginnings of New York to discover that all of these features were at least discernible, and most of them had taken firm root, before the start of the American Revolution.

From its earliest days New York has been the home of a diverse people; by the late seventeenth century, ethnic and religious identities ranged across what was for that time a remarkably broad spectrum.

New York's economy was a mixed one from the start, including agricultural and commercial enterprises of great variety. The upstate-downstate conflict was visible as early as the last quarter of the seventeenth century, and became a fixed feature during the eighteenth. As for New York's early politics, these were always spirited and contentious, particularly when evaluated against the prevailing assumptions of a deferential society. The formative years of New York's history are the central concern of this study, since the practices and habits that evolved then gave shape and direction to much that would follow.

Historians have given a good deal of attention to colonial New York over the years, but despite a substantial scholarly yield, few can be satisfied today that we have gained a true sense of the overall structure and quality of life in the province. This is most apparent in the area of politics, where a confusing tangle of factional alliances, clashing interests, and jockeyings among the elite, has led some historians to wonder whether meaningful patterns existed so early. This ambiguity has been augmented by certain problems connected with historical writing on the affairs of the province. For one thing, there are some important areas of disagreement among scholars over the meaning of various episodes and themes in New York's early life. Yet little attention has been directed toward reconciling these inconsistencies, which thus remain an integral if enigmatic part of the scholarship. Another difficulty is that the colony's history has with rare exceptions been examined in piecemeal fashion, one decade or one personality at a time. This has resulted in a number of distinguished monographic studies. But for all their detailed virtues these do not form themselves easily into a larger design, and one remains uncertain how to adjust one's vision in order to see them as anything but fragments. The history of New York Colony thus remains peculiarly a problem in perception. It is a question not simply of the facts and happenings which constitute that history, but of finding some proper range or perspective from which to view them.

Probably the most influential effort to impose some form of conceptual order on early New York life has been that made by Carl Becker. One cannot embark on any study of that subject without taking Becker's views into account; his work, in one sense microscopically detailed and in another boldly synthetic, constitutes a special problem in itself.

1. Carl Becker's View of Colonial New York

Becker's seminal study, *The History of Political Parties in the Province of New York, 1760–1776*,[1] was published over sixty years ago, but its impress upon our picture of New York Colony has been prodigious. One of the little recognized facts about Becker's book is that it claimed authority over no more than the immediate pre-Revolutionary period, as was clearly stated in the title. But because Becker, with a good historian's instinct, wanted to establish a background for the specialized side of his study, he devoted his first chapter to a brief sketch of New York's political evolution in the years from the Glorious Revolution to 1760. This was done in fairly broad strokes, much of it being based on secondary sources. The chapter was offered not so much as established fact but as a set of suggestions, a kind of hypothetical framework based on the then existing literature and reflecting what seemed reasonable to the author in the year 1909. After setting this forth as "background," Becker then proceeded in the ten chapters that followed to present his original findings about the period after 1760.

In the years since its publication, this book has had an intriguing history. As things turned out, it was Chapter I, not the others, that first made Becker's reputation. Becker's "background" chapter is the one still quoted most frequently today, while his original research concerning the period after 1760 is appreciated by only a few students of New York's very complicated immediate pre-Revolutionary history. The explanation has a certain simple beauty: no one else had, or has, ever offered such a convenient summary of eighteenth-century New York politics and society as Becker did in that opening chapter. The result has been that its well-phrased suggestions have gained an authority through the years which the author himself would probably never have claimed for them. Even the challenges that Becker's *Political Parties* has received [2] are in their way a measure of how coercive a single essay has

[1] (Madison, Wis., 1909).

[2] Three of Becker's Chapter I assertions are questioned by Milton Klein in "Democracy and Politics in Colonial New York," *New York History*, XL (July, 1959), 221–46; others are also challenged by Roger Champagne in "Family Poli-

been, and of how, in default of more extended efforts to see New York's colonial history whole, the symmetrically divided picture of colonial society that this one statement laid down could dominate the habits of mind of everyone who has since tried to think the subject through for himself.

Becker identified—or postulated—three levels of society in the colony. At the top was the aristocracy, composed of the great landed and merchant families. Next came the independent freeholders and freemen, and at the bottom were the unenfranchised mechanics and tenant farmers who, in Becker's view, composed over half the adult white male population. Because the majority of New York citizens appeared to be politically mute, Becker believed that the aristocracy was able to "control" political life, allying itself alternately with the governor or the Assembly in a continuous effort to safeguard upper-class privileges. The dominance of the aristocracy was further facilitated by the deferential habits and political apathy of the electorate. However, because the aristocrats demanded rights from the governor and the Crown in language heavy with references to "natural right and general welfare," these phrases became common coin, and from mid-century on were expressed with growing frequency "in the demands of the unenfranchised for political recognition." After 1760, the extra-legal mass activities of the common man, especially in New York City, became the "open-door" to political power, a door which the aristocrats tried to shut when they realized that their own leadership was being threatened by the new political awareness of the lower orders. Thus the Revolution became not only a struggle for "home rule" but also a contest over "who should rule at home." This much-quoted phrase is the final sentence of Becker's introductory chapter.

Many valuable insights are contained in this chapter, and indeed in those that follow. But Becker's confident emphasis on "aristocracy" and

tics versus Constitutional Principles: The New York Assembly Elections of 1768 and 1769," *WMQ,* 3rd Ser., XX (Jan., 1963), 57–79; and by Bernard Friedman, "The Shaping of the Radical Consciousness in Provincial New York," *Journal of American History,* LVI (Mar., 1970), 781–801. In later years Becker himself modified certain of his interpretations though the book on New York was never revised. See Bernard Mason, "The Heritage of Carl Becker, The Historiography of the Revolution in New York," *New-York Historical Society Quarterly,* LIII (April, 1969), 127–47.

the "common man"—characteristic, no doubt, of the era in which he wrote—and his acceptance of the then-prevalent belief that the colonial suffrage was severely restricted, have tended to blur with time and newer knowledge. On the other hand, nothing of a comprehensive nature has emerged to supplant the seeming clarity of Becker's picture, and though Becker's influence may have declined, unidentified traces of it lie everywhere around us. Meanwhile the process of fragmentation goes on. The perpetuation of small myths, successive borrowings from "background" sketches, the restricted nature of even the most careful scholarly digging—all in their way do as much, perhaps, to camouflage the historical landscape as to render its features more visible. Another effort to step back—perhaps as far back as Becker stood, but in a different place—seems indispensable.

2. The New York "Aristocracy": A Problem of Definition

One subject that certainly needs some fresh examination is that of the New York "aristocracy." It has long been recognized that one of the distinguishing features of the province, one of the characteristics that set it apart from all the other northern colonies, concerned the way in which its land was distributed. We hear much of "Patroons" and "Manor Lords," of Livingstons, Van Cortlandts, and Van Rensselaers, and have often been encouraged to think of these landed grandees as comprising a sort of neo-feudal aristocracy which imposed both economic and political restraints upon a numerous tenantry.[3] This must somehow be balanced by another body of facts, however, for it is also true that the patroonship system was a failure, with only one grant, Rensselaerswyck, lasting into the English period. And, though other large grants called "manors" were distributed by English governors to favored supporters, the greatest problem facing this nascent gentry was how to obtain tenant farmers for their estates. We have learned enough

[3] Becker, *Political Parties*, 8–10; Irving Mark, *Agrarian Conflicts in Colonial New York, 1711–1775* (New York, 1940), Chaps. II, III; Staughton Lynd, "Who Should Rule at Home? Dutchess County, New York, in the American Revolution," *WMQ*, 3rd Ser., XVIII (July, 1961), 330–59.

about the energy and enterprise of colonial immigrants to appreciate the view of one perceptive New York governor who believed that a man would be "a fool to become a base tenant" in New York "when for crossing Hudson's River that man can for a song purchase a good freehold in the Jersies." [4]

If it was so difficult to obtain tenants, how did the manors survive? The answer is that most of them did not; the majority were gradually parceled out among various family members, or broken down into smaller farms and sold outright. The few that retained their status as manors throughout the colonial period did so by surrendering nearly all the ancient privileges which historians who stress the semi-feudal character of New York land patterns rely upon to substantiate their interpretation. In addition to the manors a number of other large land patents were distributed in the colony, some to individual families and others to groups of speculators. While there is no question that this engrossment of land by a minority profoundly influenced the history of the colony, the old idea that manor "lords" and "patroons" ruled over the New York countryside seems to require further study. Concerning the political condition of residents on these manors and estates, for example, it has been shown that suffrage in New York Colony was fairly broad, and included tenants holding life leases—a class more numerous than had once been thought. Moreover, tenants did not always vote as their landlords wished, despite the obvious possibilities for intimidation in an age of open voting.[5]

A great deal more exploring needs to be done before we can ascertain with any certainty just how New York's land distribution policies affected the history of the colony. At the same time, no one taking a broad look at New York in the eighteenth century, either before or after the Revolution, can fail to be struck by the prominent part played by a number of landed magnates in the political life of the period. Alfred F.

[4] Earl of Bellomont to Lords of Trade, New York, Nov. 28, 1700, Edmund B. O'Callaghan and B. Fernow, eds., *Documents Relative to the Colonial History of the State of New York* (Albany, 1853–1887), IV, 791 (hereafter *N.Y. Col. Docs.*).

[5] Chilton Williamson, *American Suffrage, from Property to Democracy, 1760–1860* (Princeton, 1960), 27–29; Nicholas Varga, "Election Procedures and Practices in Colonial New York," *New York History*, LXI (July, 1960), 250–52, 254.

Young declares in his recent study of early New York State politics that "New York had a unique landlord aristocracy which no amount of revisionism is likely to erase from the Hudson Valley." [6] This may well be so, but "uniqueness" is itself intriguing. *How* was the New York aristocracy unique, and in comparison with what? How was it actually composed, and what was the role of the wealthy city merchant in that elite? How did the New York oligarchy, whatever its composition, differ from those, say, of Virginia and Massachusetts and Pennsylvania? And how, for that matter, did this "aristocracy" differ from that of England, after which it was supposedly modeled?

This last question, however often it may have been slurred over, is still not without interest. It was, after all, a society of Englishmen (and nominal Englishmen) and governed in some sense by English values. But it was clear from the first that no real "copy" of the British upper class would ever exist in America. No provision was ever made for a hereditary aristocracy in the colonies, nor was a specific branch of the provincial government constituted as the home of the aristocratic interest. Without a legally sanctioned sphere of influence, the colonial "aristocracy"—though it certainly existed in some form—never developed a definite function or identity. Nor was it ever certain who its members were, or precisely what the standards of admission should be. This uncertainty was made perennial by the frequency with which leaders rose from ordinary circumstances to positions of responsibility and honor, indicating that in practice talent and achievement, rather than blood lines or inherited wealth, were the essential components of "aristocracy" in the colonies. As one New Yorker put it: "Our Births are our Ancestors, but our Merit is our own." [7] Under these fluid circumstances it became impossible to preserve the restrictive class traditions which obtained in England.

This may be seen from the initial circumstances of some of those

[6] *The Democratic Republicans of New York, The Origins, 1763–1797* (Chapel Hill, 1967), viii.

[7] "The Vanity of Births and Titles; with the Absurdity of Claiming Respect without Merit," Sept. 20, 1753, No. XLIII, in Milton M. Klein, ed., *The Independent Reflector, or Weekly Essays on Sundry Important Subjects More particularly adapted to the Province of New-York, By William Livingston and Others* (Cambridge, Mass., 1963), 360.

usually referred to as "aristocrats" in the literature of New York history. Both Robert Livingston and Cadwallader Colden were sons of respectable but far from affluent Scotch Presbyterian ministers; Lewis Morris was the son of a captain in the Commonwealth army; Stephen DeLancey was a French-Huguenot refugee who arrived in New York in 1686 with the remains of his family's fortune—£300—in his pocket; William Smith was the son of a tallow chandler; the original Schuyler to settle in New York was the son of an Amsterdam baker; the first Philipse was a carpenter; and the original Van Cortlandt was a soldier with the Dutch West India Company. None of these men was from the lowest class, but neither were they "aristocrats"—not until they had made their mark on this side of the Atlantic. Once having done so, to be sure, those who had leisure and a taste for politics sought and received appointments to the governor's Council, the Supreme Court, and other high offices. This was in accord with English practice, and the public, imbued with the customs of an age of deference, offered a "becoming Regard"[8] to those who had gained positions of responsibility. In this manner a colonial "aristocracy" of a sort grew up, but compared with the true upper level of English society the colonial elite was a world apart, largely *nouveau riche* in composition, insecure in its pretensions, and infinitely less exclusive than its model.

The briefest look at the character of the New York General Assembly will indicate some of the difficulties that result from too casual an acceptance of the "aristocracy" notion. It has been said that the New York Assembly was "an exclusive gathering of merchant princes, landlords, and their spokesmen."[9] This assertion is based mainly on the frequency with which the names DeLancey, Morris, Philipse, Van Rensselaer, Schuyler, Livingston, and some others of equal familiarity appear on the rolls. Because one expects to find these men in the Assembly, their presence seems to confirm its aristocratic tone. But one cannot overlook the presence, at the same time, of many men with less familiar names—Kissam, Hansen, Snediker, Gale, LeCount, Micheaux, Miller, Seaman, Bruyn, Strong, Boerum, Groot, Wells, and Van Slyck,

[8] *Ibid.,* 359.

[9] Don R. Gerlach, *Philip Schuyler and the American Revolution in New York, 1733–1777* (Lincoln, Neb., 1964), 100; Lawrence Henry Gipson, *The Coming of the Revolution, 1763–1775* (New York, 1954), 129.

to mention but a few—whose origins were often so obscure that it is difficult to find any information about them in the sources. Perhaps, as has sometimes been suggested, they were mere "tools" of the elite. But we do not really know, because no one has ever studied the problem in depth.[10]

Cadwallader Colden is sometimes quoted on this point. The Assembly, he said in 1764, "consists of the owners of these extravagent Grants, the Merchants of New York . . . and, of common Farmers; which last are Men easily deluded and led away with popular arguements of Liberty and Privileges." Colden was not always the most reliable witness, things often being seen as it pleased him to see them at the moment. Thus in 1749, when he was locked in battle with the Assembly, he had had a different view of its members: "the generality of our Assembly consists of men of the lowest rank of People & very ignorant. . . ." [11] European observers, who often expressed surprise at the sort of men found sitting in colonial legislatures, would more likely have agreed with the 1749 assessment. Governor George Clinton declared that the New York assemblymen were an "ignorant, illiterate people, of Republican principles," while Governor Henry Moore said

[10] Irving Mark checked the landholdings of those who sat in the colonial Assembly after 1750. He asserts that the majority "were from the families of great estates," but because land categories are not clearly defined the material is less than conclusive. *Agrarian Conflicts,* 93–94. Jackson Turner Main analyzed the composition of the final Assembly elected in 1769 and concluded that nearly all of the New York legislators "had either always belonged to or had successfully entered the colony's economic and social upper class." "Government by the People, The American Revolution and the Democratization of the Legislatures," *WMQ,* 3rd Ser., XXIII (July, 1966), 394. Even if further research should confirm this, we will still need to know how many of the preceding thirty assemblies conform to this pattern. Some interesting suggestions are made about Assembly membership in the period from 1737 to 1748 in Nicholas Varga, "New York Government and Politics," though again statistical categories need to be more carefully refined. I have made a cursory check into the backgrounds of the eighty-six men who sat in the Assembly from 1750 to 1775. Using categories based largely on family connections and occupation, I find that the assemblymen were approximately one-third patrician, one-third substantial middle-class (i.e., rising lawyers, merchants, or landholders who had considerably exceeded their fathers' economic standing), and one-third moderate middle-class (i.e., substantial yeomen, shopkeepers, and country merchants).

[11] Lt. Gov. Colden to Board of Trade, Sept. 20, 1764, *N.Y. Col. Docs.,* VII, 655; Colden to Dr. John Mitchell, July 6, 1749, NYHS *Colls.,* LXVIII (1935), 33.

the Assembly was "composed of plain well-meaning men, whose notions from their education, are extremely confined. . . ." [12]

Sufficient uncertainty exists in this realm that further investigation,
not only into the social and economic makeup of the Assembly but into
other aspects of its character as well, would seem warranted. What sorts
of patterns, if any, are revealed in recorded Assembly divisions? What
effect did the small size of the New York Assembly (twenty-seven
members until 1773 when it was enlarged to thirty-one) have on the
quality of representation in the colony? As for the colonial suffrage,
we now know that the potential electorate in the colonies was much
larger than in England. Though the implications of this unplanned en-
franchisement may have taken a long time to penetrate the colonial consciousness, it would be surprising if the political life of this first modern
society to include the majority of adult white males within the electorate
were not thereby affected in significant ways. Whatever conclusions one
reaches about the "aristocratic" character of New York's leadership will
have to be measured against its remarkable responsiveness to public
opinion. [13] All of these problems will receive attention in the following
pages. Some, whose dimensions are such that the present work cannot
do them full justice, will in time, it is hoped, receive studies of their
own.

3. Political Factionalism: A "divided" and "contentious" People

Another problem area is pointed up by Carl Becker's provocative assertion that the New York aristocracy "controlled" colonial politics. "Control" connotes stability, tranquility, and order. Yet New York's early

[12] "Abstract of the evidence in the book of the Lords of Trade, relating to New
York," 1751, *N.Y. Col. Docs.*, VI, 671; Moore to Hillsborough, Jan. 4, 1769,
ibid., VIII, 143.

[13] Assemblymen frequently expressed the wish to "consult their Constituents," or
were restrained by "fear of disobliging their Constituents." In 1734 one representative warned his Assembly colleagues that their posts of honor were "but like a
fine laced Livery coat of which the vain Lacquey may be stript at the pleasure of
his proud Master [the electorate] & may be kikt out of Doors naked." *Journal of
the Votes and Proceedings of the General Assembly of the Colony of New York,*

history positively echoes with political strife: antagonistic forces were constantly in motion, seething and rumbling and periodically erupting into open conflict. New York historians devote much of their energy to sorting out the various factions or parties [14] which kept the colony's political life in an almost constant state of turmoil. And if one were to select the single most persistent theme running through the commentary of colonial politicians themselves, it would be the emphasis they put on the factiousness and volatility of their politics. Nothing about it was ever "controlled" for very long, by an aristocracy or anyone else.

It was at about the time of Leisler's Rebellion in 1689 that New York's reputation as a colony riven by "divisions and distractions" began to grow. When Governor Fletcher arrived in 1692, he reported: "A divided, contentious impoverished people I find them . . . neither Party will be satisfied with less than the necks of their Adversaries." Another observer wrote home in 1698 that New York's "discentions" had caused the new governor, the Earl of Bellomont, to be ill treated by the people. "Am sure if the Roman Catholicks have a place of purgatory," he averred, "its not soe bad as [this] place is under my Lords Circumstance." [15] The colonists themselves recognized and ostensibly deplored the prevalence of party disputes. In 1702, Robert Livingston declared: "We have a poor dispirited people, a mixture of English, Dutch, and French . . . they are not unanimous, & doe not stick to one another." Governors had learned that they could take advantage of

---

1691–1765 (New York, Hugh Gaine, 1764–66), I, June 14, 1734; Gov. Clinton to Robert Hunter Morris, Ft. George, May 19, 1751, Robert Hunter Morris Papers, NJHS; "Speech of Vincent Matthews read before the General Assembly of the Province of New York on October 21, 1735," copy, NYHS *Colls.*, LXVII (1934), 239.

[14] Because eighteenth-century New Yorkers used "party" as a synonym for faction, that practice also will be followed here. The early usage was sufficiently special, however, to require careful definition. The word party will be used in this study to identify any group of men with a temporary common interest, which assumed a stance in opposition to any other group of men with a temporary common interest.

[15] Richard Ingoldesby to the Duke of Bolton, Ft. Wm. Henry, April 28, 1692, *N.Y. Col. Docs.*, III, 834; Gov. Fletcher to Mr. Blathwayt, New York, Sept. 10, 1692, *ibid.*, 848; Margaret Kinard, ed., "John Usher's Report on the Northern Colonies, 1698," *WMQ*, 3rd Ser., VII (Jan., 1950), 101. For Bellomont's complaints to the Lords of Trade, see *N.Y. Col. Docs.*, IV, 783, 791.

this by "Striking in with one Party & they assist him to destroy the other. . . ." [16]

The decade of relative calm during Governor Robert Hunter's tenure (1710–1719) was brief, and after Hunter's departure New Yorkers resumed their former ways. They reached new peaks of factionalism during the Cosby era, which was climaxed by the famous Zenger trial of 1735. During the period that followed, Governor George Clinton and his chief adviser, Cadwallader Colden, sent a barrage of complaints about their political opponents, a "malicious faction," to Whitehall. Clinton justified his helplessness by pointing out that it was "well known that for some years before my arrival in this Government the publick affairs had been distracted by parties and oppositions which had been carried to a great hight." During the eighteenth century colonial governors were often warned in their instructions that New Yorkers were "Unhappily divided" and that "their Enmity to Each other" was undermining respect for authority. Except for rare moments of peace, discord continued to increase, reaching such a pitch in the late 1760's that James Duane's was a typical lament: "We are . . . run mad with Faction & party." [17] Even at the time of the colony's final division into Loyalists and Patriots, the factions were so evenly split that some feared the Provincial Congress would never reach any decision. "We Shall ruin all our Selves & Continent by our divisions," warned Robert Livingston, Jr., "which may be worse to us than what the Parliment can do." [18]

[16] Quoted in Lawrence H. Leder, "The Politics of Upheaval in New York, 1689–1709," *New-York Historical Society Quarterly,* XLIV (Oct., 1960), 426. See also William Smith, *The History of the Late Province of New-York, From its Discovery, to the Appointment of Governor Colden, in 1762* (New York, 1830), I, 278–82, II, 8–9, 192; Thomas Jones, *History of New York During the Revolutionary War* (New York, 1879), I, 1.

[17] Clinton to Lords of Trade, June 22, 1747, *N.Y. Col. Docs.,* VI, 352, 364; Gov. Burnet to Lords of Trade, New York, Sept. 24, 1720, *ibid.,* V, 573; "Gov. Montgomeries Instructions, Oct. 20, 1727," copy, NYHS *Colls.,* L (1917), 233; Duane to Robert Livingston, Jr., Feb. 19, 1770, Livingston-Redmond MSS, Reel 6. In 1753 the Earl of Halifax acknowledged that because of "unhappy Divisions" the government of New York had "long been in a state of disorder and distraction. . . ." Halifax to Colden, Grosvenor Square, May 17, 1753, NYHS *Colls.,* LIV (1921), 389–91. See also Gov. Moore to Earl of Hillsborough, New York, Jan. 4, 1769, *N.Y. Col. Docs.,* VIII, 143–44.

[18] Livingston to James Duane, Livingston Manor, Mar. 8, 1775, Duane Papers. See also Dr. John Jones to Duane, July 13, Dec. 7, 1775, April 14, 1776, Duane Papers, NYHS.

A fully satisfactory principle of explanation for this bellicose and unstable political climate, in which juntos formed, broke apart, and reassembled in seemingly haphazard patterns, has not yet been found. The familiar "rise of the assembly" concept still has a certain schematic usefulness when applied to the final crisis of 1776. But it gives few clues to New York's internal political development throughout the greater part of the century, during which there were at least a dozen more or less identifiable factions whose membership and allegiances were forever changing. Unlike the Virginia House of Burgesses, the New York General Assembly rarely functioned as a unit. A battleground of faction, the Assembly was often caught up in "frivolous" and "vexatious" personal debates in which the defense of Assembly prerogatives and colonial rights were not, properly speaking, the dominant themes.[19]

On the other hand, it may be unwise to view these groupings *too* narrowly, as though they were mere family factions, like Capulets and Montagues, or provincial Guelphs and Ghibellines.[20] To be sure, their quarrels often seem to boil up out of petty causes. It is difficult, for example, to discern the statesmanship of throwing the whole colony into an uproar over how to divide the salary of an acting governor, or whether the governor was entitled to replace certain provincial officeholders. And yet these conflicts may not have been quite so trifling and self-seeking as they sometimes appeared. One is struck by the frequency with which these little quarrels "skidded off their original tracks onto elevating planes of disputation and ended deadlocked in the realm of principle."[21] More seems to have been at stake here than mere per-

[19] *Journal of the Votes and Proceedings of the General Assembly of the Colony of New-York, from 1766 to 1776* (Albany, J. Buel, 1820), Dec. 16, 1768. Carl Becker long ago saw the inadequacy of this explanation for New York, and Stanley Katz has recently confirmed his judgment. Becker, *Political Parties,* 16–17; Katz, *Newcastle's New York: Anglo-American Politics, 1732–1753* (Cambridge, Mass., 1968), 44–45.

[20] Robert V. Remini, ed., *The Decline of Aristocracy in the Politics of New York, 1801–1840* by Dixon Ryan Fox (New York, 1965), xxiii; Becker, *Political Parties,* 12–14; George Dangerfield, *Chancellor Robert R. Livingston of New York, 1746–1813* (New York, 1960), 21; Gerlach, *Philip Schuyler,* 104. Jack P. Greene suggests a "rough typology" for colonial political groups in "Changing Interpretations of Early American Politics," in Ray Allen Billington, ed., *The Reinterpretation of Early American History* (New York, 1966, 1968), esp. 176–77.

[21] Bernard Bailyn, *The Origins of American Politics* (New York, 1968), 65.

sonal prestige or family reputation. We must account for the remarkable pugnacity of the contending parties, for the almost jubilant way they took up any challenge from a governor or rival faction, and for their apparent eagerness to test the limits of authority. Were there, after all, underlying themes, larger motives, an inherent direction?

4. "As the twig is bent . . ."

If the political experience of a community is indeed cumulative, and if it is possible to discern continuities in such experience over time, then it may not be entirely fanciful to connect one striking set of circumstances in that community's political history to other circumstances, equally striking, that seem to emerge at a much later stage. Political contention and political factionalism of a peculiarly virulent sort appeared very early in colonial New York, and persisted with an intensity, even in comparison with other contentious colonies, that gives a special color to its politics. And yet it was in that same New York, no longer a colony but now a republican state, that political contention was itself first institutionalized. New York, early in the nineteenth century, would be the first to learn not only that "faction" was not to be done away with but that it could actually be stabilized and made more or less predictable, even tolerable, as a political way of life.

It is generally agreed that Jacksonian New York is where one must look for the beginnings of an authentic two-party system in the United States. With Martin Van Buren and the Albany Regency one finds both the architect and the prototype of Andrew Jackson's party structure. Van Buren's techniques of political organization were very sophisticated indeed, and for a wholly informal structure the Regency possessed a cohesiveness and stability that was more than a product of happy accident.[22] Or so one is impelled to conclude. One must assume, that is,

[22] Robert V. Remini, *Martin Van Buren and the Making of the Democratic Party* (New York, 1959), Chap. I. "To stay alive in the New York political world," says Remini of the early nineteenth century, "one had to be clever, shrewd, and sometimes unscrupulous" (p. 3). As a "political manager" Van Buren was "one of the foremost in the history of this nation" (p. 2). For the importance of Van Buren and the Regency to the eventual acceptance of political parties, see Richard Hofstadter, *The Idea of a Party System: The Rise of Legitimate Opposition in the United States, 1780–1840* (Berkeley, Calif., 1969), 221–26, 238–52.

that the Regency was more than a materialization from the wand of the "Little Magician." It was the product of experience, not only Van Buren's experience but that of a long line of predecessors.

One thinks of Burrites, Tammanyites, Jayites, and Clintonians; of the Federalists and Antifederalists who battled it out for seven months in 1788; of the Whigs and Tories of Revolutionary times; and thence back to colonial factions led by Morrises, DeLanceys, Philipses, and Livingstons. With each step back the image fades somewhat, but it is nonetheless discernible, especially when compared to party development in other areas at corresponding times. It is as if each early conflict constituted a layer, and eventually a base, of political experience that was not lost. It thus may be not so much "family" as sheer experience, experience at the center of things, that forms the real tie of kinship and ancestry whereby Martin Van Buren and these many predecessors are connected.

5. "Who should rule at home"?

All of which suggests a final question: What are we to do with Carl Becker's familiar aphorism about the Revolution in New York being in part a contest over "who should rule at home"? There may be more than a little reason to guess that on this point Becker was right, though perhaps not on quite the ground he supposed. The colony, to be sure, was perennially divided, and these divisions reflected themselves in the vicissitudes of politics. Whether these are to be diagnosed in terms of "class," as Becker did, is another matter. The politics of the colony seem much too intricate, and at the same time too fluid, to be explained by such a rigid principle. But were we to suspend, or at least subordinate, the principle of class in order to survey without preconceptions some of the peak periods of factional strife, other connecting themes might very possibly emerge.

To expect that "class" can be largely supplanted by any other single principle is asking a great deal. Still, the principle of politics—simply as politics—does seem to hold a certain promise. In a colony as complex as this one—where the cultural and religious mixture was as rich as that of any province in America; where merchants, landowners, artisans, and tenant farmers all vied for economic advantage; and where rivalry between New York City and the upriver interior was an endemic irritation—the materials for contention, of all sorts, were everywhere at hand. Superimposed on all this, of course, were the familiar jockeyings for position and place among the colony's governing elite. But these, too, are a vital part of the equation. They did not occur in quite the isolated vacuum one associates with the personal politics of Walpole's England, and for that reason they deserve to be taken with some seriousness. They occurred in a context that included the internal problems of the entire province, as well as those of imperial relations, and they drew in ever larger numbers of people as time went on. Indeed, the "mere" desire for office may itself, considering the following that an energetic and ambitious man may attract, have a real unifying function.[23] There were always polarities enough in the public affairs of New York —unlike a number of other colonies where the interests were less diverse—that could, well short of tearing the colony apart, make for a chronic, and eventually more or less stable, condition of factionalism. This habitual factionalism, this politics for its own sake, laid the foundation of experience upon which such future architects of party organization as Martin Van Buren would eventually build.

[23] And a democratizing function as well; *vide* James S. Young: "[W]e have to thank that which we delight to scorn for that which we most cherish. We have to thank the thirst for power among ingenious politicians for the creation of American democracy." *The Washington Community, 1800–1828* (New York, 1966), 254.

II

~~~~~~

SETTLEMENT AND EXPANSION

In 1776 JOHN ADAMS, exasperated by the divided and sluggish response of New York to the Revolutionary crisis, wondered whether there might have been something in the very "air or soil of New York" that could explain the peculiar political behavior of its people.[1] Actually, there was. In New York, perhaps to a greater degree than in most other colonies, such primary factors as geography and climate had an important influence on the way people adapted to the land and, in turn, to each other. Patterns of settlement, economic developments, political relationships, and cultural forms were all strongly affected at the outset by the physical environment.

The importance of the Hudson River, that broad artery which penetrated 150 unobstructed miles into a fur- and timber-rich interior, was fundamental, and the immediate accessibility of those valuable resources set the initial pattern of exploitation. Later, when people began to arrive in large numbers, the Hudson River encouraged a dispersion of settlement which, from the very beginning, gave a uniquely centrifugal impetus to the colony's political and social institutions. Another important feature was New York's geographic relationship to New Eng-

[1] John Adams to William Tudor, Philadelphia, June 24, 1776, in Charles Francis Adams, ed., *The Works of John Adams* (Boston, 1850–1856), IX, 411.

land. New York's presence on the western and southern borders of the New England colonies posed a barrier to their expansion and made for a sectional rivalry that was to have political, social, and economic consequences. This proximity also contributed to the cultural and religious heterogeneity of New York's population, for the colony was subject to a continuous stream of migrating New Englanders as well as to penetration by two sets of conquerors, the Dutch and the English. The centrality of New York's location relative to the other English colonies, combined with its position as the gateway to Canada, was critical in other ways. The natural path northward formed by the Hudson River, Lake George, and Lake Champlain gave New York an unparalleled strategic value, and in no colony was the imperial presence, in the form of British troops and officials, more visible.

Such were a few of the environmental influences at work in the colony of New York. Being present from the beginning, they tended to give initial direction to a number of the social, cultural, and political patterns that would evolve in the course of time and set the essential "character" of the colony. It would thus be well to examine some of these patterns at their inception.

1. "A mixture of Nations"

New York's beginnings, as with so much else in its history, were not typical. Projected neither as a haven for religious refugees nor as a government-sponsored economic outpost, the colony's origins were narrowly commercial and singularly unidealistic. Recent investigation shows that Henry Hudson's 1609 voyage, which led to the first probing of the river that bears his name, was financed by a group of Amsterdam merchants who, though connected with the Dutch East India Company, apparently underwrote the exploration as a private rather than as a company venture. In the decade or so following that initial voyage a number of Amsterdam merchant groups, eager to take part in the vastly profitable fur trade, engaged in a competition so fierce and produced a situation so chaotic that the States General finally was compelled to intervene to restore peace. The result was the formation of the Dutch

West India Company, which was granted a monopoly of all trade to New Netherland. "The issuance of the West India Company's charter in 1621," according to Thomas J. Condon, "was not the signal for the beginning of any massive attempt to settle inhabitants of the Netherlands permanently abroad . . . for the purpose of developing a new society." Commercial exploitation continued to be the main goal of the Dutch West India Company, though that exploitation now was dedicated to the greater glory of the Dutch nation rather than to filling the pockets of a few private merchants.[2]

A handful of Dutchmen had taken up temporary residence in New Netherland in the second decade of the seventeenth century when trading posts were established at either end of the Hudson River to facilitate the fur trade with the Indians. So profitable did that trade become under the Dutch West India Company that for several years all efforts were devoted to that end alone with little heed being given to long-term development of the colony. Though the first sizeable settlement of several Walloon families was installed at Fort Orange (Albany) in 1624, and a few settlers arrived at New Amsterdam (New York City) the following year, the intended permanence of these little settlements is still uncertain. Some recent historical opinion favors the view that they were projected as fur trading posts rather than as stable colonial plantings. It was not long, however, before the home government realized that more regular settlement was essential if the colony was to hold its own against English claims to the entire area from French Canada to Spanish Florida. As an inducement to permanent settlers the company decided to exploit another resource made accessible by the beneficent Hudson River. After 1629, free land was offered to any colonist who would pay his own passage, and somewhat later the company even agreed to assume the cost of transportation. Moreover, huge tracts and

---

[2] Thomas J. Condon, *New York Beginnings: The Commercial Origins of New Netherland* (New York, 1968), 9–10, 67. This book is somewhat revisionist in its findings, stressing the commercial rather than the colonizing motives behind Dutch overseas expansion in the early seventeenth century. For another view that gives almost equal weight to commerce and agriculture in the period after 1623, consult Van Cleaf Bachman, *Peltries or Plantations: The Economic Policies of the Dutch West India Company in New Netherland, 1623–1639* (Baltimore, 1969), Chaps. I–III.

the title of "Patroon" were bestowed upon company stockholders who agreed to settle fifty persons on their estates within four years.[3]

Early patterns of settlement followed the logic of geography. New Amsterdam slowly expanded to fill in adjacent parts of Kings County and Staten Island; at the same time, the upriver fur trading center at Fort Orange grew outward to the north and west with a concentration of settlers at Schenectady. As farmlands became more scarce in the southern counties, recently arrived colonists moved out into the Hudson River counties, sprinkling settlements up and down the Hudson Valley. The Dutch effort to attract patroons was never very successful,[4] with the result that the early settlement of the Hudson Valley—that is, to about 1680—most often reproduced the familiar pattern of individual purchase of small farms or concentrated settlement by groups. Some colonists preferred the more conveniently situated east bank of the river and purchased farms or leased land in present-day Westchester, Dutchess, and Albany counties. Others sought the opportunities of the raw frontier and settled on the western bank of the Hudson in Orange and Ulster counties. The colony enjoyed a slow but steady growth and by the middle of the seventeenth century had accumulated a population of several thousand scattered along the seaboard and all the way up the Hudson River to Fort Orange and Schenectady.[5]

[3] Condon, *New York Beginnings,* 69–78; John Romeyn Brodhead, *History of the State of New York* (New York, 1853–1871), I, 158–59, 194–203, 265, 691; Alexander C. Flick, ed., *History of the State of New York* (New York, 1933–1937), I, Chap. 7. Bernard H. M. Vlekke, *Evolution of the Dutch Nation* (New York, 1945), 215; Pieter Geyl, *The Netherlands in the Seventeenth Century* (London, 1936, 1961), 158–67, 197–208.

[4] Because anything which smacked of feudalism was novel in colonial America, the Dutch patroonships have received more attention from historians than their importance merits. Only five patroonships were ever granted and only one of these, Rensselaerswyck, lasted beyond the first years of the English period. In fact, it was under English governors, especially from about 1680 to 1696, that the great landed estates of New York were patented. *Calendar of New York Colonial Manuscripts Indorsed Land Papers; in the Office of the Secretary of State of New York, 1643–1803* (Albany, 1864). For a convenient listing of the great patents with the dates of their issuance, see Irving Mark, *Agrarian Conflicts in Colonial New York, 1711–1775* (New York, 1940, 1965), 21. For judicious estimates of the transitory importance of the patroonships, consult David M. Ellis et al., *A Short History of New York State* (Ithaca, N.Y., 1957), 21–22; and Condon, *New York Beginnings,* 125–43.

[5] *Calendar of Land Papers,* 3–52.

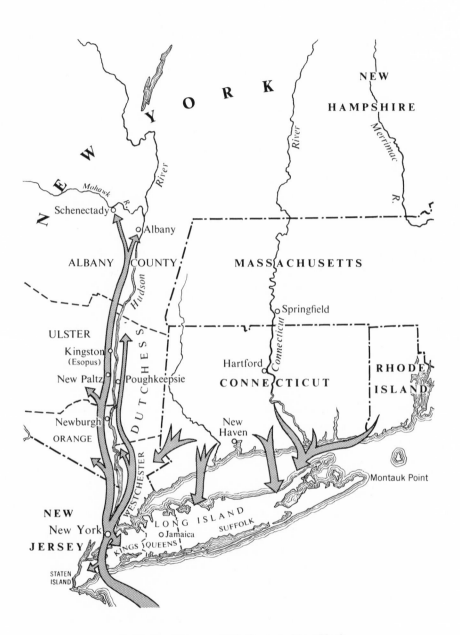

Settlement Flow—17th-Century New York

This immediate penetration of settlement far into the interior is unique in the annals of the English colonies. It was possible in New York only because the majestic dimensions of the Hudson made that river a broad natural highway into the colony's heartland. In most colonies the population clustered along the Atlantic seaboard until after 1700, when some outward movement began. Only in the Hudson and Connecticut River valleys and in parts of the Chesapeake area did interior settlement take place at the outset, and New York's extension was by far the most spectacular.

The first tide of settlers up the Hudson Valley was predominantly Dutch, but after the English conquest in 1664, a second major strain was added. Officials and other newcomers from England at first settled mainly in the southern section, particularly in New York, Westchester, and Queens counties. New York City rapidly took on a binational and then a multinational cast, with the Dutch making up slightly less than one-half of the white population by 1698. In the upriver areas, however, the Dutch remained the dominant element, in 1698 composing 66 per cent of the white population of Dutchess and Ulster counties, 75 per cent in Orange County, and an overwhelming 93 per cent in Albany County, which was to remain the stronghold of Dutch influence throughout the colonial period.[6]

Starting in the 1640's, and concurrent with the Dutch migration up the Hudson Valley, an additional stream of settlers was flowing out of Connecticut onto the eastern end of Long Island and into Westchester County. These settlers, all New Englanders, represented another special cultural strain in New York's rapidly diversifying population. The New Englanders' movement onto Long Island was relatively peaceful, they being the first to settle in that part of the colony. From their initial toehold on the island they gradually moved west, establishing typical New England towns at Southold, Easthampton, Southampton, and Hempstead, halting only when they met the Dutch settlements in Kings

[6] Brodhead, *History,* II, 156–57; American Council of Learned Societies Report of Committee on Linguistic and National Stocks in the Population of the United States, *Annual Report* of the American Historical Association for the Year 1931 (Washington, D.C., 1932), 120. Kings County also retained its strong Dutch character, that stock making up 88 per cent of the white population in 1698. In the other counties the Dutch percentages were: Richmond, 50; Westchester, 33; Queens, 7½, and in Suffolk, none.

Distribution of Colonial Population, 1650
(Each dot: approximately 200 inhabitants)

Adapted from Herman R. Friis, "A Series of Population
Maps of the Colonies and the United States, 1625–1790,"
Geographical Review, XXX (July, 1940), 464.

County. The New Englanders' migration into Westchester, which became very substantial by the 1680's, was less easily accomplished. It met resistance from established Dutch and French settlements as well as from imperial officials and favorites who had estates in the county. The New Englanders' attempt to claim parts of Westchester for Connecticut did little to ease the friction, and the situation had become so explosive by 1700 that the Crown had to intervene to uphold New York's title to the area.[7]

In addition to Dutch, English, and New England elements, still other national strains were present in New York Colony. A substantial French-Huguenot immigration occurred after 1685, "the most opulent" settling in New York City while others "planted New Rochelle, and a few seated themselves at the New Paltz in Ulster County." Twenty-five hundred German Palatines arrived under imperial sponsorship in 1710 to engage in the production of naval stores. When the program failed two years later, some of these people moved on to New Jersey or Pennsylvania while others elected to take their chances in New York. A number of them stayed in the upper Hudson Valley but most spread out into the Mohawk and Schoharie valleys in cohesive settlements such as Palatine Bridge and German Flats. In addition to these sizeable national groups there were smaller contingents of Scotch, Irish, Swedes, Portuguese Jews, and of course Negro slaves, each making its distinctive contributions to New York's polyglot character.[8]

By the early part of the eighteenth century, Dutch influence was centered at Albany, and the English were located mainly in New York County and environs. New Englanders, meanwhile, composed almost

[7] Albert E. McKinley, "The English and Dutch Towns of New Netherland," *American Historical Review,* VI (Oct., 1900), 1–18; Brodhead, *History,* I, 300–1, 322–24, 722; Dixon Ryan Fox, *Yankees and Yorkers* (New York, 1940), 60–63, 71–72, 106–9, 129–37; J. Thomas Scharf, ed., *History of Westchester County, New York* (Philadelphia, 1886), I, 25–26, 161. During the years of Dutch rule the New Englanders also tried to claim eastern Long Island for Connecticut, but these efforts diminished after the English conquest.

[8] William Smith, *The History of the Late Province of New-York, From its Discovery, to the Appointment of Governor Colden, in 1762* (New York, 1830), I, 270–71; Brodhead, *History,* II, 311–12, 625; Scharf, ed., *History of Westchester,* I, 27–28; Samuel W. Eager, *An Outline History of Orange County* (Newburgh, N.Y., 1846–47), 82–84. The story of the Huguenot settlements is summarized in Flick, ed., *History,* II, Chap. 4. The Palatines in New York are discussed in Wal-

the total population of Suffolk County and were strong in Queens, parts of Westchester and, somewhat later, in southern Dutchess County. Thus it was that during the first century of its development, New York experienced several discrete waves of settlers, each separated from the others by distinctive and sometimes hostile interests and traditions, and each becoming identified with a regional base. The degree of isolation that was possible in the more rural areas served to maintain cultural distinctions. But in the more densely settled section bordering the harbor at New York City a different sort of development was taking place.

Almost from the start, New York City had evolved along lines that were to set it off from the rest of the colony. Encompassing within a small area an ethnic and religious diversity which never failed to elicit surprised comment from visitors, the city rapidly developed the tone and style of a cosmopolitan center. Governor Dongan observed in 1686 that in addition to Dutch Calvinists, Anglicans, French Calvinists, Dutch Lutherans, and ordinary Quakers, the city also contained "Singing Quakers, Ranting Quakers; Sabbatarians; Antisabbatarians; Some Anabaptists some Independants; some Jews; in short all sorts of opinions there are some, and the most part, of none at all." One citizen complained: "Our chiefest unhappyness here is too great a mixture of Nations, & English the least part." Yet by 1698 the English had drawn equal to the Dutch in numbers and would rapidly surpass them thereafter, giving the capital at New York City a strongly English aspect by the early years of the eighteenth century.[9] The Dutch naturally continued to exercise influence in the city, as did other elements, especially the French-Huguenots; but as time passed ethnic distinctions were

---

ter Allen Knittle, *The Early Eighteenth Century Palatine Emigration* (Philadelphia, 1936), Chaps. VI and VIII. A map of the Palatine villages appears on p. 194. For the Scotch-Irish settlements see Ruth L. Higgins, *Expansion in New York* (Columbus, Ohio, 1931), Chap. VII, 89–90. The ethnic composition of New York and other states at the time of the first census in 1790 is given in American Council of Learned Societies, *Report*, 124–25, cited above.

[9] "Gov. Dongan's Report on the State of the Province," 1686, Edmund B. O'Callaghan and Berthold Fernow, eds., *Documents Relative to the Colonial History of the State of New York* (Albany, 1856–1887), III, 415; quoted in Bayrd Still, *Mirror for Gotham* (New York, 1956), 21; Carl Bridenbaugh, *Cities in the Wilderness: The First Century of Urban Life in America, 1625–1742* (New York, 1938, 1964), 5.

blurred by the familiar agents of intermarriage and acculturation. In times of economic or political stress, ethnic or religious loyalties could still be reinvigorated in the City, but these responses became less automatic with each succeeding generation.

New York Colony's political and social evolution might have been quite different if the City's ability to absorb and digest ethnic variety had extended to other parts of the province. But the well-known tendency to exclusiveness among immigrant groups seems to have been reinforced in the countryside by the dispersion of settlement which the colony's geography encouraged. With eastern Long Island and Albany each located about 150 miles—a three to five days' journey—from the capital of the colony at New York City, it is not surprising that a sectional particularism should have developed. Furthermore, within each section there existed several subcultures, and population was sparse enough to make isolation possible for those who wished to maintain a separate identity. German and French-Huguenot settlements, Quaker and Moravian colonies, and, above all, the large Dutch communities of the upper Hudson Valley retained unique language, religious, and other cultural patterns far longer than would have been possible in a more compact society.

Well past the middle of the eighteenth century William Smith found that the "Dutch counties, in some measure, follow the example of New-York, but still retain many of the modes peculiar to the Hollanders." The Dutch language was so preponderant in the upriver counties that the sheriff had difficulty empanelling a jury. As late as 1769, Richard Smith found no English-speaking people on Henry Beekman's lands around Rhinebeck in Dutchess County. A typical comment about the clannishness of another group, the Moravians, who were always viewed with suspicion because of their missionary activities among the Indians and their allegedly pro-Catholic and anti-British sentiments, noted their preference for "Setling in Bodys by themselves, they are like ever to Remain a Distinct People." The Quakers also tended to cluster together and where they were fairly numerous, as in Dutchess, Westchester, and Queens counties, they quickly learned to increase their bargaining power by voting as a bloc in local elections. In the election of 1728 they used this power to influence the outcome in Queens and Westchester counties, and in the 1750 election they made the point with

Dutchess County's leading politician, Henry Beekman, that their one hundred odd votes "would go one way." [10]

But it was in the areas where there were heavy concentrations of Dutch that chauvinism was longest and most forcefully manifested. Even Mrs. Anne Grant, normally a sympathetic observer, had harsh words for the Dutch settlements at Fishkill and Esopus (Kingston). "Their notions were mean and contracted; their manners blunt and austere; and their habits sordid and parsimonious. . . ." One way in which these narrow attitudes found expression was the tendency of each community to lodge authority solely with members of its own group. It was reported in 1752 that because the "Dutch of Esopus" wanted "to have all offices among themselves" they had protested the appointment of an outsider, a Mr. Albertson, as sheriff. In 1766 the town of Schenectady was split into two "Contending parties" when the dominant Dutch majority was challenged by a group led by John Sanders and "one Daniel Campber an Iris[h]man not above twelve years in this town. . . ." Apparently Campber was still considered a rank newcomer. Nor had the situation improved a few years later when George Smith petitioned the Governor for a grant of land near Schenectady, "your Petitioner being a Stranger, a Name given all People from the Old Country by the Dutch in general of Schenectady particularly those in power, cannot at present nor at any Time have an equal chance with the Dutch Inhabitants to get a few Acres of Land." [11] If colonial America was indeed "an open society dotted with closed enclaves" where one could settle "with his co-

[10] Smith, *History,* I, 327–28; Francis W. Halsey, ed., *A Tour of Four Great Rivers, The Hudson, Mohawk, Susquehanna and Delaware in 1769, Being the Journal of Richard Smith* (New York, 1906, 1964), 10; "Reasons for Passing the Law Against the Moravians Residing Among the Indians," by Daniel Horsmanden, May 1746, Edmund B. O'Callaghan, ed., *Documentary History of the State of New York* (Albany, 1849–1851) [hereafter, *N.Y. Doc. Hist.*] III, 1022–27; James Alexander to Cadwallader Colden, New York, May 5, 1728, *Collections* of the New-York Historical Society [hereafter NYHS *Colls.*], L (1917), 260; Henry Beekman to Henry Livingston, New York, Feb. 10, 1750, Henry Beekman MSS, NYHS.

[11] Anne Grant, *Memoirs of an American Lady, with Sketches of Manners and Scenes in America as They Existed Previous to the Revolution* (London, 1808; New York, 1901), I, 46; Colden to Gov. Clinton, Coldengham, Feb. 4, 1752, copy, NYHS *Colls.,* LIII (1920), 309; Vrooman to James Duane, Schenectady, Jan. 7, 1766, "Petition of George Smith," Feb. 4, 1771, James Duane Papers, NYHS.

believers in safety and comfort and exercise the right of oppression"
against outsiders,[12] then New York offered as fertile a soil for the
growth of competing orthodoxies as could be found in the colonies.

It is well known that New York was not the only colony where fer-
vent localism existed, but it is remarkable that separatist tendencies ran
so deep and endured so long in that province. Were there not counter-
vailing forces here, as in the other colonies, which might have moder-
ated cultural and sectional distinctions, and eventually have reversed the
centrifugal trend? They did, indeed, exist; the "melting-pot" had its effect in New York as it did everywhere else in America. But it will be
instructive to keep our attention a little longer upon those forces which
slowed acculturation, and which tended to reinforce isolation, separate-
ness, and sectionalism.

2. Local Government: A Random Growth

One of the most effective forces for social and cultural cohesion is representative government. By establishing a process whereby local needs
are referred to a central legislature, and whereby central control in turn
may be extended outward, representative government encourages both
interdependence and a degree of intercommunication among all sections
and interests. The benefits of an orderly governmental network were
recognized at an early stage in all of the colonies except one. Only in
New York were the requests, and then the demands, for a colonial legislature shunted aside. New York was not granted a permanent assembly
until sixty-seven years after its initial settlement—sixty-seven years during which localism took root and flourished in all parts of the colony.

[12] John P. Roche, "American Liberty: An Examination of the 'Tradition' of Freedom," in John P. Roche, ed., *Origins of American Political Thought* (New York,
1967), 27. The only other colonies with a comparable ethnic and religious diversity were Pennsylvania and New Jersey where, as in New York, the effort to preserve cultural distinctions often proved to be divisive. A recent study of present-
day neighborhood patterns in New York City shows that "voluntary ethnic
segregation is still a viable force," with separatism, even among such similar
groups as Norwegians and Swedes, remaining "fairly high into the second generation." Nathan Kantrowitz, "Ethnic and Racial Segregation in the New York Metropolis, 1960," *American Journal of Sociology*, Vol. 74 (May, 1969), 685–94.

No such time lag occurred in any of the other colonies. The period between first settlement and the establishment of some form of central representative government was twelve years in Virginia, four years in Massachusetts Bay, and from two to nineteen years in the other colonies. But in New York, despite persistent demands for some form of representative government, only feeble and abortive efforts were made in that direction in the early years. For nearly seven decades New York was ruled by a governor and appointive Council located at New York City, and only in 1691 was a representative assembly finally established. Prior to that time, because of the great distances involved, the central government's control of outlying areas was intermittent at best; when asserted, it nearly always encountered the opposition of local political hierarchies which protested that they had no voice in the decision-making process.[13] Predictably, after 1691, these quasi-autonomous units were reluctant to surrender power, once gained, to a central authority no matter how representative.

In the absence of firm central guidelines in the early decades, each community was thrown back upon itself to determine the structure and extent of local authority. Though English forms spread rapidly after 1664, local government developed in tandem with settlement and reflected to some degree the varying experience and traditions of each group of settlers. One consequence of this was the random and tangled growth of local forms and jurisdictions which continues to plague New York to the present day. Because of its complexity the history of local government in early New York has often been neglected or oversimplified, and this in turn has given rise to a number of myths and inaccuracies. A few examples will illustrate this. Some New York histories imply that only on Long Island did New England–type township government exist; this in turn has led to the impression that the only signif-

---

[13] Early efforts to gain representative government are described in Edmund B. O'Callaghan, *Origin of Legislative Assemblies* (Albany, 1861); Jerrold Seymann, comp., *Colonial Charters, Patents and Grants to the Communities Comprising the City of New York* (Albany, 1939), 3–72; Flick, ed., *History,* I, Chap. 8, II, Chap. 3; Ellis et al., *Short History,* 32. An article by David S. Lovejoy, "Equality and Empire: The New York Charter of Libertyes, 1683," *WMQ,* 3rd Ser., XXI (Oct., 1964), 493–515, contains some interesting suggestions about what seventeenth-century New Yorkers believed their political rights should be.

icant unit of government in the Hudson Valley was the county where, as in Virginia, government was in the hands of a local aristocracy. Or, when the existence of the Hudson Valley towns has been acknowledged, historians often discount their political importance by emphasizing, with indiscriminate use of maps, that manor "lords" and great landholders had engrossed so much of the countryside that towns had little impact on the structure of power.[14]

Regarding Westchester County, for example, three generations of historians have helped to perpetuate the myth that in the late colonial period the majority of people still lived on one of six great manors where their political views were circumscribed by their landlords.[15] But since three of these six manors no longer existed by the mid-eighteenth century such an assertion surely needs to be reexamined. In spite of all that is known about the mobility and enterprise of colonial Americans, New York historians have been reluctant to recognize how frequently land changed ownership. Most maps of the colony show all of the great land patents in their original form, though parcels were often sold off, and in some cases entire estates were subdivided. The latter occurred with three of the Westchester manors. When Caleb Heathcote died in 1714, Scarsdale Manor was distributed among his children and was gradually sold off in parcels thereafter. Fordham Manor was sold to the Dutch Church of New York City in 1696 which, in turn, sold some land and leased the rest. In 1753, the Elders sold the remaining land to several purchasers in lots of 108 to 230 acres. Two-thirds of Pelham

[14] E. Wilder Spaulding says that townships were found only in the "extreme southern counties"; *New York in the Critical Period, 1783–1789* (New York, 1932), 6. Flick does not discuss local government at all, and Ellis et al. only mention New York City government. The emphasis on aristocratic control is exemplified in Carl Becker, *The History of Political Parties in the Province of New York, 1760–1776* (Madison, Wis., 1909, 1960), 8–10; and Mark, *Agrarian Conflicts, passim.*

[15] The myth was started by Edward F. DeLancey in a chapter written for Scharf's *History of Westchester County:* "It is safe to say that upwards of five-eighths of the people of Westchester County in 1769 were inhabitants of the six manors. . . ." (I, 91). The manors cited were Philipsborough, Scarsdale, Pelham, Morrisania, Fordham, and Cortlandt. Carl Becker cited Scharf but erroneously gave the proportion of manor residents as "five-sixths" in his *History of Political Parties,* 14. Irving Mark, citing Scharf but using Becker's figure, perpetuated the myth: "In Westchester County, where by 1769 about five-sixths of the population were within the six manors. . . ." *Agrarian Conflicts,* 95.

Manor was sold to the Huguenots of New Rochelle in 1689. The residue of 3,000 acres could not have supported many tenants.[16] Of the three manors which remained relatively intact by 1769, Morrisania was quite small (about 3,000 acres), and Cortlandt Manor, though still a legal entity, had been distributed among family members and many of the farms within its bounds had been sold in fee simple. Philipse Manor did contain a good many tenants, one estimate for 1775 citing over 270. The only statement made during the eighteenth century about the number of Westchester residents living on manors was that by John DeLancey, who said that "the manors of Philipsburgh and Cortlandt [contain] at least one third of all the inhabitants" of the county—but that is a good deal less than the five-sixths figure which has gained acceptance through repetition.[17]

This is not to say that proprietors of manors and large estates lacked influence in the rural areas. In Dutchess and Albany counties, where the Livingston and Van Rensselaer manors as well as a number of large patents were located, and in Westchester County where the Morris, Philipse, and Van Cortlandt estates were situated, the New York gentry exercised considerable power. There is abundant evidence that patrician families played a prominent role in government at all levels. Yet there is reason to believe that local government was by no

[16] Rev. Robert Bolton, *The History of Westchester County* (New York, 1881), II, 60–62, 227–32, 503–24; Scharf, ed., *History of Westchester*, I, 154, 704–5. Some of the confusion about these manors comes from the continued use of their names to identify sections of the county long after the manors, as legal entities, had been broken up. Even today there is in the Village of North Tarrytown, in Westchester County, a section called Philipse Manor. Though the area was once included within the Manor of Philipsborough, the modern use of the name obviously has no significance, except to indicate the acumen of the real estate developer.

[17] *Journal of the Votes and Proceedings of the General Assembly of the Colony of New York, from 1766 to 1776 inclusive* (Albany, J. Buel, 1820), Nov. 22, 1769 (hereafter cited as *Assembly Journal* [Buel]). The latest word on Cortlandt Manor is a study by Sung Bok Kim, "The Manor of Cortlandt and Its Tenants, 1697–1783," unpubl. Ph.D. diss. (Michigan State University, 1966). For Philipsborough consult Beatrice G. Reubens, "Pre-Emptive Rights in the Disposition of a Confiscated Estate—Philipsburgh Manor, New York," *WMQ*, 3rd Ser., XXII (July, 1965), 435–56. Even the Manor of Morrisania was divided into two parts in 1762 by the terms of Lewis Morris, Jr.'s will. NYHS *Colls.*, XXX (1897), 171–74. Chapter VI below is devoted to a discussion of New York's manors and large patents.

means their private preserve, if only because there were not enough patricians available to fill all or even most of the numerous elective offices that existed throughout the colony.

After 1691 New York's provincial government had the traditional form for a royal colony: a governor, an appointive Council, and an elective Assembly. Some county lines were redrawn by the first legislature, but otherwise most local jurisdictions remained undisturbed. The colony had two cities, New York and Albany. Each had been officially chartered by Governor Dongan in 1686, though each had enjoyed several decades of viable government prior to that date. Under Dutch rule both cities had been governed by appointed magistrates—the "Eight Men," the "Nine Men"—in imitation of local government at home. The English charters provided for a system that made some offices appointive and others elective. The governor, with the approval of the provincial Council, appointed for each city a mayor, recorder, town clerk, sheriff, and a clerk of the market; other appointive positions, such as weighers and measurers, were added later as the need arose. The electors annually chose six aldermen (one for each ward), six assistants, and several constables. Governor Montgomerie granted a new charter to New York City in 1731 which raised the number of aldermen and assistants to seven when the Town of Haarlem was added to the city as the "Out ward." New elective offices for assessors and collectors were added at the same time, and the number of elected constables was increased to sixteen. In both cities the Common Council, composed of the mayor and aldermen, sat as a Mayor's Court, providing an instance of a partly elective judicial body.[18]

Another unit of local government was the township. Besides the well-known dozen and a half townships on Long Island,[19] the Hudson

[18] *The Colonial Laws of New York from the Year 1664 to the Revolution* (Albany, 1894), I, 181–216; II, 575–639 (hereafter cited as *Laws*); Albert E. McKinley, "The Transition from Dutch to English Rule in New York," *AHR,* VI (July, 1901), 693–724; McKinley, "English and Dutch Towns"; Richard B. Morris, ed., *Select Cases of the Mayor's Court of New York City, 1674–1784* (Washington, 1935), 45–48. The standard history of New York City government is George W. Edwards and A. E. Peterson, *New York as an Eighteenth Century Municipality, 1731–1776* (New York, 1917). For early forms of government at Albany, see Alice P. Kenney, "Dutch Patricians in Colonial Albany," *NYH,* XLIX (July, 1968), 249–83.

[19] In 1691 the Long Island towns were listed as Boswyck, Bedford, Brooklyn, Flatbush, Flatlands, New Utrecht, and Gravesend in Kings County; Newtown, Ja-

River counties evolved township government in areas where population was concentrated enough to support it. Westchester County had five towns by the end of the seventeenth century—Eastchester, Westchester, New Rochelle, Mamaroneck, and Bedford; three more had been added by the 1730's—White Plains, North Castle, and Rye. Ulster County contained the towns of Kingston, Hurley, Marbletown, Foxhall, New Paltz, and Rochester; the Township of Schenectady was well established in Albany County by the 1680's.[20] The manner in which New York townships were settled was described by Daniel Denton around 1670 and will have a familiar ring to students of the New England colonies. A group of people, with the governor's consent, "view a Tract of Land . . . and finding a place convenient for a Town, they return to the Governor, who upon their desire admits them into the Colony, and gives them a Grant or Patent for the said Land, for themselves and Associates." After settling on their patent they "take in what inhabitants to themselves they shall see cause to admit of [who have] equal privileges with themselves." Each person gets as much land as he needs, and "the rest they let lie in common till they have occasion for a new division, never dividing their Pasture land at all, which lie in common to the whole Town." After the English conquest, Dutch forms faded rapidly, and township government became fairly similar throughout the colony. Annual elections were held each spring to choose from six to twelve trustees and several constables and assessors, the number varying with the population. By request of any three trustees a town meeting might be held at which local ordinances were passed by a "Majority of Voices" of the "trustees the freeholders & Commonalty of the Towns." Though records are sparse, it appears that the boards of trustees, meeting on the average of once a month, ran the town governments. Matters of importance were placed before the voters at the "annual meetings" or "town meetings," which were held on the same day as the yearly elections. As the need developed, additional officials were elected, such as

maica, Flushing, Hempstead, and Oyster Bay in Queens County; Huntington, Smithfield, Brookhaven, Southampton, Southold, and Easthampton in Suffolk County. *Laws*, I, 267–70.

[20] Bolton, *History of Westchester*, traces the history of each town. For Ulster County see *Laws*, I, 267–70; and Frederick Van Wyck, *Select Patents of New York Towns* (Boston, 1938), 147. For Schenectady, Jonathan Pearson, *A History of the Schenectady Patent in the Dutch and English Times* (Albany, 1883), 21–23.

road surveyors, fence viewers, collectors, and overseers of the poor. In many of the towns the trustees chose several from among their number to serve as commissioners of "pleas of Debt & Tresspass," thereby making the court nearest the people a quasi-elective body.[21]

Nor does the list of elective offices end here. When the Assembly was finally established in 1691, New York was divided into ten counties. Dutchess, Orange, and parts of Ulster and Albany counties were too sparsely populated to support township government; instead, they were divided into larger areas called "precincts," thereby adding yet another category to New York's patchwork of local government jurisdictions. Dutchess County was divided into three precincts in 1719 and, following a rapid increase of population, was further subdivided into seven precincts in 1737. Each precinct annually elected "a Supervizor, Two Assessors & one Collector." The Southern Precinct was again subdivided into three parts in 1772 because "many of the Inhabitants cannot Attend the Annual Meetings for Election of Officers without great inconveniency." [22] Orange County was divided into the precincts of Haverstraw, Highlands, Goshen, Orangetown, and Minnisinck; when population increased, these precincts were split into smaller units as had been done in Dutchess.[23] Three precincts were established in Ulster County in 1743 to encompass the areas not included within townships;

[21] Daniel Denton, *A Brief Description of New York* (New York, 1937), 16; William G. Fulcher, "Recorded Action Taken by Freeholders and Inhabitants of the Town of Mamaroneck as Found in the Town Record," Westchester County Historical Society, *Quarterly Bulletin,* XIII (April, 1937), 39–48; Records of the Town Court, Proceedings of the Trustees, etc. of Kingston, Oct. 7, 1713–Feb. 1737, Misc. MSS (Kingston, N.Y.), NYHS; Marius Schoonmaker, *The History of Kingston, New York* (New York, 1888); Ralph LeFevre, *History of New Paltz, New York* (Albany, 1903). The charters cited are those of the towns of Kingston and Southampton; all township charters were similar in form. Frederick Van Wyck, *Select Patents of Towns and Manors* (Boston, 1938), 63–82, 83–100. For other offices see *Laws,* I, 225–26, V, 319.

[22] *Laws,* II, 955–58, V, 395–96; Isaac Huntting, *History of Little Nine Partners* (Amenia, N.Y., 1897), 4; Henry Noble McCracken, *Old Dutchess Forever! The Story of an American County* (New York, 1956). Dutchess County was provisionally annexed to Ulster until 1713 when it became a separate entity.

[23] *N.Y. Col. Docs.,* IV, 185; *Laws,* I, 1033; III, 326–27; V, 333, 391. Samuel W. Eager, *An Outline History of Orange County* (Newburgh, N.Y., 1846–47), 81–84, 452–53; Russel Headley, ed., *The History of Orange County, New York* (Middletown, N.Y., 1908), 224–25, 342.

Albany County kept adding precincts as population grew, having at least six by 1772 when the county itself was divided to create the new counties of Tryon and Charlotte. In each precinct the electors annually chose a supervisor, assessors, collectors, constables, and overseers of the poor.[24]

New York manors have often been depicted as forming distinct jurisdictions, with their own courts and officials, all under the control of the manor "lords." In fact, small manors usually joined with the surrounding area to form a precinct, while larger manors often composed a precinct or township in themselves, with the usual privileges of electing supervisors, assessors, collectors, fence viewers, pound masters, and town clerks. (The manors will be discussed in greater detail in a later chapter.) It is not entirely clear what other business besides annual elections was transacted at these meetings, but in at least one case—that of Philipse Manor—the annual gatherings were called "Town Meetings" and it is recorded that the inhabitants met to "mak town laws for that year." [25]

County offices, to be sure, were not all elective. Governors continued to appoint justices of the peace, sheriffs, and county clerks, all positions of considerable power, as well as a host of other functionaries such as militia officers and excise farmers. In imitation of English forms of local government the justices of the peace, sitting as a County Court, were originally made responsible for county government. This was altered by the first session of the General Assembly in 1691 which passed a law providing for the election of county supervisors to facilitate the assessment and collection of taxes. Though this law was repealed in 1701, it was reinstated two years later when "disputes Cavills Controversies and mistakes" made this necessary. It provided for the annual election of a supervisor by the "Freeholders and Inhabitants" of each city ward, town, and precinct, and stated that all supervisors were to meet at their county seat on the first Tuesday in October to compute

[24] *Laws*, I, 122, 998–99; III, 320–26; V, 319–23, 383–86. In addition to the offices listed above, in the counties of New York, Richmond, Queens, and Westchester, where the Anglican Church was established, the electors annually chose vestrymen and church wardens. *Laws*, V, 85–86.

[25] "The Town Book of the Manor of Philipsburgh," *New York Genealogical and Biographical Record*, LIX (July, 1928), 209; Statements of Teunis Van Slyk and Francis Salisbury, March 22, 1716, Livingston-Redmond MSS, Reel 3; *Laws*, I, 915–16; IV, 1116–19; Van Wyck, *Towns and Manors*, 101–10.

and oversee the public charges and establish the county tax rate.[26] In most counties the boards of supervisors gradually took over all executive responsibilities from the justices of the peace, who were left with a strictly judicial function. This shift of power from the County Court to the supervisors was a significant development, county administration being thereby put in the hands of an elective rather than an appointive body.[27]

As for the men who served in positions of public trust, it was a widely accepted principle at that time, in New York as elsewhere, that officials at all levels of government were to be "men of Good life . . . & of Good Estates & Ability, & not necessitous People." New York City's charter stated that officeholders were to be "persons of Good Capacity & Understanding," and by common consent this meant men of sound reputation whose permanent interest in the community was demonstrated by substantial property holdings. Because it was expected that tradition would serve to maintain standards, no minimum estate requirements were ever set forth by statute in New York Colony. It was understood as a matter of course that candidates should be freeholders or freemen, but even this was not always specifically stated. At the higher levels of government, such as the Council and the superior courts (all appointive positions), one rarely found any but men of visible affluence. The elected Assemblymen represented a somewhat broader cross-section of the population, but they too were often drawn from the higher strata, especially in the politically powerful counties of New York, Westchester, Albany, and Dutchess. The small farmer counties sent either prominent landholders like the Nicolls of Suffolk County

[26] For the establishment of the justices of the peace, see *Laws,* I, 43–44, 227–28. For information about the boards of supervisors, consult *Laws,* I, 237, 456, 498–99, 539–42; Historical Records Survey, *Minutes of the Board of Supervisors of Ulster County, New York, 1710/1 to 1730/1* (Albany, 1939), Introduction; John A. Fairlie, *Local Government in Counties, Towns, Villages* (New York, 1906), Chap. II; Cortlandt F. Bishop, *History of Elections in the American Colonies* (New York, 1893), 207–10.

[27] There is evidence that in parts of Albany County the justices of the peace continued to serve as administrators; we find them regulating municipal services, setting boundaries, and building defenses throughout the colonial era. Philip Livingston to Robert Livingston, Albany, Feb. 8, 1721, copy, "Representation of the Justices," Feb. 6, 1723, Livingston-Redmond MSS, Reel 3; Abraham Yates to Robert Livingston, Jr., Albany, Jan. 3, 1766, Livingston-Redmond MSS, Reel 6; *Laws,* V, 15–17, 403–7, 692.

or, more often, substantial yeomen such as the Lotts of Kings County.[28]

The strongest local government developed in New York City and Albany where population was concentrated and municipal services were most essential. Because the two cities were centers of powerful political interests, and because the city fathers had a good deal to say about commercial and land policies in their districts, top municipal offices, whether elective or appointive, were posts of real influence and therefore attracted men of high calibre. Livingstons, Crugers, Philipses, and Schuylers served as mayors and aldermen and took an active interest in all aspects of city government. Occasionally a younger member of one of the leading families was elected an assistant or assessor, but the less prestigious offices were usually held by men of middle rank.[29]

In the rural towns and precincts the great majority of offices were filled by the middling sort, though a few county offices attracted members of patrician families. Philip Livingston was a highway commissioner and supervisor in Albany County; Gilbert Livingston was a supervisor in Ulster; and Philipses and Van Cortlandts served as highway commissioners in Westchester and Dutchess counties. The position of county clerk also attracted some prominent citizens, and there is no question about the prestige attached to top militia offices. On the whole, however, county and local officials were more often men of narrower experience and vision whose interests and influence had only a limited sphere. Some families apparently achieved a fair degree of power within their personal bailiwicks, if we may judge by the frequency with which

[28] "Gov. Montgomeries Instructions," Oct. 20, 1727, copy, NYHS *Colls.,* L (1917), 200; *Laws,* I, 181–216, 452–54; Seymann, *Colonial Charters,* 353–55; Van Wyck, *Selected Patents of New York Towns,* 123. For the Nicoll family see Benjamin F. Thompson, *History of Long Island* (New York, 1918), III, 334–41; for the Lott family, Charles A. Ditmas, *Historic Homesteads of Kings County* (New York, 1909), 37–39. It would have required a specific and purposeful act to set minimum property requirements for officeholders and no one ever considered taking that step—at least not until the more self-conscious era of the Revolution when, in the State Constitution of 1777, property requirements were established for the first time.

[29] Edgar A. Werner, *Civil List and Constitutional History of the Colony and State of New York* (Albany, 1888), is old and contains some inaccuracies, but it is still the most convenient source for all officeholders in the colony. Some additional offices are listed in Nicholas Varga, "New York Government and Politics During the Mid-Eighteenth Century," unpubl. Ph.D. diss. (Fordham University, 1960), 421–73, which also includes a discussion of local politics in Chap. VIII.

certain names appear on the civil list. This was the case with the Haas-brouck and Hardenbergh families in Ulster County, the Hickses and Kissams in Queens, and the Schencks and Lotts of Kings, to name but a few examples. Members of these families served as supervisors, town clerks, county treasurers, justices of the peace, and trustees; some of these positions seem to have been kept within the family for two or three generations.[30] For the most part these were men who appear to have shared the middle-class outlook and ambitions of their neighbors, and local government consequently reflected with fair accuracy the atti-tudes of its constituents.

Though less tightly organized and probably less powerful than local governing bodies in New England, the petty hierarchies of New York could rise to a strong defense of local interests when challenged. A case in point is the running battle which took place between Schenec-tady and Albany over the former's attempt to move in on the fur trade monopoly in the late seventeenth century. About the same time, towns in eastern Long Island initiated a long series of protests against heavy taxation and regulation of their whaling and trading activities. Nor were local officials reticent about letting the central government know of their complaints. From all over the colony, local grievances and de-mands were expressed in resolutions and petitions drawn up by the middle-class leadership of town and precinct governments. Leading members of the gentry in each section may have had a great deal to say about who was appointed to local posts, and by cultivating the "inter-est" of regional leaders the county grandees could and did exert infor-mal pressure on local decisions. But the power of the elite was not mon-olithic in the counties of New York; it was a shared power, functioning in partnership with that enjoyed by locally elected and locally respon-sive officials.[31]

Had local government in New York been "controlled" by a prov-

[30] Werner, *Civil List;* Varga, "New York Government and Politics," 421–73.

[31] Allen W. Trelease, *Indian Affairs in Colonial New York: The Seventeenth Century* (Ithaca, N.Y., 1960), 218–19; Lovejoy, "Equality and Empire," 495–503; Charles Worthen Spencer, "Sectional Aspects of New York Provincial Politics," *PSQ,* XXX (Sept., 1915), 409–13. The most accessible source for local govern-ment documents is Berthold Fernow, ed., *Documents Relative to the Colonial History of the State of New-York,* Vols. XII–XIV; for example, XIII, 418, 556, 567; see also *N.Y. Doc. Hist.,* I, 104–5.

ince-wide network of county patricians, as apparently was the case in Virginia,[32] or had it simply been standardized at the outset and given a voice in the provincial assembly, as happened in New England, lines of communication and authority would have tended to draw the outlying regions toward the central government. Instead, for sixty-seven years the population outside the capital at New York City had little to do with the central government, except in times of stress when energies were directed mainly toward resisting it. During this period local officials naturally developed very parochial attitudes which would prove difficult to surmount in later years when a broader vision was required. It was precisely this cramped and myopic view of the public interest that William Smith, Jr., condemned when he referred to New York assemblymen as persons "whose views seldom extended farther than to the regulation of highways, the destruction of wolves, wildcats, and foxes, and the advancement of the other little interests of the particular counties which they were chosen to represent." And Philip Livingston expressed a widely held view when he declared, "We have too many narrow spirited people among us who consult nothing more than their own immediate advantage and let the public business wade through all difficulties. . . ." Though many New Yorkers undoubtedly recognized the evils of parochialism, the attitudes and habits absorbed into the grain of a society when young give way slowly, and for many years local rivalries and ambitions simply gave added impetus to the centrifugal forces already at work in the colony.[33]

3. The "City-State" of Albany

The emphasis for the present is on those forces of geographic, cultural, and political fragmentation which, it is being argued, were of fundamental importance in shaping the early history and character of New

[32] Charles S. Sydnor says gentlemen held all offices in Virginia "except such lowly posts as constable." *Gentlemen Freeholders: Political Practices in Washington's Virginia* (New York, 1952, 1965), 62.

[33] Smith, *History,* I, 367; Philip Livingston to Jacob Wendell, April 5, 1746, Livingston Papers, MCNY, quoted in Joan Gordon, "The Livingstons of New York 1675–1860; Kinship and Class," unpubl. Ph.D. diss. (Columbia University, 1959), 111.

York Colony. There is no better example of how those forces worked than in the case of Albany, a community whose experience and development stand in sharp contrast to those of New York City and its surrounding area.

Located far from the seaboard counties, where "the old leaven had given way to that liberality which was produced by a better education and an intercourse with strangers," [34] the early settlers of Albany and environs developed traits and attitudes which for a long time thereafter set that area apart from the rest of the colony. The consequence of this was a north-south, seaboard-frontier, city-country polarity—to which was added the inevitable ethnic demarcation facilitated by the concentrations of Dutch in the upper Hudson Valley. Had not the fur trade and Indian diplomatic activity been centered there, colonial Albany would almost certainly have been nothing more than an obscure backwater town. But fur and Indians, which contributed essential elements to Albany's distinctive style, at the same time assured it of political and economic power that could not be ignored in the councils of government. Thus the Albany area became a center of powerful special interests which enabled it, for at least the first hundred years of its existence, to compete on fairly equal terms with its sister city at the mouth of the Hudson. The "divided mind" that colonial New York revealed at times can surely be accounted for in part by this initial polarity.

Throughout the entire seventeenth century Albany can best be described as a city-state. Its frontier location, its almost totally Dutch character, and its fur-centered economy all conspired to emphasize a separate, special, and unique position. From the imperial point of view, Albany was the most important settlement along the whole northwestern periphery of the English colonies. Again, it was geography as much as anything that defined the role it was to play. Located at the head of the navigable part of the Hudson and looking north to Lake Champlain, the gateway to Canada, Albany was the logical jumping-off place of forays against the French. Leading west from the city was the Mohawk River Valley, which was one of the few natural furrows through the western mountain barrier offering a pathway to the Great Lakes and upper Mississippi Valley. Because of its location at this frontier crossroads, Albany was the site of greatest contact between the English and the two leading foreign powers, as it were, in the area—the French and

34 Grant, *Memoirs,* II, 69.

the Iroquois—all of which made Albany "for three quarters of a century the diplomatic center of British North America." [35]

During the years of Dutch rule Albany's policy toward the French and the Iroquois confederation was dictated by Dutch self-interest. As the only foreign intruders in an otherwise English domain, the Dutch had no interest in or capacity for enlarging their political influence or territorial possessions beyond their precarious foothold in New Netherland. Their main concern was economic, specifically the fur trade, and so long as the flow of skins into Fort Orange and down the Hudson River to New Amsterdam was uninterrupted, the home government considered the colony a success. Belligerent actions were to be avoided as disruptive of that trade, and everything possible was done to encourage a balance of power among the Indian tribes and the French. For their own part the Dutch maintained a prudent neutrality, keeping lines open to all potential sources of furs. Their main ties were necessarily to the Five Nations of the Iroquois confederacy, especially the Mohawks who occupied the territory immediately adjacent to Fort Orange. There seems to be little question that the goods traded to the Iroquois by the Dutch, conspicuous among which were weapons and powder, stimulated the rapid emergence of the Five Nations into a position of supremacy over the other tribes of the area. Though there were frequent clashes between the Iroquois and the Far Indians (the Ottawa, Huron, and other Great Lakes tribes), who trapped furs for the French, the period of Dutch rule was one of relative peace and prosperity when compared to the hostile atmosphere that would develop toward the end of the seventeenth century. The Dutch policy of abjuring political entanglements and concentrating on trade paid handsome dividends, both for the mother country and for a number of colonial merchants whose fortunes were founded on the fur trade.[36]

When the English captured New York in 1664, Albany was the area least affected by the change. An English garrison was installed at the fort, and the English governor occasionally visited Albany to pre-

[35] Arthur H. Buffinton, "The Policy of Albany and English Westward Expansion," *MVHR,* VIII (March, 1922), 327.

[36] Trelease, *Indian Affairs,* Chap. V; Buffinton, "Policy of Albany," 327–28; Condon, *New York Beginnings,* 76–77, 150. During 1656 and 1657, peak years for the fur trade, 46,000 skins a year were shipped south from Fort Orange. Trelease, *Indian Affairs,* 131.

side over the formal councils and gift offerings which were designed to keep the Iroquois loyal to the King. But beyond this, life at Albany changed very little during the first twenty years or so of English rule. The city retained its Dutch character and fur-centered economy, and Indian trade policies continued to be determined largely by the local magistrates. The city fathers, who doubled as "Indian Commissaries" or commissioners, were invariably Dutch and usually were leading *handlaers* (the Dutch word for fur merchants) who had every reason to perpetuate the successful policies of the past. Not only did the English permit this but they actually strengthened Albany's grip on the trade. One of the problems which had plagued the *handlaers* for years was the threat posed by a number of small, independent fur traders from the manor of Rensselaerswyck and the town of Schenectady who waylaid the Indians before they reached Albany, thereby cutting into the *handlaers'* source of supply. In an attempt to curb this competition the English granted Albany a monopoly of the fur trade in 1676. When Albany received its formal charter a decade later, the rule that all fur trade was to be carried on "within the Walls" of the city was confirmed, and regulation of the trade continued in the hands of the city officials.[37] The English conquest was a boon in other ways as well. The English goods which thereafter came to be used for barter proved far superior to those traded by the French, with the result that much of the trade formerly carried on with the French was diverted to Albany. One of the articles most prized by the Indians was stroudwaters, a coarse woolen cloth produced in superior quality at less cost in England, where the cloth industry was most advanced. Because the Albany merchants also paid from "two to four times as much for furs" as the single French company which monopolized the Canadian trade, even the French *coureurs de bois* began surreptitiously to carry their furs to Albany. This trade, which was contrary to all concepts of mercantilism, began as early as 1671 and became so brisk in the ensuing years that "a half or two-thirds of the total quantity of beaver produced in Canada each year" was traded at Albany.[38]

[37] *Laws,* I, 211; Trelease, *Indian Affairs,* 207–8, 212–13, 218–19; Buffinton, "Policy of Albany," 338; David Arthur Armour, "The Merchants of Albany, New York; 1686–1760," unpubl. Ph.D. diss. (Northwestern University, 1965), 76–81.

[38] Buffinton, "Policy of Albany," 337, 340; Jean Lunn, "The Illegal Fur Trade Out of New France, 1713–60," Canadian Historical Association, *Report,* 1939, p.

The *handlaers* had achieved for themselves an enviable position. Securely ensconced in their Albany warehouses, they received the furs which flowed in to them from two main directions, south from French Canada and east from the Great Lakes hunting grounds. Because these same merchants controlled the city government, they were able to fix prices and nip any budding competition from independent traders. They had important support from outside the city as well. New York City importers and their English correspondents, who supplied barter goods for the Indian trade, were more than willing to use their influence with provincial and Crown authorities to assure that the Canada trade would not be outlawed.[39] All of the merchants knew perfectly well that it would be awkward for English officials to criticize the economics, at least, of the illegal Canada trade, since it was French mercantilism, not British, that suffered.

Profitable as the fur trade was, both for the merchants fortunate enough to be part of the inner circle and for the imperial treasury, political considerations gradually moved to the fore as policies were shaped to reflect English rather than Dutch self-interest. By the end of the seventeenth century the overriding concern of British policy-makers was the rapid growth of French power, in both Europe and North America. The expansionist economic and territorial policies of Louis XIV and his chief minister, Colbert, were reflected in North America by a sharp rise in tension between the British and the French during the last quarter of the seventeenth century. As the French became more aggressive, British policy shifted away from the old Dutch preference for neutrality and plans were laid for strengthening the British position on the northwest frontier.

Everyone recognized that the support of the Iroquois confederation was crucial. The power of the Five Nations had grown until by the second half of the seventeenth century, according to Buffinton, it was "equal in fighting strength to either the French or the English, and able to incline the balance of power in one direction or the other." With the French already making overtures to the Iroquois, it was clear that the

65. English strouds became so popular with the Indians that the French were permitted to buy them in England to use in the Canada trade. Buffinton, "Policy of Albany," 356.

[39] For the steps taken by the French to stop the trade to Albany, and the permissive attitude taken by the British, see Lunn, "Illegal Fur Trade."

English had to move rapidly to strengthen their alliance with the Five Nations. For their part the Iroquois were prepared to renew their pledges of loyalty in return for British support of tribal interests. These fell into two main categories. One was a continuation of the profitable fur trade, and the other was a strong stand by the British against the French and their own Indian allies, whose increasing bellicosity had led to frequent raids into Iroquois territory and harassment of trading parties.[40] The Albany Dutch were strongly in favor of the first point, but a firm stand against the French raised the disturbing possibility of retaliatory raids by pro-French Indians against the relatively isolated and unprotected settlements on the frontier—precisely the danger which Albany's neutrality policy had been designed to avoid. To meet this difficulty a new plan was evolved in the 1680's. If the Far Indians, who had traditionally supported the French, could be drawn to the English side, this would serve both to increase the supply of furs and to weaken the French. Why, asked the English proponents of this plan, should not the Far Indians prefer to trade directly with the English instead of channeling their furs through the French *coureurs de bois?* With the latter eliminated altogether, the Far Indians would come to depend exclusively on the English, and would be less inclined to make war against them or their Iroquois allies. It was understood that this rechanneling of trade would have an adverse effect for a time on those Albany merchants whose business was geared to the Canada trade. But because this temporary displacement would presumably result in a greater volume of trade in the long run, once direct ties with the Far Indians were developed, a majority of the Albany traders agreed to give the plan a chance.[41]

Governor Dongan was a strong supporter of this program, which

[40] "Gov. Dongan's Propositions to the Five Nations," Aug. 5, 1687, *N.Y. Col. Docs.,* III, 438–41; "Answer of the Five Nations to Governor Dongan," Aug. 6, 1687, *ibid.,* 441–44; "Answer of the Five Nations to Gov. Sloughter's Address," 1691, *ibid.,* 774–77; Buffinton, "Policy of Albany," 328; Trelease, *Indian Affairs,* Chap. X.

[41] Buffinton credits Gov. Dongan with the formulation of this plan ("Policy of Albany," 343–47); Trelease, on the other hand, believes it likely that the idea originated with the Albany traders themselves (*Indian Affairs,* 269). There is disagreement among historians about the role played by the Iroquois relative to the trade with the Far Indians. McIlwain states that the Iroquois acted as middlemen, receiving furs from the Far Indians and carrying them to Albany (Charles

was completely consistent with imperial goals, and he proposed two ways to further implement it. One was that an English equivalent of the *coureurs de bois* be sent out from Albany to the Great Lakes region; the other was that a string of forts be constructed between Albany and the Great Lakes to keep the route open and to act as a barrier to French expansion southward. The first Albany trading party to go out to the Great Lakes country was a material success, but the French could not long ignore this challenge to their own imperial designs. Subsequent parties were harassed and their furs confiscated, and war fever was soon rising all along the frontier. To make matters worse the English failed to build the forts Dongan had proposed to protect the trading parties. The only new one, indeed, was built by the French. This was Fort Niagara, raised in Iroquois territory in 1687, an incursion which further inflamed tempers along the border. The failure to implement fully the new policy was not entirely the fault of New York. All the colonies that bordered the western frontier stood to benefit from strengthened defenses against the French. The task of holding the line was not the sole responsibility of New York, and there was every reason to expect the other colonies and the imperial treasury to share the financial burden. But despite the pleas of New York governors and leading citizens, the response from both sources was disappointing. The other colonies made only token contributions, while Crown officials for the most part regarded colonial defense as a matter of low priority. New York was thus left holding the purse, which could be filled only by the heavy taxes which New Yorkers themselves would have to pay. "The province," as Allen Trelease points out, "was chronically underpopulated and overtaxed by comparison with its neighbors, and the two factors were closely related." [42]

In the midst of these problems, news of the Glorious Revolution

---

H. McIlwain, ed., *An Abridgment of the Indian Affairs, by Peter Wraxall* [Cambridge, Mass., 1915], xlii–xliii). Trelease questions this in view of the frequent clashes, inconsistent with economic cooperation, between the Iroquois and the Far Indians (Allen W. Trelease, "The Iroquois and the Western Fur Trade: A Problem in Interpretation," *MVHR*, XLIX [June, 1962], 32–51; Trelease, *Indian Affairs*, 120–21, 324).

[42] Trelease, *Indian Affairs*, 294. Dongan also won the hearts of the Albany men by his firm stand against William Penn's efforts to enlarge his colony's territory and engross a portion of Albany's fur trade. *Ibid.*, 255–56.

reached New York in the spring of 1689. The ensuing upheaval led to the emergence of Jacob Leisler in June of that year as the self-appointed ruler of New York. Albany was the only center powerful enough to resist Leisler's claims to leadership. Spurred by Peter Schuyler and Robert Livingston, who feared that Leisler's lack of diplomatic delicacy might upset the Iroquois and further inflame the frontier, the city fathers refused to support Leisler's government. Instead they formed the Albany Convention, an independent governing body led by local civil and military officials; the Convention supported the new British sovereigns, William and Mary, but resisted what it regarded as Leisler's usurpation of power in the province. Leisler's year-long attempt to subdue the Albany Convention led to a number of military engagements and to an increasing estrangement between the upriver and downriver sections.[43]

Such was the grave situation which faced Albany in the winter of 1690: hostilities with the French rising all along the frontier, the fur trade at its lowest point in years, a heavy tax burden, and the city in rebellion against Jacob Leisler's putative government. At this critical juncture fell the most dreaded blow of all. In support of Frontenac's scheme to undermine English prestige with the Five Nations, a party of over two hundred French and Indians descended upon the outpost town of Schenectady shortly before midnight on February 8, 1690. Because of the deep midwinter snows that covered the ground, the townspeople had relaxed all their normal precautions in confidence that no hostile force could operate under such conditions. On the fatal night they had not even set a watch, and the gates of the town were unguarded. The enemy force stole inside the stockade undetected and then "raised their War Shout, entered the Houses, murdered every Person they met, Men, Women, and Children, naked and in cold Blood. . . ." A few saved themselves by "running out naked into the Woods in this terrible Weather"; others hid in their houses until the initial fury of the attack was spent, but when the town was set afire they too were driven into the open. In all, over sixty were slain and about twenty-seven taken pris-

[43] For more information on the Albany Convention, see *N.Y. Doc. Hist.*, II, 46–128; and Lawrence Henry Gipson, *The British Empire before the American Revolution* (Caldwell, Idaho, 1936), Vol. V, Chap. II. A convenient summary appears in Lawrence H. Leder, *Robert Livingston, 1654–1728, and the Politics of Colonial New York* (Chapel Hill, 1961), 61–69.

oner. News of the Schenectady Massacre traveled like a shudder of horror along the frontier. Wives and children, and sometimes whole families, retreated to the safety of less exposed towns, some fleeing as far as New York City. Albany's very existence seemed to be imperiled. Albany leaders once more implored the support of the other colonies: "If Albany be destroyed which is the principal land Bulwark in America against the French then there is not only an open road for French and Indians to make incursions . . . but the 5 Nations who are now for us will be forced to turn their ax the other way. . . ." [44]

As these hostilities merged into King William's War, it appeared for a time as if inter-colonial cooperation might finally materialize. The New England colonies agreed to contribute men for an overland expedition from Albany to Montreal and to lead a seaborne assault up the St. Lawrence to Quebec. The initial response of Virginia and Maryland was encouraging. But before long it became apparent that this early resolution was not to be sustained. Even New York failed to supply its promised quota of four hundred men, the more secure seaboard counties protesting the costs and inconveniences of the effort. Meanwhile the assemblies of the southern colonies, insufficiently roused to dangers threatening a distant frontier, defaulted on pledges of men and materiel. Even the Iroquois failed to press their effort fully, once they saw "that the English were lavish of Indian Lives and too careful of their own." Despite all these difficulties a poorly organized and underequipped force did finally leave Albany at the end of July, 1690, to attack Montreal. Faltering at the southern edge of Lake Champlain, the expedition was compelled to turn back after nine days of waiting for promised supplies and reinforcements that never arrived. [45]

[44] Cadwallader Colden, *The History of the Five Indian Nations* (New York, 1902), I, 139–40; "Memorial of the Agents from Albany, etc., to the Government of Connecticut," Hartford, March 12, 1690, *N.Y. Col. Docs.*, III, 694. In the case of the Schenectady Massacre the Indians involved were "Praying Indians," the name given to disaffected Iroquois who had been converted to Catholicism by French Jesuits.

[45] Colden, *Five Nations*, I, 152; "Address of the Gov. and Council of New York to the King," Aug. 6, 1691, *N.Y. Col. Docs.*, III, 796–800; "Answer of the Five Nations to Gov. Sloughter's Address," 1691, *ibid.*, 775; Gov. Fletcher to Mr. Blathwayt, New York, Sept. 10, 1692, *ibid.*, 846; "Memorial of Colonel Lodwick to the Lords of Trade," 1693, *ibid.*, IV, 53–54; Trelease, *Indian Affairs*, 302–5. The Indians also were decimated by a smallpox epidemic in the summer of 1690.

There is little doubt that the failure of these undermanned and costly efforts to take up arms against the French led directly to a resumption of the old Albany policy of neutrality. With their population depleted, their economy in disarray, and their security broken, it is hardly surprising that the citizens of Albany should begin to have second thoughts about a British imperial policy which too often left the Albany Dutch and the Iroquois standing lonely in the breach. Even so, not all of Albany's leaders returned to the neutrality policy at once. During the early years of Queen Anne's War, Peter Schuyler in particular worked to reignite patriotic fires, supporting Samuel Vetch's Canadian expedition and traveling to the Court at London with four Iroquois sachems in an effort to arouse interest in the northwest frontier and its problems. But there was now substantial sentiment at Albany against any further support for these abortive thrusts at Canada, the city preferring instead to live at peace with its neighbor, a policy which promised both physical security and renewed profits from the Canada fur trade. The wisdom of this viewpoint seemed to be confirmed in 1701 when the Iroquois joined in a treaty of peace with the French. The failure of the English to make a strong and concerted stand against the French in the 1690's left Albany, in Buffinton's opinion, "weakened, embittered, determined for the future to play a safe game." [46]

4. The "Albany Spirit"

The events of the first seventy-five years of Albany's history not only shaped many of the attitudes of the upriver population but also did much to affect the image Albany projected to its neighbors. After 1690, as Albany became increasingly reluctant to join in belligerent actions against the French, the city's reputation as a place where patriotism was regularly sacrificed for profits spread throughout the northeast. By the early years of the eighteenth century, ever-present sectional jealousies combined with ethnic rivalry to encourage a growing suspicion that the upriver center was a self-serving, money-grubbing, "foreign" enclave

[46] Armour, "The Merchants of Albany," Chaps. V and VI; Trelease, *Indian Affairs*, Chap. XII; Buffinton, "Policy of Albany," 349; G. M. Waller, *Samuel Vetch, Colonial Enterpriser* (Chapel Hill, 1960), Chaps. 7–9.

whose indifference to English interests was forever verging on the treasonable. The catch-phrase which instantly evoked the whole range of these negative images, and which served at the same time to sum up Albany's cultural and political isolation, was the "Albany Spirit."

Perhaps the foremost element of the "Albany Spirit" was its connection with the Dutch character of the upriver population. It may sound strange today to speak of English-Dutch ethnic tensions. But there were sharp stereotypes associated with the Dutch nation and people in the seventeenth century, many of which had originated during the Anglo-Dutch wars and the commercial rivalry of that period, and they were very fresh in the minds of the English-speaking colonists. They stressed the Dutchman's parsimony and shrewd trading practices, notions which have been perpetuated to this day in expressions like "Dutch-treat" and "Yankee." [47] Albany's detractors were quick to point out that the upriver Dutch were merely running true to form in continuing to trade with the enemy. Nor was it only the Canada trade that came under attack. Because it was the *handlaers* who supplied the Indians with guns, ammunition, and rum, it seemed logical enough to blame them when the same Indians raided the frontier settlements. As early as King Philip's War, Massachusetts and Connecticut had accused Albany of supplying the "comon enemy with either armes or amunition, especially the Dutch People, who you know are soe much bent upon their profit." When border raids continued during Queen Anne's War, Massachusetts accused New York of enjoying "a profound peace and profitable trade, whilst this Province has been" the victim of "bloody incursions" by the French and Indians.[48]

To the Dutch of Albany these accusations seemed unreasonable, and only showed how little outsiders understood their special problems.

[47] The preferred derivation of the word Yankee is from the Dutch Jan Kees or Kaas, a name given to Dutch pirates or freebooters of the seventeenth century. H. L. Mencken, *The American Language,* Supplement I (New York, 1960), 192–93; Jess Stein, ed., *The Random House Dictionary of the English Language* (New York, 1966); James A. H. Murray, ed., *A New English Dictionary on Historical Principles* (Oxford, 1897), I, Part II, 14.

[48] *Connecticut Colonial Records,* II, 398, quoted in Trelease, *Indian Affairs,* 232n; "Paper from Boston complaining of the Neutrality of the Five Nations," May 31, 1708, *N.Y. Col. Docs.,* V, 42–43. Armour says that Peter Schuyler and some others at Albany tried to warn the New Englanders when raiding parties were headed their way. "The Merchants of Albany," Chap. V.

The city fathers assumed that their primary responsibility was for the physical safety and economic well-being of the local inhabitants, and in their own view they followed the only course open to them. Anne Grant very likely reflected the attitude of the Schuyler family, with whom she lived in the early 1760's, when she wrote: "In all our distant colonies there is no other instance where a considerable town and prosperous settlement has arisen and flourished, in peace and safety, in the midst of nations disposed and often provoked to hostility . . . little fitted to awe and protect the whole province . . . [Albany] evidently owed its security to the wisdom of its leaders. . . ." Reasonable as this may sound today, it convinced few Englishmen in the eighteenth century. To them, Albany's Dutch leaders were "so devoted to their own private profit that every other publick principle has ever been sacrificed to it. . . ." Attitudes of this sort flourished in the xenophobic climate of New York, and once taking root were not easily dislodged. Peter Wraxall, an Englishman who became Secretary of Indian Affairs in the mid-eighteenth century, voiced the by-then familiar complaint against the Dutch traders: "Here is a Specimen of the Albanian Spirit & how little the true welfare of the publick is considered by that worthless Crew!" Wraxall referred to the Albany traders as "Dutch reptiles," and added that some might "draw their Character in blacker colors, but doubtless there have been and are many Exceptions—for my own part I know few." Some New Englanders called the Dutch "Frogs" and "Van Frogs." Cadwallader Colden gave ethnic distinctions as one basis for political alignments in the colony, inasmuch as "the prejudices which one Nation Entertains against another are often retained a long time tho' the people . . . Live in the Same Country [,] Especially where Different Languages are kept up. . . ." And indeed in Colden's own private letters he derided the "dutch boors grossly ignorant and rude who could neither write or read nor speak English." [49]

[49] Grant, *Memoirs,* I, 54; William Johnson to Lords of Trade, Sept. 24, 1755, cited in Joel Munsell, *The Annals of Albany* (Albany, 1854–1871), VIII, 54; McIlwain, ed., *Wraxall's Abridgment of Indian Affairs,* 11, 5, civ; "Memorial to his Excellency drawn by Colden," Aug. 17, 1728, copy, Rutherfurd Coll., I, 57, NYHS; "Colden's Letters on Smith's History," 1759, NYHS *Colls.,* I (1868), 205. Colden also disapproved of Peter Schuyler's "sullen Dutch manner" (*ibid.,* 199); and once wrote to Gov. Shirley of Massachusetts, "You cannot have a sufficient conception of the Ignorance & mean spirit of the Dutch members [of the Assembly] here most of them of the lowest rank of Artificers" (Colden to Shirley, New

These unfavorable opinions naturally raised the defenses of the Dutch population, which in turn produced another major feature of the "Albany Spirit," a clannish suspicion of "strangers" and their ways. Until about the middle of the eighteenth century nearly all the elective and appointive offices in the city and county of Albany were held by men of Dutch descent. Sir William Johnson's comment on this was not untypical: "There is no Justice to be expected by any Englishman in this County, nor never will, whilst the Bench of Judges & Justices is composed entirely of Dutch. . . . I could give you, Sir," he wrote Colden, "numberless Instances . . . [of their] partiality, cruelty and oppression. . . ." John Watts, a New York City resident involved in a land case at Albany, thought his treatment so unfair that he raged: "These vile Dutch will swear anything for one another." This clannishness was also shown in the hostile reception accorded to two intruding groups, British soldiers and westward migrating New Englanders. The New England migration, which had started as a trickle in the 1680's, mounted steadily as the seaboard colonies became more crowded. In 1741 Philip Livingston had tried to capitalize on this by establishing a township on frontier lands north of Albany, to which he hoped to attract both New Yorkers and New Englanders. One of the reasons this enterprise failed was that the potential Dutch settlers did not wish to mix with any but their own kin and asked Livingston (as he himself reported) "to decline N. England farmers which I have done." As it turned out the New Englanders also preferred that the lands be settled by "one Sett of People," which Livingston finally conceded "may be best." [50] The second sizeable intrusion occurred during the last two colonial wars, when expeditions launched from Albany against the French brought British troops and provisioning agents to the frontier. Friction

---

York, July 25, 1749, copy, NYHS *Colls.,* LIII [1920], 120–21). The final word on Dutch stinginess was offered by Warren Johnson, nephew of Sir William Johnson. In a diary filled with aspersions against the Dutch, young Johnson solemnly states: "The reason the Duch doe not pave the Streets of Albany is the Dread of the Stones wearing the Iron of their Cartwheels." *Journal of Warren Johnson,* 121, New York State Library, Albany. The Diary is also printed in *The Papers of Sir William Johnson* (Albany, 1921–1965), XIII, 180–214.

[50] Johnson to Colden, Ft. Johnson, Feb. 20, 1761, NYHS *Colls.,* LVI (1923), 13; Watts to General Monckton, New York, July 23, 1763, Chalmers Manscripts, New York, Volume 2, NYPL; Philip Livingston to Jacob Wendell, Albany, Jan. 15, 1742, March 16, 1741, Livingston Family Papers, MCNY.

between soldiers and the civilian population was not unusual in the colonies, but at Albany it took on the added dimension of a clash between two cultures. It was reported that "the Europian [i.e. British] Gentry have Strange notions of our Country people," and Anne Grant tells of one regiment which "turned those plain burghers into the highest ridicule. . . ." By the height of the French and Indian War in 1760, this friction had become so pronounced that the impressment of wagons and services was at a standstill, and at least one soldier was afraid to show himself in the streets "as the mob is ready to beat out his Brains." [51]

Another important aspect of the "Albany Spirit" was a profound distrust of central authority. Because the peculiar needs and problems of the upriver area so often required a special understanding, the city fathers doubted whether anyone but themselves could govern fairly. This aversion to outside control had already been shown in 1689 when Albany refused to submit to Leisler's authority. It was also shown by Albany's hot resentment of provincial laws which attempted to regulate the upriver economy. In 1678 when New York City was granted a monopoly of the export trade, and again in 1684 when it was made the sole port of entry for the colony, the citizens of Albany, whose merchants had sometimes engaged directly in overseas trade, especially to Amsterdam, protested vigorously. Only when Albany was granted a monopoly of the fur trade did their resentment partially subside. Another regulation that angered the upriver residents was the flour bolting monopoly which was conferred on New York City in 1680. The stated purpose of this act was to preserve the high quality of New York flour, a staple which was gradually replacing furs as the colony's leading export. But to the upriver millers and merchants it smacked of special interest. A concerted attack by rural leaders forced the act's repeal in 1694, but the continuing threat of its reinstatement, as well as New York City pressure for inspection of meat and wood products, kept the upriver population on constant alert. With unflagging energy Albany

[51] Philip Livingston to Jacob Wendell, New York, April 13, Aug. 25, 1747; Livingston Family Papers, MCNY; Grant, *Memoirs,* II, 285; "Petition of the Magistrates of Albany," Dec. 22, 1760, NYHS *Colls.,* LIV (1921), 385–86; General Jeffery Amherst to Cadwallader Colden, New York, Dec. 27, 1760, *ibid.,* 388–90; Lt. George Coventry to Col. John Bradstreet, Albany, July 24, 1760, copy, *ibid.,* 323–24; Gen. Amherst to Lt. Gov. James DeLancey, Oswego, July 28, 1760, *ibid.,* 324–25.

leaders continued to resist the many encroachments on their prerogatives by the central government.[52]

Such were the elements that composed the "Albany Spirit" as it
was understood in the eighteenth century. Perhaps its most succinct definition was offered by Lord Adam Gordon when he visited Albany in
1765: "The people of Albany are mostly descended of low Dutch, and
carry down with them, the true and Characteristick marks of their Native Country, Vizt an unwearied attention to their own personal and
particular Interests, and an abhorrence to all superiour powers." The
English found it hard to imagine how "foreigners . . . who know as yet
so litle of the English Constitution" could have any true love for English liberty or the glories of the British Empire. Meanwhile the "Albany
Spirit" was only the most dramatic expression of a type of parochialism
which took deep root in various localities of rural New York, inculcat-
ing attitudes which persisted over generations.[53]

This discussion of some of the manifestations and consequences

[52] Sir John Werden to Gov. Andros, St. James, Jan. 31, 1675/6, *N.Y. Col. Docs.*,
III, 238; "Gov. Dongan's Report on the State of the Province," 1686, *ibid.*, 415.
For a brief history of the port laws, see Leder, *Robert Livingston*, 19, 37–38.
Spencer, "Sectional Aspects," 400–7, discusses the flour bolting monopoly. Over
the heated opposition of upriver merchants, laws requiring inspection and brand-
ing of flour barrels were passed in 1751. At this same time inspection of meat
and wood products was instituted, giving added substance to the country merchants' fears of becoming totally subservient to the increasingly powerful New
York City merchants. Virginia D. Harrington, *The New York Merchant on the
Eve of the Revolution* (New York, 1935), 279–81, 285–87; Arthur Meier Schlesinger, *The Colonial Merchants and the American Revolution, 1763–1776* (New
York, 1918), 125, 215, 227; Flick, *History*, II, 343–44. When a bill was passed in
1771 returning responsibility for inspection of flour, pork, and beef to the upriver
counties, the only negative votes were cast by the four New York City members.
Assembly Journal (Buel), Jan. 25, 1770, Jan. 18, 1771.

[53] "The Journal of Lord Adam Gordon," in Newton D. Mereness, ed., *Travels in
the American Colonies* (New York, 1916, 1961), 416; Colden to Dr. John Mitchell, draft, July 6, 1749, NYHS *Colls.*, LXVIII (1935), 33. A number of historians
have noticed the sectional nature of New York's division over the Federal Constitution in 1788; though the explanations for this phenomenon vary, it may well
be that the "Albany Spirit" had something to do with it. Lee Benson found rem-
nants of the Albany Spirit, though he does not call it that, as late as 1840 in
Rockland County (formerly a part of Orange County). Benson tells of some predominantly Dutch towns where "ingrained resistance to change" was the fundamental political characteristic. As evidence of the staying-power of anti-Dutch attitudes, Benson cites an 1807 newspaper advertisement for laborers which

of New York's geographic, governmental, and ethnic fragmentation suggests some possible causes for the colony's political volatility. It is worth recalling that New York was the only mainland colony which had been ruled for any length of time by a foreign power, and the legacy of this was a large non-English-speaking population with deep and permanent roots in the colony.[54] New York also was the only colony whose pattern of settlement did not gradually spread outward from one primary beachhead on the seaboard. The earliest settlements at New York City, Albany, and eastern Long Island were 150 miles apart, and each developed distinctive cultural and political characteristics. Representative government with its centralizing influence was achieved only after sixty-seven years, a period during which two generations of New Yorkers had to evolve self-sufficient local government and learned to be wary of central authority. It is when one compares New York to her sister colonies that these features seem especially striking. The New England colonies encompassed a relatively homogeneous people who spoke the same language, derived from a similar background of English Protestantism, practiced standardized forms of local government, and possessed representative assemblies from a very early date. In the Chesapeake colonies, too, homogeneity of population and interest generally predominated for at least the first hundred years. The overwhelming majority of settlers were Englishmen, nominally Anglican in religion, and employed in agriculture. When substantial foreign elements started to arrive in the eighteenth century, some of the stresses which were familiar in New York began to develop, but the original settlers far outnumbered the newcomers and easily managed to maintain their early dominance over the patterns of provincial life.[55] In contrast to the New England and

---

included the qualification: "No Dutchman need apply unless he is pretty well Yankeyfied." *The Concept of Jacksonian Democracy, New York as a Test Case* (New York, 1961), 298, 302. There is a certain parallel in the restrictions against the Irish which were to be raised in Massachusetts a few years later, except that the Irish were newcomers whereas the Dutch had been in New York for nearly 200 years.

[54] New Sweden lasted only a decade and a half and involved too few settlers to make a comparable impact on Delaware society. Christopher Ward, *The Dutch and Swedes on the Delaware* (Philadelphia, 1930), *passim*.

[55] Carl Bridenbaugh, *Myths and Realities: Societies of the Colonial South* (Baton Rouge, 1952), 122–32. "Certainly the most pronounced social trait of each of the

Chesapeake colonies, New York embraced Dutch, English, German, and French peoples; its religious spectrum included Anglicans, Dutch Reformed, Presbyterians, and Quakers, to mention only the larger groups; its economic interests included landed men, fur traders, and merchants, each in substantial blocs.

It was these conditions, rather than the presence of the ruling elite so conspicuous in the pages of New York history, that imparted to the colony's politics its distinctive character. It was a character peculiarly unstable and factious. These were the conditions that confronted New York's provincial leaders, and it may well have been their very experience in dealing with them that transformed these men, whatever their social rank, from political leaders into politicians.

European nationalities was clannishness," says Bridenbaugh. "Each little group clung tenaciously to its cultural heritage and resisted with all its strength what has been called the Americanizing process." *Ibid.*, 131–32. The other middle colonies, Pennsylvania and New Jersey, would be the most like New York in both cultural heterogeneity and political contentiousness.

III

ECONOMIC INTERESTS
AND POLITICAL
CONTENTIONS

ONE OF THE MOST OBSERVABLE characteristics of New York Colony was the dual nature of its economy. With commerce and agriculture of nearly equal importance to the colony's prosperity, New York developed both a thriving merchant community and an influential body of wealthy landholders. Contemporaries took cognizance of this duality by frequent references to the "merchant interest" and the "landed" or "country interest," [1] and it is apparent from such references that the two groups sometimes found themselves in competition for political and economic advantage.

New York was the only colony where these two interests grew up

[1] For a sampling of comments on the merchant and landed interests, see Gov. Hunter to Lords of Trade, New York, Aug. 7, 1718, *N.Y. Col. Docs.,* V, 514–15; *ibid.,* 518; "May it Please your Excellency," James Alexander, 1728, draft, Rutherfurd Coll., I, 77, NYHS; Cadwallader Colden, 1728, draft statement, Rutherfurd Coll., I, 63; Lt. Gov. Clarke to Lords of Trade, New York, June 2, 1738, *N.Y. Col. Docs.,* VI, 116; Gov. Clinton to Lords of Trade, June 22, 1747, *ibid.,* 654; Robert R. Livingston to Robert Livingston, New York, Sept. 18, 1767, Robert R. Livingston Papers, I, NYHS. In eighteenth-century England the term "country party" was used to designate those opposed to the ministry in power; in New York, with rare exceptions, it simply meant the rural or upriver interest.

side by side and achieved an approximate parity of influence. In Virginia, and in the South generally, the planter interest had no competition from commercial power centers because, except for Charleston, none existed. In New England, merchants shared power with landowners and farmers, but the township pattern of land distribution prevented the growth of a class of great landholders. In New Jersey, commerce was almost nonexistent because of the overshadowing influence of the ports of New York City and Philadelphia, with the result that New Jersey's landed interest easily predominated. Pennsylvania had the potential for developing both merchant and landed interests, but so far as can be determined no clear political polarity existed between the two groups. The "Proprietary party" was not a landholding group as such, but a royalist or "court" interest that supported the Penn family and its appointees in provincial politics.[2] Only in New York, where the network of rivers draining toward the great harbor at New York City encouraged commercial development at the same time that huge parcels of land were being distributed to official favorites, did both a merchant and a landed elite of roughly equal strength emerge.

Though more than one writer has recognized that this unique economic polarity had some effect on political alignments in the colony, a full analysis of the two groups as competing interests has never been attempted. It has not always been easy to distinguish one group from the other; nor has it ever been entirely clear what inferences ought to be drawn from such distinctions. Thus despite frequent references by colonials themselves to these interests as identifiable and rival groups, most

[2] For a general discussion of each of the colonies, see Jackson Turner Main, *The Social Structure of Revolutionary America* (Princeton, N.J., 1965). Political patterns in South Carolina always varied somewhat from the southern norm, as is shown in the most recent full study of that colony. M. Eugene Sirmans, *Colonial South Carolina, A Political History, 1663–1763* (Chapel Hill, 1966). Another student of South Carolina politics has been struck by the remarkable lack of factionalism in the pre-Revolutionary period. Robert M. Weir, " 'The Harmony We Were Famous For': An Interpretation of Pre-Revolutionary South Carolina Politics," *WMQ*, 3rd Ser., XXVI (Oct., 1969), 473–501. Statistical information on landholding in colonial Pennsylvania is rather difficult to come by, but indications are that landowners did not develop a separate political interest. Gary B. Nash, *Quakers and Politics, Pennsylvania, 1681–1726* (Princeton, N.J., 1968), 52–53, 330–31; Main, *Social Structure,* 16, 25, 33–34, 192–93, 221; Theodore Thayer, *Pennsylvania Politics and the Growth of Democracy, 1740–1776* (Harrisburg, Pa., 1953), *passim.*

historians have followed Becker's lead and lumped the landholders and merchants, along with the lawyers, into a single upper class. Virginia Harrington, a leading authority on the New York merchant, offers a representative view. "Generations of inter-marriage," she writes, "had welded these first three groups [landed, merchants, and lawyers] into a large, interrelated clan whose interests could not be far separated." [3] It is only recently that we have begun to suspect that New York's ruling elite may have been less monolithic than had once been supposed. With such provocative clues as William Alexander's observation that "Interest often Connects People, who were intire Strangers, and it sometimes separats those who had the strongest natural Connections," or Philip Livingston's wry reference to his native colony as a place where "we Change Sides as Serves our Interest best not the Countries," new attention is being directed to the question of why New York leaders so often divided into rival political groupings. [4]

In the early decades of the eighteenth century the landed and merchant groups were fairly separate and distinct, and they eyed each other as competitors for place and power. Thanks to recent scholarship and newly available records, early economic rivalries may now be examined with greater precision than was once the case and a truer understanding of their influence on political alignments has become possible. [5] No

[3] Virginia D. Harrington, *The New York Merchant on the Eve of the Revolution* (New York, 1935), 11; Carl Becker, *The History of Political Parties in the Province of New York, 1760–1776* (Madison, Wis., 1909), 9–14. The best published work to date on the rivalry between the landed and merchant interests in New York is Beverly McAnear, "Mr. Robert R. Livingston's Reasons Against a Land Tax," *Journal of Political Economy,* XLVIII (1940), 63–90.

[4] William Alexander to Peter V. B. Livingston, Boston, March 1, 1756, Rutherfurd Coll., III, 93, NYHS; Philip Livingston to Jacob Wendell, July 23, 1737, Livingston Papers, Philip Livingston Box, MCNY. Philip Livingston's comment has often been misinterpreted; when read in context it is clear that he is comparing New York to Massachusetts, much to the disadvantage of the self-centered New Yorkers. For studies that question the standard view of a united elite, see Stanley N. Katz, *Newcastle's New York: Anglo-American Politics, 1732–1753* (Cambridge, Mass., 1968), 44–49; and Milton M. Klein, "Democracy and Politics in Colonial New York," *New York History,* XL (July, 1959), 238.

[5] Of greatest interest to New York historians is the material on the Philipse and Van Cortlandt families, as well as incidental records relating to other New Yorkers, being collected by Sleepy Hollow Restorations, Inc., Irvington, New York. This collection includes microfilms of seventeenth- and early eighteenth-century

crude translation of economic interest directly into political action is here suggested. *"Homo oeconomicus,"* as Marc Bloch has wisely put it, "was an empty shadow, not only because he was supposedly preoccupied by self-interest; the worst illusion consisted in imagining that he could form so clear an idea of his interests." [6] And yet under certain conditions such relationships should at least be able to tell us something. In New York economic considerations moved to the fore during the second and third decades of the eighteenth century, since that was a time of rapid growth when basic decisions were being made about fiscal policies and the direction of future development. At that time men with similar convictions on economic matters tended to close ranks, and the space between such groups widened accordingly. The sharpest polarity was that between the landed and the commercial interests, though there were sub-groups within each category. Because the goals of one group frequently could be achieved only at the expense of the other, and because the governor's support was often crucial in determining which interest would prevail, there developed a discernible struggle between the landed and merchant factions as they contended for official favor.

This contest was at the heart of New York political rivalries in the early eighteenth century. It would, to be sure, diminish in importance thereafter, and by the 1730's the New York economy was becoming so complex that lines between these interests were hard to distinguish. As early as 1732 other problems having more to do with power and legitimacy would overshadow economic concerns, and in later years a mixture of constitutional, religious, and other issues would contest for public attention. But at this earlier stage, there was no doubt that the interests of the landed and the commercial elements of New York society were not only dissimilar but were often in direct political competition.

---

shipping records in the Exchequer and Colonial Office archives in London. Also, our knowledge of early New York trade patterns has been expanded with the publication of Julius M. Block, Leo Hershkowitz, Kenneth Scott, and Constance D. Sherman, eds., *An Account of Her Majesty's Revenue in the Province of New York, 1701–09; The Customs Records of Early Colonial New York* (Ridgewood, N.J., 1966); and there is valuable information on New York's system of customs collections in Thomas C. Barrow, *Trade and Empire: The British Customs Service in Colonial America, 1660–1775* (Cambridge, Mass., 1967).

[6] Marc Bloch, *The Historian's Craft* (New York, 1953, 1964), 194–95.

1. The Merchant Interest

In the period from 1675 to about 1725 there were four families that provided the principal leadership for the New York commercial community. These were the Philipses, the Van Cortlandts, the DeLanceys, and the Schuylers. There were, indeed, other prominent merchants. But since members of these four families were political activists as well as commercial leaders, they make for the present a special claim on our attention. It may seem strange at first to find the Philipses and Van Cortlandts assigned to the merchant category; they have often been regarded primarily as landed families in view of their great estates in Westchester and Dutchess counties. But here the documents at Sleepy Hollow Restorations contain some surprises, revealing as they do that the landed concerns of these two families were always subordinate to commercial activities until at least the middle of the eighteenth century. The initial fortunes of both families were solidly grounded in commerce and, together with the DeLanceys and Schuylers, it was they who promoted with greatest vigor the interests of the commercial community.

Frederick Philipse (1627–1702), the founder of the Philipse family in the colonies, arrived in New Amsterdam about 1650 as the official carpenter and builder for the Dutch West India Company, a position which apparently carried somewhat more prestige than that of a common craftsman. It was not long before Philipse extended his activities to become a trader with the Five Nations, and in a few years he had risen to prominence as a New York City merchant. His commercial success was aided by both his first wife, Margaret Hardenbrook, and his second wife, Catharine Van Cortlandt, whose families were also active in the Indian trade. By 1674 Frederick Philipse was listed as the richest man in New York Colony, his worth of 80,000 guilders far surpassing that of his nearest rival, whose estate was valued at 50,000 guilders.[7] It has long been believed, though documentation for it has hitherto been sparse, that Philipse and other New York merchants who enjoyed a sud-

---

[7] Edward Randolph named Frederick Philipse as the "greatest trader to Albany" in 1698, and Philipse's preeminent position in early New York commerce would seem to support that assessment. "Extract of a letter from Mr. Randolph," New York, May 16, 1698, *N.Y. Col. Docs.*, IV, 311. For a listing of the wealthiest men in New York at that time, see document dated Mar. 17, 1674, *ibid.*, II,

den prosperity around that same time gained most of their fortunes by supplying English manufactured goods for the upriver Indian trade and by carrying the valuable furs back downriver for reshipment to England. But the Philipse shipping records recently made available not only give a clear picture of the large volume of that traffic; they also show that Philipse was an entrepreneur of great vision and energy who was always on the lookout for new opportunities and who by no means confined his commercial interests to one channel.

The cargoes of the ship *Beaver,* recorded in detail by customs inspectors at Dover, England, were dominated by goods shipped for Frederick Philipse and Co. Entries for the late 1670's and the 1680's show that hides and tobacco made up the bulk of Philipse's exports, varying from a cargo of 75,000 pounds of "verginia tobacco," 200 buck skins, and 200 bear skins on November 30, 1678, to a mixed listing of 1,713 beaver skins, 502 bear skins, 1,550 buck skins, 46 cow hides, 1,250 ordinary foxes, 53 timber greys, 94 timber minks, 1,100 "catts," 1,100 otters, 363 "musquashes" (muskrats), and miscellaneous others on December 7, 1686. In addition to the reshipment of Virginia tobacco, there is also frequent mention of logwood, which came from Yucatan, being shipped to Dover by way of New York. Of particular interest is the great diversity of goods which Philipse imported, many of the cargoes coming originally from Amsterdam. On February 1, 1686, the incoming cargo of the *Beaver* consisted of 537 ells of Holland linen, 72 gross tobacco pipes, 45 swords, 6 woolen night caps, 99 musket barrels, plus tools, almonds, books, children's toys, and many other items. On January 13, 1686, a cargo from Amsterdam via Dover included 1,000 ells of Holland linen, 150 iron pots, 60,000 brick stones, 100 gross tobacco pipes, 100 pairs of stockings, Holland cheese, serpentine powder, nails, and thread from Bruges. How much of this was intended for the Indian trade is not clear, but at least some items appear to have been destined for colonial homes, and a few may have been directed specifically to the Dutch market.[8]

699–700. For Frederick Philipse see the Sleepy Hollow Restoration pamphlet, *Philipsburgh Manor* (Tarrytown, N.Y., 1969); Edward H. Hall, *Philipse Manor Hall at Yonkers, New York* (New York, 1912), 45–61; *DAB*, XIV, 538 (Richard E. Day).

[8] Exchequer 190/664–17; Exchequer 190/668–18; Exchequer 190/669–4, Public Record Office, London, micro., SHR.

This general trade pattern held during the seventeenth century when the elder Philipse was in charge of the family business. But by the turn of the century when Frederick's only surviving son, Adolph, took over, a noticeable change occurred. The records show that Adolph Philipse (1665–1749) owned, in whole or in part, at least seven ships—the *Abigail, Diamond, Eagle, Phillipsburgh, Charles, Hopewell,* and the *Mayflower,* the last in partnership with Stephen DeLancey. The most apparent shifts which occurred when Adolph took charge of the business were an increase of trade with the West Indies and a greater variety of both exports and imports. At first furs continued to make up the largest share of the homeward bound shipments, but before long they were nearly equaled by such items as logwood, "Muscavado Sugar," cotton, and ginger from the West Indies. Philipse exported to the West Indies and to the other mainland colonies a growing number of New York products, especially flour, lumber, and horses. He also engaged in "the Guinea Trade," or the importation of slaves from Guinea on the west coast of Africa, receiving a shipload of 128 slaves on March 29, 1718. From about 1712 on, trade with the West Indies and the Madeira Islands began to dominate as great quantities of rum and wine were imported. By the 1720's the exportation of foodstuffs and wood products had definitely overshadowed hides, and the West Indies and reshipping trade appear to have taken up by far the largest part of Philipse's interest. This pattern was reproduced by other New York merchants as well, the Caribbean and inter-colonial trade increasing at a faster rate than that with any other area. Throughout the eighteenth century it far exceeded the total trade with England and Europe.[9]

The founder of the Van Cortlandt family, Oloff Stephen Van Cortlandt (1600–1684), came to New Amsterdam in 1638 as a soldier in the service of the Dutch West India Company. Oloff Van Cortlandt was appointed to the post of commissioner of cargoes, soon became the owner of a brewery, and in a short time was involved in other commercial ventures, including the Indian trade. In 1642 he married Anneke

[9] Philipse Shipping Records file, SHR; Exchequer 190/677–15, Exchequer 190/841–1, Colonial Office 33/15, PRO, London, micro., SHR; *The Statistical History of the United States from Colonial Times to the Present* (Stamford, Conn., 1966), 759. For Stephen DeLancey's partnership with Adolph Philipse, see E. B. O'Callaghan, ed., *Calendar of Historical Manuscripts in the Office of the Secretary of State, Albany, New York* (Albany, 1866), Part II, 286.

Lookermans, apparently a woman of some wealth, and settled down to the life of a merchant in the home he had built on Stone Street. After 1645 he served as a member of the councils which advised the Dutch governors, and he held the post of Burgomaster of New Amsterdam on two separate occasions. In 1674 Oloff Van Cortlandt was described as the fourth richest man in the colony, his worth being estimated at 30,-000 guilders. Oloff had two sons, both of whom were partners with him in the family business. Stephen Van Cortlandt (1643–1700) married Gertrude, a sister of Peter Schuyler, and Jacobus (1658–1739) married Eva DeVries, the adopted daughter of Frederick Philipse.[10]

Early Van Cortlandt shipping activities were similar to those of Frederick Philipse. The records indicate that the two families jointly owned the ship *Beaver,* and they may have had some kind of partnership arrangement. Jacobus Van Cortlandt, the sole heir after 1700 when his brother died, became particularly active in the provisioning trade to the West Indies and the other mainland colonies. His accounts for the period from 1699 to 1705 indicate that most of his trade was to Jamaica, Curaçao, and Barbados, while other ports of call included Surinam, Madeira, Amsterdam, and London. Cargoes bound for the West Indies featured pork, butter, flour, peas, staves and horses, while those headed for English and European ports included "Spanish Money," logwood, indigo, and some hides. The decline in the dominance of furs is even more noticeable here than in the Philipse records.[11]

The third great merchant family was founded by Stephen DeLancey (1663–1741), who fled Caen, France, as a Huguenot refugee in 1681, going first to Holland and then on to London. In March of 1686 when he was twenty-three years old, DeLancey set sail for New York, arriving in June, 1686, with a nest egg of £300 which represented the proceeds from the sale of some family jewels. DeLancey rose rapidly in New York City commercial circles, partly no doubt because of his marriage to Anne Van Cortlandt, daughter of Stephen Van Cortlandt. He may have made some contacts with English merchants during his stay in

[10] March 17, 1674, *N.Y. Col. Docs.,* II, 699–700; *DAB,* XIX, 161–62 (Albert Hyma).

[11] "Shipping Book of Jacobus Van Cortlandt," Aug. 12, 1699–June 30, 1702, NYHS; "Jacobus Van Cortlandt Shipping Book," Nov. 12, 1702–Dec. 28, 1705, SHR.

London which proved valuable to an enterprising young colonial merchant, if one may judge from the DeLancey family's later close ties to London mercantile houses, especially Baker and Company.[12] In 1699 Governor Bellomont accused DeLancey, along with other leading New York City merchants, including both Frederick and Adolph Philipse, of trading with pirates in goods smuggled from Madagascar. By 1711 DeLancey was prosperous enough to speculate in cocoa to the extent of some £3,000, though the plunge apparently tied up all his available capital. He also purchased wheat and flour from country traders and was active in the Indian trade. From the beginning of the eighteenth century DeLancey's name appears frequently on the shipping records, which show that he received wine from Madeira, rum and European goods from the West Indies, and European goods from England and from New England merchants. By 1728, DeLancey was described as "an eminent merchant" and "one of the richest men of the Province." [13]

The Schuyler family was founded by Philip Pietersen Schuyler, who settled at Albany about 1650. From modest beginnings as the son of an Amsterdam baker, the original Philip Schuyler chose to concentrate on commerce in the New World, trading furs with the Indians and helping to regulate that trade as one of the Albany Indian commissaries after

[12] "Memoir of the Hon. James DeLancey," by Edward F. DeLancey, *N.Y. Doc. Hist.,* IV, 627–39; J. Thomas Scharf, ed., *History of Westchester County, New York* (Philadelphia, 1886), I, 862–64. For the DeLanceys' connections with Baker and Co., see Katz, *Newcastle's New York,* 112–13, 208–9; and Chap. V below.

[13] Earl of Bellomont to Lords of Trade, Boston, July 22, 1699, *N.Y. Col. Docs.,* IV, 532; *ibid.,* 542; Gov. Montgomerie to Lords of Trade, New York, May 30, 1728, *ibid.,* V, 856–57. For DeLancey's merchant activities see Block et al., eds., *Account of Her Majesty's Revenue;* Colonial Office, 5/1222, PRO, micro, SHR; DeLancey to Robert Livingston, Feb. 14, 1710/11, Livingston-Redmond MSS, cited in Lawrence H. Leder, *Robert Livingston, 1654–1728, and the Politics of Colonial New York* (Chapel Hill, 1961), 215; *ibid.,* 217; G. M. Waller, *Samuel Vetch, Colonial Enterpriser* (Chapel Hill, 1960), 49–51; Barrow, *Trade and Empire,* 96. It has sometimes been suggested that Stephen DeLancey was the foremost New York City supplier of European goods to the Canadian fur traders at Albany. A check of the presently available records indicates, however, that DeLancey's business, like that of his fellow city merchants, was largely with the West Indies and in the reshipping trade. In 1705, DeLancey joined with other New York City merchants in pointing to wheat as the "principal staple" of New York trade, "excepting the small trade in peltry which is now so diminished as scarce worth regarding. . . ." "Petition of the Merchants of the City of New-York relating to Foreign Coin," Feb., 1705, *N.Y. Col. Docs.,* IV, 1133. The

1656. His son, and the leading family member in the period we are concerned with, was Peter Schuyler (1657–1724), who extended the family interests by means of two prudent marriages, the first to Engeltie Van Schaack of the Albany merchant family, and the second to Marie Van Rensselaer, granddaughter of the original Patroon of Rensselaers-wyck.[14] Peter Schuyler was the dominant figure in the Albany fur trade from 1686, when at age twenty-nine he was appointed the first mayor under the Dongan Charter, until his death in 1724. This preeminence was based on two main factors. By learning their language and respecting their traditions, Schuyler gained a position of influence with the Iroquois which would be equaled by no other white man until William Johnson came to Albany County in 1738. The Iroquois honored Schuyler by naming him Quidor, the Indian equivalent of Peter, and by conducting their negotiations through him whenever possible. The other source of Schuyler's power was his political position, first as mayor of Albany from 1686 to 1694, which made him a leading formulator of Indian policy, and then as a member of the governor's Council from 1692 until 1720. Throughout those years Schuyler was an outspoken advocate of the interests of Albany, the fur traders, and the Iroquois, and it seems to have been that role, rather than his personal position as a merchant, which led to his involvement with the Philipse-Van Cort-landt-DeLancey group in the early decades of the eighteenth century.[15]

---

suggestion that DeLancey almost alone engrossed the Indian trade was made in Charles H. McIlwain, ed., *An Abridgment of the Indian Affairs . . . 1678 to the Year 1751, by Peter Wraxall* (Cambridge, Mass., 1915), lxvi–lxviii, but this was only a speculation, and is backed by no evidence.

[14] *New York Genealogical and Biographical Record,* LXIX (January, 1938), 20; George W. Schuyler, *Colonial New York* (New York, 1885), I, 99–120.

[15] Allen W. Trelease, *Indian Affairs in Colonial New York: The Seventeenth Century* (Ithaca, N.Y., 1960), 209–10; Arthur H. Buffinton, "The Policy of Albany and English Westward Expansion," *MVHR,* VIII (March, 1922), 353, 359; Don R. Gerlach, *Philip Schuyler and the American Revolution in New York, 1733–1777* (Lincoln, Neb., 1964), 2; David Arthur Armour, "The Merchants of Albany, New York: 1686–1760," unpubl. Ph.D. diss. (Northwestern University, 1965), Chaps. V, VI, p. 222. Anne Grant sketches Peter Schuyler in the following manner: "The powerful influence, that his knowledge of nature and of character, his sound judgment and unstained integrity, had obtained over both parties, made him the bond by which the aborigines were united with the colonists." *Memoirs of an American Lady* (New York, 1901), I, 128.

These four families, then, constituted the leadership of the New York merchant community in the early eighteenth century. The Philipses, Van Cortlandts, and DeLanceys centered their activities at New York City, while the Schuylers spoke for the interests of the upriver merchants. That commerce rather than land was their dominant concern in the early years is shown by their urban residences and their regular public designation as "merchants," as well as their almost reflex reaction against any political threat to commercial interests. This partiality by no means precluded a desire on their parts to accumulate landed estates. In that age there was no more compelling symbol of social prestige or the rank of gentleman than the possession of land. Moreover, land was obviously one of the soundest investments one could make in the colonies. By using their influence with various colonial governors, most notably Governor Benjamin Fletcher (1692–1698), the merchant leaders pursued this goal with spectacular success. Frederick Philipse's 90,000-acre patent in Westchester, originally granted in the 1680's, was formally erected into the Manor of Philipsburgh in 1693. In 1697 Philipse's son, Adolph, received the 205,000-acre Highland Patent, which today comprises the whole of Putnam County. Adolph also received, at the death of his father in 1702, the northern section of Philipsburgh Manor known as the "Upper Mills." The Van Cortlandts had been accumulating land for some years before the 86,000-acre Manor of Cortlandt was granted to Stephanus Van Cortlandt in 1697. His brother, Jacobus, owned adjacent lands in the villages of Bedford and Katonah as well as several hundred acres at the site of present-day Van Cortlandt Park in The Bronx.[16]

Though these landed estates will be discussed in greater detail in a subsequent chapter, two points may suffice for the present purpose. Inasmuch as settlement on these great patents was sparse in the early years, the lands were valued mainly in terms of future potential. Moreover, the relationship of at least the first two generations of Philipses and Van Cortlandts to their estates was that of absentee landlords, with

[16] Frederick Philipse's will is in NYHS *Colls.,* XXV (1892), 369–74. Irving Mark, *Agrarian Conflicts in Colonial New York, 1711–1775* (New York, 1940, 1965), 21; Katherine M. Beekman and N. M. Isham, "The Story of Van Cortlandt" (New York, 1917); Rev. Robert Bolton, *The History of Westchester County* (New York, 1881), II, 616–17.

a resident overseer handling whatever details were involved in day-to-day operation. Both the Philipses and the Van Cortlandts lived in their large New York City houses, though by the eighteenth century some members of the two families apparently spent part of the summer at their country places. But life on a New York manor was far from elegant in those early years; it had virtually nothing in common with that of the English gentry. Archeological investigations show that for many years the Philipse "manor house," in present-day Yonkers, was no more than a rough outpost, the structure consisting of a cellar beneath two rooms, with each level measuring thirty-two by twenty-one feet. Additions which tripled the size of the Philipse house were made in the eighteenth century, probably in 1750, though the east parlor section may have been built as early as 1720. Similar investigation has shown that prior to 1700 the structure on Cortlandt Manor resembled a fort and Indian trading post, with gradual additions from 1700 to 1749 enlarging the main house to its present size. It was not until 1749 that a member of the family, Pierre Van Cortlandt, took up permanent residence at the manor. The date when the first domicile, "a large stone dwelling house," was built on the Van Cortlandt property in The Bronx has been established definitely as 1748. So far as can be determined, no country seat ever was constructed on the Highland Patent during the colonial era, though Adolph Philipse spent some time at the Upper Mills in Westchester County during the summer.

Philipse's relationship to his estate around the year 1740 suggests the typical pattern for a New York merchant-gentleman. He lived and worked in New York City, making the Upper Mills at Philipse Manor his "occasional home, although his mercantile pursuits in the city, for the most part required his absence from his estate. Mr. Aartse was the overseer of this establishment. The consequence of the absenteeism of the lord was of course the absence of all the usual appendages of state and social style in manorial life. . . ." [17] From all the evidence, it ap-

[17] Robert Wheeler, "Philipse Manor Hall, Yonkers," undated SHR; "Interpretive Paper of the Restoration of Van Cortlandt Manor," Prepared by the Architects Office of Colonial Williamsburg (Williamsburg, 1959); Hall, *Philipse Manor*, 108–9, 233, 245. The description of Adolph Philipse's activities is in D. T. Valentine, *Manual of The Corporation of the City of New-York for 1858* (New York, 1858), 519. Sleepy Hollow Restorations spent several years carefully restoring the

pears that the tenanting and exploitation of their vast country estates were strictly a subsidiary interest to these successful New York City merchants, the bulk of whose wealth came from enterprises which required that their activities and attention be city-centered.

Stephen DeLancey also speculated in land, though his investments and those of his descendants were most often concentrated in New York City. Second-generation DeLanceys did invest in some country properties, and one member of the family, Peter DeLancey, actually lived on his farm in Westchester. More typical, however, were Oliver DeLancey and Chief Justice James DeLancey, who had some investments in Mohawk and other upriver lands but held them mainly for speculative purposes. Peter Schuyler did not accumulate large amounts of land, despite his location on New York's northern frontier where many of the great patents were situated. He started out with a meager inheritance of a few hundred acres from his father. His holdings seemed to expand dramatically when he became one of the grantees of the 537,000-acre Dellius Patent carved out by Governor Fletcher in 1696, but this windfall came to nothing when the patent was later vacated by the Privy Council. In 1694, Schuyler had become a one-seventh partner in the Saratoga Patent and it was this, greatly supplemented through subsequent purchases by family members, which in later years formed the main Schuyler holdings. This land, however, was not developed by Peter Schuyler. It would not be fully exploited until many years later by his great-nephew, Philip Schuyler (1733–1804).[18]

Upper Mills, in present-day North Tarrytown, to its condition circa 1720–1750. In 1969 the completed project—including the stone house, a barn, a working gristmill, a dam, and an exhibition center—was opened to the public. According to SHR authorities, the Upper Mills was a "trading center," where local grain was milled before being shipped downriver to New York City.

[18] For correspondence between Oliver DeLancey and his Albany County land agents, as well as other information on DeLancey landholdings, see Bound Volumes, Miscellaneous Manuscripts, DeLancey, Box 10, NYHS. Stephen DeLancey's will is in NYHS *Colls.,* XXVII (1894), 336–38. William Johnson to Robert Leake, Ft. Johnson, April 1, 1762, *The Papers of Sir William Johnson,* X, 418; Harry Yoshpe, "The DeLancey Estate, Did the Revolution Democratize Landholding in New York?" *New York History,* XVII (April, 1936), 167–79; Gerlach, *Philip Schuyler,* 48–62, 316–18; Mark, *Agrarian Conflicts,* 21, 25–27. For a listing of DeLancey lands confiscated after the Revolution, see Alexander C. Flick, *Loyalism in New York During the American Revolution* (New York, 1901), 215–72.

2. The Landed Interest

There were, on the other hand, a number of families in New York whose prominence did derive more directly from their possession of large landed estates, and their outlook differed accordingly. These families usually resided on their country estates, and they tended over time to cultivate, at least superficially, the values and life-style of the English gentry. They took up similar positions in defense of real property interests, banding together to resist higher taxes and a variety of public pressures against land engrossment practices. From this loose alliance there emerged two families, the Morrises and the Livingstons, which were to provide the main political leadership for the landed or country interest over several generations.

The founder of the Morris family in New York was Richard Morris, a captain in Cromwell's army, who sought refuge abroad about the time of the Restoration. His son, Lewis Morris (1671–1746), was less than a year old when he was left an orphan by the unseasonable deaths of both his parents. For two years Morris was "entirely in the hands of strangers," until a paternal uncle, Lewis Morris of Barbados, arrived in New York in 1674 to assume responsibility for the boy. When the uncle died in 1691, young Lewis inherited the family estates, which consisted of two valuable parcels of land. The Westchester County tract of around 3,000 acres was erected into the Manor of Morrisania in 1697; another 3,500-acre estate, Tintern Manor, was located in Monmouth County, New Jersey. From about 1691 until 1710 Lewis Morris centered his activities in New Jersey, where he became a leading member of the Council and a judge of the court of common right. During those years he resided on his Monmouth County estate, which as early as 1680 was said to have had an iron "mill" and farms "together with 60 or 70 Negroes about the Mill and Husbandry." With the arrival in 1710 of Robert Hunter as governor of New York and New Jersey, Morris shifted many of his activities to New York. Because of his close ties to Hunter, he was appointed chief justice of the Supreme Court in 1715; he also sat in the New York Assembly, first as member from the Borough of Westchester from 1710 until 1728, and then as representative from the

County of Westchester from 1733 until he returned to New Jersey as governor in September, 1738.[19]

Lewis Morris had no particular affinity for or involvement with commerce, preferring instead the role of country squire and public servant in imitation of the style of the English gentry. How fully Morris shared the view that commerce was an inferior occupation unworthy of a true gentleman is uncertain, but some of his writings give hints of such a prejudice.[20] In any case, his own affiliations were with the land, and he was lavish in the time and energy he devoted to his estates. Morris's initial holdings, though not large, were favorably situated for settlement and cultivation and he was intimately concerned with the details of their development. When he removed from Tintern Manor in New Jersey, he placed his son John in charge but continued to exercise over it what must at times have seemed an overbearing paternal solicitude. He offered periodic advice about tenant relations, workers' wages, and additions to buildings on the property. When a new barn was to be erected, he recommended that his son make an agreement with the builder "in writing . . . down even to the drawing of a nail. . . ." He feared that John might be "too credulous" in hiring new laborers during the winter, when they would probably "eat as much as they can earn." At other times he sent detailed instructions on how to repair the mill, how to put in a new parlor chimney, where to go to have the farm tools sharpened, and how to sow the crops in correctly spaced rows.[21] Though no record of Morris's activities at Morrisania has survived, in

[19] *The Papers of Lewis Morris, Governor of the Province of New Jersey from 1738 to 1746,* New Jersey Historical Society *Collections,* 1852 (Newark, N.J., 1852), IV, 3, 5–14, 323; Katz, *Newcastle's New York,* 70–73.

[20] In one of Morris's numerous literary efforts—a long tract entitled "Dialogue Concerning Trade"—he pits a "Countryman" against a "Merchant" with results hardly flattering to the merchant. The latter is accused of not bearing his share of the public costs, engaging in shady dealings with pirates and slave traders, and generally failing to support government and the public welfare (n.d. [post 1726], Morris MSS, Box 2, Rutgers).

[21] Lewis Morris to John Morris, Morrisania, Nov. 3, 1732, Morris MSS, (John Morris Papers), Box 2; Lewis Morris to John Morris, Morrisania, April 22, 1730, March 8, 1738, Morris MSS, Box 1, Rutgers University. By the time of his death in 1746, Morris owned additional lands in New Jersey and the Mohawk Valley, but apparently he devoted his major efforts to improving Morrisania and Tintern Manor. *Governor Lewis Morris Papers,* 323–29.

all likelihood he showed a similar devotion to the improvement of his New York estate.

Morris's son, Lewis Morris, Jr. (1698–1762), continued the landed traditions of the family as second proprietor of the Manor of Morrisania. His attachment to the land may be inferred from his reply to the suggestion that he join his father in London in 1735. "I am now in the middle of my Harvest," he wrote, "and not one Soul to take any care but myself so that if I don't secure my Crop my Summer's work will be gone and the consequence of that will be the begging of my Bread." It was not until after the middle of the eighteenth century that any member of the Morris family became directly involved in commerce, when Lewis Morris III acted as one of the contractors to provision William Shirley's Niagara expedition against the French in 1755–1756. And then the venture proved abortive.[22]

One assigns the Livingstons to the landed interest almost automatically. Their great estate in Albany County, Livingston Manor, the substantial family holdings in Dutchess and Ulster counties, as well as their close ties with other Hudson Valley proprietors, all strengthen their image as a family of land barons. Nonetheless, the original Livingston to settle in New York, Robert Livingston (1654–1728), was first and foremost a merchant, and only after making his mark in trade and politics at Albany did he turn his considerable talents to the accumulation of a landed estate.

Livingston was the son of a Scotch Presbyterian minister who was forced into exile after the Restoration. Fortunately for young Robert, the family settled in Rotterdam where, in addition to learning the Dutch language, the boy plunged into the world of trade with such exuberance that by the age of sixteen he was already shipping goods on his own account. Three years later Robert Livingston decided to try his luck in the colonies. By the end of 1674, at the age of twenty, he was settled at Albany, where his fluency in Dutch soon made him indispensable to the colonial government. His marriage in 1679 to Alida Schuyler Van

[22] Lewis Morris, Jr., to James Alexander, 1735, quoted in Livingston Rutherfurd, *Family Records and Events* (New York, 1894), 15; "Order by Major General Shirley," Sept. 9, 1755, William Alexander Papers, I, NYHS; "Appointment of Geo. Craddock and others to examine accounts, by William Shirley," April 15, 1756, James Abercrombie to Messrs. Livingston & Morris, Albany, July 5, 1756, Rutherfurd Coll., III, 37, 129, NYHS.

Rensselaer, widow of Nicholas Van Rensselaer, connected him to two of the leading families in Albany County and certified him a rising star in the provincial firmament. Once established, Livingston began to look about for a means of joining the ranks of the landholders. He first cast a covetous eye toward the Van Rensselaer estate, a portion of which he claimed as the rightful property of his wife, though her first husband had died intestate. When this maneuver was thwarted by the Van Rensselaers, Livingston next began to purchase from the Indians small tracts of land, whose boundaries were conveniently vague. In a series of complicated transactions, made possible by his friendly relationship with Governor Thomas Dongan, Livingston was made the proprietor of the 160,000-acre Livingston Manor in 1686.[23]

Even after acquiring this handsome estate, Robert Livingston continued his merchandising business at Albany, being succeeded in that enterprise by his son Philip (1686–1749), who also fell heir to the major portion of Livingston Manor when his father died in 1728. The lower section of the manor, Clermont, was given to a second son, Robert, whose descendants thereafter would be known as the Clermont Livingstons. Later generations of Livingstons divided their activities among land, commerce, and the law. A third-generation Philip Livingston (1716–1778) was a prominent New York City merchant, as were Peter Van Brugh and James Livingston. William Livingston (1723–1790) was a lawyer whose biting satirical writings enlivened New York politics in the late colonial period, while Robert Livingston, Jr. (1708–1790), grandson of the founder, resided at Livingston Manor as the third proprietor. The Clermont branch of the family produced Robert R. Livingston (1718–1775), Dutchess County landowner and Supreme Court judge, and Robert R. Livingston, Jr. (1746–1813), who would be the first chancellor of New York State.[24] Despite these varied connections, however, the Livingstons' main affinities throughout the colonial period were with the landed gentry. The reasons for this are several, and bear looking into.

[23] Leder, *Robert Livingston,* 3–9, Chap. II; Mark, *Agrarian Conflicts,* 21.

[24] Joan Gordon, "The Livingstons of New York 1675–1860: Kinship and Class," unpubl. Ph.D. diss. (Columbia University, 1959); Leder, *Robert Livingston,* 256–57; Edwin Brockholst Livingston, *The Livingstons of Livingston Manor* (New York, 1910).

First, the original Robert Livingston, and later his son Philip, were never made full partners in the Albany fur trade monopoly. The Dutch fur merchants' ambivalence on this point often led the Livingstons to side with the Van Rensselaers and other upriver traders who challenged the *handlaers'* powerful grip on the Albany economy. Second, both Robert and Philip Livingston were the beneficiaries of government patronage in the form of numerous offices and military provisioning contracts, in the light of which the Livingstons tended to support the programs of the colonial governors. Because British policy generally was hostile to the French in those years, this automatically ranged the Livingstons in opposition to the merchants active in the Canadian fur trade. Third, the Livingstons were engaged in a fairly diversified trade which, in addition to furs, featured grains and wood products and thus directed their attention toward settlement and cultivation of the land. Fourth, and perhaps most important, was the increasingly central position Livingston Manor came to hold in the family's affections.[25]

In 1715 Governor Hunter confirmed the manor patent, granting with it the new privilege of a seat in the General Assembly. This was a privilege of no small importance, the Assembly at that time consisting of but twenty-four members, which meant that each one was automatically a person of consequence. Robert Livingston represented the manor until his death in 1728, though it is difficult to determine how much time he spent on the premises. There is at present no definite information on when the first manor house was built, though one writer says that Livingston and his wife, Alida, were residing on the manor as early as 1717. In any case, it was not until Philip Livingston, the second proprietor, assumed the management of the estate that a full effort to exploit its resources was undertaken. Philip Livingston made some progress in attracting tenants to the manor, increased the productivity of the saw and grist mills, and began to exploit the manor's iron ore deposits with the construction around 1740 of the Ancram furnace. This last was a favorite project of Philip Livingston and his son Robert Livingston, Jr., the third proprietor, and by the middle of the eighteenth

[25] Leder, *Robert Livingston*, 18–20, 196–98, 202–3; Trelease, *Indian Affairs*, 357; Armour, "Merchants of Albany," 163. Both Robert Livingston and his son Philip held many offices, ranging from clerk of Albany County, to secretary for Indian affairs, to membership on the provincial Council.

century the furnace employed one hundred workers. In 1765 Robert Livingston, Jr., who resided permanently on the manor and devoted all of his energy to its improvement, estimated that his "manufactoryes" (iron, grist, and saw mills) "now bring me nearly one hundred pounds per week, which I believe more than any Gentleman in America can this day Say." Just as in the case of Lewis Morris, one finds scattered throughout the correspondence of Philip and Robert Livingston, Jr., comments which show an intimate concern with the day-to-day details of running the family estate—comments upon everything from the development of a major industry like iron smelting down to the building of a small dam.[26]

The Livingstons' steady rise to wealth and power, supplemented by a taste for public office, led to their emergence along with the Morrises as leading spokesmen for the landed gentry. After about 1720, another group of men joined the Morris-Livingston faction in opposing the commercial interest. This group, falling somewhat outside the landed-merchant dichotomy, is more difficult to categorize. It contained three main figures, of whom two were lawyers, James Alexander (1691–1756) and William Smith, Sr. (1697–1769). The third was that *uomo universale,* Cadwallader Colden (1688–1776), physician, scientist, mathematician, historian, and public servant. Smith, the son of a tallow chandler, arrived in New York in 1715, attended Yale College, and was admitted to the New York bar in 1724. Alexander also came to the colonies in 1715, serving first as surveyor general of New Jersey and later settling in New York where he became a member of the bar in 1723. Colden, a protégé of Governor Robert Hunter, was per-

---

[26] Philip Livingston to Robert Livingston, Livingston Manor, April 22, 1717, Livingston-Redmond MSS, Reel 3; Philip Livingston to John DeWitt, Albany, March 5, 1741, Livingston-Redmond MSS, Reel 7; Philip Livingston to Robert Livingston, Jr., Albany, July 11, 1741, Livingston-Redmond MSS, Reel 5; Robert Livingston, Jr., to James Alexander, Livingston Manor, Jan. 22, 1753, Rutherfurd Coll., III, 203, NYHS; Robert Livingston, Jr., to James Duane, Livingston Manor, Nov. 30 1765, Sept. 21, 1767, Duane Papers, NYHS; Leder, *Robert Livingston,* 246–47. The first proprietor of the manor gained some income from his estate, particularly from Governor Hunter's Palatine naval stores scheme of 1710, but compared with later profits these early ventures reaped a small pecuniary gain. *Ibid.,* Chap. XIII. George Dangerfield says that the first manor house was built in 1692, and enlarged in 1698. *Chancellor Robert R. Livingston of New York, 1746–1813* (New York, 1960), 14.

suaded to come to New York from Pennsylvania in 1718 by Hunter's offer of the post of surveyor general.[27]

Each of the men whose careers have been so far noted was destined to play an important role in the political life of New York Colony. In the political contests of the years from 1713 to about 1732, the merchant interest was led by Adolph Philipse, Jacobus Van Cortlandt, Stephen DeLancey, and Peter Schuyler, while the landed interest was led by Lewis Morris and Robert Livingston with additional support from James Alexander, William Smith, Sr., Cadwallader Colden, and Philip Livingston. Some of those events will be discussed in the pages that follow.

3. The Backdrop: The Leislerian Upheaval— Fiscal Policies

The party rivalries of the first decades of the eighteenth century are not fully comprehensible without some sense of the political disruptions that immediately preceded them. The major one was Leisler's Rebellion, an aftershock of the Glorious Revolution in England, which kept New York in a state of political turmoil for approximately twenty years after Leisler himself had departed the scene.

One of the effects of James II's displacement by William and Mary in 1688 was an undermining of the authority of James's colonial appointees. When word of the Glorious Revolution reached North America in the spring of 1689, the colonists realized at once that they were faced with a *de facto* power vacuum until new administrators could be dispatched with full authority to speak and act in the name of the new monarchs. Thus, whereas in England the transition from James II to William and Mary was relatively swift and smooth, in the colonies the period of administrative slack and uncertainty was prolonged by the delays of communication across three thousand miles of ocean. This in turn led to sharp upheavals in several areas. In New York, the precipi-

[27] Nicholas Varga, "New York Government and Politics During the Mid-Eighteenth Century," unpubl. Ph.D. diss. (Fordham University, 1960), xix, xxiii; Alice M. Keys, *Cadwallader Colden* (New York, 1906); *DAB*, I, 167–68 (George Rose III); *ibid.*, XVII, 352–53 (Richard B. Morris).

tate flight in June, 1689, of the chief administrative officer, Lieutenant Governor Francis Nicholson, left the colony without a head and was a signal for the release of a number of pent-up tensions and rivalries.

Historians differ over the origins of the discontent which found expression in Leisler's Rebellion. Economic distress, political repression, class rivalries, ethnic and religious tensions, and regional jealousies all have been assigned as causes. But there is general agreement on the basic events of the rebellion and on the primary role played by Jacob Leisler (1640–1691), a New York City merchant and militia captain who seized the occasion of the crisis to become the leader of the colonial insurgents. The story of Leisler's twenty-one stormy months at the helm forms a dramatic episode in the history of New York. Of equal importance, however, was the legacy of rancor and reprisal which remained long after Jacob Leisler had paid the price for his brief fame with a traitor's death on the gallows on May 16, 1691. In the aftermath of the rebellion New York divided into Leislerian and anti-Leislerian factions. After 1691 the Leislerians were led by a group of moderately successful merchants—Gerardus Beekman, Abraham DePeyster, Samuel Staats, Peter Delanoy, and Abraham Gouverneur—while the anti-Leislerians were led by such solid citizens as Stephanus Van Cortlandt, Robert Livingston, Nicholas Bayard, Peter Schuyler, Frederick Philipse, and William Nicoll.[28]

Following the overthrow of Jacob Leisler in 1691, the now all-powerful anti-Leislerians determined to destroy their former rivals. Ten Leislerian leaders were indicted and tried for treason and murder. Two —Leisler and his chief aide, Jacob Milborne—were executed, and at least six were imprisoned, their property confiscated, and they themselves excluded from all offices. To stem this torrent of vengeance, which could only divide and weaken the colony further, the imperial

[28] Jerome R. Reich, *Leisler's Rebellion, A Study of Democracy in New York, 1664–1720* (Chicago, 1953); Lawrence H. Leder, "The Politics of Upheaval in New York, 1689–1709," *New-York Historical Society Quarterly,* XLIV (Oct., 1960), 413–27; Leder, *Robert Livingston,* 57–64; Michael G. Hall, Lawrence H. Leder, and Michael G. Kammen, eds., *The Glorious Revolution in America, Documents on the Colonial Crisis of 1689* (Chapel Hill, 1964), especially 83–140; Herbert L. Osgood, *The American Colonies in the Eighteenth Century* (New York, 1924, 1958), II, Chap. 18. Reich's book is the only full-scale investigation of Leisler's Rebellion to date and, though it too often slips into the "aristocracy" versus "democracy" oversimplifications characteristic of early twentieth-century writings, it is replete with interesting details.

government advocated a policy of pacification. Both the Privy Council and the Board of Trade adopted a nonpunitive attitude toward the Leislerians, recommending pardons for those in prison, prohibiting any further prosecutions, reversing the bills of attainder, and in 1695 actually upholding the legality of the late Jacob Leisler's governorship. But within the colony itself reconciliation made little headway, and whatever small chance there might have been for a détente was lost when Benjamin Fletcher was appointed governor in 1692. Fletcher, who would have done well to adopt a neutral stance, in view of what was now known in the colony about the home government's attitude, instead threw all his influence on the side of the anti-Leislerians. The usual explanation for this is that Fletcher's main objective as governor was to improve his fortune, and by allying himself with the large merchants and landholders who dominated the Council and other offices at that time, he gained a share in their commercial and speculative enterprises. The evidence would seem to bear this out. During Fletcher's administration (1692–1698) New York became notorious as a haven for pirates; this was a peak period, moreover, for the distribution of vast land grants in the Hudson Valley.[29]

Fletcher was succeeded by quite another sort of governor, for Richard Coote, Earl of Bellomont, was a firm believer in orderly imperial administration. He was appalled at the conditions he found at New York on his arrival in 1698, and though he tried valiantly to remain above party, the need to rebalance interests eventually led him into an alliance with the Leislerians. Bellomont's efforts to break Fletcher's exorbitant land grants, his enforcement of customs regulations, and his restoring of some Leislerians to office all made him the target of anti-Leislerian hostility. His enemies converted every point at dispute in the colony into an anti-administration issue, from controversies within the Anglican and Dutch Reformed churches, uneasiness over economic decline, and election irregularities, to the alleged alienation of the Iroquois tribes.

After Bellomont's death in 1701, his policies were continued during the brief tenure of Lieutenant Governor John Nanfan, but with

[29] Reich, *Leisler's Rebellion*, 117–19, 127–37. For a discussion of Fletcher's administration and of the reforming efforts, both in New York and England, of his successor, Lord Bellomont, see John D. Runcie, "The Problem of Anglo-American Politics in Bellomont's New York," *WMQ*, 3rd Ser., XXVI (April, 1969), 191–217.

the arrival in 1702 of Edward Hyde, Viscount Cornbury, the parties once again exchanged places. Cornbury seems to have been molded from the same clay as Fletcher. Upon finding that his own self-interest would best be served by joining with the great merchants and landholders of the anti-Leislerian party, the new governor supported their positions on revenue bills and trade acts, and approved the repeal of Bellomont's bills vacating a number of great land patents.[30]

Thus the political history of New York from 1692 until 1710 is a rapid series of policy and party reversals which pitted "ins" against "outs" and interest against interest, making factional strife an almost endemic condition of the colony's public life. Moreover, New Yorkers were learning the importance of gaining the ear of an incoming governor or, failing that, of developing means to obstruct his administration.

The poisonous and quarrelsome atmosphere which was thus created, though diminishing slightly as some of the leading antagonists passed from the scene, still pervaded New York in 1710 when Robert Hunter arrived to assume the governorship. Hunter turned out to be an exceptional governor; a man of integrity, wit, and tact, he easily dominates a field where mediocrity of virtue and ability was too often the norm. Of Scotch descent, Hunter had made his mark in England by means of a favorable marriage to the daughter of Sir Thomas Orby and by an outstanding record as an officer in the British army. A fondness for belles-lettres and a gift for satire had given him "an intimacy with the distinguished men of wit at that time in England." A friend of Jonathan Swift and an occasional contributor to *The Tatler,* he was attracted to "men of Learning and encouraged them whenever he had opportunity." Historians agree on the whole that Hunter broke the old factions and restored a degree of stability to New York politics, a feat which he brought off by combining an extraordinary political skill and responsiveness to colonial sensibilities with a judicious distribution of offices to both pro- and anti-Leislerians.[31]

[30] Reich, *Leisler's Rebellion,* 137–66. On Bellomont's plan of land redistribution, see John C. Rainbolt, "A 'great and usefull designe': Bellomont's Proposal for New York, 1698–1701," *New-York Historical Society Quarterly,* LIII (Oct., 1969), 333–51.

[31] William Smith, *The History of the Late Province of New-York, From its Discovery, to the Appointment of Governor Colden, in 1762* (New York, 1830), I, 232–36; Osgood, *American Colonies, Eighteenth Century,* II, Chap. 19; Leder,

While it is true that old animosities subsided after 1710, it is equally true that Hunter's administration saw and sometimes nurtured the emergence of a new political alignment—one which would pit merchants against the landed gentry. This development has been obscured by a tendency to take at face value both Hunter's memorable farewell address of 1719, in which he asserted that "the very Name of Party or Faction seems to be forgot," and the Assembly's response, which praised his "just, mild and tender Administration." [32] It should be noted, however, that by 1719 Hunter's supporters formed a majority in the Assembly, and that the panegyric to the governor was written by his most loyal political collaborator, Lewis Morris. Nonetheless it is true that the final coalescense of the new factions did not occur until the arrival of Hunter's successor, Governor Burnet. Perhaps Hunter's administration is best characterized as the lull before the storm, a lull during which the opposing forces were gathering strength. The issue which above all others divided the landed and merchant interests was finances —specifically the question of how best to raise the colonial revenue—a matter of fundamental importance to anyone with a substantial interest in the New York economy. The divisive character of this problem was inherent in the nature of New York's fiscal structure.

New York Colony had a two-part system by which it obtained the money required to sustain government. The larger portion of the colony's budget—popularly called "the revenue"—consisted of money granted by the Assembly for such standard expenses as salaries for the governor and other provincial officers and the ordinary day-to-day costs of government operation. This basic income was raised by "indirect" taxes, that is, by means of duties on trade and internal excise taxes. Duties fell most consistently on imported rum, wines, and other spirits. There was also a duty, ranging from 2 to 10 per cent, which was periodically imposed on "European goods" and articles used in the Indian trade, and after 1702 a duty was regularly charged on the importation of Negroes. The only substantial export duty was that placed on furs; after 1683 the fee was 9 pence on each beaver skin and a smaller sum

---

Robert Livingston, 241; Reich, *Leisler's Rebellion,* 167–71. For Hunter's biography see Colden to His Son, Coldengham, Sept. 25, 1759, NYHS *Colls.,* I (1868), 192–206; *DAB,* IX, 401–2 (Richard L. Beyer).

[32] *Assembly Journal* (Gaine), I, June 24, 1719.

on other peltry. A further tax on trade was the occasional "tonnage duty" levied on foreign vessels trading at New York. New York City merchants felt particularly oppressed by the tonnage duty, charging that its effect was to divert trade to the free port of Perth Amboy in New Jersey. The excise tax fell mainly on the retail sale of liquors and was collected by government-appointed excise "farmers" in each county. Another source of income was the excise irregularly placed on carriages, chimneys, and goods sold at auction.[33]

A second type of income was derived from the direct tax levied on property, though this was imposed by the Assembly not on a regular basis but "as needed," and made up a smaller portion of the colonial revenue. The property tax was usually imposed either in connection with defense requirements during the inter-colonial wars or to finance gifts to the Iroquois Nation in the continuous effort to assure friendly relations in that important quarter. Once the total amount required had been agreed upon by the General Assembly, the quota to be raised by each county was apportioned by a series of votes. The actual gathering of this tax was done by locally elected collectors on the basis of the rate set for each head of family by locally elected assessors. That rate was based on the value of the taxpayer's personal and *improved* real property, the latter being an important qualification to the Hudson Valley patentees, whose huge estates were settled and productive only in areas adjacent to the River. During the period from 1691 to 1715 the indirect taxes which made up the larger share averaged about £4,000 a year in contrast to approximately £2,700 a year raised by means of direct property taxes.[34]

[33] *The Colonial Laws of New York from the Year 1664 to the Revolution* (Albany, 1894), I, 118, 484, 675, 780, 789, 801–4, 848, 898, 904; "Minute of Brigadier Hunter's Attendance on the Board of Trade," Whitehall, July 20, 1720, *N.Y. Col. Docs.,* V, 551–52; Block et al., eds., *Account of Her Majesty's Revenue,* ix–xviii; Charles Worthen Spencer, *Phases of Royal Government in New York, 1691–1719* (Columbus, 1905), Chap. V; Osgood, *American Colonies, Eighteenth Century,* II, 109, 111–13, 418.

[34] Beverly McAnear, "Mr. Robert R. Livingston's Reasons Against a Land Tax," *Journal of Political Economy,* XLVIII (1940), 63–90; C. W. Spencer, "Sectional Aspects of New York Provincial Politics," *PSQ,* XXX (Sept., 1915), 417; Davis R. Dewey, *Financial History of the United States* (New York, 1918), Chap. I; Edwin R. A. Seligman, "The Income Tax in the American Colonies and States," *PSQ,* X (June, 1895), 221–47; John C. Schwab, *History of the New York Property Tax* (Baltimore, 1890).

This fiscal system had been in effect in New York since 1691, and despite the normal grumbling about inequitable taxation it was not until the second decade of the eighteenth century that financial policy became a major political issue. This was owing in part to the rapid emergence of New York City as a busy port and commercial entrepôt, its volume of trade more than doubling between 1691 and 1715. As New York commerce entered this new phase, it began to produce a class of wealthy and increasingly influential merchants who expected to have a stronger voice in the running of the colony. Never accepting the principle of taxes on trade as the primary source for colonial revenue, New York merchants had managed, in the relatively unregulated conditions of the seventeenth century, to evade many of the unpopular duties and trade restrictions. Toward the close of the century, however, the imperial customs service had been reorganized, collection procedures had been tightened, and it looked as if the old days of laxity were at an end. Thoroughly alarmed, commercial leaders began to cast about for other potential sources of revenue, and their eyes fell, not unnaturally, on the great estates of the Hudson Valley landed patricians. A second problem which would give to fiscal policies a special urgency during the years of Hunter's administration was that New York was heavily in debt after the mismanagement of earlier governors and the high defense costs of the second colonial war.

Thus in 1710 Governor Hunter's first task was to obtain legislation providing for the support of government and for discharging the accumulated debt. From the colonists' point of view—especially those involved in overseas trade—the arrival of a new governor provided the opportunity for a general review of, and possibly a new direction for, fiscal policy. Moreover, it was evident to all that the plan for government support adopted at this time would set the pattern for the future. As Charles W. Spencer points out, the conflict between the commercial and landed interests was at bottom "a competition in dodging the burden of this support." [35] In 1710 the commercial interests had several strong spokesmen in the Assembly, and it could be predicted that Governor Hunter would need all of his wit and ingenuity to carry his program.

[35] *Statistical History, Colonial Times to Present,* 757; Spencer, "Sectional Aspects," 407; Barrow, *Trade and Empire,* Chap. IV.

4. Politics and Governor Hunter: 1710–1719

At the outset, Governor Hunter indicated that he was amenable to suggestions for spreading the tax burden. He proposed that the system for collection of quit-rents be tightened, and he even considered supporting a suggestion that an additional land tax be imposed. Hunter had not been in New York long, however, before he began changing his views, coming more and more to favor duties and excise taxes as the most practicable sources of revenue. Why this occurred is not fully clear, but it was believed at the time that his warm friendship and growing political association with Lewis Morris, leading spokesman for the country interest, had a great deal to do with it. Osgood asserts that Hunter and Morris "struck hands" as early as 1710, and this may well be. Morris was expelled from the Assembly on November 9 of that same year after he had excoriated the House for its failure to provide for Hunter's salary. Another precipitant may have been the concentration of commercial men in the opposition which began to build as Hunter pressed the provincials to provide the necessary revenue for the government. Among the Assembly leaders were two of New York City's most prominent merchants, Jacobus Van Cortlandt and Stephen DeLancey. In addition, that body contained two of Hunter's most vocal critics, the Assemblymen from Suffolk County, Samuel Mulford and Speaker William Nicoll, whose opposition had both a sectional and a commercial basis in that "East End" economic interests were demanding greater local autonomy. The Council as well as the Assembly was divided on the question of the revenue, with Adolph Philipse and Peter Schuyler leading the merchant clique there.[36]

[36] Gov. Hunter to Lords of Trade, Nov. 14, 1710, *N.Y. Col. Docs.,* V, 177–82; Hunter to Sec. Popple, New York, July 7, 1718, *ibid.,* 512; *Assembly Journal* (Gaine), I, Nov. 9, 1710; Werner, *Civil List,* 317–18, 356; Osgood, *American Colonies, Eighteenth Century,* II, 100.. Suffolk County's grievances were of long standing. In the late seventeenth century New York City had been made the sole port of entry and customs center for the colony. This created particular hardships for the "East End" whose proximity to New England meant that its surplus products were "frequently carried to Boston," Connecticut, or Rhode Island. The costly and circuitous routing of this trade 150 miles to New York City and then on to New England made no sense to the "East Enders," and they defied the gov-

It is Osgood's view that the factional rivalry "came to full expression in the election of 1713." By that time it had been four years since the Assembly had provided for the support of government and Hunter's situation was growing so desperate that he began to wonder whether he might end his life in debtor's prison. During the 1713 election campaign Lewis Morris devoted all his considerable energies to winning control of the Assembly for the governor, and in this connection he published a pamphlet—*Address to the Inhabitants of Westchester County*—which argued the pros and cons of direct versus indirect taxation in terms similar to those he used a few years later in his essay "Dialogue Concerning Trade." Morris's general view was that duties were an equitable way to raise a revenue since they usually fell on luxury items and thus most affected those best able to pay. He did not believe they injured the merchant, who merely added the duty to the price of the goods. The farmer, on the other hand, Morris insisted, was already bearing a double burden in that he paid both a property tax and a higher price for imported goods; thus it would be patently unfair to saddle him with an additional land tax. This would be the standard argument of the landed interest throughout the colonial period.[37]

Another pamphlet, *To All whom these Presents may Concern,* attributed to Robert Hunter, was also published during the 1713 election campaign and offers the fullest statement of the government's position concerning New York's financial crisis. Demanding that the Assembly move immediately to settle the revenue question, Hunter lashed out at his opposition—"a Few Whimsical, Factious and Angry Men"—who had "Bambouzel'd" the people with charges "That REVENUE and

---

ernment's efforts to force compliance. Samuel Mulford led this fight until he was expelled from the Assembly on June 2, 1715, for printing without permission a speech against the port monopoly. Undeterred despite his seventy years, Mulford carried the case to London. It was not resolved until 1721 when, because goods had continued to be "Privately & Clandestinely" traded, with a substantial loss of government revenue, a customs collector was permanently stationed in Suffolk County and overseas trade was permitted. "Gov. Dongan's Report," 1687, *N.Y. Doc. Hist.,* I, 105; *N.Y. Col. Docs.,* III, 796–800; *Laws,* II, 38–40; Spencer, "Sectional Aspects," 410–12.

[37] "Dialogue Concerning Trade," Morris Papers, Box 2, Rutgers; Spencer, "Sectional Aspects," 409; Osgood, *American Colonies, Eighteenth Century,* II, 109, 118. Our limited knowledge of the Westchester pamphlet comes from Osgood and Spencer, who saw the copy in the PRO, London.

SLAVERY are Synonimous Terms. . . ." Noting that the "Faction" pretended that "that Terrible Bug-bear REVENUE" meant "An Impost on Goods imported and exported only," Hunter declared that he cared not how the money was raised so long as it was done in accordance with Her Majesty's instructions. Averring that the Assembly's present course would lead to "The Subversion of the Constitution" and the reduction of the Queen's power to that "of an Indian Sachim," Hunter warned that further delay would demonstrate that the Assemblymen had "With-drawn your Allegiance and————you may guess the rest." [38]

The election of 1713 resulted in several changes of Assembly membership, but the balance of pro- and anti-Hunter forces remained about the same as before, and the governor's demand for a permanent revenue continued to be turned aside. It was not until 1714 that the Hunter-Morris combination finally gained sufficient sway to crack the Assembly's resistance, and even then success was achieved only after some spirited bargaining of the sort that would increasingly characterize the relations of colonial governors and assemblies in the eighteenth century. Governor Hunter made two important concessions. One was that a provincial treasurer, appointed by the Assembly, would be given greater power over the disbursement of funds than would the government-appointed receiver-general, which was a long step toward Assembly control of the purse. The second was to support a naturalization bill confirming citizenship to New Yorkers of foreign birth, a bill which clarified the status of a number of Dutch and French-Huguenot members of the merchant group. Because the Navigation Act of 1660 excluded all aliens from employment as merchants or factors in the British colonies, the importance of this legislation cannot be doubted. The Assembly in turn provided for payment of the colony's back debt by approving an issue of over £27,000 in bills of credit, to be redeemed by an excise tax on all retail liquors. The next year, to Hunter's profound satisfaction, the Assembly granted a five-year support to the government, with the required sum to be raised by means of duties on imported liquors, European goods, and slaves, and by a tonnage duty. The pivotal role played by Lewis Morris in these negotiations was acknowledged by the governor in 1715 when, after praising Morris's "labours and industry" to which "in a great measure we owe our present settle-

[38] An original of this pamphlet is in Imprints Collection, NYHS.

ment," Hunter appointed him chief justice of the New York Supreme Court.[39]

The main resistance to the settlement of 1714–1715 apparently came from the Assembly's commerce-oriented members, and especially from the New York County assemblymen, all of whom were prominent merchants. It is even possible that these men voted against the final settlement, though Assembly divisions were not recorded until 1737, and there were no newspapers in New York at that early date, so there is no certain evidence of how the vote went. The most authoritative statement on this comes from Hunter himself, who complained in 1718 that the New York County assemblymen "have during all my time strenuously opposed all publick settlement & support of Government. . . ." But if the commercial interests were disturbed by the shape of events in 1715, their concern deepened as the final years of Hunter's tenure unfolded. By 1717 it had become apparent that the initial £27,000 issue of bills of credit would fall far short of paying the accumulated debt. Accordingly, another issue to the amount of over 41,000 ounces of plate, to be backed by an excise on liquors over the next twenty years and a duty on imported spirits, was passed by the Assembly on November 23, 1717. Assembly resistance to levies of this sort had been lowered by the 1716 election defeat of such leading merchant spokesmen as Jacobus Van Cortlandt and Stephen DeLancey. But the New York County Grand Jury—among whose members, in addition to DeLancey, were merchants Philip Van Cortlandt, John Reade, William Walton, and Robert Watts, among others—immediately swung into action, dispatching a protest to Governor Hunter with a demand that the bill be vetoed. The New York City merchants also got in touch with one of their business correspondents, "one Mr. Baker a Merchant" in London, whom they retained "to oppose some or all our money Bills at home." [40]

[39] Gov. Hunter to Lords of Trade, New York, May 21, July 25, 1715, *N.Y. Col. Docs.,* V, 402–5, 416–19; *Laws,* I, 815–26, 846–57, 858–63; Spencer, *Phases of Royal Government,* Chap. V; Osgood, *American Colonies, Eighteenth Century,* II, 99–114. The dropping of the export duty on furs may also have been a sop to the commercial interests, or it may simply have represented an effort to restimulate that trade, which had been declining for a number of years.

[40] Gov. Hunter to Lords of Trade, New York, Aug. 7, 1718, *N.Y. Col. Docs.,* V, 514; *Assembly Journal* (Gaine), I, June 5, 1716, Nov. 29, 1717; *Laws,* I, 938–91; Werner, *Civil List,* 357.

In the Assembly, meanwhile, the argument between the landed gentry and the commercial interest continued, the merchants contending that New York's trade was suffering because of high duties, while the Morris-led forces, now in the majority, thought it not unreasonable that those "who received an Advantage by our Trade, contribute their Mite to the Support" of government. The subject of a land tax was raised again, but neither that suggestion nor the effort to lower duties made much headway in an Assembly from which the commercial men were "now for the most Part remov'd." Governor Hunter, who had been fully persuaded by this time that a "land Tax is impracticable," gave unqualified support to imposts on trade as the most equitable means for raising revenue, resigning himself to the certainty that the merchants of New York and England would always oppose "every duty whatsoever" as harmful to the trade of Great Britain. He urged Whitehall to approve the money bills, pointing out that New York's trade had enjoyed a "vast increase," despite the "rage of some of these men, who formerly monopolized what is become so diffusive." Hunter had good connections to the centers of power in London and he built a strong case, emphasizing particularly that a settled revenue should not be called into question again. The Board of Trade, under conflicting pressures from merchants in London and Governor Hunter and his friends, criticized some aspects of the 1717 paper money act and noted the absence of a suspending clause, but the Privy Council finally approved Hunter's management of New York affairs by confirming the act in May, 1720.[41]

The alliance between Governor Hunter and the landed interest was further strengthened by the governor's growing friendship with Robert Livingston, which culminated in Hunter's confirmation of the Livingston Manor patent in 1715. The addition of a clause granting the manor one seat in the Assembly not only pleased the Livingstons but also promised to strengthen the governor's interest in that body. In recognition of this, opposition forces at first tried to keep Livingston—the elected manor representative—out of the Assembly, but his election was eventually confirmed in May, 1717. Just one year later, Livingston replaced the ailing William Nicoll of Suffolk County as Speaker of the House, assuring beyond doubt his position as one of Governor Hunter's

[41] *Assembly Journal* (Gaine), I, Oct. 9, 1718; Gov. Hunter to Lords of Trade, New York, July 7, Aug. 7, Nov. 3, 1718, *N.Y. Col. Docs.*, V, 512, 514, 518–20.

"chief lieutenants." Livingston's support of Hunter had a strong personal basis, for as a principal holder of the colonial debt Livingston had good reason to encourage Hunter's efforts to put New York on a solid financial footing.[42] Once he was firmly established as a member of the inner circle of advisers, Livingston joined Morris as a leader of the "court" party, using his newly won power to advance pet projects during the administrations of Governor Hunter and his successor, Governor Burnet.

When Robert Hunter returned to England in the summer of 1719, he could take satisfaction in the knowledge that he was leaving behind a more stable and prosperous colony than he had found. By administering the *coup de grâce* to the old Leislerian factions, and by holding out for a five-year support, he had restored a degree of order to New York's public affairs. Though he had made some enemies by favoring country interests over those of the commercial community, he had managed to hold the dissident element in check with small concessions and by frequent recourse to his strong "interest" in London. A sharp observer would have noticed, however, that beneath this surface calm a newly aroused and self-conscious merchant interest was accumulating grievances which posed a threat to the future tranquility of the colony. Only if Robert Hunter were to be succeeded by a person of comparable prestige and political resourcefulness would there be much chance that the fragile peace might last.

5. Politics and Governor Burnet: 1720–1727

There was a lapse of fourteen months between Governor Hunter's departure from New York and the arrival of his successor, Governor William Burnet, and once again contesting factions took advantage of the hiatus of power to assert rival claims. The merchant interest, having most to gain from subversion of the *status quo,* was especially active as it maneuvered to strengthen its position at the expense of the Morris-Livingston junto. The center of merchant power at that time was the Council, where Adolph Philipse was the main party strategist, and where Peter Schuyler, by virtue of his position as senior councillor, had

[42] Leder, *Robert Livingston,* 236–40, 247.

acceded to the post of acting governor. One of Schuyler's first moves, on September 29, 1719, was to replace Robert Livingston's nephew as mayor of Albany, appointing to the post his own relative, Myndert Schuyler. On the same day, he selected Jacobus Van Cortlandt to be mayor of New York City in place of John Johnston, a Hunter designee. Schuyler also was later accused of having used his authority as acting governor to grant lands to a number of his friends and to turn the people's minds against Governor Hunter's supporters. When Hunter, who was still the legal governor of New York, though *in absentia,* received news of these developments he immediately concluded that Schuyler and his cohorts were angling for "a dissolution of this present Assembly," which he described as "the most dutiful to their Soverign and the most attentive to the true interests of the Colony that the Province could ever boast of." Hunter immediately conveyed his fears to colonial officials at Whitehall, with the result that Schuyler was specifically ordered not to dissolve the Assembly or to replace any other provincial appointees.[43]

The arrival of Governor William Burnet in September, 1720, would under normal circumstances have triggered a scramble between the two factions for preferential status. This contest was eliminated in Burnet's case because it was known that he had been hand-picked by Hunter, that the former governor had briefed him as to which New Yorkers were the most dependable friends of government, and that he had arrived in New York with his biases in favor of the Morris-Livingston party firmly in place. A descendant of a prominent Scotch family, and the son of Gilbert Burnet, Bishop of Salisbury, the new governor was known for his intelligence and vigor. But because he followed a man of such prodigious political skill, Burnet's way of dealing with New York's political problems seems often to have been unnecessarily brusque and heavy-handed. Lacking Hunter's subtlety, Burnet apparently made no effort to balance conflicting colonial interests. In view of his decision to adhere "firmly to every one of Brigadeer Hunters friends," it is hardly

[43] "Calendar of Council Minutes, 1668–1783," New York State Library, *Bulletin,* 58, Berthold Fernow, ed. (Albany, 1902), 272; *Minutes of the Common Council of the City of New York, 1675–1776* (New York, 1905), III, 209; Gov. Hunter to Lords of Trade, London, Dec. 22, 1719, *N.Y. Col. Docs.,* V, 534; *ibid.,* 537; Gov. Burnet to Lords of Trade, New York, Nov. 26, 1720, *ibid.,* 576–81; Lords of Trade to Secretary Craggs, Whitehall, Dec. 23, 1719, *ibid.,* 535.

surprising that Burnet's attitude also guaranteed the inheritance of his predecessor's opposition. "I find the Party who have always opposed Brig. Hunter have got a head since his absence," reported the new governor a few days after his arrival.[44]

The first clash between Burnet and the opposition occurred over the question of holding new elections. It had become customary in New York to hold an election at the accession of each new governor, and the merchant party was hopeful that a new election might weaken the landed gentry's dominance in the Assembly. Burnet, on the other hand, had every reason to retain the "tractable" Assembly chosen in 1716, and by declining to call new elections he handed the opposition a ready-made issue. The governor's decision proved to be the last straw for Samuel Mulford, the fiery representative from Suffolk County, who thereafter refused to participate in the Assembly's proceedings on the ground that they were illegal. The aging Mulford was expelled from the House on October 26, 1720, and his death in 1725 finally stilled the voice of one of the most passionate defenders of "East End" interests ever to sit in the New York Assembly.[45] With Mulford's ejection, the landed party's hegemony in the Assembly was complete.

The Council was another matter, however, and two months after his arrival Burnet moved resolutely to weed out his opposition in that quarter. Apparently undaunted by fears of splitting the colony, Burnet requested permission from the Board of Trade to dismiss from the Council Peter Schuyler, Adolph Philipse, and several others "firmly combined together." He bolstered his case for dismissal by reviewing the Council's activities during the fourteen-month period between governors. He charged that Council President Peter Schuyler was "a weak ignorant man" who was easily prompted to wrongdoing by Adolph Philipse who "is known to govern him." As an "indefatigable" enemy of Hunter, Philipse was characterized as having "always tended to sour the minds of the people against a support of Government." Burnet's request that Schuyler and Philipse be replaced by Cadwallader Colden

[44] Burnet to Lords of Trade, Sept. 24, 1720, *N.Y. Col. Docs.*, V, 573; *DAB*, III, 295 (James Truslow Adams).

[45] Gov. Burnet to Lords of Trade, New York, Nov. 26, Sept. 24, 1720, *N.Y. Col. Docs.*, V, 573, 576–81; NYHS *Colls.*, XXVI (1893), 320–21; Spencer, *Phases of Royal Government*, 70–71.

and James Alexander was granted in February, 1721. With the subsequent addition to the Council of Lewis Morris, Jr., Philip Livingston, and William Provoost, an in-law of Alexander's and a New York City ally of the country party, that body also was neutralized as a center of opposition strength.[46]

Nor was Burnet yet finished with the hapless merchant faction. Having established control over the government, he and his supporters now struck another blow against the merchants, particularly those involved in the Albany Indian trade which had begun to revive after the close of Queen Anne's War. For many years there had been a body of opinion in New York which favored reorganizing the Indian trade in such a way as to improve ties with the Great Lakes Indians and at the same time to undermine their alliance with the French. The strongest colonial advocate of this plan was Robert Livingston, who as early as 1700 had urged that New York develop direct trade with the Far Indians by eliminating the French middlemen who carried furs from the distant tribes to Albany. "We shall never be able to rancounter the French," asserted Livingston, "except we have a nursery of Bushlopers as well as they." Livingston also may have believed that friendlier relationships with the Far Indians would improve frontier security and elevate land values. Efforts to implement this plan had never been more than lukewarm in the face of resistance from many of the merchants involved in the Canada trade. That Livingston had never abandoned the project is indicated by his "humble memorial" of August, 1720, in which he once again urged that restrictions, including a complete stop for three months and the posting of a guard to intercept violators, be placed on the Canada trade. Cadwallader Colden became an enthusiastic supporter of Livingston's program, which he felt should be pursued

---

[46] Gov. Burnet to Lords of Trade, New York, Nov. 26, 1720, *N.Y. Col. Docs.,* V, 578–79; Werner, *Civil List,* 357. In addition, Burnet replaced Jacobus Van Cortlandt as Mayor of New York City with his own choice in September, 1720. *Minutes of Common Council,* III, 237. Cadwallader Colden shared Burnet's opinion of Schuyler: "Col. Schuyler was so weak a man that Adolph Phillipse persuaded him to lodge the Kings seal in his hands that he might thereby be able to prevent any use to be made of it without his consent." Colden to His Son, 1759, NYHS *Colls.,* I (1868), 206. This statement and his criticism of Schuyler's "sullen Dutch manner" must be considered in the context of Colden's strong support for Burnet and his not infrequently expressed distaste for the Albany Dutch. *Ibid.,* 199.

"not-withstanding many difficultys put in the way by merchants who trade with the French," because it would offer the surest means "to strengthen the British Interest on this continent." [47]

Whereas Robert Hunter had been too preoccupied with internal problems to press imperial claims against the French, Burnet started out with the support of an Assembly which readily enlisted his interest in its plan for strengthening the frontier. After his first meeting with the governor, Robert Livingston triumphantly told his wife: "He agrees in all our feelings and he approves my [Indian trade] memorandum. . . . I cannot express enough the great friendship the new Governor shows me, he is very familiar." On November 3, 1720, Lewis Morris introduced a bill in the Assembly "for the Encouragement of the Indian Trade . . . and for prohibiting the Selling of Indian Goods to the French." Signed by Governor Burnet on November 19, the new law forbade the sale to the French of strouds, duffels, blankets, guns, kettles, flints, powder, lead or any other "Indian Goods or Commodities." [48] The reaction at Albany was immediate, the greatest anger being directed against Robert Livingston. As Philip Livingston wrote his father, the Albany Indian commissioners "grumble & Reall [rail] very much again [st] you," while the mayor complained "that you are the monarch of the whole Province." Philip himself, who unlike his father lived permanently at Albany and saw at first hand the hardships created by the law, gave only lukewarm support to the prohibition on trade, believing it "better to have it open & free for the french to bring & Send their bever to buy what they want than to be wholy without trade." Since local officials at Albany were reluctant to enforce the new law, there were frequent violations; this in turn led to a tightening up of enforce-

[47] "Mr. Robert Livingston's Report of his Journey to Onondaga," April 1700, *N.Y. Col. Docs.*, IV, 650; Mr. Robert Livingston to Colonel Schuyler, Albany, Aug. 23, 1720, *ibid.*, V, 559–61; "Cadwallader Colden on the Trade of New York; 1723," *N.Y. Col. Docs.*, V, 685–90. For an earlier discussion of the plan to strengthen ties with the Great Lakes Indians, see pp. 43–45. For the revival of the fur trade after 1713, see Armour, "Merchants of Albany," Chap. VI.

[48] Robert to Alida Livingston, Oct. 12, 1720, Livingston-Redmond MSS, quoted in Leder, *Robert Livingston*, 253; *Laws*, II, 9; *Assembly Journal* (Gaine), I, Nov. 3, 1720. The governor's speech to the Assembly supporting restrictions on the fur trade is in *ibid.*, Oct. 13, 1720. Fur trade activities during the 1720–1726 period are summarized in Osgood, *American Colonies, Eighteenth Century*, II, 419–22; Leder, *Robert Livingston*, 251–67; Buffinton, "Policy of Albany," 358–61.

ment, provision being made for search and seizure of illegal goods, fines, and rewards to informers. Particularly repugnant to the upriver traders was the requirement that anyone suspected of trading with Canada be tendered an oath, with the added provision that those who refused to take it "shall Ipso facto be adjudged Convict of having Traded" with the French.[49]

After months of unavailing protest, an opportunity to focus discontent over the Canada trade prohibition arose in 1724, when the death of an Albany County assemblyman made it necessary to call a special election. Fortunately for the historian, this election also allows some judgments to be made about the weight of the different viewpoints at Albany concerning regulation of the Indian trade. During a campaign that was all "Contrivance & Management," six candidates "Sett up" for the single seat, three of whom were "broken merchants if not bankrupts" as a result of the government's trade policies. The candidates were Myndert Schuyler, Harmanus Wendell, Johannis Beekman, Jr., David Schuyler, David van Dyck, and Robert Livingston, Jr., of the Clermont Livingstons. The strongest opponent of Burnet's policies was Myndert Schuyler, who had "Long Since made interest with the Canada traders and feeds them with hopes he [']ll open that trade," and who had openly declared his intention "to take Refenge on the Governor if he Carries it." [50] The governor's forces apparently were divided between van Dyck and Livingston. Though Livingston would have seemed the

[49] Philip Livingston to Robert Livingston, Albany, Dec. 4, 1720, Duane Papers, NYHS; Philip Livingston to Robert Livingston, Albany, March 25, 1724, Feb. 8, Feb. 20, 1721, Livingston-Redmond MSS, Reel 3; *Laws*, II, 99. Though the French for some time had tried to halt the trade with Albany, which was very detrimental to French mercantilism, this was the only time the English outlawed it. Jean Lunn, "The Illegal Fur Trade Out of New France, 1713–60," Canadian Historical Association, *Report*, 1939, pp. 63, 69–70. Robert Livingston's popularity with the Albany leaders, never very high, suffered a further decline after the fur trade bill passed. When Livingston tried to offer his suggestions about building a new courthouse for the county, he was informed that the justices of the peace "did not want Your advice nor Instructions in That affair"; the county assessors also assigned a particularly high tax quota to Livingston Manor in 1722, but the Livingstons decided it would be foolish to protest as the assessors "will do what they please." Thos. Williams to Robert Livingston, Albany, Jan. 28, 1721, Philip Livingston to Robert Livingston, Albany, Feb. 15, 1722, Livingston-Redmond MSS, Reel 3.

[50] Philip Livingston to Robert Livingston, Albany, May 20, March 16, Mar. 25, Feb. 24, 1724, Livingston-Redmond MSS, Reel 3.

most likely recipient of the governor's support, he had announced too late "and after most people were Engaged to the Governor's frind" van Dyck. Therefore, even though all the Governor's appointees in the county were instructed to vote for van Dyck, Myndert Schuyler was elected "by a majority of 40 od," a respectable margin considering the number of candidates in the race.[51]

Schuyler's election in 1724 was but another indication that the political fortunes of the merchant party were beginning to improve at last. Two years earlier, Adolph Philipse had regained his political voice by winning a special election to fill a vacancy in the Westchester County Assembly delegation. Then in 1725 Stephen DeLancey had been returned to the Assembly in a New York County by-election, adding further to Burnet's troubles. It was in that same year that Robert Livingston's age and failing health finally compelled his retirement from active political life, which included giving up his post as Assembly Speaker. It may be taken as a measure of the Assembly's mounting restiveness over Burnet's policies that Adolph Philipse was chosen to be the new Speaker on August 31, 1725. At that point Burnet decided that the time had come to move against his burgeoning opposition, but unfortunately for him, his tactics proved to be both clumsy and self-defeating. The governor chose to question Stephen DeLancey's right to sit in the Assembly on the ground that his New York citizenship was under a cloud, even though DeLancey had been naturalized under the bill passed during Hunter's administration. Even Burnet's supporters were alarmed at this challenge to the Assembly's right to judge the qualifications of its own members, and the governor's transparently political maneuver was firmly rebuffed and his authority weakened when on September 21 the Assembly unanimously voted to seat DeLancey.[52]

[51] Philip Livingston to Robert Livingston, Albany, May 7, May 15, May 20, June 10, May 30, 1724, Livingston-Redmond MSS, Reel 3. The Albany men were not all of one mind on fur trade policy, as many of the smaller traders resented the *handlaers'* monopoly. In 1723, Johannis Myndertse of Schenectady was arrested for trading illegally with the French; he escaped from custody and sued the City of Albany in a case which was to test the legality of the monopoly. James Alexander was Myndertse's lawyer; the case finally was adjudicated in 1726 with the decision favoring Myndertse and, in effect, breaking the Albany monopoly. Armour, "Merchants of Albany," Chap. VII.

[52] *Assembly Journal* (Gaine), I, Sept. 13, Sept. 20, Sept. 21, 1725.

Nor was opposition from provincial sources all that Burnet had to contend with, for the New York City merchants had again been in touch with their English correspondents, whose business also was suffering because of Burnet's hostility to commercial interests. Protests and petitions were dispatched by the English merchants to the Privy Council and the Lords of Trade, painting a dismal picture of declining trade and rising costs, all resulting from Burnet's restrictive policies. Burnet and his New York supporters staunchly defended their program as a bulwark against French expansion, but in 1726 the act prohibiting trade with Canada was repealed, being replaced by a double duty on goods bound for Canada. In 1729 even that substitute restriction was disallowed.[53]

By 1726 the clamor against Governor Burnet had become so insistent that it was no longer possible for him to ignore it. The interdiction of the Canada trade is normally stressed by historians as the single substantive grievance against Burnet, but there were in fact a number of other important complaints. For one thing, the governor's obvious bias in favor of the landed interest led to his almost unquestioning acceptance of levies on commerce as the most feasible means of raising a revenue. Imposts on trade and an excise on liquor sales became in these years the standard sources of revenue, much to the merchants' dismay. Burnet's approval of a tonnage duty was also hotly resented, for goods

[53] "Papers relating to an Act of the Assembly of the province of New-York for encouragement of the Indian trade," New York, 1724, "A Petition of the Merchants of London to His Majesty, signed by Samuel Baker, Samuel Storke, John Bayeux, Richard Jeneway [and sixteen others], Merchants of London, Trading to New-York. . . ." Imprint Coll., NYHS; Gov. Burnet to Lords of Trade, New York, Aug. 9, Nov. 7, 1724, *N.Y. Col Docs.*, V, 707–9, 711–13; "Cadwallader Colden on the Trade of New York; 1723," *ibid.*, 685–90; "Proceedings of the Lords of Trade on the New York Acts regulating the Indian Trade," Whitehall, May 5, 1725, *ibid.*, 745–56; Buffinton, "Policy of Albany," 361–62. Despite this apparent victory for the merchants, the Canada trade would never be the same again. A second aspect of Burnet's Indian policy was designed to attract the Far Indians to trade at New York by building a trading post at Oswego, on the eastern shore of Lake Ontario. This project was realized when Fort Oswego was constructed in 1727. Though there was some resistance to this at Albany, the success of the fort as an attraction to fur-laden Indians was great enough to override those objections after a short time. In any case the character of Albany was changing in fundamental ways, as the increase of population and western settlement gradually diminished the importance of the City of Albany as the center of economic and political life in the county. Buffinton, "Policy of Albany," 360; Armour, "Merchants of Albany," 168–80, Chap. VIII.

were regularly being smuggled in from New Jersey free ports. Some merchants proposed that a reasonable alternative would be to eliminate the New York tonnage duty, replacing the lost revenue by a tax on slaves. It was also suggested that some officials' salaries be reduced— that of the chief justice (Lewis Morris) being mentioned as an appropriate one with which to begin. Other grievances resulted from Burnet's failure to allow Assembly elections, his attack on Stephen DeLancey's citizenship and on the Assembly's integrity, and his resort to chancery courts.[54] Finally, in 1726, the governor agreed to hold an Assembly election, the first to take place since his arrival in the colony in 1720. In that election Adolph Philipse was chosen as one of the assemblymen from New York County; his nephew, Colonel Frederick Philipse, took over his place as assemblyman from Westchester County; and Myndert Schuyler and Stephen DeLancey won reelection. When the Assembly met in September, Adolph Philipse was again chosen Speaker. The country party's main spokesman was Lewis Morris, representing the Borough of Westchester, and Morris had some help from the representatives of Livingston Manor and Rensselaerswyck. But the landed interest was clearly on the decline, a state of affairs which was hardly improved by the transfer of its patron, Governor Burnet, to Massachusetts in late 1727.[55]

The polarization of New York economic interests into competing merchant and landed factions, which first became visible during Hunter's regime, thus reached a peak in the years of Burnet's administration. From about 1715 to 1725 the landed gentry had the upper hand, having gained the approval and patronage of two governors in succession, but after 1725 a reaction began to set in as the merchant "outs" regrouped their scattered forces. We may pause to wonder, before proceeding to

[54] George Clarke to Mr. Walpole, New York, Nov. 24, 1725, *N.Y. Col. Docs.,* V, 768–71; "To the Hon. Adolph Philipse, Esq.," "A second letter to Adolph Philipse," 1727, Imprint Coll., NYHS; Smith, *History,* I, 251, 254, 272, 277–78. Once, in pique at Robert Livingston, Burnet considered imposing a tax on untenanted land. So vociferous was Livingston's response to this suggestion that Burnet, after being pointedly reminded who his friends were, retreated to safer ground. Leder, *Robert Livingston,* 265–67.

[55] Werner, *Civil List,* 357.

the next stage of this conflict, why governors Hunter and Burnet should have aligned themselves so openly with the landed patricians. They may have harbored some of the Englishman's disdain for the commercial element which, it was alleged with growing frequency in the early eighteenth century, gained its power from stock jobbery and the manipulation of credit. The new commercial class was presumably imparting a corrupt and venal tone to English life and politics, which unsettled the ancient equation whereby public duty and honor were under the peculiar care of the landed gentry. As a friend of Swift, Robert Hunter was certainly familiar with these notions, and very likely Burnet had also been exposed to them. A second possibility is that the Scotsmen Hunter, Burnet, Livingston, Alexander, and Colden, and the Welshman Morris may have been bound together by a certain cultural affinity. We know that of the opposition leaders Philipse, Van Cortlandt, and Schuyler were of Dutch ancestry while DeLancey was of French-Huguenot descent. Colden's opinion of the New York Dutch has already been noted, and in 1728 Colden did point to cultural differences as one basis for party divisions.[56]

A further question regarding this phase of New York's provincial politics needs clarification. It concerns the tendency of historians to depict these and all eighteenth-century party conflicts as by-products of a long-running feud between the Livingston and DeLancey families. It is actually very difficult, if not impossible, to fit the complexity and sophistication of New York politics into such a simple formula. We have already seen that the foremost leader of the landed party in the early decades of the eighteenth century was Lewis Morris, with Robert Livingston and others lending valuable support in the 1720's. Turning to the merchant party, one finds a number of leaders, and if a single dominant figure had to be identified, the choice might well fall on Adolph Philipse rather than on Stephen DeLancey. Writers who have fixed

---

[56] The idea that a commercial-landed cleavage was seen by early eighteenth-century political essayists is discussed in Isaac Kramnick, *Bolingbroke and His Circle: The Politics of Nostalgia in the Age of Walpole* (Cambridge, Mass., 1968), especially Chaps. II and III. Though Bolingbroke's writings may have been too late to influence Hunter during his years in New York, the author shows that Swift and Pope, among others, "shared his [Bolingbroke's] 'style of thought.' " *Ibid.*, 4. Colden's statement on parties is in "Memorial to his Excellency, Drawn by Colden," Aug. 17, 1728, Rutherfurd Coll., I, 57, NYHS.

upon DeLancey as the party leader have done so on the assumption that he was the unnamed "Gentleman at New-York" who at the time was said to have "almost entirely engrossed the Indian Trade," and thus to have led the fight against Burnet's policies. Charles McIlwain states, though without substantiation, that the "Gentleman" was Stephen De-Lancey, and others have followed his assertion. Yet at no point in the contemporary literature is reference made to a "DeLancey party." At that early stage of New York history the parties were not identified by family names, but were designated as the "commercial" or "merchant interest" and the "country" or "landed interest." [57] It would thus appear that the Livingston-DeLancey formula is not very helpful. Party divisions in the colony did sometimes, though not always, find these two families in opposite camps, but it is a mistake to project any "feud" back to this early period.

6. Shifting Patterns: 1728–1731

When the merchant interest began to reassert its strength after 1725, and particularly after it became known that the days of Burnet's administration were numbered, it became apparent that the next skirmish

[57] McIlwain, ed., *Wraxall's Abridgment of Indian Affairs,* lxvii-lxviii; Cadwallader Colden, *The History of the Five Indian Nations* (New York, 1902), II, 58. A check of McIlwain's citations reveals no instance in which DeLancey was named as the leading trader. The only authority for naming DeLancy as the main party figure comes from Colden, who stated in 1760 that during Burnet's administration DeLancey was "at the head of the party in the Assembly." ("Comments on Smith's History," NYHS *Colls.,* I, [1868], 220–21.) This must be viewed with skepticism, however, inasmuch as DeLancey was not in the Assembly from 1716 to 1725, and after 1725, he must at least have shared leadership with the Speaker, Adolph Philipse. Becker emphasized the Livingston-DeLancy party lines in his *History of Political Parties,* and in two articles, "Growth of Revolutionary Parties and Methods in New York Province, 1765–1774," *AHR,* VII (Oct., 1901), 56–76, and "Nominations in Colonial New York," *AHR,* VI (Jan., 1901), 260–75. For later examples see Klein, "Democracy and Politics," 223; Alfred F. Young, *The Democratic Republicans of New York, The Origins, 1763–1797* (Chapel Hill, 1967), 9–10; George Dangerfield, *Chancellor Robert R. Livingston of New York, 1746–1813* (New York, 1960), 20–24; Gerlach, *Philip Schuyler,* 104–6. These modern scholars are all well aware, as their own studies testify, that New York Colony's politics cannot be reduced to simple formulas. Even so, the impression of the Livingston-DeLancey dichotomy remains strong.

would occur as the two factions vied to gain favor with the incoming governor. That competition proved to be indecisive. Governor John Montgomerie, who arrived in April of 1728, was an uncertain leader whose administration was cut short by his death in July, 1731. Yet the party sparring which took place during those three years is of special interest. The provincial politicians were quite aware that their "Animosities . . . were occasioned by the Struggle which Some rich men made after power. . . ," and the forthright acknowledgment of such a struggle seemed to signal the release of a great store of creative political energy.

James Alexander and Cadwallader Colden were particularly active during Montgomerie's tenure in formulating strategy for the country interest. They concentrated their fire on Adolph Philipse, whom they labeled "the head" of the merchant party. Dubbing the Speaker "Ape," from his initials A—P—e, Alexander and Colden set to work turning out propaganda pieces which they had printed up in pamphlet form. Even Alexander at one point wondered whether Colden's zeal might be running away with him. "I think in the further Letters to Ape there should be rather more reservedness of Epithets," he advised, "no passion but clear truth & reason." Suggesting that Colden urge his readers "to Enquire themselves into the truth & not be led aside by idle tales told at Cocks & other Corners," Alexander added, "I believe it would not be amiss . . . however to lay their Credulity to their good Nature." This correspondence is instructive, not only for the growing awareness it reveals of the need to court public opinion for the election contests ahead, but also for the insights which occasionally flash forth regarding the arts of political persuasion. "Be not allways wiser than your Company but suit your self to their present humour," was Colden's advice to Alexander. "The despising of these fooleries begets an aversion in the common herd. . . ." [58]

[58] "Summary statement on parties," Cadwallader Colden, [circa 1728], draft, Rutherfurd Coll., I, 63; James Alexander to Colden, New York, May 5, 1728, NYHS *Colls.*, L (1917), 259–61; Colden to Alexander, Coldengham, Nov. 19, 1728, Rutherfurd Coll., I, 81. For additional information on Colden's and Alexander's attitudes toward partisan rivalry, see "A Letter from a Gentleman in New York to his friend in the Country," James Alexander, Oct. 22, 1728, draft, and "May it Please Your Excellency," James Alexander, draft, [circa 1728], Rutherfurd Coll., I, 59, 77, NYHS. The printed pamphlets are in Imprints Coll., NYHS.

But Colden's and Alexander's efforts were not sufficient to displace Adolph Philipse. To their partisan thrusts Philipse declared he would answer "by the voice of the people" in the next election, which in effect he did, being returned as assemblyman from New York County in the spring of 1728. In this same election Lewis Morris lost his seat in Westchester County, leaving no one in the Assembly "to head any Project" for the landed interest and assuring Philipse's control, there being now "none to oppose him." Still hopeful of regaining some of their waning strength, the landed party leaders made plans to improve their position. Noting "what great pains Ap-e & others joined with him take to make a party," James Alexander suggested to Lewis Morris that their party too should "Consult together . . . So that each may act his part in Concert." Colden agreed that "one reason of our having often failed is that we never concerted our Measures together but acted upon the sudden Emergents that happened. . . ." [59] Colden, who was residing at that time on his estate in Ulster County, took it upon himself to strengthen the party's interest in that area, while Alexander was to court Henry Beekman of Dutchess and persuade assemblyman Hicks of Queens "to use all his Interest" to enhance the position of the country group.[60]

At this point the two parties were still vying for the favor of Governor Montgomerie, a factor which in the coming contest might well be decisive. As late as November, 1728, Colden wrote that the governor "continues to show me abundance of Civility," but he feared that Philipse might be gaining the upper hand. A few months later, the landed party's troubles grew when the Philipse-led Assembly voted to set Chief Justice Lewis Morris's salary at a rate lower than he expected. This occasioned an intemperate outburst in the Council from Lewis Morris, Jr.,

[59] Alexander to Colden, New York, May 5, 1728, NYHS *Colls.*, L (1917), 259–61; Colden to Alexander, Coldengham, June 30, 1728, Alexander to Lewis Morris, draft, [circa 1728], Colden to Alexander, June 21, 1728, Colden to Alexander, Coldengham, Sept. 6, 1728, Rutherfurd Coll., I, 53, 51, 81, NYHS. It is apparent that Colden felt a typical eighteenth-century ambivalence toward partisan activities; for on the same day that he suggested concerting measures, he wrote another letter to James Alexander advising that they "let the world see that we hate Contention." Colden to Alexander, Coldengham, June 21, 1728, Rutherfurd Coll., I, 53, NYHS.

[60] Colden to Alexander, Coldengham, June 21, June 30, Nov. 19, 1728, Rutherfurd Coll., I, 53, 92, NYHS.

which was promptly followed by his dismissal from that body by Governor Montgomerie. Colden and Alexander were severely irked with young Morris for thus damaging their prospects. "I abhor this furious procedure," fumed Alexander, "where friends no more than foes are Safe." By 1729 Governor Montgomerie had definitely swung over to the side of the merchant party. The only two Council appointments he made during his tenure were those of James DeLancey, Stephen's oldest son, in 1729, and of Philip Van Cortlandt in place of the ousted Morris in 1730.[61]

The term "merchant party" is now being used mainly for convenience. By 1729 the contest between factions in New York was for power, and economic issues *per se* were declining in importance. This displacement was abetted by certain shifts in economic patterns which were to have a permanent effect on subsequent political alignments. For one thing, there had been a gradual rapprochement between New York City and eastern Long Island after 1721, when the "East End" was finally granted separate port privileges and its own customs collector. No longer subservient to the port of New York, Suffolk County's natural affinity with the other seaboard counties of Kings, Queens, Richmond, and New York was increasingly recognized. Each of those counties had strong commercial interests, and all shared the sense of well-being inherent in their secure location far from the dangers of an exposed frontier. One consequence of this was a rising resentment over the high cost of maintaining defenses in the frontier counties. Back in 1717 Samuel Mulford had protested the high property tax on Long Island, which he felt received little benefit since most of the money was used "up the river." As Anglo-French rivalry grew in the eighteenth century, this sectional division became more noticeable; not untypical was Philip Livingston's lament that "the [Assembly] members of the Lower Coun-

---

[61] Colden to Gov. William Burnet, Coldengham, Nov. 19, 1728, copy, NYHS *Colls.,* L (1917), 273; Gov. Montgomerie to Lords of Trade, June 30, 1729, *N.Y. Col. Docs.,* V, 877–82; Werner, *Civil List,* 318. For Colden's fears that Philipse was becoming too friendly with Montgomerie, see also Colden to Alexander, Coldengham, Nov. 29, 1728, March 1, 1729, Rutherfurd Coll., I, 93, 107. For comments about Lewis Morris, Jr.'s dismissal, see Alexander to Colden, New York, June 28, 1729, NYHS *Colls.,* I (1868); and correspondence in Rutherfurd Coll., I, 125, 127, NYHS.

ties Seem against doing any thing Effectually for the Fronteers which is really a most maloncholy Case." [62]

The loosening of old ties between the New York City and Albany merchants engaged in the Indian trade was another factor contributing to this sectional realignment. In the early eighteenth century the leading Albany *handlaers* had obtained their trading goods from a few large New York City import houses, thereby forging a chain of interests between those two merchant groups. Near-monopolies of this sort had been common in New York during the early years, but all this had begun to change as the colony's economy became more complex. After 1720 or so an increasing number of Albany traders imported their goods direct from England, using factors or family members located in New York City as their agents instead of working through the big importers. The Indian traders, said Adolph Philipse in 1730, "now have almost all their Indian Goods from England on their owne accountes, whereas they formerly bought the Same from the merchants & Traders at New York." [63]

Another development which affected the northern section was the continuing diversification of its economy, as food products rapidly outdistanced furs in the export ratio. As the volume of grains, meats, and dairy products rose, New York City exporters interested in maintaining the high quality of these staple goods renewed their efforts to impose restrictive regulations. These efforts were dramatically successful after 1750 when a series of acts provided for the regulation and inspection at New York City of outbound beef, pork, fish, lumber, naval stores, and sole leather, as well as the main staple, flour.[64] Thus the "merchant interest" no longer ran along the New York City–Albany axis, tying

[62] *N.Y. Doc. Hist.,* III, 363–71, Smith, *History,* I, 232; Philip Livingston to Jacob Wendell, New York, Jan. 14, 1746, Livingston Papers, Philip Livingston Box, MCNY. See also Philip Livingston to Jacob Wendell, Sept. 4, 1744, April 5, 1746, June 2, 1746, Livingston Papers, Philip Livingston Box, MCNY; Colden to Archibald Kennedy, Nov. 17, 1756, copy, NYHS *Colls.,* LXVIII (1935), 165–67. For the stationing of a customs collector on eastern Long Island, see *Laws,* II, 38–40.

[63] Adolph Philipse to Mr. Leheup, Agent at New York, New York, Dec. 23, 1730, CO 5/1055, PRO, micro., SHR; Harrington, *New York Merchant,* 237.

[64] Harrington, *New York Merchant,* Chap. II, 279–81; Spencer, "Sectional Aspects," 406–7.

those distant points together. Instead, the Hudson Valley became a staple producing center whose people were concerned with the total development of the region, a goal which was threatened by the often successful attempts of New York City to extend controls up the river. Growing up to the south was a rival seaboard interest which was concerned mainly with inter-colonial and overseas trade, and which supported the central government's efforts to maintain the high quality of New York's products. Though issues of an economic nature continued to affect New York politics after the 1720's, the landed-merchant dichotomy lost much of its force as sectional and other rivalries moved to the fore.

On the New York City leaders, moreover, the lessons of the Hunter-Burnet years had not been lost. The key to success was power, and power was achieved by means of the right political connections. Getting the ear of the governor was obviously of great value, but the merchants also knew that influence at the seat of all power—London—was responsible for their victory over Burnet's Indian trade restrictions. The New York City–centered seaboard interests had a distance to go before they could overtake the power of the long-entrenched Hudson Valley grandees, but the methods by which they might best pursue that goal were well understood by 1730.

IV

~~~~~~

THE MORRIS-COSBY DISPUTE: A POLITICAL AND CONSTITUTIONAL CRISIS

AN EARLIER GENERATION of scholars has salted the literature of American history, at times almost imperceptibly, with hundreds of character analyses and minor interpretations which continue to exert a subtle influence today. This is true even in the relatively circumscribed realm of New York history. The process may certainly be seen in various treatments of the character and motives of Lewis Morris—particularly in relation to the part Morris played in the political crisis of the 1730's, the subject of this chapter. To some of the earlier writers, Morris's motives and actions during those years when he led a vigorous opposition to Governor William Cosby were tainted by self-interest and an unseemly lust for power, and even today his historical reputation is impaired by some of these associations.[1]

---

[1] An example of the earlier evaluation can be found in John E. Stillwell, *Historical and Genealogical Miscellany* (New York, 1916), where much is made of Morris's "lack of principle, greed of self-advancement . . . autocratic nature . . . [and his] arrogant and overbearing" attitude toward inferiors (p. 32). One of the most balanced evaluations of Morris is in Gordon B. Turner, "Governor Lewis Morris and the Colonial Government Conflict," *Proceedings* of the New Jersey Historical Society, new series, LXVII (Oct., 1949), 260–304. See also Donald L. Kemmerer, *Path to Freedom: The Struggle for Self-Government in Colonial New*

No one who has studied the career of Lewis Morris can fail to discern that the man was a politician to his marrow. Every age has known leaders of this sort—men whose blood runs faster when they are engaged in partisan disputation, and who gain their deepest satisfactions simply from the knowledge that they are moving in the midst of things and making some difference there. Perhaps it is because partisan activities were theoretically frowned upon in the eighteenth century that Morris's zest for political contention has so often been deprecated. Lewis Morris was an early example of a political type that would not really come into its own until about a hundred years later, though he was not the only man of his time to display the kind of political precocity which is of more than passing interest to the present study. As for the self-interested aspect of Morris's activities, this of course must be evaluated in context. It is true that his decision to form an opposition to Governor Cosby followed hard on the heels of assaults on his judicial prerogatives and land interests, though these were certainly vital concerns to Morris and he defended them in the same way that other patricians defended their personal interests when under attack. Historians may have been harder on Morris because of their tendency to rely rather more than they should on the dyspeptic views of his foremost political enemy, Governor Cosby, or because there are some very quotable contemporary descriptions of Morris's waspish temperament. Much has been made of William Smith, Jr.'s assertion that Morris was expert in "the arts of intrigue"—as indeed he was. Taken as a whole, however, Smith's analysis of Morris's personal qualities is not unfavorable. It shows him to have been a man of strong character and opinions, as well as an able politician. Morris was "a man of letters, and though a little whimsical in his temper . . . grave in his manners and of penetrating parts. . . . Through the love of power he was always busy in matters of a political nature." [2] In the highly charged political atmosphere of colonial New York this last need not be read as a condemnation.

Jersey, 1703–1776 (Princeton, 1940), 149, 153, 154; Stanley N. Katz, *Newcastle's New York* (Cambridge, Mass., 1968), 49, 72–73, 84.

[2] William Smith, *The History of the Late Province of New-York, From its Discovery, to the Appointment of Governor Colden, in 1762* (New York, 1830), I, 208–10. Colden claims that Morris was "far from being a popular man Nor was his Temper fitted to gain popularity." "History of Gov. William Cosby's Administration and of Lt.-Gov. George Clarke's Administration through 1737," NYHS *Colls.*, LXVIII (1935), 299.

Perhaps Morris would have had a stormy career in any age. But it is also possible that certain conditions and tensions prevalent in the colonial milieu may have reinforced his native contentiousness. When Morris was next to the seat of power, as he was during Hunter's administration, he showed himself to be capable of a cool-headed and rational leadership. But when he moved into the opposition, as he did during Cosby's regime, Morris and those equally rational men who supported his cause became the masters of a rhetoric and a style of political combativeness whose ferocity eventually embroiled the whole colony in a partisan struggle until, in the words of Cadwallader Colden, "we had all the appearance of a civil War." [3] How can one reconcile, or at least understand, the Morris of the Hunter years and the Morris of the Cosby era? How, for that matter, can one explain the shifts from court to popular party, and back again, of any number of New York politicians of this time? It may be that the well-worn terms of "mere" self-interest and absence of consistent principles are not enough.

The frequency with which such passions seized colonial politics, with their accompaniment of shifting parties and seemingly petty cabals, has recently attracted new interest. The question has been raised as to whether this surface volatility might have been symptomatic of a more fundamental malaise in provincial life, of endemic imbalances that caused conflict "to rise irresistibly from deep-lying sources." From this perspective, the old questions about individual motives and consistency of principles lose some of their point, for "action becomes not the product of rational and conscious calculation but of dimly perceived and rapidly changing thoughts and situations" which take on a life of their own and accelerate toward unpredictable consequences.[4]

The Morris-Cosby conflict may be an archetypal case, and a kind of test. Starting as a minor salary dispute, it soon became involved with larger questions concerning the colonial court structure; it then jumped another level when censorship and freedom of the press became an issue; it ascended still farther when an open break developed between

[3] Colden, "History of Cosby and Clarke," 349.

[4] Bernard Bailyn, *The Origins of American Politics* (New York, 1968), 65; Gordon S. Wood, "Rhetoric and Reality in the American Revolution," *WMQ,* 3rd Ser., XXIII (January, 1966), 23. Wood suggests that we may be reaching the point in our writing about the Revolution "where idealism and behaviorism meet." *Ibid.,* 4.

the governor and an increasingly vocal popular opposition; it was next carried to England, and it ended up on the lofty heights of constitutional principle. Judging from the number of people involved—to say nothing of the passionate rhetoric and furious party activities of the leading figures—it would appear that before it was over this episode signified something more than narrow self-interest or personal pique. It is unlikely that the issues raised by the Morris forces against the government would have evoked the response that they did from the people of New York had there not been at stake matters of the most serious public concern.

1. The Resurgence of Parties: Governor Cosby and the Van Dam Affair

William Cosby was a man of imperious temperament who was ill-equipped to take on the responsibilities of a colonial governorship. As such, he provides the model for much that was wrong with the British method of choosing colonial administrators during the eighteenth century. Suited "neither by training, aptitude, nor temperament" to be governor of New York, Cosby nonetheless was awarded that key place because he was married to a woman with the right political connections. Grace Montague Cosby was a first cousin of the Duke of Newcastle and the sister of the first Earl of Halifax, impeccable credentials in an age when official preferment depended in large part on whom one knew. Cosby had eagerly solicited the New York post, and though he claimed to have the colony's true interests at heart, it was not long before New Yorkers began to suspect that his real interest was "to repair his broken fortune." His crude efforts to squeeze every shilling from the anticipated emoluments of office, taking little account of provincial sensibilities, precipitated clashes. Any hint of resistance to his authority threw him into a rage, all of which soon caused New Yorkers "to conceive a dislike to his Person & to his Administration." [5] Contemporar-

---

[5] Colden, "History of Cosby and Clarke," 286, 287; Katz, *Newcastle's New York*, 33. It is always advisable to take colonists' evaluations of their governors with a degree of skepticism, but in Cosby's case the verdict seems to be quite clear, even though this could be asserted with real conviction only if we had corroboration

ies claimed that Cosby was ruled by his wife; [6] if so, he made up for his lack of authority at home by playing the petty tyrant in public affairs.

Governor Cosby had arrived in New York on August 1, 1732. The customary party jostling for preferential treatment was of fairly short duration in his case, for a rapport quickly developed between the new governor and Assembly Speaker Adolph Philipse, Stephen DeLancey, and their friends, possibly because of their willingness to comply with Cosby's requests for money. The governor not only obtained a five-year grant but also managed to extract an additional £1000 from the Assembly for services he had allegedly rendered to the colony while still in England. Nor did Cosby call for new elections at his accession to the governorship. That this omission was passed over without comment from the Assembly leaders was probably not unconnected with their eagerness to bind their interests to those of the new governor, as well as to preserve their party's majority in the House.[7] The cordial relation-

from some of Cosby's supporters. Because of the paucity of Philipse, DeLancey, and Van Cortlandt political papers, such corroboration is not available. One neutral observer, New Yorker Abigail Franks, noted that Cosby was "Very much disliked," and that Supreme Court Justices DeLancey and Philipse had "Lost a great deall of good Will by being in the Gov[ernor]s Interest." Abigail Franks to Naphtali Franks, Dec. 16, 1733, Leo Hershkowitz and Isidore S. Meyer, eds., *The Lee Max "Friedman Collection of American Jewish Colonial Correspondence": Letters of the Franks Family (1733–1748)* (Waltham, Mass., 1968), 16–17. This is one case where Colden's views take on a special importance, for Colden was most reluctant to criticize constituted authority; Cosby was the only governor who aroused his ire in all his many years in New York politics.

Many of the complaints against Cosby had to do with his land speculations. Edith M. Fox, *Land Speculation in the Mohawk Country* (Ithaca, N.Y., 1949), 19–21. Of course, the opportunity to acquire a landed estate was one of the accepted fringe benefits of colonial governorships (*ibid.*, 4), but Cosby's attempts to do this at the expense of prominent colonials could not at best have won him many friends among that group.

[6] Smith, *History*, II, 10, 26.

[7] *Journal of the Votes and Proceedings of the General Assembly of the Colony of New York, 1691–1765* (New York, Hugh Gaine, 1764–1766), Oct. 7, 1732; Katz, *Newcastle's New York,* 62. Colden says that the £1000 gift was approved by "a party that intended to ingratiat themselves in his favor." "History of Cosby and Clarke," 288. Cosby considered Supreme Court Justices Frederick Philipse and James DeLancey to be "Men of good Characters." Cosby to the Duke of Newcastle, May 3, 1733, *N.Y. Col. Docs.,* V, 943. The most perceptive and scholarly analysis of this period is contained in Stanley N. Katz's book, *Newcastle's New York,* and in his unpublished doctoral dissertation "An Easie Access: Anglo-

ship between Cosby and the Philipse group may have been enough to put Morris and his friends on their guard, but it was not until more substantive issues arose that a real opposition to Cosby began to form.

Following the death of Governor Montgomerie in 1731, Rip Van Dam, senior member of the Council, had taken over as acting governor during the thirteen-month interval before Cosby's arrival. In accordance with an irregularly observed custom, Cosby insisted in November, 1732, that Van Dam pay over to him one-half of the salary he had received during his tenure as acting governor. When Van Dam refused, Cosby determined to pursue the matter in a court of law. Unwilling to trust his chances with a jury of New Yorkers, Cosby turned instead to the New York Supreme Court in December, 1732, asking that it sit as a court of exchequer in order to try the case on the equity side. This proved to be a twofold error. Equity courts, which sat without juries and were governed by more arbitrary legal concepts than courts based on the common law, had always been feared in the colonies as potential star-chamber tribunals. The threatened or actual use of such courts to strengthen the governor's hand regarding land grants, the collection of quit-rents, and other governmental prerogatives had made them very unpopular with a great many of the colonists. Secondly, the man who was chief justice of the New York Supreme Court, Lewis Morris, was also president of the New Jersey Council and had served as acting governor of that colony pending Cosby's arrival. Assuming that Cosby might also demand one-half of Morris's interim salary, as indeed he did in February, 1733, Morris in a sense was being asked to render a judgment contrary to his own interests.[8]

Important as these considerations undoubtedly were in determining Morris's position on erecting a court of exchequer, there were still others, having to do with the old "landed party's" failure to gain favor with

American Politics in New York, 1732–1753" (Harvard University, 1961). While Katz is particularly concerned with how this dispute was affected by imperial pressures and relationships, my emphasis will be on its effect on provincial politics and attitudes.

[8] The people's dislike of chancery courts is described in Colden, "History of Cosby and Clarke," 290–91. See also Katz, *Newcastle's New York,* 63–64, 73–74.

the new governor. Because former governor Robert Hunter was an "Old Acquaintance" of Cosby, Morris and his friends had initially expected that the new governor would be friendly to them. Such a relationship would have been exceedingly helpful in 1732, for James Alexander, William Smith, Cadwallader Colden, and the Morrises had joined with others in a move to obtain title to "the Oblong," a tract of choice land recently ceded to New York by Connecticut, and their scheme would have been much enhanced if Cosby could be persuaded to fall in with it.[9] The governor chose instead to join his interest with a group of counter-claimants. By January, 1733, Alexander, Smith, and Lewis Morris, Sr., were stirred by misgivings. The governor, Alexander declared in March, "makes Little Distinction betwixt power & right, of which he has given Sundry proofs in the Small time he has been here. . . ."[10]

Another hint that party tensions were building was the appearance of James Alexander and William Smith as lawyers for Van Dam in the matter of his salary dispute with Cosby. In addition to their other concerns Alexander and Smith, as leading members of the New York bar, were alert to possible executive encroachment on their professional territory, and they strongly opposed a court of exchequer. It might be supposed that the opposition to Cosby, being so far largely of a personal nature, would continue to be restricted to a small circle, outside of which it would attract relatively little attention. Such was not to be the case.

On April 9, 1733, the salary dispute between Van Dam and Cosby was heard before the Supreme Court, with Chief Justice Lewis Morris

[9] Robert Hunter to James Alexander, Jamaica, June 13, Sept. 9, 1732, Rutherfurd Coll., I, 151, 153, NYHS. For information on "the Oblong," consult Colden to Micajah Perry, n.d., copy, NYHS *Colls.*, LI (1918), 26–30; "Agreement between the Patentees of the Equivalent Lands," *ibid.*, 65–71; Colden, "History of Cosby and Clarke," 305–12; Katz, *Newcastle's New York*, 80–81; Fox, *Land Speculation*, 17–18. There is some indication that the above-named group might themselves have been willing to press their claim in a court of equity if they could have counted on a friendly governor.

[10] William Smith to Lewis Morris, New York, Jan. 2, 1733, James Alexander to F. J. Paris, March 19, 1733, Rutherfurd Coll., I, 157, 159. Alexander also said later that Cosby's refusal to repay a personal loan had contributed to the New Yorker's decision to oppose him. Alexander to Peter Collinson, New York, June 4, 1739, draft, Rutherfurd Coll., IV, 63, NYHS.

presiding. The two other judges on the court at that time were James DeLancey, son of Stephen, and Colonel Frederick Philipse, nephew of Adolph Philipse, both of whom had been appointed to the bench in 1731 by Governor Montgomerie. Van Dam's lawyers, Alexander and Smith, argued that the case could not be tried in equity as Cosby desired, and Morris, in a prepared opinion, supported that view. The chief justice went on, moreover, to assert a novel position. He declared that "no less or other Authority than that of the whole Legislature [including the Assembly] can erect a Court of Equity," and that any other method was "unlawfull." Things drew toward a climax when Judges DeLancey and Philipse predictably took the opposite view, upholding the right of the Supreme Court to function as a court of exchequer. Morris thereupon roundly censured his younger associates for the perversity of their opinion, and refused to hear the case further.[11]

The next move was up to Cosby, and whereas with rare prudence he decided not to press his suit against Van Dam, he was hardly prepared to overlook Morris's challenge to his authority. In a long letter to the Duke of Newcastle, Cosby compiled a list of complaints against Morris which he claimed dated back to the earliest days of his administration, though prior to Morris's decision on the court of exchequer the governor had made no mention of any dissatisfaction with him. Now Morris was denounced for "excessive pride and his oppression of the people," for his "intemperate drinking," his "partiality" in the courtroom, and "his delay of justice" caused in part by late arrivals at court. Cosby also felt affronted that Morris had not visited him once since his arrival in the colony. The governor finished off his letter urgently recommending that "this Madman" be dismissed from his post as chief justice.[12]

When the governor had asked him for a copy of his opinion, Morris took the occasion to have his full statement on equity jurisdiction published in pamphlet form. He now defended his conduct in increas-

---

[11] For Morris's opinion see *Proceedings* of the New Jersey Historical Society, new series, LV (1937), 98, 105, 113, Katz, *Newcastle's New York*, 65–67.

[12] Cosby to the Duke of Newcastle, May 3, 1733, *N.Y. Col. Docs.*, V, 943. A few months earlier Cosby had written that James Alexander was "the only man that has given me any uneasiness since my arrival. . . ." Cosby to Lords of Trade, New York, Dec. 18, 1732, *ibid.*, 939.

ingly popular terms. Allowing that he might have been "impertinent" in some of his actions, "for old men are too often so," Morris denied that he intended any rudeness or disrespect to the governor "either in your public or private capacity." Declaring that his court opinion had been delivered "upon a point of law that came before me" as a judge, Morris suggested that "if judges are to be intimidated so as not to dare to give any opinion but what is pleasing to a *governor* . . . the people of this province" might well feel concern about the independence of their courts. Morris, secure in the thought of his own integrity and impartiality during nearly twenty years as chief justice, solemnly declared: "I have served the public faithfully and honestly according to the best of my knowledge, and I dare, and do, appeal to it for my justification." [13]

Morris had apparently anticipated as early as November, 1732, that all might not go well in his relations with Cosby, and he had told his son that he believed he could "parry everything but a poke." On August 21, 1733, the poke came. Cosby suspended Morris from his post as chief justice, elevating in his place the thirty-one-year-old second judge of the court, James DeLancey.

Morris's reaction to this blow is well worth noting. Far from being staggered by it, he seemed galvanized, even transformed. It was as though he were now released from all restraints. He now becomes the party leader, a role he embraces with zest, and he proceeds to challenge Cosby's authority with a persistence that must have surprised even those who best knew his pugnacious temper. Morris received prompt support from James Alexander and William Smith, Sr., and eventually a number of other prominent New Yorkers were drawn to his cause.[14] Few of them could have imagined at the outset how far the struggle would carry them from their originally limited goals. But before the conflict finally subsided in 1738, Morris and his supporters were to found an

---

[13] *Proceedings* of the New Jersey Historical Society, new series, LV (1937), 114–15; Lewis Morris, Esq., to Lords of Trade, Aug. 27, 1733, *N.Y. Col. Docs.,* V, 951–55.

[14] Lewis Morris to John Morris, Morrisania, Nov. 3, 1732, Morris MSS (John Morris Papers), Box 2, Rutgers. Though Cadwallader Colden wasted little sympathy on William Cosby, his strongly royalist sentiments deterred him from taking an active part in the Morrisite opposition, possibly because he deplored the "personal" tone of the propaganda directed at the governor and court party. Colden to James Alexander, Aug. 1, 1735, Rutherfurd Coll., II, 125, NYHS.

opposition newspaper, to fashion a program specifically designed for broad popular appeal, to launch a colony-wide petition campaign, and to involve large numbers of New York citizens in something resembling, at least embryonically, a party organization. All of this would be done in the name of a faction which opposed the legally constituted government, and on grounds which at the end appeared to challenge the very nature of the imperial relationship.

If their roles as popular party leaders raised internal anxieties or value conflicts in these normally restrained and prudent New Yorkers, they did not allow them to show. But whether this puts them down as mere opportunists and men without principle is quite another question. Today's social psychologist will tell us that "certain types of role-playing experiences can facilitate changes in personal opinions," especially when the role is socially rewarded by popular approval. Even opinions expressed initially "in the absence of a supporting attitude" may acquire inner conviction if sufficiently reinforced by public acclaim.[15] That such support was available to the Morrisites in their role of popular leadership cannot be doubted. Their public following exceeded any the colony had experienced to that time, or would experience for many years to come. And the techniques and ideas which gradually took shape in the course of this conflict were sufficiently precocious, sufficiently in advance of their time, that a comparable level of political development would not again be reached until the last decade of the colonial era.

2. A Twofold Strategy: The Founding of Zenger's New-York WEEKLY JOURNAL; the Westchester Election of 1733

By the time Morris was suspended as chief justice in August, 1733, he, Alexander, and Smith were already considering ways to increase the effectiveness of their opposition to Cosby. Aware of the value of public

[15] Irving L. Janis and Bert T. King, "The Influence of Role Playing on Opinion Change," *Journal of Abnormal and Social Psychology*, XLIX (April, 1954), 211; William Abbott Scott, "Attitude Change Through Reward of Verbal Behavior," *ibid.*, LV (July, 1957), 72, and "Attitude Change by Response Reinforcement: Replication and Extension," *Sociometry*, XXII (Dec., 1959), 328–35. Janis and King sug-

opinion, especially in New York City where direct pressure could be brought to bear on the governor, Council, and Assembly, the three men made plans to carry their case to the people. The publishing of Morris's opinion in pamphlet form had been the opening shot, but a more regular and popular mode of communication was wanted. There was at that time but one newspaper in New York, William Bradford's New York *Gazette,* which had begun publication in November, 1725. Because Bradford was also the official government printer for the colony, a post which paid £50 a year and was held at the pleasure of the governor, the *Gazette* often served as a vehicle for government views. The printer was "not Suffered to insert any Thing but what his Superiors approve of. . . ." To circumvent this monopoly of communication, Morris and his friends decided to start a second newspaper, one specifically designed to apply "the Lash of Satyr," as they boldly declared in an early issue, to "wicked Ministers." To print their paper they hired John Peter Zenger, a young man who had formerly been an apprentice to Bradford and had but recently set up his own shop. Pending establishment of the newspaper, Alexander and Smith busied themselves preparing anonymous polemical essays belaboring Cosby and the court party.[16]

Lewis Morris, meanwhile, prepared to open a second front in his war with the governor. Morris decided to dramatize the popularity of his opposition to Cosby by challenging the court party to a test of

---

gest that "the gain from role playing may occur primarily because the active participant tends to be impressed by his own cogent arguments, clarifying illustrations, and convincing appeals which he is stimulated to think up in order to do a good job of 'selling' the idea to others." Or an alternative explanation may rest in the "rewarding effects of the individual's sense of achievement or feelings of satisfaction with his performance in the role of active participant" (p. 218).

[16] New-York *Weekly Journal,* Dec. 17, 1733; Clarence S. Brigham, *History and Bibliography of American Newspapers, 1690–1820* (Worcester, Mass., 1947), I, 633–34; Vincent Buranelli, "Peter Zenger's Editor," *American Quarterly,* 7 (1955), 174–81. In their statement of purpose the editors of the *Weekly Journal* described a free press as "a Curb, a Bridle, a Terror, a Shame, and Restraint to evil Ministers." See issue of Nov. 12, 1733. For drafts of some party propaganda, see Rutherfurd Coll., II, 161, 163, 165, NYHS. By far the fullest and most learned analysis of Zenger's newspaper, his trial, and all of the surrounding political and legal ramifications is contained in Stanley N. Katz, ed., *A Brief Narrative of the Case and Trial of John Peter Zenger, Printer of The New-York Weekly Journal, by James Alexander* (Cambridge, Mass., 1963); see especially the Introduction, 1–35.

strength in the Westchester County by-election of October 29, 1733. A great deal of interest centered on this election, which soon took on a colony-wide significance; it continued, moreover, a local rivalry between two of Westchester's leading families, the Morrises and the Philipses. As both Adolph and Frederick Philipse were already members of the Assembly, that family's candidate was one William Forster, a schoolmaster for the S.P.G. whom the governor had recently appointed to the post of county clerk, no doubt hoping to give him some added lustre with which to face his opponent, Lewis Morris. It was, consequently, an occasion "of great Expectation," at which the "court and Country's Interest was exerted (as is said) to the Utmost. . . ." [17]

As was customary in those years, all of the electors gathered at one central spot—in this case the village of Eastchester—to record their votes. Because of the considerable distances involved, Morris's supporters began to assemble the night before the election, riding in from outlying parts of the county and gathering up followers as they went. By midnight one group had reached New Rochelle, where "a large Fire was made in the Street, by which they sat 'til Day-Light, at which Time they began to move." This first contingent was soon met by "about 70 Horse of the Electors of the lower Part of the County," and when they all converged upon the Eastchester green they numbered "above 300 Horse of the principal Freeholders . . . (a greater Number than had ever appeared for one Man since the Settlement of that County.)" Led by "two Trumpeters and 3 Violines," they rode three times around the green. At about eleven o'clock Forster's detachment arrived. At the head of that band was "the Honourable James Delancy, Esq., Chief Justice of the Province of New-York, and the Honourable Frederick Philipse, Esq., second Judge of the said Province, and Baron of the EXCHEQUER, [this was intended as a dig, the account having been written by Morris's supporters], attended by about 170 Horse of the Freeholders and Friends" of Forster and the two judges. When the two groups passed, Philipse "very civilly" saluted Morris "by taking off his Hat, which the late Judge returned in the same Manner." After assembling on the green, the electors publicly indicated their choice when the question was put to them by the sheriff.

It was soon apparent that Morris had won. But the opposition de-

17 New-York *Weekly Journal,* Nov. 5, 1733.

manded a poll, and the election was delayed for two hours while tables and chairs were obtained and set up. The court forces tried to cut Morris's margin by insisting that the sheriff reject thirty-eight Quaker votes. When he did so, the Morrisites accused him of "a violent attempt on the Liberties of the People." (The sheriff, it may be recalled, was an appointee of the governor.) The poll continued until about "Eleven o'Clock that Night," at which time the count stood at 231 for Morris —without the thirty-eight Quaker votes—and 151 for Forster. "The Indentures being sealed, the whole Body of Electors, waited on their new Representative to his Lod[g]ings, with Trumpets sounding, and violins playing. . . . Thus ended the Westchester Election to the general Satisfaction." [18]

Morris, of course, interpreted this victory as a public vindication of his stand against Cosby, and when the newly elected assemblyman returned to New York City on October 31, his supporters greeted him as a conquering hero. His arrival "was announced by the explosion of the cannon of the merchants ships in the harbour, and by the citizens meeting and conducting him, with loud acclamations, to a public and splendid entertainment" at the Black Horse Tavern. In the midst of this, Cosby began to fear the spread of the "Boston spirit," as he called it, to the province of New York.[19]

The opposition newspaper, the New-York *Weekly Journal,* began publication on November 5, 1733, just in time to devote most of its first issue to a report of Morris's Westchester triumph. The political parentage of the paper left its mark on every page. In addition to the tracts of the local polemicists, selections from the popular English essayists Addison and Steele, as well as from the "spirited papers" of Trenchard and Gordon, were prominently featured. Past and present governors

[18] New-York *Weekly Journal,* Nov. 5, 1733. Milton Klein has calculated that the total vote of 420 electors represented approximately 32.9 per cent of the adult white males residing in Westchester County at that time. This is not as high a turnout as that stimulated by New York County elections, but it is a substantial response considering the rural setting of Westchester County, which at that time also encompassed much of present-day Bronx County. Klein, "Democracy and Politics in Colonial New York," *New York History,* XL (July, 1959), 237. For more on New York elections, consult Nicholas Varga, "Election Procedures and Practices in Colonial New York," *New York History,* XLI (July, 1960), 249–77.

[19] Smith, *History,* II, 9; New-York *Weekly Journal,* Nov. 5, 1733; Cosby to Lords of Trade, New York, Dec. 6, 1734, *N.Y. Col. Docs.,* VI, 21.

were castigated openly or by implication. One article noted that governors whose names started with the letter C had "always proved unhappy" for the province. After describing the corrupt activities of former governors Coote and Cornbury, the writer concluded pointedly: "What has once been may be again." In other articles Governor Cosby was accused of cronyism, of "concerning himself in elections," and of land jobbery which deprived "many of His Majesty's good and Loyal Subjects" of "a Part of their Property." Cosby's supporters were alleged to have sacrificed the public welfare for private advancement, and in at least one article impeachment of these "courtiers" was broadly suggested. Not even the advertisement page was neutral ground, as notices for lost animals, bearing remarkable resemblances to leading court politicians, enlivened what would normally have been dull reading. As Stanley Katz has suggested, it would seem that the *Journal* "was looking for trouble." It did not take Cosby long to realize that an opposition newspaper which regularly attacked the competence and affronted the dignity of the King's representative could not be suffered to continue without seriously undermining imperial authority. As the governor informed Newcastle, the Morrisites were trying to provoke him into a "paper war" by demanding that he justify "my owne conduct, and his Majesty's authority, which ought not to be prostituted to the censure of the mob." [20]

As early as January, 1734, Cosby attempted to get the New York County Grand Jury to move against the *Journal* for libel, but neither then nor during the jury's October term was he successful. The governor next turned to the Council and the Assembly for orders to have the most offensive issues of the *Journal* publicly burned. The Assembly, its popular faction newly strengthened by the presence of Lewis Morris, refused to comply, and Cosby had to act with the acquiescence of the Council only, a procedure which further alienated public opinion. By

[20] Smith, *History*, II, 9, Cosby to Newcastle, New York, Dec. 17, 1733, *N.Y. Col. Docs.*, V, 974; New-York *Weekly Journal*, Dec. 24, 1733, April 8, Oct. 21, Dec. 23, 1734, Feb. 17, April 14, 1735; Katz, ed., *Zenger*, 9. One *Journal* advertisement for "A Large Spaneil, of about Five Foot Five Inches High" was intended to raise the vision of Francis Harison, one of the leaders of the court party. New-York *Weekly Journal*, Nov. 26, 1733. For a convenient sampling of the *Journal's* style, see Katz, ed., *Zenger*, Appendix A. Although Cosby rejected the idea of a "paper war," his supporters employed the pages of Bradford's *Gazette* to answer the *Journal's* polemics.

order of the Council, Zenger was arrested and imprisoned on November 17, 1734, though the *Journal,* pending the outcome of Zenger's trial, continued to appear. James Alexander and William Smith, Sr., immediately offered their legal services to Zenger, as well they might, since it was their own inflammatory writings in the *Journal* that had led to his arrest. In a series of motions before Chief Justice James DeLancey and the Supreme Court, Alexander and Smith tried to turn Zenger's defense, according to Stanley Katz, into "an impeachment of the Cosby administration," by implication charging Governor Cosby with "tyrannically flouting the laws of England and New York and of setting up personal henchmen with unlawful powers to control the judicial system of New York." DeLancey's response to these attacks on his patron was to disbar Alexander and Smith on April 18, a move which he may later have regretted, for Alexander thereupon obtained for Zenger the services of the most brilliant trial lawyer in the colonies, Andrew Hamilton of Philadelphia. The Zenger case was heard on August 4, 1735, before a jury of ordinary· New York citizens. Andrew Hamilton, overriding current legal concepts, argued that truth was a legitimate defense against accusations of libel. He further argued that colonial juries had —or should have—broader prerogatives in the rendering of general verdicts than did their English counterparts, this latter point being based on the *practical* differences between the government in England and its paler image in America, a novel point of view sure to appeal to the colonists. Not unexpectedly, the jury deliberated only a few minutes before finding Zenger innocent.[21]

The Zenger case has been a perennial object of interest and comment through the years. But though it was hailed in the nineteenth century as a milestone in the development of freedom of the press, the im-

[21] Katz, ed., *Zenger,* 18–20. Hamilton's defense is summarized on pp. 22–26; James Alexander's version of his full argument is presented on pp. 61–101. It was customary at that time for juries in libel cases to render only special verdicts, which would have limited this jury to determining only whether or not Zenger had in fact printed the allegedly libelous papers. A general verdict extended the jury's authority to include a determination of whether or not a libel had in fact occurred. Though the New York court denied the jury's right to return a general verdict, that is in effect what it did, for there was never any doubt that Zenger's press printed the issues of the *Journal* in question. *Ibid.,* 22–23.

portance of the case was then gradually downgraded to the point where it could be asserted, as Leonard Levy recently has, that "the Zenger case had no appreciable effect upon the freedom, or rather lack of freedom, of the press in colonial New York." [22] It is true that with regard to its direct effect on Anglo-American legal practice the Zenger case marked no sharp turning-point, for the law of libel remained essentially the same until the early nineteenth century. Katz has noted in his recent edition of the trial papers that while the Zenger case "significantly contributed to neutralizing seditious libel in the armory of weapons used to restrict speech, [it] by no means guaranteed respect for freedom of the press in colonial New York." When it comes to evaluating the case as a political phenomenon, however, he finds that its fame is "by no means undeserved," for it indirectly helped to establish "the connection between law and politics in a popularly based society." In effect, the political point stressed by the Morrisite party at every opportunity was that "the government was the servant of the people and that open criticism was one of the important ways in which magistrates could be kept responsible to them." [23] In an age when the concept of a loyal opposition was virtually unknown, New Yorkers demonstrated once again that they were capable of a remarkably imaginative and innovative approach to politics—even if their application of new principles was inconsistent. As we know, when in power the Morrisites had been no more willing to accept criticism than was the Cosby court party.

Leonard Levy further points out that after the Zenger case in 1735, responsibility for restraining the New York press shifted from the courts to the General Assembly, and he cites several examples where government critics were haled before the House to answer charges of seditious libel. Professor Katz suggests that this shift in itself represented a progressive step, "for it is one thing to be prosecuted and judged by one's elected representatives and quite another to be assailed by the surrogates of the Crown." Even here a good deal of caution is required in evaluating the real significance of the Assembly's role, for it

[22] Leonard W. Levy, "Did the Zenger Case Really Matter? Freedom of the Press in Colonial New York," *WMQ*, 3rd Ser., XVIII (Jan., 1960), 36. For a summary of nineteenth-century views, see Katz, ed., *Zenger*, 1.

[23] Katz, ed., *Zenger*, 30, 34.

seems often to have been dictated by political expediency.[24] Such "inconsistencies of principle" cannot be evaluated outside of a political framework. Indeed, very few events in the history of colonial New York are fully comprehensible unless they are related to the political currents of the time.

There is no question that New York's colonial press, both before and after the Zenger case, was subject to a variety of restrictions, even if the application of them was often uneven or dictated by party strategies. Yet perhaps the most remarkable thing was that New York's newspapers developed as much latitude and vitality as they did. After the founding of Zenger's *Journal* in 1733, New York City would never again be a one-newspaper town.[25] Also, as will become evident, after 1735 the New York presses continued to pour forth political commentary in every way as libelous as that which had led to Zenger's arrest. It

[24] While it is true that the Assembly occasionally issued warrants for the arrest of critics who had printed derogatory comments about government figures or policies, the handling of these cases was fairly mild. The offenders were usually dismissed after entering an apology and paying all costs. There were a few instances, as Levy shows, where citizens were actually jailed by the Assembly, but these actions more often stemmed from political rivalries than from any consistent definition of libel or policy of censorship by the Assembly. Not untypical was the case of the Reverend Mr. Watkins of Ulster County, who as Levy states was arrested and jailed in 1756 for writing an article in the New York *Gazette* which criticized the Assembly for failing to provide adequately for frontier defenses. According to William Smith, Jr., however, the Assembly had moved to apprehend the author of that article in the belief that the culprit was Cadwallader Colden, who at that time was a political opponent of the Assembly majority. When the article was traced to Mr. Watkins, says Smith, "the wrath of the house vanished into smoke," for Watkins was an Anglican clergyman who supported the current effort by the Assembly to assure Anglican control of the newly founded King's College. In another well-known case, Alexander McDougall was jailed in 1770 for publishing two broadsides attacking the Assembly for provisioning the King's troops. Yet a close look at the case shows that McDougall's main crime was that he attacked the party which controlled the Assembly. *Assembly Journal* (Gaine), I, Nov. 14, 1753, II, Mar. 16, 18, 19, 23, 30, 1756, and pp. 746–47; Smith, *History,* II, 279; Levy, "Did the Zenger Case Really Matter?" 41–49; Katz, ed., *Zenger,* 30. For more details on McDougall, see pp. 267 ff. below.

[25] Brigham, *History of Newspapers,* I, 527–57. Even when Zenger was in jail awaiting trial, the tone of the *Weekly Journal* remained the same, with Cosby's courtiers being criticized by name, and Zenger's letters from jail being given full play. See issues of Dec. 23, 1734, Jan. 6, 1735, and others to August, 1735, when the printer was acquitted.

is altogether likely that in a society which focused so much of its energy on politics, a spirited press would have developed with or without Zenger—or rather, with or without Alexander, Smith, Morris, and company. The Zenger case was more a symptom than a cause; the New York press reflected a society periodically sundered by political factions. Those factions attempted, by the printed word and by every other means at their disposal, to justify their opposition and to expand the base of their popular support.

3. A Flanking Maneuver: Lewis Morris in London; Petitions in New York

If Governor Cosby had had any of the ordinary skills of tact, diplomacy, or conciliation, he might have found a way to avert the factional split which developed after 1733. It was still a precarious business to oppose a governor, and the deposing of a chief justice and imprisoning of a printer were not such obviously popular causes as to guarantee under any conditions the mobilization of public sentiment in their behalf. But Cosby had no political instincts. Despite some clumsy efforts to gain popularity, his artless manner and impulsive actions served to swell the ranks of the opposition. In little more than a year Cosby had made himself sufficiently odious by one means or another that the Morris junto was emboldened to draw up a list of thirty-four complaints against him, and they sent it off to London with a request for Cosby's removal. Among the more serious charges was that Cosby had ignored the Council's right to sit separately from the governor when acting in its legislative capacity, thereby rendering the Council useless as a "check and ballance in Government." He had failed to notify certain Councilmen (i.e., Alexander, Colden, and Van Dam) when meetings were to be held, and he had displaced judges and sheriffs without consulting the Council. He was further charged with having appointed non-residents as sheriffs in the counties, having appointed a man "in necessitous circumstances" to the Council, and having encouraged the Westchester sheriff to deny Quakers the vote in the 1733 by-election. Cosby had allowed a French sloop to enter New York harbor to obtain provisions, an action which the Morrisites solemnly claimed might well have compromised the colony's security. Crowning the list of complaints was the charge that Cosby had participated in the destruction of the "Albany deed." [26]

This last charge concerned a 1,200-acre section of land near Albany which the Mohawk Indians had deeded to the Albany Corporation in 1730 with the provision that it be held in trust for their tribe. By 1733, at the supposed instigation of Cosby, the Indians were complaining that the agreement was not being observed, whereupon Cosby, in what must have been a singular ceremony, had returned the deed to them and had then stood by while the Indians tore it up and threw it in the fire. From a legal viewpoint Cosby may well have had some reason to question the transaction's validity. Although the Albany people had generally been on good terms with the Mohawks, they were not above occasional sharp practices in matters of land. But whatever the merits of the case, Cosby chose an unnecessarily picturesque way of dealing with it. He failed to consult the Albany magistrates and made no attempt to work out an amicable settlement. Cosby's abrupt action in this matter raised a great clamor at Albany and led to a permanent rupture with the governor.[27]

In addition to demanding Cosby's recall, the popular party, as it was now called, had been active on other fronts. In October, 1734, the Morrisites had injected themselves into the New York City Common Council elections, where their slate of candidates had swept all but one of Cosby's supporters from office.[28] Their progress was slower in the

[26] "Articles of Complaint against Governor Cosby by Rip Van Dam, Esq.," Dec. 17, 1733, *N.Y. Col. Docs.*, V, 975–78. Although Van Dam signed the articles, Cosby was probably correct when he charged that they were written by Morris and Alexander. Cosby to Newscastle, New York, Dec. 17, 1733, *N.Y. Col. Docs.*, V, 974–75. Regarding Cosby's attempts at popularity Colden says he "invited many of low rank to dine with him such as had never pretended or expected so much respect." "History of Cosby and Clarke," 298. For more on these dinners, see Abigail Franks to Naphtali Franks, June 9, 1734, Hershkowitz and Meyer, eds., *Friedman Collection of American Jewish Colonial Correspondence*, 25–26.

[27] Gov. Cosby to Lords of Trade, New York, June 6, Dec. 7, 1734, *N.Y. Col. Docs.*, VI, 6, 25; *ibid.*, 15–16. Colden charged that Cosby destroyed the deed in order to get the land for himself, and that his design was defeated because of the protest this raised at Albany. "History of Cosby and Clarke," 304–5. See also Edith Fox, *Land Speculation in the Mohawk Country* (Ithaca, N.Y., 1949), 16–20.

[28] *Minutes of the Common Council of the City of New York, 1675–1776* (New York, 1905), IV, 217–19, 228–30. Two election songs which were printed in the

Assembly, however, for no general election had been held since 1728, and the court party remained strong in that body. By stimulating petitions from various counties, the Morris party had managed in June, 1734, to force an Assembly debate on the validity of equity courts. This had so aroused public interest that "the doors [of the House] were thrown open to satisfy the general curiosity." With the eyes of the people upon them even Cosby's supporters had to watch their step. As William Smith, Jr., described it, "popular motions were also made by the court party; a bill was brought in to introduce the balloting of jurors," and "Mr. [Stephen] DeLancey moved . . . for limiting the continuance of assemblies" to three years. Smith, whose sympathies of course were with the popular party, adds that the "multitude" put no faith in these "appearances" and "petitions were circulated to stimulate their representatives to real services." [29] Short of a new election, however, there was not much the opposition could do except keep the Assembly under public scrutiny.

Outside of the Assembly, on the other hand, the popular party continued to make substantial headway. Philip Livingston, the second proprietor of Livingston Manor, finally swung over to the opposition party in December, 1734. The burning of the Albany deed was the deciding factor for the cautious Livingston. "Now I have layd my Self open," he explained, "to all the Malice & Revenge of the Court but I could not avoid it, unless I did Calmly Submitt to all their Illegall proceedings & Suffer myself & neighbours to be . . . tore to peices. I think I have Choisen of Two Evils the Least." Once having made his choice, however, Livingston assumed a vigorous role in party activities. To protest the governor's action regarding the deed, he circulated at Albany a petition which, as he reported on December 6, 1734, "this

Journal, and are reprinted in Katz, ed., _Zenger,_ 109–11, form part of the libelous material attributed to Zenger. One of the songs, whose first line reads "To you Good Ladds that Dare oppose all Lawless Power & Might," was written by Lewis Morris. See folder marked "Miscellaneous Verse and Prose" in Morris MSS, Box 2, Rutgers. The songs were also distributed in the form of broadsides. See Broadside Collection, Rare Book Room, NYPL.

[29] _Assembly Journal_ (Gaine), I, May 23, 28, June 7, 12, 21, Nov. 16, 1734; Cosby to Lords of Trade, New York, June 19, 1734, _N.Y. Col. Docs.,_ VI, 4–7; Smith, _History,_ II, 16–17; Osgood, _American Colonies, Eighteenth Century,_ II, 457–58. So far as can be determined, this was the first time the public had been admitted to Assembly debates.

morning above 110 had signed & how many more before night I Cant tell." To keep Livingston staunch to the cause in the ensuing months, James Alexander reminded him that Cosby was trying to "Set aside the oblong patent in a Court of Equity" and that if he succeeded no man's property would be safe.[30]

Another party adherent was gained in late 1734 when Governor Cosby ousted Assemblyman Vincent Matthews from his posts as chief judge and clerk of Orange County. Matthews had made a speech which was critical of Francis Harison, one of the leading members of the court party, and Cosby retaliated by removing Matthews and all of his supporters from office. It is a measure of Cosby's unpopularity that Matthews, in the face of the governor's ire, nevertheless managed to retain the support of nearly all his constituents, who, as he told Alexander, "Stand Verry Manfully to their Entegrety & Show a firm Spirrit of Defending the Liberties of their Cuntry." [31]

But by late 1734, it was becoming increasingly apparent that despite these gains in popular party strength it would be impossible to topple Cosby from power so long as he retained the support of his patrons at Whitehall. It was in London that the real decisions about Cosby's future and Morris's displacement as chief justice would be made, and the Morrisites recognized that a more forceful presentation of their case was essential. Besides, many of the problems which had taken

[30] Philip to Gilbert Livingston, Albany, Dec. 6, 1734, Misc. Livingston MSS, Box N-P, NYHS; James Alexander to Philip Livingston, Sept. 29, 1735, draft, Rutherfurd Coll., II, 131, NYHS. In 1735 Livingston urged his brother, Gilbert, representative from the manor, to attend the opening of the Assembly "to prevent Some Schemes . . . by the Court party." Philip to Gilbert Livingston, Albany, Oct. 11, 1735, Misc. Livingston MSS, Box N-P, NYHS.

[31] Vincent Matthews to James Alexander, Matthewsfried, Jan. 5, 1735, Rutherfurd Coll., II, 103; "Speech of Vincent Matthews . . . Oct. 21, 1735," draft in Colden's hand, NYHS *Colls.,* LXVII (1934), 226–40. The implication is that Cadwallader Colden wrote Matthews' speech. A letter in support of Matthews from 78 of his constituents appeared in the New-York *Weekly Journal* on Oct. 7, 1734 (and is reprinted in Katz, ed., *Zenger,* 129–31). When Gov. Cosby retaliated by turning Matthews' friends out of office, including some whose only error had been to sign the letter of support, Colden commented that this showed political resentment against those "daring to thank their Representative for acting according to the Sentiments of his Constituents," and could be construed as "an attempt against the Liberties & Freedoms of the People in their Representative Capacities," Colden to James Alexander, Aug. 1, 1735, Rutherfurd Coll., II, 125, NYHS.

shape during the turbulent months since Cosby's arrival touched upon broad questions of constitutional relationships within the empire, and the colonists sensed, correctly, that their point of view was not well understood at home. Knowledgeable New Yorkers had realized for some time that their constitution was "very sickly," and the events of the 1730's had pointed up a number of critical questions. What were the rights of Englishmen in the colonies, and how were they to be preserved against an insensitive and obdurate governor? Could the English court system be imposed intact upon a distant colony, or did different conditions require that adjustments be made? How were the colonists to gain a fair hearing and a just solution of their grievances? Hopeful of finding answers to some of these questions, Lewis Morris embarked for London on November 23, 1734, in order to plead the opposition cause personally before the Privy Council.[32]

Inasmuch as Morris's trip would make possible the direct presentation of a number of New York grievances, the party leaders spent considerable time drafting and re-drafting a set of instructions for his guidance in London. So far as can be judged by the much-revised copies of these instructions, it appears that eleven points were considered most essential. Assembly elections should be annual or triennial; the Council should be allowed to sit separately from the governor; the courts should be "Established by Law" (that is, by an act of the Assembly); and judges should be appointed during good behavior. Morris was also to request a new act to govern the appointment of councillors and the ap-

[32] New-York *Weekly Journal,* Nov. 25, 1734. "Our Constitution is very sickly & I am affray'd we shall have a fever before a Crisis," wrote Colden to James Alexander. Coldengham, June 22, 1729, Rutherfurd Coll., I, 125, NYHS. The applicability of English legal precepts to the colonies was of continuing concern to the provincials. At one point a list of 48 rules was drawn up to guide the administration of the court of oyer and terminer. The last clause stated that in cases of conflict over whether to proceed according to "the Laws of this Province or according to the Laws of England, it is always to be understood . . . that . . . where the Laws of this Province have made any Provision therein . . . the Court will Proceed according & not otherwise & that wherein the Laws of this Province are Silent the Court is to be Regulated by the Laws of England." "Rules and orders for the Court of oyer & Terminer throughout this Province appointed by the Judges," n.d., Livingston-Redmond MSS, Reel 9. Charles Andrews says that this was the prevailing attitude toward the law in all royal colonies. *The Colonial Background of the American Revolution* (New Haven, Conn., rev. ed., 1931), 54–55.

pointment or election of sheriffs and coroners, a ruling that land in the colony be patented without the governor's receiving "exorbitant fees," and the reapportionment of Assembly seats in accordance with population growth. Special attention was given to the influential centers of New York City and Albany, in that new charters were to be recommended "with the annual Election of Mayors, Sheriffs & other officers of the Corporation by the people," and efforts were to be made to gain encouragement for manufacturing. This last point was designed to appeal to the commercial interests, which were now being wooed by the popular party. In addition, of course, Morris was to work for his own restoration as chief justice and for Cosby's removal as governor.[33]

By January, 1735, a fall-back position had been devised in the event Morris were unable to obtain Cosby's removal. Annual elections were considered to be "of most Consequence" along with a general emphasis on constitutional reforms which would limit the governor's power over the judiciary and Council. As Alexander observed, "the Compromise proposed is in Substance what Englishmen are entitled to by the original Constitution of their mother Country" and would preserve "this peoples rights & Liberties" by making certain that power would be "Distributed & justly ballanced & checkt by an independent Council, independent frequent assemblys independent judges etc." [34]

While Morris was pressing the cause in England, his New York supporters worked hard to keep up the spirit of opposition and to broaden the party base. Aware that Morris would have to demonstrate that he spoke from more than personal pique, and denied the important weapon of an appeal from the Assembly because their position in that body was still a minority one, the Morrisites launched a petition cam-

---

[33] "Proposals of what Col. Morris Shale go home for," Lewis Morris, Jr., n.d., "Coppy Instructions to Col. Morris for his Conduct in England," Nov. 19, 1734, "Considerations and alterations in the instructions to Col. Morris," William Smith, n.d., "Instructions proposed for Col. Morris Conduct in Great Britain," [James Alexander], Nov. 19, 1734, Rutherfurd Coll., II, 71, 73, 75, NYHS. Morris was accompanied to London by his son, Robert Hunter Morris, whose record of the trip is reproduced in Beverly McAnear, ed., "R. H. Morris: An American in London, 1735–1736," *Pennsylvania Magazine of History*, LXIV (1940), 164–217, 356–406.

[34] James Alexander to R. Pacheco, New York, Jan. 17, 1735, draft, Rutherfurd Coll., II, 95, NYHS.

paign to produce visible evidence that their views had wide public support. In December, 1734, Alexander wrote Morris that "the Petitions from the people to Supply your want of a Legislative power" were being prepared. In Queens County petitions were circulated by members of the Hicks family and by Thomas Cornell; one received more than eighty signatures and it was claimed that many more could have been obtained if necessary. In order to gain support in Albany, Alexander had sent Philip Livingston a copy of Morris's instructions showing that a new charter for Albany was one of the points Morris was "to insist on." A petition circulated by Peter V. B. Livingston in June, 1735, drew fifty-one subscribers, while a second one, which specifically requested the return of the lands included in the "Albany deed," was circulated by Philip Livingston in October and found the populace "So unanimous . . . Eager and Ready . . . to Sign. . . . if this had been a fair day could have had most if not all the hands in Town to it." Lewis Morris, Jr., was in charge of the campaign in Westchester County, though there is no record of how many signatures were obtained there. In New York County, where petitions had long been used to express demands and grievances, approximately three hundred signatures were gathered, including those of many prominent citizens.[35]

The signers were asked not only to lend the authority of their names to Morris's efforts in London, but also to give money where possible to defray the costs of his trip. Rip Van Dam and James Alexander

---

[35] James Alexander to Lewis Morris, New York, Dec. 30, 1734, draft, Jan. 17, June 16, 1735, Philip Livingston to Alexander, Albany, Oct. 15, 1735, Rutherfurd Coll., II, 95, 97, 139. A copy of the New York County petition, "Names of those agreeing to sustain Col. Morris," n.d., is in the Rutherfurd Coll., II, 75, NYHS. Peter V. B. Livingston was a new recruit to the cause in 1735. He had made a visit to London in late 1733 and, though requested by Morris to convey New York's dissatisfaction with Cosby to the Board of Trade, Livingston had begged off on the ground that he had to catch a ship. Lewis Morris, Jr., interpreted this excuse as showing "a Little of the Albany Spirit." By June, 1735, however, Livingston had had a change of heart: "He behaves very well here and has carried a propper Petition to Albany," which was to be signed and sent to Morris in London. Lewis Morris, Jr., to Robert Hunter Morris, New York, June 3, 1735, Morris MSS, Box 3, Rutgers. We know that New York County was familiar with such campaigns because of the hundreds of petitions, dating back as far as 1681, on deposit at the Municipal Archives and Records Library in New York City. All are individual petitions until 1728, when the first of a series of group petitions can be found.

each pledged £200 while William Smith was down for £50. One of
Morris's Westchester in-laws complained that some "Party persons"
were slow about raising money, and it is evident that the success of the
fund-raising effort was tied to reports of Morris's progress in London.
Indeed, the success of the opposition in general rose and fell with the
news from England, for "as in all Oppositions, there is a necessity of
taking some Men into the party whose Merits are not considerable" and
"who are ready to fly off, the moment they hear any little idle tale from
the Adverse party. . . ." Nonetheless in May, 1735, party hopes were
still high, and it was reported that "where we Loose one, we gain
five." [36]

But despite the optimistic expectations of the party leaders that
Morris's trip would help to "Setle our Liberty on a Solid foundation," a
few weeks in London had made Morris less sanguine. "Your instructions are good," he wrote to Alexander in March, 1735, "but you have
Verry imperfect notions of the world on this Side of the water. . . .
they are unconcerned at the Sufferings of the People in America. . . ."
Morris goes on to describe a world of corruption and influence-peddling
where "the most Nefarious Crime A governor can commit is not by
Some counted So bad as the crime of Complaining of it, the last is an
arraigning of the ministry that advised the Sending of him Exposing
them to Censure. . . ." Regarding the Privy Council, Morris found that

[36] Alexander to Lewis Morris, New York, Jan. 17, 1735, draft, Rutherfurd Coll.,
II, 95, NYHS; James Graham to R. H. Morris, New York, May 30, 1735, Morris
MSS (Robert Hunter Morris Papers), Box 3, Mathew Norris to Lewis Morris,
New York, Nov. 6, 1735, Morris MSS, Box I, Rutgers. Nor was the court party
inactive on the political front. Alexander reported that they were spreading ru-
mors that Morris was giving up the case, and that the British might send troops.
Furthermore, "the two judges [James DeLancey and Frederick Philipse] went
. . . to every one of the Countys" where "they Endeavoured as much as possible
to be popular . . . those Assemblymen whom they could not gain over they Endeavoured to prevail on to Stay at home, accordingly Gilbert Lvingston, Henry
Beekman, Van Cleek, & the Patron" ["Patroon" Van Rensselaer] stayed away
from the fall Assembly session. The governor had also made it a point to visit
with Beekman, Gaasbeck, and Pawling (the last two, Assemblymen from Ulster
County), "who before were pretty firm with us." Alexander's assessment of the
situation was that the court party had "Lost ground amongst the people," especially after the Zenger trial, though they still had a majority in the Assembly. Alexander to Lewis Morris, New York, Nov. 6, 1735, draft, Rutherfurd Coll., II,
145, NYHS.

it was "difficult to get them there [to a meeting] on Plantation affairs
than which nothing takes up So little of their thoughts. . . ." Nor did
Parliament escape his critical eye, for Morris advised Alexander that if
he could observe that body himself "you would perhaps form another
idea of a British Parliament than what you at present have. . . ." That
his choicest invective was reserved for officials concerned with colonial
affairs was a measure of the isolation and spiritual fatigue which Morris
experienced in the early weeks. In February he had told his son John
that "the meanest cottage in America with peace is preferable to anything here [.] Would to God we were with you and free from Cosbys
Rule in any Station of life not Slaves [.] Oh happy Americans too
happy if you know your own blest state." London, on the other hand,
was a city where "an universale avarice and corruption Predomin-
ates," particularly in any matter which touched the interests of the
colonies.[37]

Morris's initial despair did not last long, however; he was hardly
an innocent (he had been in England in 1701 as a solicitor for New Jersey interests), and he himself was by no means inexperienced at the
game of "influence." Morris's efforts to gain support in high places
against Cosby's powerful relatives and friends have been described fully
by Professor Katz. Without a strong family "interest" or the distinct
benefits of commercial ties, Morris had to depend on chance acquaint-
ances and a few second-level figures to cultivate his cause in the all-important antechambers and precincts of informal politics. By October,
1735, he believed he had made some headway, though he still questioned whether justice would prevail in a land where "every thing is
Said to go by interest. . . ." [38] The hearing on Morris's charges against
Cosby was held before a committee of the Privy Council in November,
1735. Morris and his counsel appear to have made a strong presentation against Cosby, for the committee majority agreed that the governor

[37] Philip Livingston to James Alexander, Albany, Jan. 7, 1735, Lewis Morris to
Alexander, London, March 31, 1735, Rutherfurd Coll., II, 103, 115; Lewis Mor-
ris to John Morris, London, Feb. 9, 1735, Morris MSS (John Morris Papers),
Box 2, Rutgers; Lewis Morris to Alexander, Chelsea, Aug. 25, 1735, Rutherfurd
Coll., II, 129. See also Morris to Alexander, London, Feb. 24, 1735, Rutherfurd
Coll., II, 113, NYHS.

[38] Morris to Alexander, London, Oct. 24, 1735, Rutherfurd Coll., II, 141, NYHS;
Katz, *Newcastle's New York,* Chap. 5.

had given insufficient reasons for removing Morris as chief justice and there was even some hint that Morris might regain his post. As Peter Collinson wrote James Alexander, the only criticism directed at the New Yorker was his "writing his own Case & appealing to the Country —this (Enter Nous) was not well Taken & looked on as a very wrong Step," likely to "make Divisions & Stir up Anemosities." (This was a reference to the publication of Morris's opinion regarding equity courts and his appeal to the people for vindication.) [39] In England squabbles between government officials were expected to be settled *in camera,* and were not on the whole considered fit subjects for public debate.

Though Morris had gained a form of vindication from the committee, it soon became apparent that this would not be translated into any direct action against his antagonist, Governor Cosby. Yet Morris had already invested eleven months in the quest, and he was not one to give up easily. He decided to remain in London a while longer in the hope of something more concrete. After November, 1735, he broadened the attack on Cosby, bringing forward all possible evidence, including the petitions gathered by his New York supporters, to show that the government of the colony had been badly mismanaged and that Cosby had lost the confidence of the people. His main tactic in this second phase of the campaign was to dispatch a series of appeals to both the King and the Privy Council praying for relief regarding such matters as the Albany deed and the general reform of New York's governmental structure. At this same time Morris began to realize fully the high cost and uncertain result of colonial solicitations. As he informed Alexander, every grievance had to be filed in an affidavit, with fees attending each form. "If you complain of 20 things, there must be 20 references—20 orders, 20 duplicates, which will Stand in about £10 Sterling on Each petition. . . ." Even then "the matter may End with a gentle or rough admonition to the Governor . . . which he'll do as far as he thinks fit." As Morris concluded: "This must mend Sometime; but when, God

[39] Peter Collinson to Alexander, London, Nov. 8, 1735, Rutherfurd Coll., II, 145; Katz, *Newcastle's New York,* 116. According to another English correspondent of Alexander's, Ferdinand J. Paris: "There was nothing Stuck with any of the Lords of the Council in Coll. Morris's Affair but the printing and publishing of his Opinion, which was endeavoured by some Persons to be magnifyed as tending to Sedition." Paris to [Alexander], London, Nov. 21, 1735, Rutherfurd Coll., Small Scrap Book, NYHS.

knows. . . . In a word, if we cannot help our Selves on our own Side of the water we must learn to beare our miseries as well as we can till chance or providence relieves us. . . ." [40]

In New York, meanwhile, the opposition party was doing everything it could to distress Cosby and to promote "the common cause of Liberty." Cosby, now in failing health, protested to Whitehall that the Morrisites held "Nightly Corrispondence and secret meetings," and it is quite likely that the intrigues of the junto contributed significantly to the governor's worsening condition.[41] On March 10, 1736, William Cosby died. One of the most turbulent administrations in the colony's history was thereby closed, but the unlamented Cosby was barely off the scene when another dispute, one which raised party antagonisms to an even higher pitch, erupted.

The two most senior members of the Council, Rip Van Dam (whom Cosby had finally suspended the previous November) and George Clarke, each claimed the right to head the government pending the arrival of a new governor. A majority of the Council sided with Clarke, and he was promptly installed as president of the Council. But the Morrisites, as on an earlier occasion, continued to press Van Dam's claim, dramatizing it with skillful propaganda in Zenger's *Weekly Journal* and by stimulating popular agitation. The dissidents continued to question the legitimacy of Clarke's leadership throughout the spring and summer of 1736, while tensions on all sides mounted. When it appeared that the fall session of the General Assembly might be used to ratify the Council's choice of Clarke, the popular party leaders took alarm. Philip Livingston felt that "a vigorous attempt to prevent them might be of Service" and suggested that "all those who are for the Liberties of the people ought to meet 2 or 3 days before" the Assembly session. Even with prior consultation the party's chances were uncertain; as Livingston saw it, "my Brother Gilbert will Stand firm to his Sentiments. So may Colonel Phill [ipse]" on the other side, "but as for the Rest they are for the Raiseing Sun." It was at this critical juncture, on September 18, that the popular party's spirits were revived by news that Lewis

[40] Morris to Alexander, London, Jan. 4, 1736, Rutherfurd Coll., II, 171, NYHS.

[41] Lewis Morris, Jr., to Alexander, Morrisania, Dec. 24, 1735, Robert Hunter Morris to Alexander, Westminster, Oct. 16, 1735, Rutherfurd Coll., II, 91, IV, 43, NYHS.

Morris had landed in Boston and was on his way to New York. Fear of a popular uprising against the Clarke government had become so great by the first week of October that additional gunpowder was obtained for the troops garrisoned at Fort George, while Clarke and his family joined them inside its protecting walls.[42]

On October 9, 1736, Lewis Morris returned to New York City, "being met by Mr. Van Dam & many of His friends with whom he marched thro' the Streets to a tavern where a supper was prepared." He was welcomed by his supporters as a staunch defender of colonial liberty, a role in which, by now, Morris had probably already cast himself. The eighteen long months in London had been filled with agonizing delays and frustrations, and had produced few tangible results. Morris had failed to gain more than a reprimand for Cosby; he had not been restored to his post as chief justice; and his efforts to achieve reforms in colonial administration had been adroitly deflected, smothered in red tape, or ignored. Nonetheless he had pursued his goals with resolution, and though his personal problems were never far from his thoughts, he seems to have pictured his mission in a more and more elevated way as time went on; he was now the spokesman for colonial reform. In the second year of his stay, despite the bleak prospects of the moment, he had stoutly declared that his "Sollicitation" would yet "turne out for the great benefit of my countrymen in future." [43] A short time earlier he had loftily rejected the Duke of Newcastle's offer of the newly created post of governor of New Jersey in exchange for dropping his charges against Cosby. Morris must have been sorely tempted by this bribe, for the New Jersey governorship was a choice plum which he had been trying to promote for himself since 1702. Perhaps he suspected that Newcastle would not keep his word once the Cosby furor should subside. But it also seems that he was somehow animated by a sense of higher duty, if only in that having gone so far in the name of his fellow-citizens he could hardly back down. Peter Collinson, who was on the scene in London at the time, cast the intrepid New Yorker in a heroic light. "Col.

---

[42] Philip Livingston to Alexander, Aug. 14, 1736, Rutherfurd Coll., II, 185, NYHS.

[43] Lt. Gov. Clarke to Lords of Trade, New York, Nov. 27, 1736, *N.Y. Col. Docs.*, VI, 85–88; Morris to Alexander, London, Jan. 4, 1736, Rutherfurd Coll., II, 171, NYHS.

Morris," he wrote to Alexander, "is a gentleman that Deserves the Most gratefull Returns His Country Can Bestow for his great & Examplary Integrity—(A Government is a high Bribe) But He as Nobly Refused it, No Temptation Should be able to Make Him Desert His County & their Cause." [44] It was only after he had completed his work as informal agent for New York Colony, and was once more free to seek his personal advantage, that Lewis Morris returned to the subject of the New Jersey governorship. He obtained it in 1738. [45]

Morris's return to New York in October, 1736, did little to soothe party heats. He promptly joined Alexander and the others in supporting Van Dam's claim to interim leadership, and political pressures rose to the danger point; it was to this time that Colden referred when he said New York was on the verge of civil war. However, with the arrival of royal orders on October 13 confirming Clarke as president of the Council, and then on October 30 naming him Lieutenant Governor, the crisis was eased and a semblance of peace restored.

But though the Morrisites lost on Van Dam's claim to the Council

[44] Collinson to Alexander, London, Feb. 27, 1736, Rutherfurd Coll., IV, 57, NYHS. The suggestion that Morris was suspicious of Newcastle's dependability is made in Donald L. Kemmerer, *Path to Freedom: The Struggle for Self-Government in Colonial New Jersey, 1703–1776* (Princeton, 1940), 151–53.

[45] Morris's acceptance of the New Jersey governorship, and his resolute defense of government prerogatives during the eight years of his administration, have caused some historians to view his liberal professions during the Cosby conflict as mere sophistry. It is indeed true that after an auspicious start, Morris sank rapidly in popular esteem and within a short time found himself locked in battle with an unmanageable Assembly. But perhaps we have been too eager to scold Gov. Morris for his "courtly conduct"; it may be only human to see executive power quite differently depending upon whether one is competing with or wielding it. Morris did introduce some innovations in New Jersey, such as the acceptance of a one-year support and withdrawal from the Council when sitting in its legislative capacity, which were fully consistent with his earlier views. He also made the first "good behavior" judicial appointment, though some of the shine is taken off of that action when one notes that it was his son, Robert Hunter Morris, who was the beneficiary of his favor. If one were to select Lewis Morris's two most fundamental character traits, one might choose, first, his sense of duty in office and, second, his self-righteous belief in his own point of view. Neither of these qualities prepared him for a graceful acceptance of political opposition, leading one to wonder if his problems in New Jersey, and elsewhere for that matter, might have stemmed more from his rigid personality than from inconsistency of principles. For information on Morris's administration in New Jersey, see Kemmerer, *Path to Freedom,* especially 151–54 ff.

presidency, their party and its program gained public vindication in the election called by Clarke in the spring of 1737. (It was the first Assembly election since 1728.) Adolph Philipse and Stephen DeLancey lost their seats for New York County, while James Alexander came in for New York and Lewis Morris and his son, Lewis, Jr., were both re-elected in Westchester. The Morrisites had a majority at last, and Lewis Morris, Jr., was chosen as the new Speaker. For a time the Morrisites continued to wear the popular party label, pressing their program in the Assembly with the introduction of bills for frequent elections, for the establishment of courts by statutory enactment, and by standing firm for Assembly control of the revenue. But when Clarke let it be known that he would welcome a reconciliation, the Morrisites, particularly the Lewis Morrises, moved into the court fold, displacing the Cosbyites, who in turn began to identify themselves with the popular opposition. All this occurred after the Morrisite election victories in May, 1737, but when a New York County by-election was held that September, an outlet for popular dissatisfaction with the Morrisites was provided. Adolph Philipse, now of the popular party, was one candidate, while Cornelius Van Horne stood for the Morrisite party. Of this election Cadwallader Colden wrote: "Mr. Philipse has carried it by 15 votes [.] Such a struggle I believe was never [seen] in America and is now over with a few bloody noses. . . . The sick the lame and the blind were all carried to vote [.] They were carried out of Prison and out of the poor house to vote [.] Such a strugle I never saw and such a hurraing that above one half of the men in town are so hoarse that they cannot speak this day [.] The pole lasted from half an hour after nine in the morning till past nine at night [.] There was upwards of 800 persons poled [.]" [46]

Though party competition continued through the next election, that of 1739, its feverishness tended to subside thereafter. George Clarke's own skill had much to do with this. Ideally suited for the task of calming political excitements, Clarke managed to balance off and eventually to undermine the competing factions. Moreover, he enjoyed strong support at Whitehall, and having resided in New York since 1703, he had

[46] Colden to Mrs. Colden, New York, Sept. 11, 1737, NYHS *Colls.*, LI (1918), 179; New-York *Weekly Journal*, June 27, Sept. 5, 1737, Mar. 19, 1739; Colden, "History of Cosby and Clarke," 352–55; Smith, *History*, II, 41–42, 55–58.

a shrewd awareness of colonial susceptibilities.[47] His administration, which lasted from 1736 to 1743, provided a much-needed respite from the intense level of political irritability that had gripped the colony during Cosby's hapless stewardship.

4. A Crisis of Identity in the Making

It has recently been observed that the constitutional results of the Morris-Cosby conflict were few, and it is true that no radical structural changes occurred. Yet long-term effects there must have been; it is inconceivable that the political strife of the 1730's should have left no traces. Certain alterations in administrative practice, indeed, can be traced directly to the Morrisite agitation. For example, the new requirement that New York governors withdraw from the Council when it was sitting in its legislative capacity was in response to Morrisite criticism of Cosby's behavior in this regard. Within one month of Cosby's arrival in the colony, the Assembly had devised "a new method of carrying our bills To the upper house" which challenged Cosby's right to sit with the Council. "We carry them to the council," explained Lewis Morris, Jr., "Deliver them at The lower End of the Table and Desire their concurrence without Taking any notice of The governor att all. . . ." The separation of legislative and executive powers was one of the points urged most strongly by Morris in London, and Cosby was instructed by the Board of Trade in 1736 to absent himself when the Council was considering legislation. Cosby had died before the order arrived, but from the time of the Clarke administration on, the integrity of the Council as an upper house of the legislature was respected.[48] Another example of subtle change concerned the court system, for it is a fact that after Morris's

---

[47] For a detailed description of the Clarke administration, see Katz, *Newcastle's New York,* Chap. 6.

[48] Lewis Morris, Jr., to Colden, New York, Sept. 24, 1732, NYHS *Colls.,* LI (1918), 81; James Alexander to Colden, New York, Aug. 26, 1736, draft, Rutherfurd Coll., II, 185, NYHS; Smith, *History,* II, 39; Sec. Popple to Cosby, Whitehall, Jan. 23, 1736, *N.Y. Col. Docs.,* VI, 39–40 ff. Katz asserts that the Morris-Cosby conflict "did not significantly affect the constitutional arrangements of the colony. . . ." *Newcastle's New York,* 69; see also Katz, ed., *Zenger,* 29.

refusal to establish a court of exchequer the New York Supreme Court "ceased to sit in equity." [49]

An even more direct legacy of the Morrisite agitation was the subsequent approval of a septennial election bill. A triennial bill had been proposed by New Yorkers from time to time, but not until it became an issue in the party contentions of the 1730's was it pressed with any consistency. As has been seen, another of Morris's key instructions concerned the colonists' desire for more regular elections. After the popular party's Assembly victories in 1737, the new Speaker, Lewis Morris, Jr., reintroduced the triennial bill, which was approved by the Council and governor in December, 1737, but disallowed in London on November 30, 1738. Finally, in 1743, a septennial bill was enacted, and it gained approval in England. That this success was owing in no small measure to the demands raised by the Morris junto can hardly be doubted. Another important deviation from earlier practice occurred in 1739 when George Clarke accepted a one-year grant of revenue from the Assembly, being the first New York governor to do so. Though Clarke's reasons for giving in to the Assembly were several, his explanation to the Board of Trade stressed the "pernicious precedent" set by Lewis Morris as governor of New Jersey in accepting a one-year grant from his Assembly.[50]

But despite these not insubstantial changes, it is more in the area of informal arrangements and procedures that the greatest impact of the Morrisites was registered. Unlike earlier party struggles, such as those during Leisler's Rebellion or at the time of Governor Burnet's administration which focused mainly on intra-colony rivalries, the opposition to Cosby ended up challenging some of the most fundamental assumptions of the imperial system—challenges which prefigured in basic ways the final rupture of 1776. Organizing and participating in popular resistance to the arbitrary rule of an insensitive governor was an experience that was not lost on the people of New York. They had undergone something both intense and unusual, and political techniques became sharper and markedly more sophisticated in the province after 1733.

---

[49] Katz, *Newcastle's New York*, 68.

[50] *The Colonial Laws of New York from the Year 1664 to the Revolution* (Albany, 1894), II, 951–52, III, 295–96; Smith, *History*, II, 42–45; Lt. Gov. Clarke to Lords of Trade, New York, June 13, 1740, *N.Y. Col. Docs.*, VI, 158–59, 160.

The Morrisites had shown how to simplify and popularize issues, and how to suit themselves, as Colden had once advised, to the public humor. They had learned to appeal to the public for vindication of their views and to concert the energies of many people in widely separated places. They had contributed directly to the growth of the press and had effectively used printed propaganda as an opposition weapon. They had aroused general interest in legislative issues to the point that the doors of the Assembly, on at least one occasion, were thrown open to the public. And they had directed attention to the representative nature of elective government by making Assemblymen more strictly accountable to their constituents, for in response to the Morrisites' efforts, the Assembly agreed in June, 1737, to publish the names of those voting "aye" and "nay" in Assembly divisions.[51]

It is, to be sure, important not to overemphasize popular involvement in politics; it was still a gentlemen's game.[52] Governor Cosby's remark that the popular party's ranks were made up of "the meanest labourers, tradesmen and Artificers" was more a rhetorical flourish than an accurate analysis of the party's composition. The leadership, the propaganda, and most of the opposition energy came from men like Morris, Alexander, and Smith; the ordinary citizens of New York were still quite willing in the 1730's to defer to their betters for political direction. Yet something has happened when demands for constitutional clarification and expansion of colonial rights are made in the name of *all* the people. No elite, as Carl Becker has noted, could long sustain an opposition "by pleading the natural rights of a class or the general welfare of the few." Some of the Morrisite propaganda developed a distinctly leveling tone. One piece of their literature, which bears the title "The Almighty made us equal all . . . ," excoriates "people in Exalted Stations" who look with contempt on "those they call the Vulgar, the Mob, the herd of Mechanicks." The essay goes on to declare

[51] *Assembly Journal* (Gaine), I, June 16, 1737; New-York *Weekly Journal,* March 19, 1739.

[52] Even in New York City public apathy toward politics was common. In the winter of 1734, when the Morrisites were still trying to whip up an opposition to Cosby, Henry Beekman reported that "our paper war Still Goes on by the parties but the people here Look only on them (being a Dull time of year) as party affairs & amnosomty [animosity]." Beekman to Gilbert Livingston, New York, Feb. 29, 1734, Beekman MSS, Box I, NYHS.

that "greatness of Birth, Riches and Honours . . . can add no reall praise to a Man. . . ." [53] Such prose cannot be bandied about, as it was in New York with growing frequency after 1733, and leave political perceptions exactly as they were.

By far the most significant legacy of the Morris-Cosby struggle was the attention it directed toward the many imbalances within the British imperial system. As the colonies grew in wealth and political maturity, the inferior status imposed on Englishmen abroad became a source of increasing irritation. True, demands for constitutional reform did not mount in a steady chorus; in New York, much of the excitement subsided after 1737 with the removal by death of Cosby and the advent of a more flexible governor. But so long as the fundamental constitutional problems remained, colonial anxieties could now be reactivated and the rhetoric of opposition resumed, on very little notice.[54]

For a test, one need only look at New York in January, 1745, a time of relative factional calm. Word had just reached the colony that Parliament was about to attach two highly offensive clauses to a paper money bill, the effect of which would have been to make all instructions from the Crown and Privy Council obligatory on colonial councils and assemblies. According to Henry Beekman, the somewhat conservative Assemblyman from Dutchess County, these amendments would strike "Emedietly at the Liberty . . . and Establish arbetrary power" in the colonies, and therefore "hath alarmed the American world. . . ." When news of Parliament's intentions reached New York City, the Assembly was not in session and emergency procedures had to be put into effect. A meeting was called among those assemblymen who resided in town and "the principal inhabitants without Distinction of parties." James

---

[53] Cosby to Lords of Trade, New York, Dec. 6, 1734, *N.Y. Col. Docs.*, VI, 22–24; "The Almighty made us equal all . . . ," n.d., Rutherfurd Coll., II, 169, NYHS; Becker, *History of Political Parties,* 17. For typical party appeals to the workingman and the "industrious poor," see New-York *Weekly Journal,* April 8, 1734 (reproduced in Katz, ed., *Zenger,* 134–38) and Sept. 12, 1734.

[54] Bernard Bailyn compares this conditioned response to "an intellectual switchboard wired so that certain combinations of events would activate a distinct set of [danger] signals. . . ." *The Ideological Origins of the American Revolution* (Cambridge, Mass., 1967), 22. One of the interesting things about the Morris-Cosby conflict is that it shows how early the essential elements of this response were in place.

Alexander reported that "never was there so nearly an union in any place as there was in this against these clauses. . . ." The New Yorkers decided that in addition to writing to their friends and business associates in London, they should employ "an agent Sollicitor & Council" to lobby against passage of the amendments. Stephen DeLancey & Co. immediately donated £150, which was dispatched to the Messrs. Baker in London for that purpose. That another constitutional crisis was brewing escaped no one in New York. James Alexander averred that "tho' the King has now no faster friends nor better Subjects," the colonists would not be "put under the absolute power of any prince, & would of Course Leave no Stone unturned to free themselves from the thought of Such Slavery." [55]

These phrases now came quite readily to Alexander's tongue. He had employed them in the 1730's against Cosby—just as his son, and the sons of Lewis Morris, Jr., Philip Livingston, and others would rely on them again in the 1770's. The 1745 episode, as it happened, did not set off a full-scale reaction, for the offensive amendments were soon withdrawn. As before, an uneasy calm was restored. But now the words were there, as were the gestures; they had already been said, and were available to be used again. How truly stable things might remain from here on was problematical, now that the provincials could no longer be quite certain who they were or where they belonged. They were suspended between two worlds, and which rules applied was no longer quite so clear—especially since, without quite realizing it, they were now making so many of their own. This confusion of roles, this crisis of identity, may account in part for the undercurrent of malaise that has been observed in provincial society. It may well be that the volatility of New York colonial politics was indeed chronic and inherent.

Much of this ambiguity was dimly sensed, though only rarely articulated, by New Yorkers in the 1730's. A few discerning men perceived, even that early, that unless fundamental questions concerning the applicability of the English Constitution to the New World setting were examined and resolved, the stresses in the imperial system might become

---

[55] Beekman to Henry Livingston, New York, Jan. 7, 1745, Henry Beekman MSS, NYHS; James Alexander to Colden, [Jan., 1745], NYHS *Colls.*, LII (1919), 101; Alexander to ?, Jan. 4, 1745, draft, Rutherfurd Coll., III, 15, NYHS; *Assembly Journal* (Gaine), II, Mar. 13, 15, 1745.

intolerable. As Lewis Morris expressed it from the depths of his frustration in London: "I believe the Seeds are sown which will one day rise of maturity either in the destruction of the constitution or fixing of it on so firme a foundation as not to be Shaken." [56]

[56] Morris to Alexander, London, Feb. 25, 1736, Rutherfurd Coll., III, 15, NYHS.

V

JAMES DELANCEY, ANGLO-AMERICAN: THE POLITICS OF NEW YORK AT MID-CENTURY

EFFORTS TO DISCERN the patterns and purposes of New York political affairs in the mid-eighteenth century have always been impeded by the need to account for a number of abrupt shifts of allegiance by certain major political figures of the time. The most notable case is that of Chief Justice James DeLancey, whose erratic path was marked by sudden transpositions from avowed "courtier" in the 1730's to opposition leader *par excellence* in the 1740's, and thence back to royal spokesman in the 1750's, when he became lieutenant-governor and then acting governor. Another look at this particular case—that of the most influential provincial politician of his time—may reveal that the path was not so "erratic" after all.

A descendant of James DeLancey has charged that his ancestor's name "has passed into history under colors which take their hues rather from the passions of the day than from the light of truth." [1] The com-

---

[1] Edward F. DeLancey, "Memoir of the Hon. James DeLancey," *N.Y. Doc. Hist.*, IV, 638.

plaint has a certain validity. Though DeLancey seems to have been highly regarded by most of his fellow New Yorkers, his enemies proved both implacable and articulate, and they left behind them a trail of damaging appraisals.

Governor George Clinton and his chief adviser Cadwallader Colden, who after 1746 believed DeLancey had tricked and betrayed them, were perhaps his most relentless critics. In their view DeLancey was a man of "indefatigable art and Cunning" who displayed "Pride & Insolence," "violent passions," an "Arbitrary Disposition," and was "capable of every thing that Caesar Borgia was." William Livingston, the chief justice's main antagonist after 1753, employed all his literary talents to impugn DeLancey's motives and character. DeLancey's "thirst after popularity," he claimed, "which in him is a mere engine of state, hath almost banished all public spirit." "He will only stand by a governor while at his devotion . . . but, in case of a rupture, instantly sacrifice prerogative on the altar of popularity. His own interest is his idol. . . . By hints, by threats and blandishments, by emissaries, by dark insinuations and private cabals, he is able to render any measure hateful or popular; to put down, or raise up, whom, when, and what he pleases." But Livingston did have to admit that the chief justice was a "political genius." "His uncommon vivacity, with the semblance of affability and ease; his adroitness at a jest, with a shew of condescension to his inferiors, wonderfully facilitated his progress." But "he knows no such thing as Friendship abstracted from political Views, and the purposes of Trimming and popularity." As if reciting a kind of creed, Livingston declared in 1754: "I believe he cares not a Groat for . . . any Man living. That always was my Opinion about him; now is so, and ever shall be, world without End Amen." [2]

Such round pronouncements have strongly influenced subsequent historical evaluations. One student of New York history, for example, confidently asserts: "With the intrigues of a schemer and the arts of a

[2] Clinton to Robert H. Morris, Ft. George, Aug. 29, Sept. 8, 1750, Robert Hunter Morris Papers, NJHS; Clinton to Newcastle, May 30, 1749, NYHS *Colls.*, LII (1919), 393; Colden to Gov. Wm. Shirley, New York, July 25, 1749, NYHS *Colls.*, LIII (1920), 124; [William Livingston], "A Review of the Military Operations in North-America . . . ," Massachusetts Historical Society, *Collections,* 1st Ser., VII–VIII (1801–1856), 84, 85, 79; William Livingston to Robert Livingston, Jr., New York, Feb. 4, 1754, Livingston-Redmond MSS, Reel 5.

demagogue," DeLancey seemed "to step direct out of the supple politics and exaggerated postures of [the] Italian Renaissance. . . ." Cadwallader Colden's biographer paints DeLancey as an "unscrupulous" manipulator whose political actions were shaped almost solely by personal ambitions.[3] Until very recently no effort has been made to reexamine this one-dimensional view of DeLancey, even though in the opinion of one scholar the history of mid-eighteenth-century New York without a full-scale study of this central figure is like "a *Hamlet* without the Prince." [4]

Not that the many slurs upon the man's fame are entirely without foundation. James DeLancey was another of those early New Yorkers who enjoyed power, and he probably had more of it at his disposal than any other politician in the colony's history. There is evidence of a robust ego and a fondness for popular acclaim. But the obvious passion which infused his eighteenth-century critics invites a certain skepticism; nor, indeed, was DeLancey without his contemporary defenders. A eulogy delivered at the time of his death told of the "uncommon dignity and lustre" he brought to high office. "His Genius, provident, active, fertile in Expedients, and capable of averting or improving the most unexpected Occurrences, joined to a perfect Knowledge and Esteem of our happy Constitution, and a zealous Attachment to his Majesty's illustrious House, rendered him a most able and faithful Counsellor of the Crown; and, to the Rights and Liberties of the People, a cordial and unshaken Friend." His brother-in-law, John Watts, described him as "a man of uncommon abilities . . . and an elegant, pleasant companion— what rarely unites in one person; it seemed doubtful which excelled, his quick penetration or his sound judgment: the first seemed an instant guide to the last. . . . No man in either office, (Chief Justice or Lieut.

---

[3] Arthur Pound, *Johnson of the Mohawks* (New York, 1930), 30; Alice M. Keys, *Cadwallader Colden* (New York, 1906), 208. Keys asserts that after a quarrel with Governor Clinton, "Delancey flung himself out of the room vowing that Clinton's life should be made miserable. . . ." *Ibid.,* 142.

[4] Milton M. Klein, "Politics and Personalities in Colonial New York," *New York History,* XLVII (Jan., 1966), 11. Stanley N. Katz's recent book on Anglo-American aspects of New York politics brings some balance into the picture, and provides valuable information about James DeLancey's English connections and his struggle with Governor Clinton. *Newcastle's New York: Anglo-American Politics, 1732–1753* (Cambridge, 1968), especially Chaps. 7 and 8.

Governor,) had more the love and confidence of the people, nor any man, before or since, half the influence." [5]

There is much in DeLancey's career to suggest that no other eighteenth-century New Yorker understood so well as he the delicate equilibrium required to sustain imperial power relationships, or was so well equipped to harmonize conflicting interests. James DeLancey managed to blend two cultures—provincial and metropolitan—and to combine a masterful appreciation of the exigencies of colonial politics with an admiration for the imperial concept and a love of things English. That this was the very elixir needed to ease New York's political fevers is shown by the relative calm which prevailed in public affairs during the years DeLancey was in charge of the government. He was one of a rare breed of eighteenth-century Englishmen—a true Anglo-American —whose bonds to the mother country and to the colony of his birth exerted such nearly equal pull that his personal ambitions were best served when both worlds were in balance. DeLancey's career was shaped by his efforts to maintain that alignment.

1. Building an Anglo-American "Interest"

James DeLancey was the eldest son of Stephen DeLancey, a French-Huguenot refugee who emigrated to New York in 1686, and Anne Van Cortlandt, daughter of the wealthy New York City merchant Stephen Van Cortlandt. Stephen DeLancey had built one of the greatest fortunes in the colony in the early days of New York's commercial growth. Born on November 27, 1703, James grew up in patrician comfort, and as a young man of rank was groomed for leadership in accordance with the expectations of that day. His father sent him to England at the age of eighteen, where he entered Cambridge in October, 1721. After several years at Corpus Christi, he read law for a brief term at Lincoln's Inn, returning to New York at the end of 1725 prepared to take his position in provincial society. After being admitted to the bar of New York, he began the practice of law on the solid foundation of a £3,000 gift from his father. In 1728 he married Anne Heathcote, daughter of

[5] New York *Mercury,* Aug. 4, 1760; Edward DeLancey, "Memoir," 637.

the late Caleb Heathcote, a landed proprietor of Westchester County. The next year, at the age of twenty-six, DeLancey was appointed a member of the governor's Council, and in 1731 he was commissioned second judge of the New York Supreme Court.[6]

In August, 1733, when Governor William Cosby dismissed Lewis Morris as chief justice, DeLancey was elevated to Morris's vacated place. Thus at the age of thirty James DeLancey had achieved one of the highest offices at the disposal of the governor, an office he would hold for the next twenty-seven years, and which he would convert into a base of power sufficiently strong to challenge the authority of a subsequent governor. DeLancey was able to do this, in part, because the post of chief justice conferred influence not only in the highest circles of government but at the county and local levels as well. First established by the Judicature Act of 1691, the New York Supreme Court gradually assumed its full powers by the early years of the eighteenth century. Consisting of a chief justice and two or (after 1758) three puisne judges, it exercised jurisdiction over all civil and criminal cases as well as "appellate and transfer jurisdiction over judgments (in civil cases over £20), indictments or informations removed from the inferior courts by warrant, certiorari or writ of error." After 1704 the court met four times a year at New York City, in January, April, July, and October. In 1692 provisions had been made for an annual circuit through the counties, with one Supreme Court justice and two or more local justices of the peace comprising the bench for the county terms. Because the Supreme Court "enjoyed almost unlimited power to hear, try and determine Crown pleas no matter how serious or how trivial," and because it came to have a powerful voice in cases pertaining to commerce and land titles —matters close to the hearts of all New Yorkers—its weight could be brought to bear on all ranks in all parts of the colony.[7] Set into this

[6] Edward DeLancey, "Memoir," 627–39; William Smith, *The History of the Late Province of New-York, From its Discovery, to the Appointment of Governor Colden, in 1762* (New York, 1830), I, 288 n. Edgar A. Werner, *Civil List and Constitutional History of the Colony and State of New York* (Albany, 1888), 318.

[7] Julius Goebel, Jr., and T. Raymond Naughton, *Law Enforcement in Colonial New York: A Study in Criminal Procedure, 1664–1776* (New York, 1944), 27–30, 73–74, 141–47; Stanley N. Katz, "An Easie Access: Anglo-American Politics in New York, 1732–1753," unpubl. Ph.D. diss. (Harvard University, 1961), 216; Werner, *Civil List,* 297. For the Supreme Court's involvement with commer-

framework a chief justice with the political acumen of James DeLancey, and it is not difficult to understand why he was regarded by some as having the power of a Pope.

Eighteenth-century New Yorkers generally agreed that the office of chief justice, particularly during DeLancey's tenure, was possibly the most influential post in the colony. William Smith, Jr., refers to DeLancey's "amazing power" as chief justice; he had, according to Cadwallader Colden, more "influence on the public affairs in this Country than can well be imagined." "No man that has any Property," Colden explained, "can think himself independent of the Courts of Justice however carefull his behaviour in life may be. There are in this Country numbers of Lawyers who's bread & fortune depend on the Countenance of a Chief Justice & who may serve as his emissaries & spies in every part of the Country [.] When then a Chief Justice puts himself at the head of a party . . . he becomes as formidable . . . as the Popes formerly were in the days of Ignorance at the head of the Monks & friers." William Livingston asserted that "as chief justice great is his [DeLancey's] interest in the counties: with that interest he commands elections; with his sway in elections he rules the assembly; and with his sovereignty over the house controls a governor." [8]

DeLancey's influence was further augmented by the active political involvement of various members of his immediate family. His father, Stephen, was an assemblyman from New York County for several periods between 1702 and 1737. His younger brother, Oliver, though busy operating the family's mercantile business in New York City, was one of his political managers and found time to solicit "the Election of particular persons" in support of his brother's interest at Esopus (Kingston) and other upriver towns. Oliver DeLancey served as New York City alderman from the Out Ward from 1754 to 1757, as Assembly representative from New York County from 1756 to 1761, and as a member of the Council from 1760 until the Revolutionary War. Peter DeLancey, another brother, was the first member of the family to reside out-

---

cial matters, see Goebel and Naughton, *Law Enforcement in Colonial New York,* 236–38; for land cases see *ibid.,* 87–89, 203–22.

[8] Smith, *History,* II, 171–72; Colden to Gov. Wm. Shirley, New York, July 25, 1749, copy, NYHS *Colls.,* LIII (1920), 124–25; *ibid.,* 163; [William Livingston], "A Review of Military Operations," 85.

side of New York County. Sometimes called "Peter of the Mills" because of his large farm and mills at West Farms, Westchester County, by mid-century he had built an influence in the county equal to that of either the Morris or Philipse families. From 1750 to 1768, he was continuously elected Assembly representative from the Borough of Westchester.[9]

Helpful as this network of influence within the colony was, James DeLancey would have been only another provincial politician, much like Lewis Morris and Adolph Philipse before him, had he not enjoyed the additional advantage of a luminous galaxy of patrons at the all-important imperial level. It is no doubt true that "New Yorkers were incredibly sensitive to the winds of political favor in England." [10] During the most critical stages of DeLancey's career those winds were unfailingly favorable.

Marital connections provided two of DeLancey's most important channels of influence. His own marriage to Anne Heathcote had tied him to a large and distinguished family in England. His wife's first cousin, Sir John Heathcote, Bt., was a member of Parliament "and one of Walpole's political managers for the county of Rutland." Sir John's assistance had been particularly helpful during the 1730's, when Lewis Morris was soliciting his own reinstatement, and DeLancey's removal, as chief justice. An even more crucial tie came through DeLancey's sister Susannah, whose marriage to Commodore Peter Warren in 1731 connected the DeLanceys to a man whose career was soon to experience a meteoric ascent. Warren had entered the British navy at the age of twelve, and by his middle twenties was commander of a ship patrolling the waters off North America and the West Indies. With the encouragement of the DeLanceys he had developed aspirations to the governorship of New Jersey, or possibly even that of New York. In 1745 his fortunes and his political ambitions soared when, as fleet com-

[9] Colden to Clinton, Coldengham, Feb. 19, 1749, copy, John Ayscough to Colden, Ft. George, Sept. 11, 1749, NYHS *Colls.*, LIII (1920), 102, 141; *Assembly Journal* (Gaine), II, Nov. 9, 1756; *DAB*, V, 214–15 (Charles Worthen Spencer); Werner, *Civil List*, 355–60. Though Peter DeLancey's wife was Alice Elizabeth Colden, daughter of Cadwallader Colden, this relationship apparently did not inhibit Peter's party activities after 1746, when he supported James DeLancey's opposition to the policies of Clinton and Colden.

[10] Katz, *Newcastle's New York*, 57.

mander at the siege of Louisbourg in the War of the Austrian Succession, he captured not only the fort and many valuable prizes but the affections of the British people as well. His naval prowess having been again confirmed at the battle off Cape Finisterre in 1747, he was showered with honors by a grateful ministry. He was made a knight of the Bath in May, 1747, and in July was promoted from rear admiral to vice-admiral and chosen a member of Parliament from Westminster. Thus Warren had become a national hero, "one of the richest men in England," and a power in politics at the very moment when James DeLancey, having just broken with Clinton, had need of a friend at court to counteract Clinton's efforts to remove him from office and influence. This fortuitous convergence of Warren's and DeLancey's careers proved of inestimable benefit to the New Yorker. Warren provided him with one of his strongest links to Whitehall, and was instrumental in obtaining the lieutenant governorship for him in 1747.[11]

Another of DeLancey's English connections had been forged years earlier by his father and other New York merchants and importers. Historians have noted that as far back as the 1690's the export trade to New York was in the hands of a small group of English merchants. This pattern continued into the eighteenth century, and whenever New York commercial interests were threatened, the call would go out to these English correspondents, who would then act as informal lobbyists in the mutually beneficial effort to maintain the thriving condition of New York trade. We have already seen this lobby at work in the contest over Governor Burnet's Canada trade prohibitions of 1720, when twenty London merchants, headed by Samuel Baker, successfully petitioned for repeal of the Burnet policy. New Yorkers continued to call upon the good offices of Baker and Company from time to time, even when grievances concerned political questions. In 1745, for example, Stephen DeLancey and Company sent £150 to the Messrs. Baker to finance opposition to Parliament's effort to tighten control over colonial assemblies and councils. William and Samuel Baker had the reputation in London of being well informed on American affairs, and their opinions were received with courteous attention from the government. As

[11] Warren Johnson to William Johnson, New York, Sept. 13, 1747, *Johnson Papers,* I, 117; Katz, *Newcastle's New York,* 111–13, 116, 210–12, 252; *DAB,* XIX, 485–87 (L. Harding Rogers, Jr.).

London correspondents of the DeLancey family, the Bakers were able to render valuable services to James DeLancey in the 1740's, especially in the matter of his opposition to Governor Clinton's policies during King George's War.[12]

DeLancey had two other advocates in London. Robert Charles, onetime private secretary to Sir Peter Warren, was appointed agent for the New York Assembly in 1748. Charles was instructed by the Speaker to follow Warren's advice on New York affairs, and this meant that the DeLancey-led government opposition had a full-time spokesman on duty in London. Furthermore, Charles "kept the DeLancey party in America informed of proceedings in England." Finally, no one could have foreseen that DeLancey's Cambridge tutor, Thomas Herring, would rise from that relatively obscure beginning to become Archbishop of Canterbury in 1747.[13] The timing was such that James DeLancey might truly count his blessings.

DeLancey's English interest was cultivated not only for its influence on opinion in London, but also for its effect within the province of New York, "evidence of political influence in England" being "the prerequisite for political mastery in America." So successful were DeLancey's London solicitations in the late 1740's that both Clinton and Colden feared that the people of New York credited him with having greater power than the governor himself. "Men's minds in this province," Colden informed the governor in 1749, "are prepossest of the Chief Justice's Interest at home." Apparently DeLancey's supporters had noised it about "that the Chief Justice has a better Interest at court than the Govr," and while that opinion prevailed, Colden warned, "people will adore the . . . rising sun." [14]

Such were the main supports of James DeLancey's Anglo-Ameri-

---

[12] Curtis P. Nettels, "The Money Supply of the American Colonies Before 1720," Univ. of Wisconsin Series in Social Sciences and History, XX (Madison, 1934), Reprints in Economic Classics (New York, 1964), 74. For the earlier activities of Baker & Co., see pp. 94n and 138 above.

[13] Katz, *Newcastle's New York*, 207–10.

[14] Colden to Clinton, Nov. 9, 1749, copy, Colden to John Catherwood, Nov. 21, 1749, copy, NYHS *Colls.*, LIII (1920), 150, 159; Katz, *Newcastle's New York*, 56.

can power base: wealth and family status; a strong influence over the provincial judiciary, the Council, and the Assembly; and a solid interest in London. How "accidental" these various advantages were must be judged against the skill—one might say the political genius—with which James DeLancey was able to improve every opportunity that came his way.

2. James DeLancey versus Governor George Clinton

In the early years of his political career DeLancey was a "courtier"— that is, he supported the governor and worked to uphold the prerogatives of his office. Governor William Cosby had appointed him chief justice in 1733, and in the days of the Morris-Cosby struggle DeLancey had stood by his patron. During the more relaxed years of Lieutenant Governor George Clarke's administration (1736–1743), DeLancey had strengthened his position in the Council and had gradually gained a following in the Assembly. When George Clinton became governor in September, 1743, DeLancey was able to put his considerable influence at the service of the new executive, thereby assuring him a smooth beginning or, as they said in the colonies, an "easie" administration.

It was customary for new governors "to confide into some one person for private advice," and from all indications Clinton was well satisfied with DeLancey's counsel. In September, 1744, Clinton awarded him a "good behavior" commission as chief justice, replacing the "at pleasure" appointment required by the governor's instructions, and in the early years of his administration Clinton appointed DeLancey's friends to four of the five available Council seats. In November, 1743, the Assembly voted Clinton a £1,560 salary grant, though only after he acceded to DeLancey's recommendations that he accept the salary on an annual basis and that he permit the Assembly greater control over appropriations of salaries for other government officers. Thus within a short time of Clinton's arrival DeLancey had expanded his already great influence over the judiciary, Council, and Assembly to include the governor's office. Though Colden overstated the case, there was some truth in his assertion that Clinton "had inadvertently put the whole executive powers" into the hands of "the Chief Justice & his Faction in the Assembly. . . ." [15]

During the autumn and winter of 1746–1747 a falling-out occurred between Clinton and DeLancey, and from that time until Clinton's departure from New York in 1753, the chief justice was to lead the most effective opposition ever formed against a New York governor —an opposition that would, in Clinton's own words, make him a "ridicule" to the people "instead of an Awe over them." William Livingston's explanation for the Clinton-DeLancey rupture was for many years the standard account. Livingston claimed that DeLancey, having obtained "a new commission for his office of chief justice *during good behaviour;* and flattering himself with the hopes of another, appointing him lieutenant-governor, through the interest of his friends in England, he cared not how soon his excellency abdicated the province, nor how tempestuous he rendered his administration." Thus "he put off all that humble devotion, by which he had so fatally deceived his too credulous master, and openly set himself at defiance against him." But this explanation is not fully satisfactory, for if a thirst for power and for the lieutenant-governorship had been DeLancey's only motive, it might be supposed that his best course would have been to stay at the governor's side, thereby encouraging Clinton to add his "superb" English interest (he was closely related to the Pelhams) to DeLancey's own in the effort to obtain the appointment. Though DeLancey's personal ambitions must be conceded, there is every reason to believe that he differed with Clinton over substantive policy matters as well, particularly the question of what New York's role should be in King George's War.[16]

The concern most New Yorkers felt at the approach of another Anglo-French war was acute, and it is only necessary to recall their earlier experiences with the French in Canada to appreciate this. They

[15] Clinton to Board of Trade, June 22, 1747, *N.Y. Col. Docs.,* VI, 352 (though this letter is signed by Clinton, it was drafted by Cadwallader Colden: see Colden Papers, Box 12, NYHS); Colden to Dr. John Mitchell, July 6, 1749, draft, NYHS *Colls.,* LXVIII (1935), 21.

[16] Clinton to Robert H. Morris, Greenwich, July 20, 1752, Robert Hunter Morris Papers, NJHS; [William Livingston], "A Review of Military Operations," 79; Katz, *Newcastle's New York,* 201. Katz sees a "genuine division" between the two men over war policy (171).

knew perhaps better than any other colonists what dangerous enemies the French and their Indian allies could be, having lived in closest proximity to them. This was felt with particular immediacy in Albany County, where frequent border clashes had occurred from the outbreak of King William's War in 1690 to the close of Queen Anne's War in 1713. Past experience had taught them that the other colonies could not be relied on in time of war, and this had always led to a disproportionate drain on New York's manpower and financial resources whenever aggressive actions had to be undertaken. Moreover, whenever the alarm was raised along the northern border, New Yorkers would suffer an interdiction of the profitable Canada trade.[17] It was just such disagreeable circumstances that had led New York into a policy of neutrality with its French neighbors, and it was this informal accommodation that had produced three decades of relative peace and prosperity along the northern frontier. Thus with their physical security, their tax rate, and their economic well-being all at stake, it is no wonder that New Yorkers could generate so little enthusiasm when King George's War broke out in 1744, or that they reacted so coolly to the government's plans for a land expedition up the Hudson Valley–Lake Champlain route to Quebec in 1746.

DeLancey was fully attuned to these anxieties. When in June, 1746, Governor Clinton proposed a meeting at Albany with the Six Nations to obtain their support for the overland assault later that summer, DeLancey, along with most other members of the Council, found an excuse not to go. Only three councilmen attended Clinton at the Albany meeting—Philip Livingston, John Rutherfurd, and Cadwallader Colden. Livingston resided in Albany County, was secretary for Indian affairs, and by 1746 had come to believe that "the French aim at nothing less than to have the whole Continent." Rutherfurd, a captain in the British army, was already at Albany organizing troops for the proposed

[17] New York's experiences with the French on the northwestern frontier are discussed on pp. 40–48. During King George's War, owing to British superiority on the high seas, the French Canadians came to depend on Albany to supply many of their own needs as well as goods for the Indian trade. "Remarks on the Subject Matter of the papers sent me by his Excellency April 5th 1748," by Cadwallader Colden, NYHS *Colls.*, LIII (1920), 37; Colden to Dr. John Mitchell, July 6, 1749, draft, NYHS *Colls.*, LXVIII (1935), 34.

expedition. Colden had not been active in politics for some time, and
Clinton had to persuade him to come out of semi-retirement at his country estate to attend the Albany conclave.[18]

One cannot but wonder whether Clinton later may have privately
regretted his success in calling Colden back into public life. During the
three months Clinton remained at Albany, Colden replaced DeLancey
as his chief adviser, their cordial relations being based on similar imperialist attitudes. And yet this created another dilemma for the governor,
for in embracing Colden so heartily Clinton at the same time cut himself off from the majority of New Yorkers who opposed a firm policy
against the French. All of which led to a real disruption of the political
life of the colony. To perceive how the mere substituting of one "prime
minister" for another could have such an extraordinary effect, one must
have some acquaintance with Cadwallader Colden.

Born in 1688 in Dunse, Scotland, Colden was the son of a Presbyterian minister. He was educated at the University of Edinburgh, gradu-
ating in 1705 at the age of seventeen, following which he studied for a
medical degree in London. Not wishing to put his father to the further
expense required to "make that figure which it is necessary for a young
Physician to do in Gr. Brittain on his first appearing in the World,"
Colden decided "to try my fortune in America." Settling first in Philadelphia in 1710, he moved on to New York in 1718, his talents apparently having attracted the attention of some persons of note, with the
promise of an appointment as surveyor general. He assumed that post
in 1720, and the next year was made a member of the governor's Council. Colden's work as surveyor general gave him a first-hand acquaintance with New York's northwest frontier, the fur trade, and the Iroquois tribes, all of which were discussed in his book, *The History of the
Five Indian Nations,* published in two parts, in 1727 and 1747. He
purchased an estate, Coldengham, in Ulster County, to which he moved
his growing family in 1728, and there he indulged his love for science,
concentrating particularly on botany and astronomy. Colden was a man
of exceptional intelligence: his botanical discoveries were highly re-

[18] "Representation to Clinton of seven members of the Council in reference to
Colden's pamphlet on the Treaty with the Six Nations," New York, Dec. 16,
1746, Colden to Mrs. Colden, New York, July 3, 1746, NYHS *Colls.,* LII (1919),
222, 294–305; Philip Livingston to Jacob Wendell, New York, Jan. 14, 1746,
Livingston Papers, Philip Livingston Box, MCNY.

garded by the Swedish scientists Carolus Linnaeus and Peter Kalm, with whom he corresponded regularly; and he exchanged astronomical and other scientific observations with a number of prominent Europeans as well as many colonials, including Benjamin Franklin. Anne Grant once described him as "diminutive, and somewhat more than high-shouldered," adding that "the contrast betwixt the wealth of his mind, and the poverty of his outward appearance, might remind one of Aesop. . . ." That Colden should have had time and energy left for politics may surprise the modern reader, and even Colden knew times when he longed to restrict his activities solely to scientific and scholarly researches. But as Benjamin Franklin once advised him, statesmanship should always take precedence over science. "Had Newton been Pilot but of a single common Ship," wrote Franklin, "the finest of his Discoveries would scarce have excus'd, or atton'd for his abandoning the Helm one Hour in Time of Danger; how much less if she carried the Fate of the Commonwealth." [19] And Colden heeded Franklin's advice, returning time and again from his country retreat to resume his public duties.

Always a man of serious mien and intensity of purpose, Colden seems to typify the dour Scot. His "indefatigable diligence" and "rigid" sense of justice made him a trusted servant of the Crown and a zealous administrator, though these same qualities also made it difficult for him to see the other side of almost anything. By the time he became allied with Clinton in 1746, Colden had managed to offend some of the most powerful segments of New York society. His 1721 recommendation for a resurvey of the province, the goal of which was the opening up of many privately held but uncultivated lands, had won him no friends among the landholding interests; his unconditional support for Governor Burnet's restriction of the Canada trade had alienated many in the merchant community; and his suggestion in 1726 that colonial governors be paid out of the quit-rents, thereby rendering them independent of the Assembly, was little calculated to increase his popularity among the colony's politicians. Throughout his public life Colden showed a remarkable facility for stirring up dissension. As General Gage said of

[19] Colden to Peter Kalm, Jan. 1751, copy, Franklin to Colden, Philadelphia, Oct. 11, 1750, NYHS *Colls.*, LIII (1920), 259, 227; Anne Grant, *Memoirs of an American Lady* (New York, 1901), II, 5; Keys, *Cadwallader Colden*, 2; Brooke Hindle, "Cadwallader Colden's Extension of the Newtonian Principles," *WMQ*, 3rd Ser., XIII (Oct., 1956), 459–75.

him near the end of his long career, "the Old Gentleman th'o Eighty five years old, does not dislike a little Controversy, which he has been engaged in for the greatest part of his life." [20]

Thus, by choosing Colden as his counselor, Clinton replaced a man who was in touch with all interests and shades of opinion in the colony with one who was looked upon, to say the least, with misgivings. The process whereby Clinton and Colden gradually alienated potential supporters is revealed by the experience of Philip Livingston, who was in attendance throughout the Albany sessions with the Six Nations. Livingston, an initial advocate of the projected expedition against Canada, at first blamed the Assembly for its reluctance to provide funds for the assault, though he did take account of their fears that the money might not "be Rightly applyd" and added that "this is a dolefull Case." [21] By September 18, 1746, when the Albany meetings had been going on for about a month, Livingston's attitude had begun to change. The governor seemed "always out of humour" and would not listen to Livingston's advice that the attack should be launched before the weather grew any colder. This had always been a sore point in connection with past expeditions, and Livingston felt the governor should pay some heed to those who from experience knew whereof they spoke. By November, when the troops still had not set out from Albany, Livingston was reaching the end of his patience. He knew the soldiers were ill-prepared for a winter campaign, that though the Six Nations had agreed to support the attack they were hardly as firm as might be wished, and that the result would be the laying out of "much money for nothing at all." In Livingston's opinion "all the Gentry about the Grandee can do nothing at all but Slander their neighbours & gett over heated with madera." Though

[20] Grant, *Memoirs,* II, 5; "Representation of Cadwallader Colden, Surveyor-General . . . to Gov. William Burnet . . . Nov., 1721," NYHS *Colls.,* LXVII (1934), 164; Gage to Barrington, New York, July 1, 1772, Clarence E. Carter, ed., *The Correspondence of General Thomas Gage with the Secretaries of State, 1763–1775* (New Haven, 1931), II, 611; Keys, *Cadwallader Colden,* 33–37; Siegfried B. Rolland, "Cadwallader Colden, Colonial Politician and Imperial Statesman, 1718–1760," unpubl. Ph.D. diss. (University of Wisconsin, 1952).

[21] Philip Livingston to Jacob Wendell, June, 1746, Livingston Papers, Philip Livingston Box, MCNY. Even Colden admitted in later years that Clinton was not above reproach when it came to money matters. One of his worst offenses was the "selling of offices." Colden reports that the Albany county clerk's post "was put to a kind of open Vendue." Colden to Peter Collinson, Coldengham, Oct. 4, 1754, NYHS *Colls.,* LIII (1920), 468.

Livingston had little use for Clinton, his odium was directed mainly toward Colden, whom he considered a "most dangerous" man who had given "pernicious advice"—despite which, as was becoming apparent, nothing would move Clinton "to part with his darling Councellor." In December, 1746, the governor requested the removal of Livingston from his post as secretary for Indian affairs, and that same month Livingston joined the Council majority in an open break with Clinton and Colden.[22]

When the governor finally had to abandon plans for a full-scale attack because of the onset of winter, he tried to spread some of the blame by charging that the Council had refused to accompany him to Albany, and that the Albany Indian commissioners had made only halfhearted efforts to gain the cooperation of the Six Nations. The Council hotly denied the implied derelictions. As for the Albany commissioners, it was true that they had advised the governor back in July that the Indians were "Unwilling" to attack the French. Clinton had only managed to gain the support of the Iroquois through the intercession of William Johnson, proprietor of a large estate in the Mohawk Valley, whose reputation for honest dealings with the Indians had given him an influence over them which exceeded that of the Albany magistrates.[23] Johnson became one of the few prominent New Yorkers to side with Clinton in the rapidly deepening political schism,

[22] Philip Livingston to Jacob Wendell, Nov. 24, Sept. 18, Dec. 16, 1746, May 25, June 8, 1747, Livingston Papers, Philip Livingston Box, MCNY; "Representation to Clinton of seven members of the Council . . . ," Dec. 16, 1746, NYHS *Colls.,* LII (1919), 294. Clinton cannot be blamed for everything that went wrong with the 1746 expedition, for he was in many ways a victim of the ministry's shifting policies. The 1746 campaign has been called "one of the least creditable episodes in British colonial history" by Arthur H. Buffinton, who charges that "its whole course was determined by political considerations" in England. "The Canada Expedition of 1746: Its Relation to British Politics," *AHR,* XLV (1940), 579.

[23] "The Commissioners of Indian Affairs Answer to his Excellencys Order in Council 23 July 1746," July 24, 1746, NYHS *Colls.,* LII (1919), 230; Philip Livingston to Jacob Wendell, Dec. 6, 1746, Livingston Papers, Philip Livingston Box, MCNY. Johnson, a nephew of Peter Warren, had come to New York only in 1738, but his bonds with the Indians had grown so strong that in winter he wore "almost entirely their dress and ornaments." He was formally adopted into the Mohawk tribe in a solemn ceremony, and being a widower "connected himself with an Indian maiden," who lived with him "in great union and affection all his life." Grant, *Memoirs,* II, 16; James Thomas Flexner, *Mohawk Baronet, Sir William Johnson of New York* (New York, 1959); *DAB,* X, 124–28 (Wayne E. Stevens).

and after 1746 the governor leaned almost exclusively on him for advice regarding Indian affairs.

Though the 1746 expedition was canceled, Clinton expected to
reschedule the attack for early 1747. He therefore kept the soldiers en-
camped about Albany all winter, sending them off from time to time on
scouting missions through the heavy snows. These troops were to have
been supplied by commissioners appointed by the General Assembly,
but when the commissioners refused to make provisions available, the
British officers at Albany broke open the warehouses and took what
they needed. This gained them the eternal enmity of "the Faction," as
Clinton and Colden now called the DeLancey-led opposition. Philip
Livingston was at Albany in February, 1747, when another effort was
to be made against Canada, though as might have been predicted, Livingston reported "our Chiefe Justice is of opinion that it is a Rash &
hazardous undertaking. . . ." Livingston himself was more critical than
ever of Clinton. Again in 1747 the attack on Canada—that "Infamous
Scandolous Expedition," as Livingston now called it—bogged down. As
the year wore on toward another winter, the soldiers "without any pay
from the time they were levied & allmost naked without cloaths began
to mutiny." At that point Clinton made one of his most ill-advised
moves. He sent "Orders to the Several Regiments of Militia in this
Province to choose every tenth man by lot to hold himself in readiness
to March on an hours warning." [24] Clinton no doubt imagined he was
thereby enabling himself to rush men to the frontier in case of emergency, but the result was only a further drop in the governor's authority.
As Colden later explained, the people of New York "questioned
whether the Governor can March any company out of their own County
without Express power from the Assembly, and there is Reason to
think that the Militia would Refuse obedience without Such power or
authority." According to Philip Livingston, almost no one in New York
was volunteering for the militia "after Such vile treatment." "Our assembly will not I think dare *not* make a Bill to detach men," asserted

[24] Colden to Dr. John Mitchell, July 6, 1749, draft, NYHS *Colls.,* LXVIII (1935),
24–25, 30–31; Colden to John Catherwood, Nov. 21, 1749, copy, NYHS *Colls.,*
LIII (1920), 165; Philip Livingston to Jacob Wendell, Feb. 13, Dec. 8, 21, 1747,
Livingston Papers, Philip Livingston Box, MCNY. According to Livingston, the
governor "used me So Ill, nay abuzd me," that it was clear no one could be his
friend except those "who will do, say, and think, as he doth. . . ."

Livingston, adding forlornly, "We Seem to be on the brink of extinction." [25]

The province was spared such a fate by the termination of the war in 1748, though this did little to alter New Yorkers' opinion that the war had been a wretched mistake from the first. The return of Louisbourg to the French by the terms of the treaty of Aix-la-Chapelle undoubtedly reinforced their suspicion that the colonists were little more than pawns, to be moved about and sacrificed at will in the distant game of empire building.

Clinton had been placed in a difficult position from the start. Caught between an indecisive ministry and a recalcitrant provincial Assembly, he had tried to do his duty; in the end he managed only to arouse doubts at home about his administrative ability and to inspire the widest animosity in New York. It is not surprising that the unhappy governor should begin to suffer "not only the pains of the Body but those of the mind. . . ." [26] As for James DeLancey, it must have been fairly obvious by the summer of 1746 what his choices were. He could stand by Clinton and put all his prestige on the line in support of a strong war policy, the result of which he no doubt believed would be the loss of his popular following, the disruption of the New York economy, and the ravaging of New York's northern frontier. (Saratoga had already been burned by Indians in 1745.) Or, he could oppose Clinton and the Canada expedition, frustrate the governor's administration, and possibly force his recall and replacement by a more congenial appointee —say, Sir Peter Warren, or perhaps even DeLancey himself. Had DeLancey's outlook been simply that of a British imperialist, he would have chosen the first alternative; as an Anglo-American, he could not have failed to share the colonists' anxieties. Thus he made the valid Anglo-American choice. He could still serve his King by averting a potentially disastrous defeat, his fellow-colonists by preserving their peace and prosperity, and himself by demonstrating—and in all likelihood increasing—his power in the province.

[25] Colden to Mr. Catherwood, Coldengham, Nov. 22, 1750, Robert Hunter Morris Papers, NJHS; Philip Livingston to Jacob Wendell, New York, Nov. 23, 1747, Livingston Papers, Philip Livingston Box, MCNY; Colden to Clinton, Jan., 1747/8, copy, NYHS Colls., LIII (1920), 4.

[26] Clinton to Gov. Knowles, April 22, 1747, Clinton MSS, V, Clements Library, Ann Arbor, quoted in Katz, Newcastle's New York, 170, n18.

Clinton's conduct of New York's share of the war effort was almost completely frustrated by the local opposition. But once the war was out of the way the governor's spirits lifted, and he began to cast about for ways to restore his own authority and to diminish that of the chief justice.

3. Governor Clinton Builds a Party: 1748–1752

The underlying premise of British imperial administration was that the King's representative in each colony should be endowed with sufficient authority to assure the people's subordination to and support of long-range imperial aims. Though lacking a formal and standardized statement of their constitutional powers, the governors, especially in the royal colonies, were nonetheless possessed of considerable authority. In New York the governor could veto legislation, dissolve or prorogue the Assembly, appoint officials, establish a court of chancery, grant land titles, and distribute military supply contracts. His patronage powers, which included appointments from the top levels of government down to local militia officers and justices of the peace, and his authority over land titles, were probably his most effective devices for tying provincial interests to those of the government.[27]

In New York as elsewhere during the first half of the eighteenth century, a number of these powers had been worn away as governors made concessions in the hope of assuring peaceful administrations. The process whereby fiscal initiative was gradually transferred from the governor to the Assembly is already familiar. Not only the governor's salary, but also appropriations to other officials, as well as funds for provincial defense and military needs, had by mid-century all become dependent on Assembly action. Regarding land, though the governor still had to certify new titles, his authority over existing grants had been largely transferred to the Supreme Court, especially after courts of chancery had fallen into such ill-repute in the 1730's. As for local patronage, it was widely acknowledged that New York governors had adopted the practice "of intrusting blank commissions with certain fa-

[27] For a general survey of New York's government structure, see Rex M. Naylor, "The Royal Prerogative in New York, 1691–1775," New York State Historical Association, *Quarterly Journal,* V (July, 1924), 221–55.

vorites in the respective counties, [who were] impowered to place and displace civil and military officers at their pleasure." In Colden's opinion this custom was clearly "destructive of Good Govt & of his Majesties Authority in this Province." [28] During the years of Clinton's administration the power that slipped from the governor's hands was gathered up by James DeLancey, resulting in a *de facto* shift in constitutional relationships; by 1746 DeLancey's power within the province equaled or excelled that of the governor.

In the beginning Clinton did not take this threat very seriously, being confident that as an officer of the Crown he could count on the backing of Whitehall. As he informed Colden in January, 1747, "I don't doubt but carry my point [in London] even to turn out the C. J. tho' he fancys himself so great a Man. . . ." But once the strength of DeLancey's English interest became apparent, as it did when the governor not only failed to have him dismissed as chief justice but found to his dismay that DeLancey had been appointed lieutenant governor, Clinton began to worry. By 1750, when he still had made no headway against DeLancey, Clinton declared that it would be "impossible for me to support His Majesty's Authority and Right, unless they redress my grievances," for DeLancey's continuance in office would "overset all my endeavours to support His Majestys Dignity, or my being servicable to him or my Country by staying here." It may be difficult in retrospect to comprehend the ministry's reluctance to give Clinton the support he needed to fight DeLancey's encroachments on the prerogative, but it seems that such neglect in the Newcastle era was not unusual.[29]

When the war ended in 1748, Clinton deemed it a propitious time

---

[28] [William Livingston], "A Review of Military Operations," 83; "Colden's Observations on the Balance of Power in Government," (1744–45), draft, NYHS *Colls.*, LXVIII (1935), 257. In 1754 William Livingston proposed as a possible future subject for one of his essays, "The mischievous tendency of the conduct of former Governours, in delegating their power of appointing civil and military officers, to their creatures in the counties," Milton M. Klein, ed., *The Independent Reflector, or, Weekly Essays on Sundry Important Subjects More particularly adapted to the Province of New-York, By William Livingston and Others* (Cambridge, Mass., 1963), 444.

[29] Clinton to Colden, New York, Jan. 14, 1747, NYHS *Colls.*, LII (1919), 334; Clinton to R. H. Morris, Ft. George, Aug. 29, 1750, Robert Hunter Morris Papers, NJHS; Katz, *Newcastle's New York*, 197, n13. Katz notes that the Board of Trade wrote Clinton "only once in each of the years 1744, 1745, 1746, 1748, 1750, and 1752, and not at all in the intervening years."

to regain something of what he had earlier given or bartered away. "I am now determined," he wrote Newcastle, "to embrace the first opportunity of letting the assembly know that I expect they should put an end to all their late innovations, and encroachments upon His Majesty's government, which have been introduc'd at the beginning of my administration: and which I acquiesced to during the war, and shall insist in general upon resetting His Majesty's government in this Province upon the same foot it was upon, in the time of my predecessors." The tactics he employed in the attempt to achieve this goal were fairly orthodox at the beginning. In the fall of 1748 he refused to accept the Assembly's annual salary offer, and for the next two years he maintained this position in an effort to compel Assembly compliance with the old policy of a five-year support. The governor also set about to reestablish his majority in the Council. Rather than rely solely on Colden for advice, he began to court New York City leaders James Alexander and William Smith, Sr., as well as other men who had stood apart from the DeLancey-led opposition to Clinton's war policies. In September, 1748, he suspended two opposition members, Stephen Bayard and Daniel Horsmanden, from the Council and appointed his own favorites to these and subsequent vacancies. As he told another of his newly acquired supporters, Robert Hunter Morris, who was then aiding some of Clinton's solicitations in London, one of the best ways to "Crush . . . the Pride & Insolence" of the chief justice would be to get Alexander restored to his Council seat, an objective which was accomplished in 1750. William Johnson and William Smith, Sr., as well as two other Clinton supporters, were also appointed to vacancies in the postwar years, thereby assuring Clinton a majority in the Council.[30]

So far, Clinton was following a well-worn path in attempting to regain the initiative. It was becoming evident, however, that the old methods were no longer sufficient. The support of an elite of executive officers and councilmen was still important to a successful administration, but by 1748 it was even more essential to have a majority in the

[30] Clinton to Newcastle, Sept. 30, 1748, Add. MSS 32716, fol. 399, British Museum, London, quoted in Katz, *Newcastle's New York,* 185; Clinton to R. H. Morris, New York, Sept. 8, 1750, Robert Hunter Morris Papers, NJHS. Clinton gained Robert H. Morris's support by offering to back him for DeLancey's replacement as lieutenant governor. Clinton to R. H. Morris, New York, Sept. 26, 1751, Robert Hunter Morris Papers, NJHS.

General Assembly, where the power to tax and to appropriate funds was lodged. Since the Assembly was still in the hands of the opposition faction, Clinton decided to build his own party—from the county level up—in the hope of gaining control of both houses and beating DeLancey at his own game. Thus in 1748 Clinton plunged into local politics with a fervor unmatched by any previous New York governor.

In September Clinton adjourned the Assembly, and "in order to bring things to some pass" began to assert his power over local appointments. "I am beginning to make a thorough change in the County of Albany, as to Mayor recorder & Sherriff etc etc.," he wrote to Colden; "I have agreed with [William] Johnson for Recorder but that not to be known yet & I believe have got a judge. . . ." Colden was given an almost free hand in nominating justices of the peace and other officials in Ulster and Orange counties, and his advice was sought regarding appointments in other places. By the summer of 1750 Clinton believed he had made enough progress to call a new election, and he confided to Colden that he had already given "private notice to Coll. Hicks, Morriss & the persons who are in my interest in Kings County that I proposed a dissolution." But the opposition was not taken by surprise. Clinton had already discovered that "several Yorkers & others had been canvassing for Members from this Place [New York City] up to Albany (as they expect a dissolution) and working up the People to their own seditious way of thinking, among them was Robt. Livingston of the Mannor, James Livingston, John Livingston, Nich. Bayard," and others.[31]

The impending election signaled the start of "a Voilent paper war," which according to William Alexander produced "a Dozen different papers" in New York City within a few days, and Alexander's father predicted that there was "like to be more Strugle in the Elections than of Late." One hot spot was the Borough of Westchester, where the incumbent, Lewis Morris, Jr., now a supporter of the governor, was to be opposed by the chief justice's brother, Peter DeLancey. James Alex-

[31] Clinton to Colden, Ft. George., Sept. 7, [1748], Colden to Clinton, Coldengham, May 9, 1748, copy, Feb. 19, 1748/9, copy, Clinton to Colden, Ft. George, July 19, 1750, Feb. 9, 1749/50, NYHS *Colls.*, LIII (1920), 76, 62, 103, 222, 189. For additional information on provincial politics in this period, consult Nicholas Varga, "New York Government and Politics During the Mid-Eighteenth Century," unpubl. Ph.D. diss. (Fordham University, 1960).

ander at first believed Morris would win easily, despite the efforts of Frederick Philipse, second judge of the Supreme Court, who had "about 15 of the voters much under his power . . . & insisted on their votes for Peter." But after the election he had to report ruefully that "the threatenings & bribery used barefacedly" to overturn Morris "did prevail by about 8 or 10 votes." Another reason offered for Morris's defeat was that "there appeared one hundred & odd voters, a number Considerably beyond what voters were Supposed to be there." [32] (Here is an indication of the many uncertainties that were now creeping into the election process, even in the rural areas.) Having lost the borough election, Morris then decided to stand for one of the county-wide seats. Again he was defeated.[33] The second loss, according to Clinton, was brought about by the personal efforts of "the C. J." who "actually headed into East Chester a Party from Rye. . . . He had his two Bullies, Peter and Oliver to frighten those, that his artful Condesention & dissimulation could not persuade to vote against their Conscience." The governor was of course much incensed when he wrote this letter, but he leaves no doubt of his awe at DeLancey's power. Noting the chief justice's claim that he had enough "Influence and Interest" to "sway every Election, thro' the Province," Clinton added: "Which I believe he will do; for he has in every County his Emissaries . . . sounding out his praise by his pretended Endeavours, for the Liberties and Properties of the People; which he says, must be in danger of being swallowed up by *Hungry Dogs.*" So discouraged was Clinton by his failure in the 1750 election that he wrote Robert Hunter Morris in London to urge the ministry to "either get the C. Justice or myself removed, for it is impossible, that I can maintain his [Majesty's] Prerogative in opposition to

[32] William Alexander to John Stevens, New York, Aug. 23, 1750, William Alexander Papers, Oswego Box, NYHS; James Alexander to [Robert Hunter Morris], New York, Aug. 2, 1750, copy, Rutherfurd Coll., Small Scrapbook, NYHS.

[33] In the eighteenth century, elections were often held on different days in each jurisdiction. In the County election the vote was Col. Philipse, 268; John Thomas, 257; and Lewis Morris, Jr., 53. It was reported that more than 300 Philipse and Thomas supporters were waiting to vote when Morris gave up. (New-York *Weekly Journal,* Sept. 3, 1750.) Statistics are also available for the 1750 Queens County election. Speaker Jones and Thomas Cornell polled 452 and 477 votes respectively, while the governor's friends, Judge Hicks and David Simmons, got only 293 and 288. New-York *Gazette: or, The Weekly Post-Boy,* Sept. 3, 1750.

the Influence & crafty Wiles of him at the head of the Faction. . . ." [34]

By the fall of 1750 the picture had brightened momentarily. The new president of the Board of Trade, the Earl of Halifax, had brought a fresh spirit into imperial administration and appeared ready to furnish more dependable support. Clinton meanwhile decided to accept the Assembly's offer of a one-year salary grant when it also agreed to pay the arrears of other official salaries and a portion of the accumulated war debt. Earlier that fall, concern over continuing dissension in New York had led the Privy Council to order that the Board of Trade submit a "white paper" report on the condition of the province, and this too had helped to subdue the opposition. The report was many months in preparation, but in October, 1751, Robert Livingston, Jr., observed that "Some private hands" seemed in a mood to compromise, and thought this might bring a "better understanding" if not a full "Reconsiliation." [35]

The undeclared truce was broken on November 25, 1751, when Clinton, perhaps believing that he had the opposition on the defensive, resumed hostilities by dissolving the Assembly and calling for new elections. Sighed John Livingston: "Good G-d Help us & deliver us etc." Philip Livingston [II]'s information was that "the Principal reason of the Assemblys Dissolution . . . is to gett Collo. Schuyler [of Albany County] out of the Assembly. . . . I Suppose [William] Johnson will Exert himself in the Election. I Hope He May be Disappointed." Another reason for the dissolution may have had something to do with James Alexander's suggestion that the only way to counter DeLancey's "great influence" was to enlist a man "of good Sense Spirit and independent Estate" who might wrest the Assembly from the chief justice's grip. Such an individual was Robert R. Livingston of the Clermont Livingstons, who, it was rumored, would seek the approval of Robert Livingston, Jr., to stand for election to the Livingston Manor seat. Alexander confessed that Robert R. Livingston's "relations in blood" to the

[34] Clinton to R. H. Morris, Ft. George, Aug. 29, 1750, Robert Hunter Morris Papers, NJHS.

[35] James Alexander to Colden, New York, Nov. 7, 1750, "Drafts relating to the Proposals," [Clinton and John Ayscough], n.d., NYHS *Colls.*, LIII (1920), 230–32, 233–36; Robert Livingston, Jr., to Jacob Wendell, New York, Oct. 17, 1751, Livingston Papers, MCNY.

chief justice, to James Livingston, and to Henry Beekman (the latter
two being firm members of the opposition party), "staggered me a little,
but upon the whole we believed that RRL's good Sense Spirit and independence, could over balance that relation." Clinton, too, thought it
"Something odd" that Robert R. Livingston would agree to such a
scheme, but he gave his approval and made plans to call the election.
The governor's party was once more to be disappointed. Robert Livingston, Jr., a strong supporter of the DeLancey opposition, refused to
relinquish his manor seat, and thus his cousin, Robert R. Livingston,
was unable to run in the election called for February, 1752.[36]

Clinton nonetheless gave the election his best effort for, having requested permission to return to England, he knew this would be his
final contest with DeLancey. He did everything he could to put up a
strong opposition to DeLancey's candidates in each of the counties. He
urged John Chambers to stand for assemblyman in New York County,
though to his chagrin he found Chambers so "affraid of the C. J. &
Oliver [DeLancey]" that "he has not been able to eat or drink for this
two days." Chambers finally agreed to stand, but it appeared to be "a
Common Saying now amongst the people that if Oliver would but Sett
up his Four Coach Horses" they would be elected. The governor believed he had a good chance in Orange, Ulster, and Richmond counties,
though in "Albany, Dutchess, Westchester & the Manner as also in
Kings & Queens Countyes," he expected a "Strong opposition." To improve his chances in Westchester, Clinton gave "directions for a New
Sett of justices . . . & also Militia officers according to desire." He also
had a lively concern for the propaganda war, noting at one point that in
response to the opposition's "Grubsheet," his own supporters would
"come out with a hummer next Week." [37]

[36] John Livingston to Robert Livingston, Jr., New York, Nov. 25, 1751, Philip
Livingston [II] to Robert Livingston, Jr., New York, Nov. 29, 1751, Livingston-
Redmond MSS, Reel 5; James Alexander to Colden, New York, Dec. 5, 1751,
Jan. 21, 1752, Clinton to Colden, New York, Jan. 6, 1752, NYHS *Colls.*, LIII
(1920), 303–4, 306, 307–8. This second Philip Livingston (1716–1778) was a
New York City merchant, the son of Philip Livingston, second proprietor of Liv-
ingston Manor who died in 1749, and a brother of Robert Livingston, Jr., and
William Livingston. In order to differentiate him from his father, the son will be
referred to as Philip Livingston II in these pages.

[37] Clinton to R. H. Morris, New York, Jan. 17, Jan. 21, 1752, Robert Hunter
Morris Papers, NJHS.

Governor Clinton's high hopes were once more dashed when the election resulted in a near rout. "With a great deal of Bullying and Noise joyned to Numbers of Lyes Spread against me and my friends & for want of those Instructions I was to have had so long ago they have carryed their point in most places of Election. . . ." The only bright spot was Albany County, where "Coll. Johnston's interest" had been sufficient to oust the old members, Schuyler and Hansen, after a scrutiny of the votes. In other contests the opposition won handily. Henry Beekman was delighted that "David Jones & Thos. Cornell [of Queens] were Elect'd by a Great Majority. 2 to one. Staten Island & oringe the Same & So it will be in New York & Westchester." Philip Livingston happily reported to his brother that for "all the [governor's] party Can do they do not Gain Interest any where that I know of." [38]

There was probably no other time in New York colonial history when one man enjoyed such vast influence as did James DeLancey in the middle years of the eighteenth century. And yet one should hesitate a little, even here, before taking the next step and assuming that one man, however skillful, "controlled" the politics of the province. For the very dynamics of that "control"—if such it really was—as well as the responses it evoked, were full of uncontrollable consequences. The dominant quality of New York politics was its extreme competitiveness —whether in a contest between the governor's "court" party and an opposition "popular" party, or between rival provincial factions to win either the governor's favor or an Assembly majority—and in the course of this competition all manner of unanticipated things happened. As political leaders tended more and more to reach down to the local level to broaden their support, ordinary men accustomed to think of politics as something high-toned and remote might now find themselves being courted by a governor and a chief justice. DeLancey was constantly intruding himself into local elections, as he did in the 1750 New York

[38] Clinton to R. H. Morris, New York, Mar. 11, Ft. George, Feb. 19, 1752, Robert Hunter Morris Papers, NJHS; James Alexander to Colden, New York, Feb. 15, 1752, NYHS *Colls.*, LIII (1920), 311; Henry Beekman to Henry Livingston, New York, Feb. 17, 1752, Henry Beekman MSS, NYHS; Philip Livingston [II] to Robert Livingston, Jr., New York, Feb. 15, 1752, Livingston-Redmond MSS, Reel 5. One reason for the opposition's success, Clinton believed, was the rumor that DeLancey might "get the government." Clinton to R. H. Morris, Ft. George, Feb. 19, 1752, Robert Hunter Morris Papers, NJHS.

City aldermanic contest when, according to Clinton, he did not scruple to set up "the most profligate, stupid, ignorant Person" to oppose the governor's candidate. The governor was jubilant when in one Assembly contest in Ulster County the opposition "was forced to take in a Shoemaker . . . for the best of the County declare they wont Sett" with such a "turbulent" party. Yet the governor himself was accused of commissioning "Judges and Justices of known ill Characters," and "so shamefully ignorant and illeterate, as to be unable to write their own Names. . . ."[39] Whatever else such hyperbole might mean, there can be little doubt that as the circle of politics expanded the people were becoming less tractable and elections were becoming less predictable.

Other by-products of this political competitiveness included a heightened awareness of the potential value of special-interest blocs, as well as an increasing resort to politics by the people as a means for addressing problems at all levels of provincial life. Some of these themes may be observed at close hand in Dutchess County, where Henry Beekman, prominent assemblyman, member of the gentry, and cohort of DeLancey, found that to stay in power he had to roll up his sleeves and be willing to fight.

4. Henry Beekman and the Politics of Dutchess County

For a sense of what was taking place in Dutchess County politics around the middle of the eighteenth century, a few words about Henry Beekman and the community he served may be in order. Beekman was born in 1688 and lived most of his life in Dutchess County, where his family owned the Beekman and Rhinebeck patents as well as other scattered holdings. When Beekman came of age, he further solidified his position as a landed patrician by marriages, first to Janet Livingston, of the Clermont Livingstons, and after her death to Gertrude Van Cortlandt. For a number of years Beekman devoted most of his time to managing and enlarging the family properties. He did not enter provin-

[39] Clinton to R. H. Morris, Ft. George, Aug. 29, 1750, New York, Jan. 21, 1752, Robert Hunter Morris Papers, NJHS; *Assembly Journal* (Gaine), II, Nov. 6, 1753.

cial politics until 1724, when at the age of thirty-six he was elected an assemblyman in place of a deceased member. Dutchess was sparsely populated in those years and life proceeded at a leisurely pace, disturbed only by an occasional squabble over land between the two leading families in the county. Though Beekman's holdings dominated the northern part of Dutchess, Adolph Philipse's Highland Patent encompassed most of the southern third. Cadwallader Colden observed in 1728 that Beekman might be "willing to have Mr. Phillipse's Power lessened For I know that in some places they have disputes about the Boundaries of their lands." [40]

Henry Beekman possessed all the better attributes of a country squire. Sincerely concerned for the welfare of his tenants and neighbors, and well informed about the problems of his community, he earned and accepted without affectation the esteem and respect of his constituents. Not a man of partisan temperament, Beekman was far better attuned to the sedate rhythms of eighteenth-century deferential politics than to the frustrations and anxieties of factional conflict. But Dutchess County could not remain forever unaffected by the tremors that were altering political life in the more settled parts of the colony. The population of the county began to increase rapidly in the 1730's, more than doubling in each of the next two decades. Many of the newcomers were New Englanders who spilled over the border from Connecticut and Massachusetts, seeking land and bringing with them attitudes markedly more egalitarian than those characteristic of the original Dutch and German settlers. About this time, Adolph Philipse began to challenge Beekman's leadership in Dutchess County. With all this, the well-ordered world that had been so satisfying to Henry Beekman was undergoing bewildering and unwelcome alterations. [41]

When it became evident in 1745 that Beekman might have competition for his Assembly seat from a hand-picked candidate of the Phil-

[40] Colden to James Alexander, Coldengham, Nov. 19, 1728, Rutherfurd Coll., I, 81; Philip L. White, *The Beekmans of New York, in Politics and Commerce, 1647–1877* (New York, 1956), 162–63; Werner, *Civil List*, 357–59.

[41] Smith, *History*, I, 311–12; Evarts B. Greene and Virginia D. Harrington, *American Population before the Federal Census of 1790* (New York, 1932), 98–101; Staughton Lynd, "Who Should Rule at Home? Dutchess County, New York, in the American Revolution," *WMQ*, 3rd Ser., XVIII (July, 1961), 334–35. For further information on the New England migration, see pp. 201–3 below.

ipse forces, his first impulse was to withdraw from the election. "If other good men Can be fixed on," he told his cousin and confidant Henry Livingston, "I had rather be out than in." But he was prevailed upon to stand, and as things turned out he and one of the Philipse candidates, Johannis Tappen, were elected to the two county seats. Later that year when a dispute was in the making between Beekman and Tappen over the naming of militia officers, Beekman, a colonel and commanding officer in the county, wrote, "I would act the Causious peacefull part, for it Seems that the Sead of Discord is very prevellant, & would reather Suffer a Smal Indignity than Inflame the Community." By the election of 1748, Beekman thought it was becoming impossible to "avoyd malice Invye & Slander," and decided to "take no payns" to be elected "unless a great majority wil have it So." [42] But again, for a variety of reasons, things went quite smoothly. That was the first election to be held since Governor Clinton's abortive Canada expedition of 1746. Because Clinton and his chief adviser Colden had so outraged public opinion by their highhanded methods of raising troops and obtaining supplies, most leading provincial politicians had united with James DeLancey in popular opposition to the governor. This, together with the illness of Adolph Philipse which resulted in his death in 1749, encouraged a rapprochement between Henry Beekman and his fellow assemblyman Johannis Tappen. Both men were reelected in 1748, and from that time on their differences were gradually reconciled. [43] Yet no sooner had that rift been mended than a new threat to the political peace arose. It was in the fall of 1748 that Clinton determined to capture an Assembly majority from the opposition.

To build his party in Dutchess, the governor made a particular effort to cultivate the support of the farmers and small merchants living in the central part of the county, men whose deferential habits were gradually being undermined by the strong anti-landlord views of the incoming New Englanders. Frustrated in their search for land by the prior

[42] Henry Beekman to Henry Livingston, New York, May 15, Dec. 3, 1745, Nov. 24, 1747, Henry Beekman MSS, NYHS.

[43] Henry Beekman to Henry Livingston, Jan. 19, 1749, Feb. 10, Mar. 22, 1750, Henry Beekman MSS, NYHS. Philipse had been able to control Tappen because he had "an asandent [ascendancy] over those men that Mr. Tappen mostly must depend [on]," presumably residents on the Highland Patent. Beekman to Livingston, Mar. 22, 1750, Henry Beekman MSS, NYHS.

claims of the great proprietors, many of the New Englanders had chosen to squat on the unimproved fringes of the large patents, thereby initiating conflicts with the landlords which ultimately led to the land riots of the 1760's. Clinton and Colden held no brief for the great landholders who helped swell the ranks of their opposition, and by identifying themselves with the small farmers they may have hoped to win support away from Beekman and Tappen. The governor courted various lesser leaders from the Poughkeepsie-Fishkill area, notably the Brinkerhoff family, Martin Hoffman, and "priest [Chauncey] Graham," a Presbyterian minister from New England who was pastor of an English-speaking congregation at Brinkerhoffville near Fishkill.[44] Beekman first expressed concern about this new coalition early in 1749 when Clinton appointed Isaac Brinkerhoff sheriff, and then replaced the justices of peace with a new slate consisting of Martin Hoffman, Theodorus Van Wyck, and John Brinkerhoff. Clinton's secretary had also asked Colden to "think of a proper person to supersede [Henry] Livingston, as Clarke of the Peace for Dutchess County . . . that his Excellency's Interest may be supported against the damd opposing Faction. . . ." Beekman maintained an exterior calm as these maneuvers took place, though he noted privately that in the next election "there necessarily will be 2 hot parties." [45]

Beekman had been aware for some time that the Poughkeepsie people were nursing resentments against the large landowners in the county, and he had taken certain steps to disassociate himself from the latter. As early as 1743 he had agreed to assist four Poughkeepsie freeholders in an ejectment suit brought against them by the patentees of the Nine Partners tract. Beekman's private letters show that he undertook to aid the small farmers as "a mater of Consiance," and because

[44] Henry Beekman to Henry Livingston, Rhinebeck, Jan. 23, 1752, *Yearbook* of the Dutchess County Historical Society, 1921, pp. 35–36, 51–52. Members of the Brinkerhoff family were farmers, millers, and small merchants; Hoffman was a county supervisor and a militia officer. James H. Smith, *History of Dutchess County, New York* . . . (Syracuse, 1882), 184–85; Varga, "New York Government and Politics," 456, 458; Staughton Lynd, *Anti-Federalism in Dutchess County, New York* (Chicago, 1962), 39–40.

[45] Henry Beekman to Henry Livingston, New York, Jan. 6, 1749, Henry Beekman MSS, NYHS: John Ayscough to Colden, Ft. George, Sept. 11, 1749, NYHS *Colls.*, LIII (1920), 141.

he believed "the Cause is Just." Though he told them he would "expect no other reward for this than your friendship," Beekman was not unaware that his siding with the freeholders rather than the landlords would enhance his political standing among the small farmers. It was with this in mind that he advised his brother-in-law, Gilbert Livingston, to "git Conserned also for the people of Poghkeepsie," predicting that his own position in the ejectment case "most lykly will put it out of their h[e]ad to Snarrole at us." [46]

Though Beekman seemed fairly confident of winning reelection in 1750 despite the governor's efforts to defeat him, he nonetheless made sure that his fences were in good order. "We have takin care to have us Entered Defandants" in another ejectment case, he informed Henry Livingston in February, and he was more solicitous than ever about local interests, wanting to know "if the County Stands in need of acts." About the same time he also asked Livingston to "git as much as its can be got the Caracter of one Wm. Moore, a quacker Preacher, if he be Honest I bleive he Could be usefull to me." He appears to have been quite aware of a potential bloc vote. "Yesterday; after meeting," he wrote Livingston shortly before the election, a group of "quaker frinds . . . payd me a visit. I treated them well, & th[e]y Signified that all the frinds would go one way" and vote for the incumbent Assemblymen. From "what I could Learn they can make out above 100 Vots in our County. . . . we Seemed to part very frindly." [47]

By means of these and similar efforts Beekman managed to maintain, and perhaps even to enlarge, his influence over Dutchess County politics. But the strain was beginning to tell. As the Poughkeepsie party grew more shrill and factious, going to such lengths in the fall of 1750 that Sheriff Brinkerhoff had Tappen arrested and jailed for debt, Beekman confessed that he was growing "tyered of all these things." He confided to Henry Livingston in 1751 that if "our frinds could thinck of

[46] Henry Beekman to Henry Livingston, New York, Dec. 28, 1743, Henry Beekman to Gilbert Livingston, New York, Dec. 29, 1743, Henry Beekman MSS, NYHS; Henry Beekman to Messrs. LaRoy, Veiln, Parmentier & Peltz at Poghkeepsie, New York, Dec. 29, 1743, DCHS *Yearbook, 1927, pp. 41-42.*

[47] Henry Beekman to Henry Livingston, New York, Feb. 7, 1749, Feb. 10, Sept. 11, 1750, Oct. 23, 1751, Henry Beekman MSS, NYHS; White, *Beekmans of New York,* 204. For more information on the Beekman-Clinton party contest, see *ibid.,* 185–99.

any other person in my sted . . . so Hoffman was kipt out" he would gladly step down. But he added in the true spirit of *noblesse oblige,* "how Ever if I must I will come & not for saake my frinds." When Beekman finally did retire from the Assembly in 1758, his personal power was still so great that he was able to nominate his cousin and long-time political agent, Henry Livingston, and his son-in-law, Robert R. Livingston, to both county assembly seats and to see them both elected.[48]

And yet by the end of the next decade the Poughkeepsie party, riding the crest of a new political awareness and exploiting popular resentment against the landlords, would manage to oust the political heirs of Henry Beekman, electing in their place two Poughkeepsie men, one of them Dirck Brinkerhoff.[49] Political excitement would reach a higher level than ever from that time on. But it should be clear that the rivalries and issues which divided the people of Dutchess County in the Revolutionary era had had their beginnings years earlier, when a new element of the population came to figure in the party contests of the 1740's and 1750's. Such participation was stimulated by the efforts of political leaders to outbid each other for public support; and popular interest, once aroused, was not easily laid to rest again.

5. James DeLancey Becomes Acting Governor of New York

The supreme test of James DeLancey's many political talents came in 1753. George Clinton was finally notified in the spring of that year that he could soon return home, Halifax having concluded that New York's

---

[48] Henry Beekman to Henry Livingston, Sept. 18, 26, 1750, Henry Beekman MSS, NYHS; Henry Beekman to Henry Livingston, New York, Dec. 19, 1751, DCHS *Yearbook,* 1921, pp. 34–35. Beekman managed to get Tappen released from jail and reinstated in the Assembly despite the opposition of the "Grandees of this town" (i.e., Clinton and his party). The next year, Tappen absconded and was immediately dismissed from the Assembly. Though embarrassed by Tappen's irresponsible behavior, Beekman was able to name his successor, Henry Filkin, former Dutchess County sheriff and a staunch supporter of Beekman. White, *Beekmans of New York,* 195–97.

[49] The 1768 election is discussed below, pp. 239 and 245.

affairs were too hopelessly tangled to be resolved by anything less than a fresh start under new leadership. As he wrote in response to one of Cadwallader Colden's ponderously detailed letters about the colony's internal confusions, "The affairs of the Government of New York have long been in a state of disorder and distraction before I was in a Situation to apply any remedy to them, [and therefore] I must be excused entering unnecessarily into so disagreeable a Detail, and recapitulating the variety of Incidents that occurred, and variety of measures pursued thro' the Course of such unhappy Divisions." Instead, the Board of Trade would simply send out a new governor, Sir Danvers Osborne, armed with a set of instructions designed to restore the integrity of the executive office. A few months earlier, Colden's own hopes of becoming lieutenant governor had been dashed by the confirmation of DeLancey's commission for that post, and though Halifax now expressed appreciation for Colden's past services to the Crown, it seemed that future preferment would depend on the inclinations of the new governor. Some events, however, are beyond the calculations of men. On October 12, 1753, a few days after his arrival in the colony, Sir Danvers Osborne was found hanging from a tree in the garden of the governor's mansion, having taken his own life in despondency over the recent death of his wife. Thus it was that James DeLancey became acting governor of New York. He would hold that office, except for a twenty-one-month interval, until his own death in 1760.[50]

This surprising turn of events placed DeLancey in the delicate position of being responsible for enforcement of the very prerogatives he had attempted to undermine as opposition leader. Nor was his dilemma made any easier by the clause in Osborne's instructions which charged the executive to reestablish the "royal Prerogative and Authority" which had been "trampled upon, and invaded in a most unwarrantable and illegal Manner" by the Assembly. It was suggested that the governor regain the upper hand by insisting on "a permanent Revenue settled by Law. . . . without Limitation."[51] A lesser politician might have

---

[50] Earl of Halifax to Colden, Grosvenor Square, May 17, 1753, NYHS Colls., LIII (1920), 390. Sir Charles Hardy, governor from the fall of 1755 until the summer of 1757, seems to have depended on DeLancey for advice on most matters.

[51] Assembly Journal (Gaine), Oct. 31, 1753.

been unsettled by this sudden transition, but DeLancey crossed the line from opposition leader to royal spokesman without breaking stride. Thenceforth he proceeded with much astuteness to strike a workable balance between colonial and imperial demands.

His first address to the Assembly, on October 31, 1753, was a model of decorum. "You will perceive, by the thirty-ninth Article of his Majesty's Instructions to Sir Danvers Osborne (Copies of which, I shall herewith deliver you)," he began, "how highly his Majesty is displeased. . . . On this Head, I must observe to you, that by our excellent Constitution, the executive Power is lodged in the Crown; that all Government is founded on a Confidence, that every Person will discharge the Duty of his Station." Thus "I must earnestly press it upon you," he continued, "that in preparing your Bills for the Support of Government, and other public Services, you pay a due Regard to his Majesty's Pleasure signified in his Instructions; and frame them in such a Manner, as when laid before me for my Assent, I may give it consistent with my Duty to his Majesty." Pointing out that "my Inclination and Interest lead me to study and pursue the Welfare of this Country," DeLancey promised his "chearful Concurrence" with all bills "that have his Majesty's Service and Prosperity of the Province for their Object." Thus DeLancey graciously requested compliance from the Assembly, though he knew perfectly well that long-term grants had not been made for many years. The assemblymen seem to have had some feeling for his predicament, if we may judge from the report of Robert Livingston, Jr., that the House was "very much ambarassed with his Majestyes Instructions to Sir Denvers which his Honor our Lieut Governour thinks himself obliged to Insist on. . . ." [52]

When the Assembly refused funds for any period longer than one year, as DeLancey knew they would, he declined the limited grant but at the same time forwarded the Assembly's explanations and resolutions to the Board of Trade with his own recommendations that the Board review its policy on this matter. Time and again DeLancey urged the as-

[52] *Ibid.*; Robert Livingston, Jr., to Jacob Wendell, New York, Nov. 12, 1753, Livingston Papers, MCNY. Livingston expressed the belief that the Assembly would not "Quarl with our Lt. Governour, on the Contrary I have all reason in the world to Expect that we Shall agree very well & Live in peace & unity." Livingston to Wendell, New York, Oct. 29, 1753, Livingston Papers, MCNY.

semblymen to provide long-term support, but he never showed any dis-
pleasure at their failure to act, nor would he hold them in session, like
previous governors, to force compliance. Benignly sending them home
for the harvest, he would urge that they consult their constituents and
return with a new outlook. His letters to the Board of Trade always put
the best possible face on the Assembly's actions, stressing its fundamental loyalty to the Crown despite its tenacious insistence on annual support bills. This stalemate continued for three years, until in September,
1756, Whitehall finally gave in. One-year grants would henceforth be
allowed, in view of the Assembly's willingness "to concur in every other
Measure which might be proposed for his Majesty's Service." [53]

Everything DeLancey did as acting governor was designed to reduce tensions. His new role, to which he brought all his art, was now to
conciliate and mollify. One of his first acts as governor was to extend the
hand of friendship to his former arch-rival, Cadwallader Colden. The
day after he was sworn into office DeLancey sought out Colden, who
reported with satisfaction that "nothing but mutual civilities passed between us." The lieutenant governor asked Colden to delay his return to
Ulster County for a few days "because he wanted to advise with me on
some affairs of Consequence. He shews as much regard to me as to any
of the Council & takes every opportunity to do it." DeLancey had read
Colden correctly, and after October, 1753, the old enmity between them
faded rapidly. In similar manner DeLancey cultivated the support of all
interests in the province, including that of the sometimes antagonistic
upriver landed proprietors. To be sure, he proposed to tighten the
collection of quit-rents, a policy they had generally resisted, but he balanced this off by initiating efforts to establish a permanent line along
the disputed New York-Massachusetts border, and he encouraged rapid
settlement of the northwest frontier, a program designed to appeal to
New York's many land speculators.[54]

[53] *Assembly Journal* (Gaine), II, Sept. 24, 1756. To gain the full flavor of DeLan-
cey's ingratiating manner, see his addresses to the Assembly and letters to the
Board of Trade. *Assembly Journal* (Gaine), II, Nov. 6, 8, Dec. 11, 12, 1753,
April 9, 12, May 2, 4, Aug. 20, 22, Nov. 20, 21, 25, 27, 1754, Feb. 4, May 27,
Aug. 5, Sept. 1, 1755; Lt. Gov. DeLancey to Lords of Trade, New York, Jan. 2,
May 21, Dec. 15, 1754, Mar. 18, 1755, *N.Y. Col. Docs.*, 819–21, 838–40,
925–29, 940–41.

[54] Colden to Mrs. Colden, New York, Oct. 14, 1753, NYHS *Colls.*, LIII
(1920), 407. For DeLancey's policies on land, see p. 208.

The most difficult problems DeLancey had to deal with concerned defense, for once again in the 1750's Anglo-French hostility was becoming acute. As early as 1754 DeLancey was called on to take a stand, for it was his *ex officio* duty to act as host and presiding officer of the Albany Congress. The main purpose of the Congress was to shore up the deteriorated alliance between the English and the Iroquois confederation, a goal supported by all New Yorkers. DeLancey believed then, as he had a decade before, that the key to securing the frontier against French encroachments was a fully coordinated and well-financed inter-colonial defense program. He proposed to the Albany Congress that two forts be built in Iroquois territory, and that three others be raised around Crown Point athwart the invasion route from Canada. As had happened so often in the past, the colonies proved unwilling to share the cost of such a program or to centralize the planning which it would require, and it looked as if the fourth colonial war would be no more decisive then those that had preceded it.[55] DeLancey nonetheless continued in the early years of the war to press his plan for the construction of forts and a united colonial effort. His zeal cooled somewhat in 1755 when a former political rival, Governor William Shirley of Massachusetts, was named second in command to General Braddock and was placed in charge of the projected Niagara expedition. DeLancey's antipathy to the Massachusetts governor was such that he refused to loan or help transport cannon for the Niagara campaign though requested, and then ordered, to do so by Shirley.[56]

The enmity was further heightened by Shirley's policy on supply contracts. There was a great deal of money to be made by provincials fortunate enough to be chosen to outfit and provision the troops, and because supply contracts were considered choice items of patronage, it was customary for commanding officers to consult the local governor when such contracts were to be let in his colony. Oliver DeLancey had

---

[55] "Copy of the Chief Justice Plan July 29, 1747," NYHS *Colls.*, LII (1919), 408–9; Robert C. Newbold, *The Albany Congress and Plan of Union* (New York, 1955), 77–79. For the proceedings of the Albany Congress, see *N.Y. Col. Docs.*, VI, 853–92.

[56] *Assembly Journal* (Gaine), II, Aug. 20, 1754; Gov. Shirley to DeLancey, Boston, May 26, June 1, 1755, Rutherfurd Coll., III, 61, 63, NYHS. For additional information on the DeLancey-Shirley rivalry, consult Katz, *Newcastle's New York*, 205–6; and John A. Schutz, *William Shirley, King's Governor of Massachusetts* (Chapel Hill, 1961), 190.

already been selected by the New York Assembly to provision the local
militia units, but Shirley excluded the DeLanceys from all contracts for
the Niagara campaign, turning instead to a rival group consisting of
William Alexander, Lewis Morris [III], Peter V. B. Livingston, and
John Erving of Massachusetts. This affront, as well as other evidences
of discrimination against the DeLanceys and their friends, raised opposition to Shirley in New York and probably contributed to the failure of
the Niagara campaign and the recall of Shirley himself in 1756. Even
before that time, however, the DeLanceys had set their London friends
to work. "Some of our Townsfolks have been very busy & Impertinent
in England," William Alexander wrote Peter V. B. Livingston, "in
hopes of Getting a Contract to Supply Contingencies, and have said
many dirty things of us. . . ." By mid-1756 these solicitations had done
their job. When new contracts were let that year, it was the London firm
of Baker-Kilby, and its New York correspondent Oliver DeLancey, that
got them. This sudden reversal created considerable hardship for the
displaced group of Alexander, Morris, Livingston, and Erving, and
made for anything but sweet feelings between them and the DeLancey
brothers.[57] James DeLancey's closer connection with the prosecution of
the war, however, as well as the improved prospects for victory after
Pitt came to power in 1758, led him once more to step up his support
for it in the final years of his administration.

Though the war and the acting governor's political skill tended in
general to restrain internal conflicts during DeLancey's years at the
head of the New York government, the dispute over military contracts
was certainly a disturbing influence. Nor was it the only one. Another
was the storm that arose in 1753 over the chartering of King's College.
Anglican leaders hoped to establish the college "upon a Foundation,
that may give a Prospect of promoting religion in the way of the National Ch [urch]," [58] and seven of the ten trustees were members of the

[57] William Alexander to Peter V. B. Livingston, Boston, Mar. 20, 1756, Gov.
Shirley to Oliver DeLancey, Oswego, Sept. 29, 1755, Rutherfurd Coll., III, 95,
69, NYHS; Schutz, *William Shirley,* Chap. XI, 233–34, 237–38; Theodore
Thayer, "The Army Contractors for the Niagara Campaign, 1755–1756," *WMQ,*
3rd Ser., XIV (Jan., 1957), 31–46. As Robert Livingston, Jr., counseled his
brother, "If we could but gitt our money we Should be well Satisfyed never to
have anymore to do with Expeditions." Livingston to [Peter V. B. Livingston],
Livingston Manor, Nov. 26, 1756, Livingston Misc. MSS, R-W, NYHS.

[58] Quoted in Klein, ed., *Independent Reflector,* 34.

Church of England. When the Anglicans' intentions became known, William Livingston, also a trustee but a leading Presbyterian, launched a crusade to assure that the college would be controlled by no single denomination. Livingston's effort relied heavily on the printed word, especially the *Independent Reflector,* a New York City periodical established by him in company with William Smith, Jr., and John Morin Scott. This "triumvirate" of literary lawyers also addressed public meetings, circulated petitions in the outlying counties, and, in the words of the eighteenth-century historian Thomas Jones, put the whole province into a "ferment," as "presbyterian pulpits thundered sedition, and every engine was set at work. . . ." Robert Livingston, Jr., observed in 1754 that "the Colladge affair has been the Grand topcheck. . . . this affair of the Charter makes most people in this Province very uneasey." The person most discomfited by the uproar was James DeLancey. As a member of the Church of England and a friend of the Archbishop of Canterbury, the acting governor came under much pressure to support the aspirations of local Anglican leaders. On the other hand, Anglicans composed only about 10 per cent of the colony's population, and DeLancey had no wish to be identified with an unpopular cause. The college was eventually chartered and placed under Anglican direction, though without the support of public funds, and by the end of 1756 the controversy was fading. But if Livingston could claim only a partial success, DeLancey himself was not entirely unaffected by "the breaches upon his popularity without doors." [59]

At another and possibly deeper level of concern was the relocation of power that had taken place during the years of DeLancey's administration, as the upriver region had gradually lost influence to the New York City–seaboard area. DeLancey, being of a New York City merchant family, had carefully protected the interests of the downriver community. It was during the decade of his power that long-term legislation had been passed to control the quality and packing of the colony's staple products. Flour, beef, pork, fish, wood products, and shoe leather, all produced in the upriver section, were included within the

[59] Thomas Jones, *History of New York During the Revolutionary War* (New York, 1897), I, 7, 13; Robert Livingston, Jr., to Jacob Wendell, Claverack, Dec. 13, 1754, Livingston Papers, MCNY; Smith, *History,* II, 289; Klein, ed., *Independent Reflector,* 32–39, 44–45, 171–214. For the circulation of petitions in Dutchess County, see William Livingston to Henry Livingston, n.d., DCHS *Yearbook,* 1921, pp. 52–53.

purview of regulatory agencies located in New York City. The purpose
of this legislation was to guarantee the reputation and competitive position of New York products, but the Hudson Valley merchants and
farmers felt themselves much put upon by the new restrictions. Another
check upon the influence of the upper Valley had occurred in 1755
when William Johnson was permanently appointed the sole commissioner for Indian affairs. This eliminated any further need for the local
Albany officials who had supervised Indian relations and trade since the
seventeenth century.[60]

It has sometimes been suggested that the New York election of
1758, when four members of the Livingston family gained seats in the
General Assembly, marked the beginning of a Livingston–landed party
opposition to the DeLancey-merchant majority. Whether any sharp division arose so early is a moot question, as will presently be discussed,
though against the known background of sectional jealousies and earlier
landed-merchant conflict, it may be supposed that upriver political leaders would be looking for ways to regain some of their former influence.
The most propitious time for such a resurgence would have been after
July 30, 1760, for it was on that date that James DeLancey was sud-
denly struck down by a fatal heart attack at the age of fifty-seven. With
the removal of a man so preeminent in New York politics for a decade
and a half, public life would loosen up once again as new leaders vied
to replace the old. And though upriver politicians did what they could
to exploit this new fluidity, they were never entirely successful. The reasons had much to do with the disruptive effects of problems relating to
land—a question of the most fundamental importance in the public affairs of eighteenth-century New York.

[60] Virginia D. Harrington, *The New York Merchant on the Eve of the Revolution* (New York, 1935), 279–82; David Arthur Armour, "The Merchants of Albany, New York: 1686–1760," unpubl. Ph.D. diss. (Northwestern University,
1965), 253–59. See also pp. 42–43 above.

VI

~~~~~~

NEW YORK'S LAND SYSTEM: PROBLEMS AND OPPORTUNITIES

NEW YORK'S EARLY HISTORY was profoundly influenced by the patterns of landholding that were set in the late seventeenth and early eighteenth centuries. In New York, as in the other northern colonies, small farms dotted the countryside and constituted the most typical form of land ownership. But the colony did contain a number of huge patents which were under the exclusive control of a few families. So much more extensive than the largest southern plantations as almost to defy comparison, the greatest of the New York patents each encompassed several hundred thousand acres of the choicest land in the colony.[1] One result of this was the emergence of a provincial "gentry," whose prominence and power were identified in the public mind with their great holdings. Historians have usually studied these New York landlords in terms of their influence on the social and economic life of the colony, a field so

[1] A few large patents in the South ran from 10,000 to 20,000 acres, but this was most unusual. Thomas J. Wertenbaker, *The Planters of Colonial Virginia* (Princeton, 1922), 46–49, 144; Jackson Turner Main, *The Social Structure of Revolutionary America* (Princeton, 1965), 46–47, 54–55, 64–65, 169. In New York, Rensselaerswyck encompassed one million acres and the Philipse Highland Patent was 205,000 acres.

rich and extensive that it has still not been thoroughly plowed. On the other hand, analysis of the relationship between landlord power and politics—a matter of special interest here—has fallen well short of being either sufficient or satisfactory.

There are, to be sure, obstacles, especially with regard to the period after 1750. Over the years a number of myths have grown up around the subject of New York's colonial land problems, which means that one must begin by questioning most of the presently held assumptions. Many of the great patents have never been studied at all; others have received no more than superficial treatment. Moreover, the widespread tendency to cast New York's great landholders as neo-feudal "manor lords" and close cousins of the English gentry has obscured some fundamental distinctions between the two societies.

1. Problems of Interpretation and Definition

Those drawn to the "conflict" rather than "consensus" aspects of American history always have found the study of New York Colony particularly rewarding, inasmuch as New York was almost continuously riven by one form or another of internal strife. That much, indeed, is indicated in the pages of the present study. Moreover, in the immediate pre-Revolutionary period New York was further shaken by that classic expression of social discontent—land riots—as recurrent and violent clashes took place between small farmers and the land barons of the Hudson Valley. When the long-simmering dispute between these two interests finally erupted in a general and widespread uprising in 1766, New Yorkers experienced the phenomenon of armed bands, consisting in some estimates of as many as 500 to 2,000 men, roaming about the countryside and engaging in clashes with sheriff's posses and British regulars. During these disturbances a number of men were killed, others were seriously wounded, houses were burned, and crops were destroyed. A threatened march on New York City by over five hundred "levellers," as they sometimes were called, was narrowly averted when the governor, in a show of force, dispatched British troops to disperse the mob gathered at the city's outskirts.[2]

[2] Irving Mark, *Agrarian Conflicts in Colonial New York, 1711–1775* (New York, 1940, 1965), Chap. V.

All this is heady drink for those who support a more radical view of the American Revolution, and it is not surprising that New York's land riots have frequently been cast as "peasant rebellions" against the "neofeudal society" of the Hudson Valley.[3] Though some of the evidence certainly offers support for a class analysis, a comprehensive survey of the riots of 1766, and of the other land disturbances which preceded and followed them, reveals other elements of such importance and weight as to suggest that any simple "class" formula needs significant modification. Parallels between European and colonial American societies regarding conflicts over land can hardly be drawn in a classic way in view of the sharp distinctions between European and colonial assumptions about landholding itself. Centuries of land engrossment in Europe by a privileged nobility, upon principles that went well beyond those of simple "property"—embracing those of governance, military protection, and justice as well—had, over those centuries, made for a pattern of landlord-tenant relationships and a hierarchical order of rural society that would have very little counterpart in America. One of the legacies of such a tradition was a whole set of historic limits on the holdings of the peasant class; no such "history" could be imposed on the American colonies. There, small landholders always outnumbered the large by a heavy majority, and long before Thomas Jefferson drew breath it was the independent freeholder who was being proclaimed the true and representative American. The few efforts to transfer feudal land patterns to the colonies almost all miscarried, mostly for the same reasons. The traditional landlord-tenant relationships, on the one hand, and the ready availability of land, on the other, were fundamentally incompatible.[4]

Conceivably New York might be regarded as not a typical case.

---

[3] Mark, *Agrarian Conflicts*, 131; Staughton Lynd, *Anti-Federalism in Dutchess County, New York* (Chicago, 1962), 38. See also E. Wilder Spaulding, *New York in the Critical Period, 1783–1789* (New York, 1932), Chap. III.

[4] Percy W. Bidwell and John I. Falconer, *History of Agriculture in the Northern United States, 1620–1860* (Washington, D.C., 1925), 60–66; Main, *Social Structure*, 24, 66–67, 273–77. The failure of the patroon system in New York has already been mentioned; one thinks also of the short-lived efforts to establish neofeudal patterns in the Carolinas, Maryland, and New Hampshire. R. R. Palmer says that in France, one of the more enlightened countries on the continent, peasants held only about 30 per cent of the land in the eighteenth century. *The Age of the Democratic Revolution* (Princeton, 1959), I, 440.

There, a number of the great proprietors indeed expected to operate their estates as quasi-feudal baronies, and it might be supposed that the anti-landlord *gestalt* would be more fully developed in New York than elsewhere. But again, the New World was not the Old; in colonial New York there were a number of factors that tended over time to inhibit the growth of a true landed aristocracy. One of the most substantial was an imperial policy which after 1696 consistently, though not always effectively, opposed the engrossment of the land by a minority and sought to break up the largest holdings. Many of the great New York patents, moreover, were subject to challenge because of unextinguished Indian titles or overlapping claims by adjacent colonies. Also, because of the enormous size of some New York grants, only the most accessible portions were under cultivation, which meant that thousands of potentially productive acres were allowed to lie idle. The pressure that built up against this wasteful system may well be imagined, coming as it did from several directions—not only from colonial yeomen seeking land to till, but also from the imperial government looking to exploit its overseas possessions to the fullest.

The great landlords, consequently, were forever on the defensive, and it might even be said that the greatest sufferers from "insecurity of tenure" were they themselves. Their anxieties became so acute after mid-century that the proprietor of Livingston Manor could ominously predict that unless the interests of the landlords received greater protection from the government it might be necessary to "bid adieu to all Estates." [5] When all is added up, the land riots in New York appear less as the desperate acts of an oppressed peasantry than as a series of self-confident thrusts at the shaky and anachronistic remnant of a "neo-feudal" system that had never achieved a very secure foothold in the first place. Moreover, the rioters themselves, when one takes a closer look at them, appear more like the precursors of the "expectant capitalists" [6] of nineteenth-century America than like descendants of the *jacquerie* of medieval Europe. The small farmers wanted nothing so much as to get their hands on the proprietors' vacant lands so that they

[5] Robert Livingston, Jr., to William Alexander, Livingston Manor, Mar. 26, 1753, William Alexander Papers, Vol. I, NYHS.

[6] This is Richard Hofstadter's term for the energetic entrepreneurs of the Jacksonian era. *The American Political Tradition and the Men Who Made It* (New York, 1948, 1962), 55–56.

too might begin building up estates. That there were class overtones, of a sort, is undeniable. But they must be considered in their very special American context.

The history of land distribution in New York, and of the large patents and manors carved out by a number of astute colonials, has usually been studied in piecemeal fashion. For many years the main source of information about the large estates was a series of pamphlets published by the Order of Colonial Lords of Manors in America, an organization made up largely of descendants of the old colonial families who sought to preserve some of the memories and traditions of their ancestors. This society published twenty-three separate studies of New York patents, and despite the mellow glow that emanates from some of them, they at least represented a first step in the organization of this complex subject. One of the earliest efforts at objectivity had been made by Edward F. DeLancey in the late nineteenth century, and his essay on the colony's land patterns is still one of the better statements on this subject. DeLancey was not tempted to stress the aristocratic and feudal aspects of New York's land system, and his study generally avoids the romanticism which marks some of the other early efforts. "The term Lord of a Manor," DeLancey admonished, "is a technical one, and means simply the owner,—the possessor,—of a manor, nothing more. Its use as a title is simply a work of intense or ignorant republican provincialism." [7]

In the early decades of this century there was a flurry of interest in colonial New York's land system on the part of professional historians, no doubt stimulated in some degree by Frederick Jackson Turner's emphasis on the frontier.[8] Then in 1940 appeared two monographs which

[7] Edward F. DeLancey, "The Origin and History of Manors in New York, and in the County of Westchester," in J. Thomas Scharf, ed., *History of Westchester County, New York* (Philadelphia, 1886), I, 87; Order of Colonial Lords of Manors in America, New York Branch, *Publications,* nos. 1–14, 17, 20, 21, 23, 25–26 (1914–1935). The proprietor of Gardiner's Island in 1798 pointed out that in former days the manor proprietor "by common custom had the title of Lord," but that he himself preferred freedom with his fellow men above "any empty titles whatever." "Gardiner's East Hampton, Etc.," NYHS *Colls.,* (1869), 267–68.

[8] Several studies of specific areas resulted from this, as well as the first serious attempt to make sense out of the land riots of the late colonial era. See Oscar Handlin, "The Eastern Frontier of New York," *New York History,* XVIII (Jan., 1937), 50–75.

explored the problem of the small farmer rebellions. Irving Mark's book, *Agrarian Conflicts in Colonial New York, 1711–1775,* quickly became the standard work, and did much to bring some order into a difficult subject. Recognizing that the land controversies were not simply a question of "rich and poor" or "conservative and radical," Mark strove to take into account their many complexities. He could not entirely escape from the climate of the period in which he was writing, however, and his tendency to invoke the categories of Progressive thought still left a heavy emphasis on class conflict as the motive force behind New York's land disputes. The other monograph published in 1940 was Dixon Ryan Fox's *Yankees and Yorkers,* and there the part played by geographic and political factors, as well as the problem of cultural clash between New Yorkers and New Englanders, was fully and objectively treated.[9] The elements which Fox introduced to the subject have not as yet, in the present writer's opinion, been assimilated into a full and proper analysis of it.

From 1940 to the present, two major additions have been made to the literature on this subject. One is Staughton Lynd's prize-winning master's essay, *Anti-Federalism in Dutchess County, New York.* The author devotes one chapter to a discussion of the 1766 land riots in Dutchess County, and despite a number of valuable insights, Lynd, like many earlier writers, also inclines heavily toward a class interpretation of these events. The other, a recent doctoral dissertation on the Manor of Cortlandt—the only full-scale examination of a single estate—challenges many of the earlier class-conflict assumptions, and provides more than a hint that the last word on this complex subject is very far from having been said.[10] Much remains to be done, and for the subject as a whole, we lack as yet the most rudimentary statistics and information. Nevertheless, it should at least be pos-

[9] Fox's book argues that the land conflicts were part of a larger regional struggle between New York and New England which started in the colonial period and lasted well into the nineteenth century.

[10] (Chicago, 1962). Material drawn from Lynd's study appeared as "Who Should Rule at Home? Dutchess County, New York, in the American Revolution," *WMQ,* 3rd Ser., XVIII (July 1961), 330–59. Sung Bok Kim, "The Manor of Cortlandt and Its Tenants, 1697–1783," unpubl. Ph.D. diss. (Michigan State University, 1966). Some of Kim's main points are summarized in a recently published article, "A New Look at the Great Landlords of Eighteenth-Century New York," *WMQ,* 3rd Ser., XXVII (Oct., 1970), 581–614.

sible to make a few projections as to the form a new synthesis might take.

The mere physical dimensions of the problem are in themselves quite formidable. Approximately fourteen separate manor grants and at least an equal number of very large non-manorial patents were given out by various New York colonial governors to individual families or small groups of speculators. But this hardly means that those tracts were maintained intact throughout the colonial period, and in this respect the many existing maps of colonial patents are highly deceptive. The great majority of patents did not retain their original dimensions but were gradually broken up as land was distributed among family members, or sold off as speculators realized profits on their original investments. It has already been shown that three of the six original Westchester County manors were subdivided at a fairly early stage, and most of the Long Island manors experienced a similar fate.[11] By about the second third of the eighteenth century only Rensselaerswyck, Livingston Manor, Philipsborough, Morrisania, the Manor of Cortlandt and, apparently, the 3,300-acre Gardiner's Island in Long Island Sound any longer existed as manorial entities—the Manor of Cortlandt in name only, and Gardiner's Island so much on the periphery as to be of little importance to the economic or political life of the colony. Regarding the non-manorial patents there were also many variables. Some of the largest early grants, such as the Dellius and Evans patents, were canceled by the Crown; others were divided among the original partners or among family members, and still others were sold off in individual lots.[12] A few, such as the Philipse and Beekman patents in Dutchess

[11] See, e.g., Rev. Melancthon Lloyd Woolsey, "The Lloyd Manor of Queens Village," and C. H. Brown, "The Smiths of Smithtown," Order of Colonial Lords of Manors in America, New York Branch, *Publications,* nos. 13, 17 (1925, 1927). One of the better maps of colonial landholdings is Claude J. Sauthier, "A Chorographical Map of the Province of New York in North America" (London, 1779), which is reproduced in *N.Y. Doc. Hist.,* I, 774. Cortlandt Manor is erroneously placed in Dutchess County, but otherwise it is relatively accurate. The only way colonial land patterns could be charted with full accuracy would be to draw up a series of maps, perhaps one for every ten years, to show the changes that took place in individual holdings. For the breakup of the three Westchester manors, see pp. 30–31 above.

[12] Ruth L. Higgins, *Expansion in New York with Especial Reference to the Eighteenth Century* (Columbus, Ohio, 1931), 26, Chaps. VII and VIII. This is the

County or the Schuyler and Johnson holdings in Albany County, remained relatively intact.

Attention here will be centered upon the great estates located on the east bank of the Hudson River in the counties of Albany, Dutchess, and Westchester. There are six major grants which fall in this category —Rensselaerswyck, Livingston Manor, the Beekman Patent, the Philipse Highland Patent, Cortlandt Manor, and Philipse Manor—together with several smaller ones: the Oblong patent, the Great Nine Partners and the Little Nine Partners patents, and Beekman's Rhinebeck patent. (See map.) Most of these lands were patented in the seventeenth or early eighteenth centuries to prominent individuals or groups of speculators who sought land both as a mark of current status and in anticipation of the future profits and power that an increase of land values would bring. The holders wanted to maintain their estates intact if possible, leasing rather than selling land, for as Philip Livingston expressed it, "Selling I am not fond off att all." [13]

So far as can be determined, throughout the English period the neighboring manors and non-manorial estates of the Hudson Valley patricians were operated along similar lines, the only differences being the form of the deed and the lack of Assembly representation for the non-manorial patents.[14] The distinguishing feature of colonial New York's land system, then, was not the presence of manors or manor "lords." As

---

best chronological account of the patenting and settlement of colonial New York lands.

[13] Philip Livingston to Jacob Wendell, Albany, May 10, 1739, Livingston Papers, Philip Livingston Box, MCNY.

[14] Even the manors differed in this latter respect, with only Rensselaerswyck, Livingston Manor, and the Manor of Cortlandt having the privilege of a seat in the Assembly.

Land Patents on East Bank of Hudson River
—18th-Century New York

Outlined here are the dimensions of the major patents as they were believed to exist in the early eighteenth century. Parts of Cortlandt Manor, the Oblong, and possibly of Beekman and Great and Little Nine Partners Patents were sold off in the course of the century.

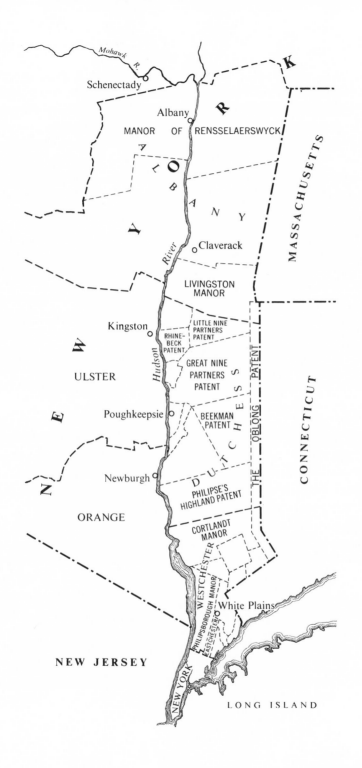

will be shown, the form of the grant is of little or no significance beside the fact of an exclusive land policy pursued by a few rich and powerful New Yorkers who chose to withhold from the market several million acres of prime land, to the great exasperation of small farmers who saw themselves excluded from one of the most fertile regions in the New World. This was the source of New York's land problems, and although "feudal" privileges were not involved, there can be little doubt that the landlords frequently relied upon political office or raw political power to guard what must have seemed an arbitrary economic position.

2. Legal and Economic Aspects of the Great Patents

New York landlords without doubt had originally hoped to operate their estates as quasi-baronies. Throughout the early years by far the most desirable form of patent was the manor grant, which conferred, at least on paper, a distinctly privileged position on the proprietor. There is still no agreement among legal historians as to the "feudal" character of the manor grants. Following the form of His Majesty's "Manor of East Greenwich in our County of Kent," New York manors were granted in "ffree and Common Soccage" [12 Charles II, c.24], which technically meant freehold tenure. But all land in New York was subject to quit-rents, which implied a feudal connection to the Crown, and which may in turn have initially imparted a quasi-feudal tone to land-lord-tenant relationships.[15] Of greater importance, perhaps, was that the manor patents conveyed a number of privileges and exemptions which were clear legacies of the feudal past. Several manor proprietors were authorized to hold courts leet and baron, which would have given them jurisdiction over both civil and criminal infractions occurring on their estates. A number of deeds also reserved to the landlords control over hunting, fishing, milling, timber-cutting, and mineral deposits

---

[15] See, for example, "Governor Hunter's Patent, 1715, for Livingston Manor," *N.Y. Doc. Hist.,* III, 414–20. For a discussion of the erosion of neo-feudalism in New York, consult Robert Ludlow Fowler, *History of the Law of Real Property in New York* (New York, 1895), Chap. II. For more information on quit-rents, see Beverly W. Bond, Jr., *The Quit-Rent System in the American Colonies* (New Haven, 1919), Chap. IX.

within manor boundaries. The right of advowson, or the appointment of a clergyman for the manor and the tithing of tenants for his maintenance, was included in some deeds. Escheat, which confirmed the automatic reversion of land to the proprietor at the death or removal of a lessee, was another common feature; and of course the right of distraint, or repossession for non-payment of rent, was always specified. In addition, landlords were entitled to require several days' work each year from their tenants on manor roads and fences.[16]

All of these clauses have been cited in the past to show the feudal nature of New York land grants, and though there can be little doubt that the manor deeds were at least quasi-feudal in form, the key question is whether they were feudal in application. It has to be determined whether the privileges and immunities granted to the manor proprietors were translated into actual practice, how onerous these obligations were, and to what extent they restricted the activities and opportunities of the tenant farmers upon whom they fell.

Regarding the courts leet and baron, it appears that if they existed at all it was only during the shadowy early years of English rule. Only one reference to such courts has ever been discovered, whereas there is abundant evidence that during most of the colonial period the manors were regularly included within the county judicial system. Among the factors that discouraged the erection of such courts, perhaps the most important was the jurisdictional jealousy of strong county and local governments, which not only circumscribed manor judicial power but also set administrative and tax policies for the manors with little reference to the wishes of the proprietors.[17] It has been pointed out earlier

---

[16] The deed for Rensselaerswyck is reproduced in Samuel G. Nissenson, *The Patroon's Domain* (New York, 1937), 381–85; parts of other deeds can be found in the studies of New York patents in Order of Colonial Lords of Manors in America, New York Branch, *Publications;* the Fordham Manor deed is in Harry C. W. Melick, *The Manor of Fordham and Its Founder* (New York, 1950), 70–72.

[17] Not that manor proprietors would not have liked to establish such courts of privilege; as late as 1748 Philip Livingston included in his leases a reference to courts leet and baron "when Erected." Lease between Philip Livingston and Salomon Schutte, April 14, 1748, Livingston-Redmond MSS, Reel 5; *The Colonial Laws of New York from the Year 1664 to the Revolution* (Albany, 1894), I, 226–31; Julius Goebel, Jr., "Some Legal and Political Aspects of Manors in New York," Order of Colonial Lords of Manors in America, New York Branch, *Publications,* no. 19 (1928), 18–21; Nissenson, *Patroon's Domain,* 272, 308–10; Sung

that manors rapidly acquired full township or precinct political status, replete with annual town meetings and the election of all local officers. As manor population increased, moreover, the number of local elective officials was raised proportionately. An indication of the process whereby the landlords' political power was steadily eroded is a 1673 petition from the Manor of Fordham in which the residents demanded the right to elect their own local magistrates "as is allowed to all the other inhabitants of this government." John Archer, the manor proprietor, granted self-government to the residents with the declaration that he "desists from the government, authority and patroonship of said town, reserving alone the property and ownership of the lands and houses there." [18]

On the three manors that had representation in the Assembly, the landlord was no doubt able to influence, though probably not to "control," his tenants in political matters. None but family members were ever elected to those seats, and until the more politically self-conscious period of the 1760's there is no evidence that these elections were ever contested.[19] The term of a tenant's lease was an important factor in determining political rights on manors and patents, for in accordance with a 1701 law all holders of life leases were qualified to vote in Assembly elections provided they met the £40/40s property requirement. On the other hand, leases for a stated number of years did not convey this right.[20]

Bok Kim, "Manor of Cortlandt," 53–54; Mark, *Agrarian Conflicts,* 57–58. It is true that courts baron were not courts of record, but one would expect to find some sort of reference to them if they had ever existed.

[18] *N.Y. Col. Docs.,* II, 625; *Laws,* IV, 85–86, 1056, 1116–19; Nissenson, *Patroon's Domain,* 312. For a detailed account of the dissolution of a manor, see Melick, *The Manor of Fordham.* For the earlier discussion of manors and local government, see p. 35 above.

[19] During a typical election at Livingston Manor in 1717, presided over by Philip Livingston in the absence of his father, the son reported, "all those who were present did *nimene Contradicente* Choise you for their Representative after that was done they were very merry." Philip Livingston to Robert Livingston, Albany, April 25, 1717, Livingston-Redmond MSS, Reel 3; Mark, *Agrarian Conflicts,* 65. In 1768, however, there was a contested election on the Manor of Cortlandt, and though the two rival candidates were both members of the Van Cortlandt family, they may have had differences over the political issues of the day. 1768 Election Talley, V1645, Van Cortlandt Papers, SHR.

[20] "Memorandum," Livingston Manor, March 7, 1753, and other leases in Misc. MSS, Livingston, Box R-W, NYHS; *Laws,* I, 453; Mark, *Agrarian Conflicts,*

Regarding some of the other "feudal" privileges granted in the original manor charters, the record is seldom entirely clear. Landlords sometimes tried to obtain resident clergymen for their estates; in 1745 Philip Livingston hoped he might "succeed in my Resolution to have a minister here and oblige the Tenants to pay part but that will Cost me a Vast deal of trouble however I Shall try it as soon the Ensueing Election is over." Some Livingston and Van Rensselaer leases included clauses regarding tithes, but there is little evidence that these were ever collected.[21] Most leases required that lessors give from one to three days' work or "riding" on the manor roads and fences. Tenants usually fell behind in this obligation, and its "feudal" nature was in any case hardly unique, inasmuch as other jurisdictions, such as towns and precincts, also required work from their citizens. If anything, the obligation in those jurisdictions was more onerous.[22] In the realm of political and judicial privileges, therefore, the position of the grantees was not especially distinctive. The same cannot be said, however, of purely economic matters, where the landlords exercised considerable control over the affairs of their tenants, and maintained their power in the face of mounting pressure. Such was the case not only with regard to manor tenants but with those on the ordinary patents as well.

There were two basic kinds of leases in colonial New York. One was the conveyance of a plot of land in "fee simple" with the reserva-

---

67–72. Although some leases were for a specific term of years—such as three, seven, or thirteen—many, and perhaps the majority, were for from one to three lives. A lease for "two lives" was the most common, and it usually referred to a man and wife, which indicates that in most cases the "lives" ran concurrently and not sequentially. There was, for example, one Livingston Manor lease for "2 very old lives." Apparently a 21-year lease qualified as a life lease.

[21] Philip Livingston to Robert Livingston, [Jr.], Livingston Manor, June 1, 1745, "Indenture between Robert Livingston, [Jr.], and John Peter Lowry," March 19, 1760, Livingston-Redmond MSS, Reels 5 and 6; Mark, *Agrarian Conflicts,* 65, 67.

[22] In towns and precincts, residents had to contribute from three to six days' work per annum. *Laws,* I, 534, 632, 797, II, 71; Beverly McAnear, ed., "Mr. Robert R. Livingston's Reasons Against a Land Tax," *Journal of Political Economy,* XLVIII (1940), 69–71; Kim, "Manor of Cortlandt," 146–50; Mark, *Agrarian Conflicts,* 67. When some Livingston Manor tenants balked at working on the roads in 1741, the proprietor told his overseer to have the "next Justice to order them to do it," and if they refused he would "take Care to have them punished. I am obliged to make Some pay for their Insolence to deter others." Philip Livingston to John DeWitt, Feb. 13, 1741, Livingston-Redmond MSS, Reel 7.

tion of a token perpetual rent, often something as trifling as "3 pepper-corns" per annum.[23] But if the rents were insignificant in these leases, other qualifications were not and, as will be shown, these leases fell far short of offering secure tenure. The other standard form was a lease for life or years which specified a rent to be paid either in cash or in kind. Many landlords charged "the annual rent of a tenth of the produce." Tenants at Rensselaerswyck paid their "tenths" in wheat, as was also the custom with Henry Beekman's tenants in Dutchess County.[24] Philip Schuyler reserved "a fourth or, more commonly, a tenth of all produce as a rent" on his Saratoga estate; and Philip Livingston specified a rent of "4 fatt hens" and "24 stiple of wheat" in a typical manor lease, while Robert Livingston, Jr., the third proprietor, leased a seventy-two-acre farm for the annual rent of "4 fatt hens" and, after three years, "25 stipple of wheat" and the "fruit of 10 choice apple trees." [25]

[23] This form of lease, peculiar to New York, was inherently contradictory inasmuch as fee simple in the common law traditionally was the most absolute and unconditional mode of land conveyance. Its apparent purpose was to enable the proprietor to retain a semblance of overriding domain to the land within his original patent. Henry Noble McCracken, *Old Dutchess Forever! The Story of an American County* (New York, 1956), 39. There were many subtle variations of the two basic lease forms. For a detailed discussion see Don R. Gerlach, *Philip Schuyler and the American Revolution in New York, 1733–1777* (Lincoln, Neb., 1964), 324–27; Mark, *Agrarian Conflicts*, 62–72; Fowler, *History of Law of Real Property*, 40–42.

[24] Philip Livingston to Robert Livingston, Albany, April 21, 1724, Livingston-Redmond MSS, Reel 3; Henry Beekman to Henry Livingston, New York, Dec. 19, 1743, Jan. 21, 1747, Nov. 7, 1752, Henry Beekman MSS, NYHS; McCracken, *Old Dutchess Forever*, 39–40. Because of the scarcity of coin, most leases provided that payment be made in crops or livestock, or both. Early Van Rensselaer leases state the annual rent in guilders but usually translate the sum into bushels of wheat or other produce. A. J. F. van Laer, ed., *Van Rensselaer Bowier Manuscripts* (Albany, 1908).

[25] Leases between Philip Livingston and Salomon Schutte, April 14, 1748, and Francis Sale, April 28, 1748, "Indenture between John Peter Lowry and Robert Livingston, [Jr.]," March 19, 1760, Livingston-Redmond MSS, Reels 5 and 6; Gerlach, *Philip Schuyler*, 61. A stipple was equivalent to three pecks. *Journal of Warren Johnson*, 99, New York State Library, Albany. A student of Philipsburgh Manor says that by 1776 most rents were stated in monetary terms (averaging from $15 to $20 a year for a farm), though before 1750 they were usually expressed in terms of wheat. Beatrice G. Reubens, "Pre-Emptive Rights in the Disposition of a Confiscated Estate—Philipsburgh Manor, New York," *WMQ*, 3rd Ser., XXII (July, 1965), 440. On the Philipse Highland Patent in 1768 rents were

A rent of one-tenth of a farm's yield does not seem excessive, particularly since payments frequently fell far behind and many landlords —if Henry Beekman was any example—were somewhat casual about collections. Beekman never seemed quite sure what was owed him, and he often took his tenants' word on that score. "Johannes Dollson blive is honest," he wrote his rent collector in 1744, "& Say what paid & what not." And again, regarding William Henry's rent, "I blive may have paid more than I can find Credited"; in another case, the tenant "may have paid part," Beekman conjectured, "but I know not to hoo." William Smith, Jr., believed that the "tenths" on Livingston Manor and Rensselaerswyck were "neither exacted nor paid." [26]

But if the *cost* of leasing land in New York does not appear unreasonable, there were other aspects of both the "fee simple" and the term leases that were distinctly burdensome. The most onerous restriction pertained to alienation fees, those fees charged at the time of resale of the lease, when the tenant was usually required to pay the landlord one-quarter or one-third the going price of his farm. This practice, which became known as the "quarter-sale," was described by Richard Smith, a visitor to Philipse Manor in 1769. "The tenant for Life here tells me he pays to Col. Philips only £7, per Annum for about 200 acres of Land & thinks it an extravagent Rent," Smith reported, "because, on his demise or Sale, his Son or Vendee is obliged to pay to the Landlord one Third of the Value of the Farm for a Renewal of the Lease." Philip Schuyler believed this was the most profitable way to manage lands, since in the "course of a few years, from the frequent transmutations of tenants, the alienation fines would exceed the purchase of the fee-simple, though sold at a high valuation." [27]

---

given in pounds and shillings. "List of Tenants on Lott no. 8 Belonging to Mrs. Margret Philipse," May, 1768, Philipse-Gouverneur Land Titles, CU. Oliver DeLancey leased a 200-acre lot in 1767 for £10 per annum. Misc. MSS, DeLancey, 49, NYHS.

[26] Henry Beekman to Henry Livingston, New York, Dec. 19, 1744, Jan. 7, 1745, Rhinebeck, Nov. 7, 1752, Henry Beekman MSS, NYHS; William Smith, *The History of the Late Province of New-York, From its Discovery, to the Appointment of Governor Colden, in 1762* (New York, 1830), I, 314. Regarding Dutchess County, McCracken says that debts were not taken seriously even though warrants were frequently sworn out for delinquents. *Old Dutchess Forever,* 218.

[27] Francis W. Halsey, ed., *A Tour of Four Great Rivers, The Hudson, Mohawk, Susquehanna and Delaware in 1769, Being the Journal of Richard Smith* (New

Another annoying restriction was the requirement that tenants take their crops to the landlord's mill for processing, thereby giving the proprietor a monopoly which allowed him to fix prices at will. From the turn of the eighteenth century on, grains—particularly wheat—were becoming the staple export of the colony, and the great proprietors now ran their domains as commercial enterprises. One of the most oppressive requirements was that tenants offer their landlords "first refusal" on their crops. Only if the proprietor chose not to buy could they then be sold on the open market. How widespread this practice was is difficult to determine, though a Dutchess County historian says it was a standard requirement in Beekman leases, and it clearly occurred on Livingston Manor. Philip Livingston instructed his overseer to enforce the rule, it being "our Right to have the Refusall of the wheat of our Tenants. . . ." On January 2, 1741, the free market price for wheat was three shillings/three pence and Livingston told his agent to "keep pace . . . [if you] cant gett it cheaper." Yet five days later Livingston was paying a flat three shillings, claiming that this was "as good as they do gett from others" and that the tenants should not "Sell it to others when I want the Same." Not surprisingly, there was dissatisfaction, and in February Livingston instructed his overseer that tenants who would not abide by the rule could "leave the manner." [28]

The "quarter-sale" and "first-refusal" privileges were probably the most nettlesome, but other restrictions added to the pressure. Most tenants were required to pay all taxes on their property, and in many cases landlords also made them responsible for quit-rents. Philip Livingston,

---

York, 1906, 1964), 5; Leonard, *Life of Charles Carroll,* 282, 284, quoted by Gerlach, *Philip Schuyler,* 61, n40. See also "Memoranda between Robert Livingston, Jr., Johannis Arkenbregh, and Peter Athuysen," Livingston Manor, March 7, 1753, and with Andries Shurts, Nov. 4, 1774, Misc. MSS, Livingston, Robert Livingston Folder, NYHS; Kim, "Manor of Cortlandt," 116–17; Gerlach, *Philip Schuyler,* 61–62. Also on the whole question of resale fees, see Mark, *Agrarian Conflicts,* 64, 67, 71–72. All leases provided for reentry for non-payment of rent, and if the lessor died, the land in many cases automatically reverted to the landlord.

[28] "Indenture between John Peter Lowry and Robert Livingston, [Jr.]," March 19, 1760, Philip Livingston to John DeWitt, Albany, Jan. 2, Jan. 7, Feb. 10, 1741, Livingston-Redmond MSS, Reels 6 and 7; Mark, *Agrarian Conflicts,* 51, 56, 64, 67; Gerlach, *Philip Schuyler,* 62; McCracken, *Old Dutchess Forever,* 39–40. Staughton Lynd says Gilbert Livingston's leases required that his tenants' grain be ground at his mill and that he be offered first refusal. *Anti-Federalism in Dutchess County,* 41.

who along with his son Robert Livingston, Jr., was particularly fastidi-
ous about landlord rights, even tried to get his tenants to share the expenses of a manor election. He recommended to his overseer that
"What is Expended in Liquor . . . charge to the Manor that it may be
paid out of the Tax [.] Its not Just I Should bear that Charge alone." [29]

All these demands and restraints combined to relegate tenant
farmers to a subordinate position on the manors and patents of New
York. That a man with sufficient means would avoid tenant status if he
could has been attested many times over. Governor Hunter saw in 1710
that the great landholders would have difficulty getting tenants "in a
Country where the Property may be had at so easy Rates," and Cadwallader Colden perceived the issue clearly when he said that "the hopes of
having land of their own & becoming independent of Landlords is what
chiefly induces people into America. . . ." And indeed, settlement on
the great patents did proceed very slowly in the early years. In 1701
Livingston Manor had only "4 or 5 cottagers," Philipse Manor had
about "20 families," and the Manor of Cortlandt had only about "4 or
5" tenant families. Henry Beekman's lands in Dutchess County apparently had a few settlers in the Rhinebeck area.[30]

Yet if an aversion to tenant status was a dominant theme among
New York farmers, it appears not to have been the only one. Something
is needed to account for the substantial increase of population on the
Hudson Valley manors and patents during the eighteenth century. In
1720 Rensselaerswyck had at least eighty-one heads of families; the
northern part of Livingston manor had twenty-eight, a number that
would increase rapidly as the century progressed; and by the end of the
colonial period Philipse Manor would have over 270 families.[31] What

[29] Philip Livingston to John DeWitt, Albany, March 17, 1741, Livingston-Redmond MSS, Reel 7; Mark, *Agrarian Conflicts,* 68–69.

[30] Gov. Hunter to Lords of Trade, Nov. 14, 1710, *N.Y. Col. Docs.,* V, 180; Colden to Micajah Perry, n.d., copy, NYHS *Colls.,* LI (1918), 32; Colden to Board
of Trade, New York, May 15, 1761, NYHS *Colls.,* IX (1876), 82; Earl of Bellomont to Lords of Trade, Jan. 2, 1701, *N.Y. Col. Docs.,* IV, 822–23; Philip L.
White, *The Beekmans of New York in Politics and Commerce, 1647–1877* (New
York, 1956), 161.

[31] *N.Y. Doc. Hist.,* I, 244–46; Reubens, "Pre-Emptive Rights . . . Philipsburgh
Manor," 438. If John DeLancey's estimate in 1769 that one-third of the population of Westchester County lived on manors is correct, that would amount to
about six thousand people. See *Assembly Journal* (Buel), Nov. 22, 1769.

induced these farmers to accept tenant status, and did they look upon it as a degrading subordination? Or were there benefits in the leasing system that have been obscured by most studies of New York's land practices?

3. A Favorable View of Tenancy

Many settlers came to America with enough cash to buy a small farm and establish an immediate independency. Others, destitute when they arrived, nonetheless cherished high expectations in what William Smith, Jr., called "the best poor mans country in the world." [32] If the impoverished immigrant had no trade, he turned naturally to farming, but his dream was to till his own land rather than turn his labor to the benefit of someone else. In this respect his interests coincided with those of New York's great landholders. Throughout the eighteenth century the patentees were periodically told by imperial authorities to settle and improve their estates if they wished to retain title. And the patentees, accordingly, sought to make tenant farming as attractive as possible to landless newcomers.

The sort of inducements offered may be inferred from the terms of one of Philip Livingston's leases for the land he was developing north of Albany. In 1737 Livingston leased a farm to two Palatines whom he first had "ransomed" for "42 pistoles," apparently the amount of their outstanding debts. According to Livingston's description the lease ran "for two lives. 9 years [rent] free and after that to pay half Stiple wheat per Morgan but I Supply them with Provisions for 12 months With 3 horses & 2 Cows all to pay again when they are Able." As Livingston put it, "these Conditions are favorable [.] What induces me to do it is that I think to Prevail on one of them to go to Germany next Year after he has seen the land to Incourage a good Number to Come Over to settle our Lands." It was not at all unusual for landlords to lease land

---

[32] William Smith, Jr., *Information to Emigrants, Being the Copy of a LETTER from a Gentleman in North-America: Containing a full and particular Account of the Terms on which Settlers may procure Lands in North-America, particularly in the Provinces of New-York and Pensilvania* (Glasgow, 1774), 5.

rent-free for the first few years in order to attract settlers. Livingston Manor leases regularly offered from three to seven years free rent; James Duane let farms with no rent for from five to ten years; and Philip Schuyler often did not collect rent until after the first five years when the land had started to return a profit to the tenant.[33] Considering that landlords often started new lessees off with dwellings, livestock, wagons, and tools, tenancy must in any case have been something of a boon to those without means to purchase farms at the outset.

The few families on Livingston Manor in 1701 were described as "too poor to be farmers having not wherewithall to buy Cattle to stock a farm," and those on Philipse and Cortlandt manors at about the same time were also known to be "poor people." Many of the tenants after 1712 were impoverished Palatine Germans cast adrift when Governor Hunter's naval stores program failed. Sometimes a number of people would immigrate together, as when seventeen "high-land families" took up leases on Livingston Manor in 1741, to the delight of Philip Livingston, who knew "its no Easy matter to gett 17 families at once." In another examplé "a Number of Irish Families . . . who are able to pay their Passage & settle themselves but not able to buy Lands" were hoping to locate a "Large Tract w[h]ere they may settle on a perpetual Rent." [34] For these people, tenancy apparently offered sufficient advantages to offset the restrictions imposed by the landlords.

The benefits of leasing are discussed by St. John de Crèvecoeur in Number III of his *Letters from an American Farmer*. Though he describes the system as it existed in Pennsylvania, Crèvecoeur also lived for a time in New York, and he must have been familiar with similar practices in that colony. Crèvecoeur tells the story of Andrew, a Scot from the Isle of Barra in the Hebrides, who arrived in Pennsylvania

---

[33] Philip Livingston to Jacob Wendell, New York, Oct. 17, 1737, draft, Livingston Papers, Philip Livingston Box, MCNY; Mark, *Agrarian Conflicts,* 73; Gerlach, *Philip Schuyler,* 61–62; Higgins, *Expansion in New York,* 4.

[34] Earl of Bellomont to Lords of Trade, Jan. 2, 1701, *N.Y. Col. Docs.,* IV, 822–23; "Petition of Jacob Sharpe etc. in Behalf of the Palatines in The Manor of Livingston," June 13, 1724, *N.Y. Col. Hist.,* III, 430–31; Philip Livingston to John DeWitt, Albany, Mar. 5, 1741, Livingston-Redmond MSS, Reel 7; Robert R. Livingston to Robert Livingston [of Clermont], June 7, 1764, Robert R. Livingston Coll., Box I, NYHS; White, *Beekmans of New York,* 162.

during the third quarter of the eighteenth century with a wife, one child, and eleven and a half guineas in cash. For the first year Andrew worked as a common farm laborer, but desiring to "have land of his own" he asked Crèvecoeur's assistance in finding a small farm to purchase. A landowning friend of Crèvecoeur's, a Mr. A. V., was approached, but as the latter did not wish to sell, it was suggested that Andrew and his family take up a lease. "I will lease them an hundred acres for any term of years you please," Mr. A. V. told Crèvecoeur, "and make it more valuable to your Scotchman than if he was possessed of the fee simple. By that means he may, with what little money he has, buy a plough, a team and some stock; he will not be incumbered with debts and mortgages; what he raises will be his own." The farm was described as "good arable land, that shall be laid out along a new road; there is a bridge already erected on the creek that passes through the land, and a fine swamp of about twenty acres." The lease provided that "the first seven years you shall pay no rent, whatever you sow and reap, and plant and gather, shall be entirely your own . . . the remaining part of the time you must give me twelve dollars and an half a year; and that is all you will have to pay me. Within the first three years you must plant fifty apple trees, and clear seven acres of swamp within the first part of the lease . . . The term of the lease shall be thirty years. . . . If ever you are dissatisfied with the land, a jury of your own neighbourhood shall value all your improvements, and you shall be paid agreeably to their verdict. You may sell the lease, or if you die, you may previously dispose of it, as if the land was your own."

Crèvecoeur viewed the results of these negotiations with obvious satisfaction. "Here then is honest Andrew, invested with every municipal advantage they confer; become a freeholder [sic], possessed of a vote, of a place of residence, a citizen of the province of Pennsylvania. Andrew's original hopes and the distant prospects he had formed in the island of Barra, were at the eve of being realised." And, if Crèvecoeur is accurate, Andrew was so overcome by the turn in his fortune that it "took him above a week before he could be sure, that without disturbing any money he could possess lands." [35]

[35] Crèvecoeur, *Letters from an American Farmer* (New York, 1912), 78–83.

Crèvecoeur listed the value of Andrew's property after four years as follows: [36]

	Dollars
The value of his improvements and lease	225
Six cows, at 13 dollars	78
Two breeding mares	50
The rest of the stock	100
Seventy-three bushels of wheat	66
Money due to him on notes	43
Pork and beef in his cellar	28
Wool and flax	19
Ploughs and other utensils of husbandry	31
2401. Pennsylvania currency—dollars	640

Whether Andrew sold his lease at that time in order to purchase land of his own, Crèvecoeur does not say, but had he done so, he would have been following a pattern that was quite familiar throughout the middle colonies.

There is considerable evidence, indeed, that tenant farmer mobility was fairly high, that many farmers, much like Crèvecoeur's Andrew, leased land for a period of years while accumulating enough profits to purchase land in their own right. Robert R. Livingston claimed that "a Men [Man] seldom sits down on a Piece of Land a Whole Year, before he is able to dispose of his Improvement for £50, or 100£ and sometimes for much more." Future studies might thus give to tenant farming a very different aspect from those that assumed to be dealing with a more or less permanent peasantry. A check of seventeenth-century Van Rensselaer leases shows a considerable turnover even that early, a typical case being that of Thomas Chambers, who leased a farm from 1647 to 1654, thence moving to Esopus (Kingston), where he had bought his own land on June 5, 1652. Another suggestion of this comes from Henry Beekman's rent lists and correspondence, which often mentioned that leases had been or were about to be sold. Philip Schuyler's comment on the frequency with which leases changed hands has already

[36] *Ibid.*, 86.

been noted. In his study of the Manor of Cortlandt, Kim is impressed by the way in which tenancy facilitated mobility, and he concludes that on the whole tenants were just as "bourgeois-minded" as their land-lords. In one sample group of Cortlandt leases, nearly half were sold with improvements after an average period of little over ten years.[37] In a "List of Tenants on Lott no. 8 Belonging to Mrs. Margret Philipse" on the Highland Patent in Dutchess County, a comparison of the names of the farmers holding the initial leases with those in possession in 1768 (when the list was made) shows that about half the farms had changed hands at least once.[38]

Let us assume that such evidence is as yet too fragmentary to be more than indicative. But if further investigation should show that most leaseholders viewed tenancy as a temporary condition—as a way station on the road to an independency—this might invite a reconsideration of the old view that New York tenant farmers constituted an oppressed class.

4. The Causes of Agrarian Unrest

But if tenancy in colonial New York was not the New World form of villeinage that has sometimes been depicted, the land riots of the late colonial period still require an explanation. If they were not tenant up-risings against oppressive landlords, why did they occur? An alternative

[37] McAnear, ed., "Robert R. Livingston's Reasons Against a Land Tax," 90; van Laer, *Van Rensselaer Bowier Manuscripts,* 755–56; Henry Beekman to Henry Livingston, New York, Dec. 19, 1744, Jan. 7, 1745, Feb. 2, 1749, Henry Beek-man MSS, NYHS; Henry Beekman to Henry Livingston, March 13, 1752, *Year-book* of the Dutchess County Historical Society, 1921, p. 37; Kim, "Manor of Cortlandt," 191–96, 269, and for lease turnover, 200–1.

[38] The Philipse records give little indication as to when those farms were initially "run out," an exception being Moss Kent's 118-acre farm (#47), which was leased for a yearly rent of £8 on August 1, 1766. Lease between Philip Philipse and Moss Kent, Aug. 1, 1766, Philipse-Gouverneur Land Titles, CU. This collection was re-catalogued in 1969 and therefore items will be identified by calendar listing rather than by the old folder numbers. Regarding the "List of Tenants," May, 1768, Philipse-Gouverneur Land Title, CU, a certain amount of caution may be advisable, as some of the farmers listed as initial tenants may have been ejected at the time of the re-bellion of 1766. See Mark, *Agrarian Conflicts,* 133 n6.

formula has been suggested by scholars who have studied this problem in a sectional context, and who have found that "the land system of New York and the expansive forces of New England" [39] were the true catalyzing agents of New York's small farmer uprisings in the second half of the eighteenth century.

It has already been noted that people of Dutch descent made up by far the largest part of the upriver population, and it was farmers of that stock who first took up leases on the great Hudson Valley patents. A 1709 tax list for Rensselaerswyck, probably the most populous patent in the early years, shows that the great majority of tenants were of Dutch extraction. New York landlords expressed a distinct preference for Dutch or German tenants; they were regarded as more "industrious" farmers than New Englanders, who "usually just raise stock." [40] The New York Dutch, moreover, appear to have been generally disposed to accept the restrictions imposed upon tenants by the landlords, and on the whole life was peaceful on the Hudson Valley estates in the early decades of the eighteenth century. Dutch tenants, according to Dixon Ryan Fox, were "not inclined to agitation"; [41] nor was it, indeed, the Dutch who initiated the struggle against the New York patentees. The true source of that turbulence lay in another direction altogether. It was not a movement for reform from within but an attack from without, threatening the privileged position—and in some cases the aristocratic pretensions—of the Hudson Valley landed elite.

It is of crucial significance that all the estates experiencing tenant conflicts were located on the east bank of the Hudson River and had contiguous borders with the New England colonies of Massachusetts and Connecticut. [42] When migrating New Englanders began their push to the west, the lands they came upon first were those owned by the New York patentees, and this fact of geography provides the first clue to the fundamental nature of the New York land conflicts. New York, as

---

[39] Handlin, "Eastern Frontier," 50. Besides Handlin, Dixon Ryan Fox offers a sectional interpretation in *Yankees and Yorkers*.

[40] "Tax List of the Manor of Rensselaerswyck," 1709, Livingston-Redmond MSS, Reel 9; Philip Livingston to Jacob Wendell, Albany, Feb. 27, 1740, March 16, 1741, Livingston Papers, Philip Livingston Box, MCNY.

[41] Fox. *Yankees and Yorkers*, 142.

[42] See map, p. 187.

Dixon Ryan Fox put it, "was in the way of the New England swarm."
In the beginning, New York had no difficulty accommodating the flow
out of New England, for there was good land available for lease or purchase in parts of Westchester, Dutchess, and Albany counties, and
across the river in Orange and Ulster as well. But by about 1740 this
situation had changed, and "there was very little unpatented land in the
Hudson Valley south of Albany, or along the banks of the Mohawk." [43]
At the very time that unclaimed land was becoming scarce, moreover,
the movement of New Englanders to the west took a sharp increase. A
combination of exhausted soil and black stem-rust, which was infecting
wheat in Connecticut and Massachusetts, forced many families to move
on in search of better land. The ensuing "perpetual emigration," as
Mrs. Grant called it, from New England into New York helped swell
the population of the east bank counties. Dutchess County's population
more than doubled between 1737 and 1749, while the more densely settled county of Westchester increased by nearly 50 per cent. Albany's
population in the 1740's was held down by fears engendered by the
third inter-colonial war, but between 1749 and 1756 that county grew
from a population of around 10,000 to over 17,500. [44]

Decades of experience with township government and with land
policies quite different from those of New York had conditioned these
migrating New Englanders to the habit of private ownership of property
and had instilled in them a strong self-confidence. Upon reaching the
Hudson Valley, the newcomers, with characteristic energy, set about to
change the system they found in ways that might better suit their preferences. This New England élan, since admiringly ascribed to the "Puritan Ethic" or the "Yankee Spirit," was seen in a different light by colonial New Yorkers. The Hudson Valley patricians, long accustomed to
the more deferential habits of their Dutch and German tenants, found

[43] Fox, *Yankees and Yorkers,* x; Higgins, *Expansion in New York,* 70. This
shortage of patentable land continued until after the close of the French and Indian War, when new lands were opened to settlement. Higgins, *Expansion in
New York,* Chap. VIII.

[44] Anne Grant, *Memoirs of an American Lady* (New York, 1901), II, 137; Bidwell and Falconer, *History of Agriculture,* 92–94; Evarts B. Greene and Virginia
D. Harrington, *American Population before the Federal Census of 1790* (New
York, 1932), 98–101; and Richard L. Bushman, *From Puritan to Yankee* (Cambridge, Mass., 1967), 83–84.

the New Englanders an alien and abrasive people. Their aggressiveness seemed to spring from an excess of republican zeal, and more than once they were characterized as "levellers." Lewis Morris, Jr., sought to shield his son, Gouverneur, from the taint of New England ideas by specifying in his will that the boy was not to be educated in Connecticut "lest he should imbibe in his youth that low craft and cunning so incident to the People of that Colony" and "interwoven in their Constitutions." James Duane feared the New Englanders would "spread over the whole continent," disturbing "the political and religious principles . . . of their Neighbors." Even the generally temperate Anne Grant lost her restraint in sketching the character of the New Englanders, whom she described as "conceited . . . litigious. . . . vulgar [and] insolent." "They flocked indeed so fast, to every unoccupied spot, that their malignant and envious spirit, their hatred of subordination . . . began to spread like a taint of infection." Moreover, she declared, "all tendencies to elegance or refinement were despised as leading to aristocracy." [45]

To be sure, not every New Englander who crossed into New York brought trouble. Some became ordinary tenants on the New York patents, and many stopped only briefly before moving on into New Jersey and Pennsylvania. A sizeable number, however, including land speculators supported by the Massachusetts General Court, pursued a different course, and it was this group which eventually forced a direct showdown with the landed grandees of Albany, Dutchess, and Westchester counties. Several factors were working in the New Englanders' favor, each of which suggests that the landlords' position was far more vulnerable than has usually been supposed.

In the first place, the great patents of the Hudson Valley had been

[45] Morris's will is in NYHS *Colls.*, XXX (1897), 171–74; James Duane to Robert Livingston, [Jr.], New York, May 29, 1773, Livingston-Redmond MSS, Reel 6; Grant, *Memoirs,* II, 137–38; Mark, *Agrarian Conflicts,* 99–100, 137, 140. As Mark points out, Mrs. Grant's opinion of New Englanders was undoubtedly influenced by her father's loss to New England squatters of a 4,000-acre plot in the New Hampshire Grants region. Duane, too, lost some of his land in a dispute with New England claimants. Prior to that time, his overseer on the Duanesburgh Patent northeast of Albany told of his efforts to get each tenant family to supply one man for occasional help at the saw mill. The tenants called a meeting and then turned down the proposal: "Their whole fear was, drawing their Posterity into Bondage. Silly People!" John McFarland to James Duane, Duanesburgh, Dec. 21, 1771, James Duane Papers, NYHS.

under attack from imperial officials since the end of the seventeenth century. The notorious land-jobbing of Governor Benjamin Fletcher (1692–1698), who granted away hundreds of thousands of choice acres during his tenure, had stimulated the first imperial effort to purge New York land policies of their inequities. Fletcher's successor, the Earl of Bellomont (1698–1701), was instructed to restrict grants and to oblige patentees to plant and improve all lands "within the space of three years" or be subject to forfeiture. And had Bellomont been given his head, he would have broken all land patents above 1,000 acres. He soon realized, however, that this would be impossible unless the Board of Trade were willing to "send over a good Judge or two and a smart active Atturny Generall" as well as "a peremptory order from the King." Such measures, as it turned out, London was not yet prepared to take.[46] Accordingly, Bellomont's efforts at reform were suffered to lapse, and many of the great landowners retained their massive holdings.

The attention of the Board of Trade had nonetheless been directed to the problem. New York governors were thereafter instructed to limit land grants to a maximum of 2,000 acres, to require that the land be systematically improved, and to provide for the collection of quit-rents. Enforcement varied with each governor. Hunter and Burnet observed their instructions scrupulously, though many of the others, especially Cornbury (1702–1708), Cosby (1732–1736), and Clarke (1736–1743), enforced the rules loosely, if at all. A favorite evasion was the patenting of land to dummy partners, who would subsequently turn over their shares to a single owner. By this means a few very large tracts were

[46] Bellomont had been astonished and dismayed on his arrival to discover that three-quarters of the province was "in the hands of ten or eleven men," and he had briefly gained the cooperation of the colonial Assembly in annulling several of Fletcher's most extravagant grants, including the Dellius, Evans, and Bayard patents. After this auspicious start, which incidentally helped to even some old Leislerian scores for several Assemblymen, the zeal of the "reforming" Assembly quickly began to flag. Bellomont suspected the reason: other owners of "unmeasurable grants, fancie I shall push at them the next time. . . ." "Instructions from the Lords Justices to the Earl of Bellomont," Nov. 10, 1698, *N.Y. Col. Docs.*, IV, 424–25; Earl of Bellomont to the Lords of Trade, Boston, May 29, 1699, *ibid.*, 528–29, and 384, 392; Bellomont to Board of Trade, April 27, 1699, New York, May 3, 1699, *ibid.*, 510, 514, 535, 553–54. John C. Rainbolt, "A 'great and usefull designe': Bellomont's Proposal for New York, 1698–1701," *New-York Historical Society Quarterly*, LIII (Oct., 1969), 333–51.

carved out in the eighteenth century. On the whole, however, the trend was toward more moderate-sized holdings, often jointly owned by a number of speculators.[47]

One of the most persistent advocates of a more equitable land policy was the surveyor general, Cadwallader Colden. In 1721 Colden recommended that New York make "a Resurvey of the Province," following the example of Virginia and Pennsylvania, in order to open some uncultivated parts of the great estates to settlement. The power of the landholders was once again sufficient to bury the plan. But Colden and others continued to press for reform, it being obvious that the presence of good land lying vacant and unproductive would sorely try the self-restraint of land-hungry settlers. "A Stranger," Colden wrote, "could not believe that some men in this Province own above two hundred thousand Acres of Land each which neither they nor their Great Grand Children can hope to Improve. . . ."[48] Just as Colden predicted, even by mid-century large sections of the great patents had not been settled, there never being sufficient numbers of farmers willing to accept tenant

[47] Typical of the Board of Trade's point of view during this period are articles 36, 37, and 38 of Gov. Montgomerie's instructions which stated, "Whereas It has in all times Been a very Great Hindrance to the peopling & Settling of our said province, that large tracts of land have been Ingrossed by Particular Persons, A Great Part whereof remain Uncultivated. . . . to provide against so great an Evil for the future" grants were to be limited to 2,000 acres per person, quit-rents were to be collected, and patentees were "to plant Settle and effectually Cultivate, at least three Acres of Land for every fifty Acres, within three years, after the Same shall be so granted, Upon penalty of forfeiture of every Such Grant." "Governor Montgomeries Instructions," Oct. 20, 1727, NYHS, *Colls.,* L (1917), 210–11. One of the difficulties with enforcement was the conflict of interest inherent in administrative procedures, for one of the governor's key fringe benefits was the fees he earned processing land grants during his tenure. Higgins, *Expansion in New York,* 30–31. Also, government officials at all levels used their positions to acquire personal landed estates, without necessarily being tainted with corruption. "They considered themselves, and were considered to be, men of integrity, and they were merely following the customs of the day in reaching out for and building up their estates." Edith M. Fox, *Land Speculation in the Mohawk Country* (Ithaca, 1949), 4. As the Fox study reveals, some officials exceeded the bounds of propriety, even by the standards of the time.

[48] "Representation of Cadwallader Colden . . . to Gov. Burnet. . . ," Nov., 1721, NYHS *Colls.,* LXVII (1934), 164; Colden, "The Second Part of the Interest of the Country in Laying Duties," 1726, draft, NYHS *Colls.,* LXVIII (1935), 268. Colden was not opposed to land speculation or to moderate-sized estates (his own estate, Coldengham, was about 3,000 acres), but the presence of enormous uncultivated tracts disturbed him, as it did many others.

status. Those willing to take leases were settled first on land nearest the Hudson River, where transportation was available; as additional tenants arrived, the area of cultivation gradually spread eastward. Nonetheless, some of the patents were so vast that the most easterly lands bordering the New England colonies were virtually untouched, being used only for grazing and wood-cutting, if at all. It was these lands, obviously fertile and temptingly vacant, which first met the covetous gaze of westward-migrating New Englanders.

A second challenge to the New York landowners, particularly with respect to their title over the easternmost lands, was that presented by conflicting border claims. The colonies of Connecticut and Massachusetts claimed lands on their western borders which were regarded by New York as clearly within her own eastern boundary. Various joint commissions were set up to arbitrate these disputes, with results that were usually favorable to New York. The Connecticut–New York boundary was more or less settled in 1725 and 1731, when lines were run approximately twenty miles east of the Hudson. Some settlers from Ridgefield and other western Connecticut villages nonetheless continued to encroach on the Oblong Patent, which encompassed equivalent lands surrendered by Connecticut when the line was established. Far more disturbing was the conflict that erupted between New York and Massachusetts. The charters of the two colonies included overlapping claims that were especially contradictory in the section forming the eastern boundaries of Livingston Manor and Van Rensselaer lands in Albany County. It was not until nearly mid-century, when the line of Massachusetts settlement reached the western borderlands, that the rivalry over these lands broke into the open. Here it was the General Court that was most adamant in pressing Massachusetts' claims. The General Court encouraged the laying out of townships west of the Housatonic River, and sent agents and land speculators into the disputed area in an effort to preempt title by prior settlement. After 1750 the agents extended their activities inside the borders of Livingston and Van Rensselaer lands, with the apparent purpose of seducing manor tenants with Massachusetts deeds and thereby further strengthening Massachusetts' claim to title.[49]

[49] Handlin, "Eastern Frontier," 51–52, 54–57; Fox, *Yankees and Yorkers,* 141–46; Mark, *Agrarian Conflicts,* 116. As Fox points out, it was not until the

Questions of title were further complicated by the old problem of unextinguished Indian claims. Some of these difficulties arose over the Indians' culturally conditioned inability to grasp the concept of private property, but more often they resulted from the corrupt practices of the white man. Many New York grandees are known to have engaged in fraudulent, or at least questionable, land dealings with the Indians. The techniques included the familiar lavish hospitality and free flow of spirits; the obtaining of deeds from one or two hand-picked sachems when the approval of the tribal council was required; and—probably the most common of all—the stretching of boundaries by intentional misreading of their vague terms. It was claimed in a lawsuit, for example, that Adolph Philipse added over 190,000 acres to his Highland Patent by omitting to mention a marked tree which delimited one side of his patent in the original deed. The Livingstons, Van Rensselaers, and others used similar devices.[50] This stretching of boundaries was made easier by the government's failure to devise a program of orderly purchase, and by the haphazard manner in which boundaries were described in the deeds. The impermanent nature of some of the designated limits—a "heap of Stones," or a "marked tree"—opened the way for much chicanery. In a deed between one Indian tribe and Cornelius Van Rensselaer, the land was described as "beginning at the beaver creek, going on northward, to the great fallen plane tree, where our tribe slept last summer; then eastward, to the three great cedars on the hillock; then westward, strait to the wild duck swamp; and strait on from the swamp to the turn in the beaver creek where the old dam was." That conflicting interpretations should arise after the decease of the last elders who remembered exactly where the tribe had slept, or where the old dam had stood, might have been anticipated. Mrs. Grant was struck by the num-

---

twentieth century that the Connecticut–New York border was finally settled. *Yankees and Yorkers,* 138–39.

[50] Handlin, "Eastern Frontier," 52–53; Higgins, *Expansion in New York,* 83–87, 103–4; Allen W. Trelease, *Indian Affairs in Colonial New York: The Seventeenth Century* (Ithaca, N.Y. 1960), 62–64, 330–31, 337–40; Lawrence H. Leder, *Robert Livingston, 1654–1728, and the Politics of Colonial New York* (Chapel Hill, 1961), 32–35; Mark, *Agrarian Conflicts,* 32–41, 133–35, 155–58. Like his father, Philip Livingston used his position as Indian commissioner at Albany to buy lands from the Indians. Philip Livingston to Jacob Wendell, Albany, May 10, 1739, Livingston Papers, Philip Livingston Box, MCNY.

ber of lawsuits which stemmed from clouded titles in New York, "where all conversation begun to be infected with litigious cant." [51]

The landlords' position was made still more precarious after 1750 by the increasingly unsympathetic attitude of the imperial government. It will be recalled that New York Colony was the subject of a "white paper" in 1751. Though land policies were not specifically discussed in it, there was a general tightening of administrative procedures after that time. When the new governor, Danvers Osborne, was sent to New York in 1753 his instructions included no fewer than six articles which dealt in one form or another with land matters. The upper limit on individual grants was reduced from 2,000 to 1,000 acres, the quit-rent of two shillings/six pence per hundred acres was to be enforced, and great emphasis was placed on the systematic settlement and improvement of patented land. After deploring the continued existence of large grants which obstructed the "settling and improving the Province," the government directed Osborne to "enquire into the state of these Grants, and to take all lawful methods for vacating them. . . ." [52] After Osborne's death the implementation of this policy fell to Acting Governor James DeLancey. With characteristic diplomacy DeLancey made no direct attempt to break any existing patents. He pressed the Council instead to strengthen his power to collect quit-rents, on the ground that this would "compell those who hold large Tracts of uncultivated Lands, to a speedy Settlement." DeLancey also evolved a plan whereby township settlement would be stressed in future land patents. It "tends to make a Country strong," he told the Assembly, to have lands "speedily and closely settled." [53]

The imperial government was naturally chary about launching direct assaults on the privileges and property of leading New York citi-

[51] Grant, *Memoirs,* II, 152–53, 155; Mark, *Agrarian Conflicts,* 36.

[52] Osborne's instructions are in "Representation of the Lords of Trade to the King," Whitehall, July 5, 1753, *N.Y. Col. Docs.,* VI, 788–91 (see especially articles 56 and 59). Extracts of the two key articles are also included in Colden's papers, NYHS *Colls.,* LXVIII (1935), 125–26, and were inserted among the official land papers, *Calendar of New York Colonial Manuscripts Indorsed Land Papers; in the Office of the Secretary of State of New York, 1643–1803* (Albany, 1864), 280. For the "white paper" report see p. 163 above.

[53] "James DeLancey to the Council," New York, Oct. 29, 1754, DeLancey Papers, 2, MCNY; *Assembly Journal* (Gaine), II, Aug. 22, 1754. The collection of quit-rents was tightened in 1755. *Laws,* III, 1107–21.

zens. But when clear legal questions regarding title arose, the Crown co-operated in pressing them in the courts. The government's strongest stand was taken in a 1767 case, *King* v. *Van Rensselaer,* which challenged Van Rensselaer's title to a part of the family estate in Albany County. Other grandees were much alarmed, it being apparent that the Crown "seem determined to have a part of that Tract," and that it would cost Van Rensselaer considerable to defend his title in court. "Madness," according to Judge Robert R. Livingston, "seems to prevail on the other side of the water; melancholy & dejection on this. The order to try the Renssalaers' title seems to be a fire that endangers every neighbor." [54] The Crown lost the case before the New York Supreme Court, which may have been inevitable in view of the ties between the New York judiciary and the landed families. Yet in none of this was there much encouragement for the owners of great landed estates in New York.[55] Nor would there be much from either the government or

[54] Peter R. Livingston to Robert Livingston, [Jr.], New York, Sept. 5, 1767, Livingston-Redmond MSS, Reel 6; Robert R. Livingston to Robert Livingston [of Clermont?], Sept. 18, 1767, Robert R. Livingston Papers, Bancroft Transcripts, NYPL; New-York *Gazette; and The Weekly Mercury,* Nov. 14, 1768; Julius Goebel, Jr., and T. Raymond Naughton, *Law Enforcement in Colonial New York: A Study in Criminal Procedure, 1664–1776* (New York, 1944), 249–55, 665, 668; Gerlach, *Philip Schuyler,* 72–73. The case arose when a French and Indian War veteran named Campbell discovered that a tract of land he had obtained as a bonus at the time of his discharge was subject to conflicting claims by John Van Rensselaer. The Crown took Campbell's side in the suit. The lands involved in this suit also were invaded by New England squatters. Gov. Francis Bernard to Gov. Henry Moore, Boston, Sept. 8, 1766, copy, Dec. 12, 1767, Jared Sparks MSS, Bernard Papers, V, 199–203, 246, Houghton Lib., Harvard. Robert R. Livingston noted that Surveyor General Colden's "enmity is most pointed at the landed interest. The suit against Mr. Rensselaer is to be at the King's expense & an appeal they tell me is directed; but in what manner I know not. Mr. Colden has furnished 12 folio pages against the Manor of Livingston occasioned by Robert's attack on the Oblong. . . ." Robert R. Livingston to Robert Livingston [of Clermont?], Sept. 18, 1767, Robert R. Livingston Papers, Bancroft Transcripts, NYPL.

[55] One of the members of the New York Supreme Court in 1767 was Robert R. Livingston, whom Gov. Moore described as one of the "greatest Landholders" in the province. Moore to the Earl of Hillsborough, New York, Jan. 21, 1769, *N.Y. Col. Docs.,* VIII, 148–49. For an interesting discussion of Cadwallader Colden's efforts to pursue a consistent policy regarding land and other matters which concerned Crown prerogatives, see Carole Shammas, "Cadwallader Colden and the Role of the King's Prerogative," *New-York Historical Society Quarterly,* LIII (April, 1969), 103–26.

the common law when it came to evicting the New Englanders who
were squatting in large numbers on the vacant fringes of the Hudson
Valley patents. Ejectment suits brought by the New York landlords
were often tried by the county courts where a favorable verdict might
be expected, but as Robert Livingston, Jr.'s lawyer pointed out, "the
Statute for Regulating the Proceedings of Justices in Regard to forcible
Entries . . . Required that the Party Grieved Prove the Actual Possession (that is Improved or Enclosed Possession). . . ." [56] Governor
Tryon's advice to Livingston in 1772 might be taken as some measure
of the extent to which the Crown had by then aligned itself with the
small farmers on this issue. Where title was in dispute, he said, squatters should not be ejected but "should continue in possession of the
Lands; [and] be no longer Prossicuted at the King's Sute," pending further instructions from London. [57]

So long as the landlords retained their political influence in the
Assembly and Council, and to the extent that they remained on good
terms with the governors, their interests were hardly in danger of being
swept away. And so long as they were strongly represented on the
courts that heard the land cases, the likelihood of wholesale revocations
of titles was most remote. Cadwallader Colden may have had his own
biases, but he was probably right when he said that "the Gentlemen of
the Law, both the Judges and the principal Practitioners at the Bar are

[56] Abraham Yates to Col. Robert Livingston, Jr., Albany, Dec. 4, 1766, Livingston-Redmond MSS, Reel 6. Efforts to locate the statute cited have been unavailing; other laws regarding trespass are contradictory, though they seem more often
to favor owners over squatters. *Laws*, I, 401–3, 473–74, 712, II, 206–14, V, 786.
To date we have no study of how such laws were actually enforced in New York.
Such information is more readily available for Massachusetts, however, and it
tends to support the view that title alone did not guarantee landowners' rights
against trespassers. *Moor* v. *Spencer*, Berkshire Common Pleas, Feb., 1769, p.
270; *Powers* v. *Powers*, Worcester Common Pleas, Dec., 1776, p. 457; *Spaulding*
v. *Green*, Middlesex Supreme Judicial Court, Oct., 1771. I am indebted to Professor Stanley N. Katz for sharing with me his knowledge of eighteenth-century law;
the Massachusetts case citations were kindly provided by William E. Nelson, who
is presently completing a dissertation on Massachusetts at Harvard University.

[57] James Duane to Robert Livingston, [Jr.], New York, June 2, 1768, Livingston-Redmond MSS, Reel 6; Robert Livingston, Jr., to James Duane, Livingston
Manor, Aug. 28, 1772, James Duane Papers, NYHS. In view of this it is little
wonder that so many New York farmers were Loyalists at the time of the Revolution.

either, Owners, Heirs or strongly connected in family Interest with the Proprietors." [58] But to the landlords themselves all this must have appeared in rather a different light as they saw the legitimacy of their position being steadily chipped at by such diverse elements in the life of the province. Their position was full of anomalies, and these added up to something a good deal short of feudal privilege.

5. A "Drove of Banditt Rovers"

Vacant lands, overlapping colonial boundaries, unextinguished Indian titles, and an unsympathetic government all conspired to make New York land titles among the most assailable in North America. It was hardly a wonder that the New Englanders should feel encouraged to challenge the New Yorkers' claims to the border area. Finding the eastern sections of the patents uninhabited, some New Englanders simply squatted in expectation that occupancy and use of the land would prove in the long run the strongest evidence of title. Though such squatters were to be found all along the border area by the middle of the eighteenth century, the first clashes occurred in the southern section where New Englanders moving westward were met by eastward-expanding tenants of the Dutchess County patentees.

From about 1749 on, Henry Beekman was plagued by disputes over his lands in the Beekman Patent and the Oblong. Because he deplored controversy and avoided it whenever he could, Beekman's first reaction to the squatters who began working vacant sections of his tenants' lands was that "I would thinck my Self obliged" to grant them leases. But his attitude hardened when four men, "John Monroe, Joseph Burch, Benjamin Burch and John Bradshaw . . . forceably Entered & have moved of[f] Capt. Bemes [a Beekman tenant] . . . in a riotious manner." Promising to "Stand by" Bemis and to "bear all Charges," Beekman prepared to defend his tenants and his lands. As colonel of the Dutchess County militia, he dispatched Captain Tenbroeck and some Poughkeepsie militiamen to act as his "Ambassadors," and they

[58] "Mr. Colden's Account of the State of the Province of New-York, New York," December 6, 1765, *N.Y. Col. Docs.*, VII, 796. For other comments by Colden of similar tenor, see NYHS *Colls.*, IX (1876), 231, and X (1877), 70.

in turn were met by an "Assambly of rioters" numbering "about 16—
mostly with Clobbs." After harsh and probably colorful words,
"Th[e]y parted Every one to his tents. O. Sumthing how Ever must be
don." Regarding his Oblong lands, Beekman wrote: "If [I] Could git
Honest Good Chaps, beter to Sell Sum part there then to be for Ever
plaged," and in at least two cases that was just what he did.[59] But the
"Drove of Banditt Rovers" continued their harassment, invading lands,
cutting timber, and in general creating "Great Havek." Beekman gave
his tenants permission to destroy the squatters' structures and to carry
off all cut wood, promising to "defend and Bear them harmless." Meanwhile, true to their "litigious" reputation, the New England squatters
began resorting to the local courts, and by the fall of 1751 Beekman
was seeing himself "Dayley heep't up with Showers of Law Suets." In
1752 the encroachers claimed some Dutchess County lands "under a
neuw fair field Right," to the further chagrin of the belabored Beekman.
"So . . . they Trump up more & more tytells against us." [60]

By 1753 several of Henry Beekman's own tenants were becoming restive, infected no doubt by the relentless pressure of the New Englanders. It is not clear whether these were long-term tenants or more recent arrivals from New England who had accepted leases from
Beekman, but judging from similar situations on other patents it was
probably the latter. In any event Beekman instructed his agent, Henry
Livingston, to tell his tenants to "pay their rent in arrear . . . or must
Expect I will re Enter in Default thereof: which if we had done from
the beginning, would [have] prevented these rebelions we now meet
with." On hearing that the Philipses were also pressing claims against
squatters on the Highland Patent, Beekman observed, "So . . . now
there is oppen war proclaimed & Each Side Shoe title." Though some-

[59] Henry Beekman to Henry Livingston, New York, Jan. 16, Aug. 16, Aug. 31,
Dec. 8, 1749. For Beekman land sales, see Beekman to Henry Livingston, New
York, n.d. [circa 1749], and Beekman to Henry Livingston, New York, Feb. 17,
1752. All of the above letters are in Henry Beekman MSS, NYHS. Cadwallader
Colden also had trouble with New Englanders encroaching on his tenants' land
in the Oblong. See letters and memos of Aug. 23, 24, Sept. 7, 9, Dec. 11, 26,
1749, NYHS *Colls.*, LIII (1920), 132–36, 139–40, 168–69, 179–80.

[60] Beekman to Henry Livingston, New York, Dec. 29, 1750, March 20, Oct. 10,
1751, Henry Beekman MSS, NYHS; Beekman to Henry Livingston, New York,
April 7, 1752, DCHS, *Yearbook,* 1921, pp. 37–38.

what premature, he proved to be right. In a few years Dutchess County would be the storm-center of the great riots of 1766, though it would be the Philipse Highland Patent rather than Beekman lands that would be the scene of most of that tumult. Beekman himself was very aged and long retired by then, and though the political career of his son-in-law and heir, Robert R. Livingston, suffered from the taint of "landlordism," the Beekman lands were largely spared in the 1766 upheavals. The relative tolerance and flexibility of Henry Beekman, and his willingness to sell off lands, may account for the comparative quiet which prevailed on his estates while great turbulence erupted elsewhere.[61]

Beekman's troubles around mid-century had a more exaggerated parallel on the Albany County estates of the Livingstons and the Van Rensselaers. There, too, manor life had been fairly placid until the tide of New England settlers began to overflow upon lands claimed by the New York proprietors. Agents of the General Court distributed Massachusetts deeds to settlers and made a concerted effort to discourage farmers from accepting leases or paying rents to the New York patentees, referred to by the General Court as "persons pretending titles as Patroons or Lords of Manors." Even after 1756, when the General Court was finally prevailed upon to withhold official sanction from the New England agents, the latter turned to the Stockbridge Indians, who never had surrendered their claims to much of eastern Albany County, and "bought" two-thirds of Livingston Manor from them.[62]

Robert Livingston, Jr., the third proprietor of the manor and a leading spokesman for the landlords, left a remarkably full record of the

[61] Beekman to Henry Livingston, New York, Jan. 9, 1753, Rhinebeck, Nov. 7, 1752, Henry Beekman MSS, NYHS. Apparently there were some disturbances on Beekman lands in 1766, but compared with those on adjacent patents they were relatively mild. William H. W. Sabine, ed., *Historical Memoirs from 16 March 1763 to 9 July 1776 of William Smith* (New York, 1956), 33; Mark, *Agrarian Conflicts,* 139. The same may also have been true on the Manor of Cortlandt, where some land was also sold. Kim, "Manor of Cortlandt," 93–103, 223–30.

[62] Massachusetts Bay General Court, *Acts and Resolves* . . . (Boston, 1907–13), Vol. XV, App. X, 313, quoted in Handlin, "Eastern Frontier," 61; Robert Livingston, Jr., to Peter V. B. Livingston, Livingston Manor, April 27, 1757, Rutherfurd Coll., III, 45, NYHS. Robert Livingston, Jr., reported in the above letter that "these people give me much trouble they have lately bought about ⅔ of my part of the mannor of the Stockbridge Indians. . . . I am determined to oppose it with all my might, be the Consiquence what it will."

riotous activities which took place in Albany County. He never doubted that the source of his troubles was New England, specifically the colony of Massachusetts. "I Shall look upon all the Blood that may be Spilt in this Affair," he wrote to his Boston friend Jacob Wendell, "to lay at the doors of your people as being the Contrivers and Supporters of it." [63] Here, as with the Beekman case, the word of all parties confirms that it was migrating New Englanders, rather than long-term tenants protesting rack-rent or insecurity of tenure,[64] who first sought to challenge the Hudson Valley landlords. Since the main instigators were not actually lease-holding tenants, but were either squatters or holders of rival Massachusetts or Indian deeds, New York's small farmer disorders do not qualify in the usual sense as "tenant rebellions," at least not until a later stage when a few of the long-term tenants cast in their lot with the New Englanders. Thus the contesting forces should be divided not into two groups, tenants and landlords, but rather into three: the landlords, the New England claimants, and the long-term New York tenants who held leases from the landlords.

The regular tenants, the great majority of whom were of Dutch and German origin, had up to mid-century managed to coexist with their landlords in relative harmony. If disturbed in the peaceful possession of their farms, they had been known to seek the protection of their landlords, who were expected to "redress the wrongs of such as pays rent and has leases under you. . . ." Although the tenants were apparently annoyed by some of the economic restrictions, and no doubt would have preferred to own their lands outright, there is no evidence that they believed rents were too high or that they contemplated violence against their landlords. The latter were nonetheless under no fond illusions. In 1752, Livingston reported that "this affair [of the Massachusetts intruders] gives me trouble, [and] makes my Tenants Insolent. . . ." A year later the situation had deteriorated further: "Those folks are Still daily troubleing me & my Tennents, Some of the Latter are Indeed near as

[63] Robert Livingston, Jr., to Jacob Wendell, Livingston Manor, Mar. 4, 1755, Livingston Papers, MCNY.

[64] Irving Mark believed that the Livingston Manor troubles stemmed from "small farmer dissatisfaction with tenure and rent," and that the leaders were Livingston tenants who were "advised by shrewd Massachusetts land grabbers. . . ." *Agrarian Conflicts*, 118–19.

bad as the N. England people. . . . I fear the Infection will very Soon
be general and then no man that has an Estate in this Province or perhaps in North America, will be Safe. . . ." Some of Livingston's tenants had attended a meeting called by the New England agents at which
"Boston government," that is, the invitation to accept Massachusetts
deeds, was cheered. To Livingston this represented "the utmost
Insolence." [65]

In the history of New York's small farmer conflicts it is often implied that "many" tenants turned against their landlords because of dissatisfaction with the terms of their leases. Again, the confusion on this
point arises in part because the term "tenant" has been applied too
broadly. Only those holding leases from the landlords fully qualify as
tenants; landlords sometimes gave squatters verbal permission to remain
on their property, and these people were sometimes called "tenants at
will." But they and the leaseholding tenants stood in very different categories. Livingston obviously feared that many of his regular tenants
would be enticed over to the enemy, especially with the Massachusetts
agents telling them they were "fools" to pay rent. In his view, "tho'
none of them have yett been so dareing as to Refuse paying," the instigators' efforts "are too dareing and dangerous in this young Country
w[h]ere there are many Tennents & no army to Quel in Case of an In-
surrection; they may at Last take it in their heads to rebell. . . ." [66] As
it turned out, however, only a "few" tenants were actually moved to
join the New Englanders. Two of these were Josiah Loomis, whose
fields Livingston destroyed in retribution, and Michael Hallenbeck, a
tenant of Dutch descent whom Livingston jailed as a riotous person in

[65] Uzziah Harvey to Philip Livingston, Feb. 8, 1735, Livingston-Redmond MSS,
Reel 5; Robert Livingston, Jr., to Jacob Wendell, New York, April 16, 1752, Livingston Papers, MCNY; Robert Livingston, Jr., to William Alexander, Livingston
Manor, Mar. 26, 1753, William Alexander Papers, I, NYHS. The people from
Sheffield, Massachusetts, were "daily Instilling prejudices in my tenants against
me," complained Livingston, "advising them not to pay me their Rents . . . and
many more Such Idle tales. . . ." Robert Livingston, Jr., to Jacob Wendell, Livingston Manor, April 12, 1753, Livingston Papers, MCNY. Most of the lease-
holding tenants on Livingston Manor had Dutch names; see sworn statements regarding the land disputes, 1753, Livingston-Redmond MSS, Reel 5.

[66] Robert Livingston, Jr., to Jacob Wendell, Livingston Manor, April 12, 1753,
Livingston Papers, MCNY; N.Y. Doc. Hist., III, 729; Mark, Agrarian Conflicts,
118, 124; Handlin, "Eastern Frontier," 55, 68.

the fall of 1753. A few months later a compromise was struck with Hallenbeck, and Livingston wrote his friend Wendell that the tenants close to Hallenbeck "do now Seem to be pretty Easey and I have all the reason in the world to believe they will Continue so if your folcks will but lett them alone." [67] Some other Livingston tenants nonetheless appear to have caused trouble. In 1755 Livingston wrote that he would have to punish six of them, which is the largest number mentioned in any of his correspondence. The ratio of disaffected tenants to New Englanders may to some extent be inferred from Livingston's comment on the 1757 riots in the Taconic area: "This Last Company of vagabonds I hear was 97 Strong and only 4 of my tenants among them & those were they I had dispossessed." John Van Rensselaer said that "several" of his tenants had been lured by promises of Massachusetts leases, though he named only Robert Noble, who had been a tenant for six or seven years.[68]

[67] Robert Livingston, Jr., to Jacob Wendell, Oct. 2, 1753, Livingston Papers, MCNY; *N.Y. Doc. Hist.*, III, 755, 764, 767; Robert Livingston, Jr., to Jacob Wendell, Claverack, Dec. 13, 1753, Livingston Manor, April 29, 1754, Livingston Papers, MCNY. Loomis also was imprisoned and this seemed at least temporarily to subdue him, if one may judge from a very self-effacing letter he wrote Livingston from jail in which he blamed all his troubles on "Several of the Great men that belong to Boston." Josiah Loomis to Robert Livingston, Jr., Albany, April 15, 1755, copy, Livingston Papers, MCNY. Livingston claimed that some of his tenants' names were placed on Massachusetts petitions without their permission. *N.Y. Doc. Hist.*, III, 745.

[68] Robert Livingston, Jr., to Jacob Wendell, Livingston Manor, Mar. 4, 1755, Mar. 21, 1757, Livingston Papers, MCNY; "Affadavit of John Van Rensselaer," *N.Y. Doc. Hist.*, III, 78–82. The present writer has checked the sources for the conflicts of both the 1750's and the 1760's and finds only nine rebels on Livingston Manor who are named at any time as tenants. These are Michael Hallenbeck, Josiah Loomis, George Robinson, Joseph Paine, William Rees, Andries Janse Reese, Jonathan Darby, Hendrick Brusie, and Christopher Andries Brusie. *N.Y. Doc. Hist.*, III, 739–49, 768–72, 780–82, 817–19; Robert Livingston, Jr., to Jacob Wendell, Livingston Manor, Oct. 2, 1753, Livingston Papers, MCNY; Mark, *Agrarian Conflicts,* 119, 121, 125, 127; Handlin, "Eastern Frontier," 58–63. Even some of these are in doubt, as for example George Robinson, whom Mark calls a tenant but whom Livingston describes as a squatter encouraged to encroach on his land by the Massachusetts agents. Robert Livingston, Jr., to James Alexander, Livingston Manor, Jan. 22, 1753, Rutherfurd Coll., III, 203, NYHS. This may also have been the case with Joseph Paine, *N.Y. Col. Hist.*, III, 768–72. But even if all nine were tenants, this is still a very low number, particularly since by the French and Indian War Livingston claimed that his manor had as large a population as the counties of Richmond or Kings if one judged by militia quotas. Robert Livingston, Jr., to James Duane, Livingston Manor, April 6,

The landlords' main antagonists in the upriver area, in addition to the New England squatters, were Massachusetts land speculators like David Ingersoll, an agent of the General Court described by Livingston as a "monster of a man" who deserved a "halter [around] his Windpipe." Typical of such agents' activities was their laying out a tract on Livingston Manor in early 1753, on which they "gott one George Robinson to build a house . . . in order to keep possession for them." Livingston's response was to have Robinson's house pulled down. The house was rebuilt and pulled down twice more, whereupon Livingston had Robinson placed in the Albany County jail on a writ from the New York Supreme Court. In retaliation the New Englanders planned to take Livingston's clerk and overseer from the Ancram ironworks and carry them to the jail in Springfield, Massachusetts, a scheme that was foiled by the intervention of armed Livingston tenants. In the face of more expected trouble, Livingston declared, "My people are determined to defend themselves." He was warned a few months later that "the New England People Intirely Intendeth to Take you Dad or Alife," but Livingston stuck to his guns. "I Shall not Suffer any man to take possession of a foot of my Land by force of arms," he declared; "In Short, Sir, I am determined to defend my property against all Invaders. . . ." In another skirmish at about this time, the New Englanders did manage to carry off some of Livingston's tenants, one Van Deusen and his sons, and place them in a Massachusetts jail. The New Englanders then gave the Van Deusens' manor lands to a farmer who was willing to accept a Massachusetts deed.[69]

Matters went from bad to worse during 1754 as the violence spread to Van Rensselaer lands at Claverack. Both the New Englanders and the New York proprietors armed their adherents, who then raided,

---

1772, Misc. MSS, Livingston, NYHS. In the census of the 1756 Kings had a white population of 1,862 and Richmond had 1,667. Greene and Harrington, *American Population,* 101.

[69] Robert Livingston, Jr., to Jacob Wendell, Livingston Manor, April 12, May 26, 1753, Livingston Papers. MCNY; Robert Livingston, Jr., to James Alexander, Livingston Manor, Jan. 22, 1753, Rutherfurd Coll., III, 203; Mr. Van Rensselaer to Mr. Livingston, Claverack, Aug. 1, 1753, *N.Y. Doc. Hist.,* III, 753; Robert Livingston, Jr., to Jacob Wendell, Livingston Manor, Oct. 2, 1753, Livingston Papers, MCNY; "Depositions to Justice of Peace of Albany City and County," Nov. 16, 1755, Livingston-Redmond MSS, Reel 6.

arrested, and kidnapped their opponents, each side meanwhile staging dramatic rescues of their jailed cohorts. By February of 1755, according to Irving Mark, "the controversy was fast becoming a miniature border war." This indeed seems the best way to characterize it. Houses and fields were burned, contingents of armed men clashed in a number of bloody skirmishes, and the inevitable fatality occurred when William Rees was killed in an exchange of shots with a New York sheriff's deputy in April of 1755. Despite the efforts of officials in both New York and Massachusetts to restore calm, the clashes sporadically continued. In 1757 two more fatalities occurred, and Robert Livingston, Jr., who had received threats that his house would be burned "over his head," asked for a guard of fifty soldiers.[70] The French and Indian War began in earnest at just about this time, and fighting spirits were temporarily absorbed in broader concerns.

6. The Riots of 1766

It was not until 1766 that agrarian conflicts once again embroiled the New York countryside, but by that time newly intensified passions and heightened sensibilities were altering the entire spectrum of colonial life. The close of the French and Indian War in 1763 has always been recognized as a turning point in American colonial history, and its effects were especially pronounced in the upper Hudson Valley. In addition to permitting the return of attention to internal problems, the end of the war also saw the final conquest of the French and their Indian al-

---

[70] *N.Y. Doc. Hist.,* III, 789–824; *N.Y. Col. Docs.,* VII, 206–8; Mark, *Agrarian Conflicts,* 124, 129. James DeLancey was acting governor for two fairly long stretches in the 1750's, and some historians have asserted that a presumed Livingston-DeLancey political rivalry caused DeLancey to defer pressing Massachusetts for a settlement of the border dispute. Irving Mark, for example, claims that when DeLancey became acting governor in 1753 he brought to the job "a bitter hostility to Livingston." (*Agrarian Conflicts,* 123, n89; see also Handlin, "Eastern Frontier," 63.) If this were true, Livingston did not seem to be aware of it, for he believed DeLancey was doing his best to get Massachusetts to establish a joint commission to settle the dispute, and this writer can find no instance in which he expressed anything but satisfaction with DeLancey's efforts. Robert Livingston, Jr., to Jacob Wendell, Livingston Manor, Feb. 8, April 22, May 6, 1754, May 10, 1755, Livingston Papers, MCNY.

lies, always a barrier to westward expansion. The removal of that obstacle released a new wave of settlers and land speculators across the northern part of New York Colony. The opening of new areas to settlement might have drained off some of the discontent, but it also attracted many new settlers and elevated land values throughout the whole region. At about this same time the colonists began to mount a new series of challenges to imperial authority, a preliminary peak being reached in the Stamp Act riots of 1765. As has often been the case with popular movements, the excitements aroused tended to spill over into very different areas. That the ambitions of the small farmers gained new encouragement from the urban riots is shown by the farmers' inclination to cast themselves as rural "Sons of Liberty." [71]

In a situation as inflammable as that on New York's eastern frontier, only a spark was needed to set it off. That spark was supplied by the Philipse Highland Patent proprietors, Philip Philipse, Beverly Robinson, and Roger Morris, who in the early 1760's began vigorously to assert their claims to the eastern reaches of the patent. This was the section that had never been developed by earlier proprietors, and its vacant lands had acted as a steady attraction to migrating New Englanders. When the New Englanders began to move into the area around 1740, a number of them were allowed by the New York proprietors to squat there. This was apparently part of an effort to strengthen the Philipses' rather dubious claim to the eastern borderlands. As the relationship between the Philipse heirs and the New Englanders was later described, "none of the then Tenants had taken any Leases under the said Patentee Claimants, nor made any specific agreement with them Respecting said Possessions: but only had been told by them that they might go and Possess the same, pretending that the same belonged to them. . . ." The eastern section of the Highland Patent was also subject to rival claims by the Wappinger Indians. As the Indians themselves told the story, their lands were seized by the proprietors while they were away fighting for the King in the French and Indian War. When the Indians returned in the early 1760's to reclaim their land, the New Englanders saw an

[71] Irving Mark and Oscar Handlin, eds., "Land Cases in Colonial New York, 1765–1767, The King v William Prendergast," *New York University Law Quarterly Review,* IX (Jan., 1942), 183; NYHS *Colls.,* IX, 99, 111–12; Higgins, *Expansion in New York,* Chap. VIII.

opportunity to strengthen their own position, and a number of them obtained deeds to their farms from the Indians while others accepted leases which ran from 99 to 999 years. This was the state of affairs in 1763 when the Philipse proprietors began a series of successful lawsuits, by which they ejected a number of farmers holding Indian titles and replaced them with loyal tenants holding Philipse leases. The New Englanders, some of whom had lived on their farms for two or three decades and "had thereon with much Labour and Expence Erected Houses, Barns, Mills, Granaries, and made Great Improvements," resisted with all their strength.[72] The Indians themselves petitioned the New York government for aid, and in March, 1765, were granted a hearing before a panel composed of Lieutenant Governor Cadwallader Colden and the Council. This "court" rejected the Indians' claims and in effect confirmed title to the Philipse heirs.[73] By the fall of 1765 the dissident farmers were organizing to oppose the Philipse demands, and by the spring of 1766 the entire border area was in an uproar.

Once again the conflicting forces resolved themselves into three major categories: the landlords; migrants from New England, most of whom were either squatters, tenants at will, or claimants under Indian deeds; and the loyal tenants "sent in by the landlords" to maintain proprietary claims. There is a hint that some leaseholding Philipse tenants were "seduced" by the New Englanders, but owing to the loose way in which the term "tenant" was used, it is almost impossible to de-

[72] Mark and Handlin, eds., "King v. Prendergast," 165–66; Handlin and Mark, eds., "Chief Daniel Nimham v. Roger Morris, Beverly Robinson, and Philip Philipse—An Indian Land Case in Colonial New York, 1765–1767," *Ethnohistory*, XI (Summer, 1964), 201, 206–7. Robinson and Morris were former British officers who had married Susanna and Mary Philipse, heiresses of the Highland Patent.

[73] Handlin and Mark, eds., "Chief Daniel Nimam v. Roger Morris et al.," 193–246. Mark's assertion (*Agrarian Conflicts,* 133) that the members of the Council were all "great landlords" overstates the case, but as land speculators and men of property they might be expected to favor the gentlemen proprietors over the Indians and small farmers. As John Morin Scott, one of the proprietors' attorneys, pointed out at a subsequent hearing, if the Wappingers' claims were allowed it would be a "Dangerous Tendency; 'Twill open a Door to the greatest Mischiefs, inasmuch as a great part of the Lands in this Province are supposed to lie under much the Same Scituation. . . ." Handlin and Mark, eds., "Chief Daniel Nimham v. Roger Morris et al.," 240.

termine who these may have been.[74] In any case, it is as clear in the Philipse disturbances as in the others that the rebels' grievances were inspired less by conditions of tenancy than by the hope that they might force the proprietors to surrender some of their land.

In November, 1765, the dissident farmers, led by William Prendergast, Samuel Munroe, William Finch, Stephen Crane, and others, called a meeting at which they vowed to reinstate the farmers evicted by the proprietors and to pay "no Rents" until the dispute were equitably settled. It was further agreed that if any of the agitators were sent to jail for nonpayment of rent, the rebels would "fetch them Out if it cost them their Lives." [75] In the following months mobs varying in size from one hundred to five hundred men, armed with clubs, swords, and pistols, ranged about eastern Dutchess County ejecting loyal tenants, burning barns, threatening backsliders, and stirring up general rebellion against the proprietors. For a mob, the Dutchess County rebels were remarkably well organized. The men were divided into several companies, with captains and lieutenants at the head of each, a "Committee of Twelve" was chosen to direct their activities, and all decisions were to be made by majority vote. A quasi-judicial tribunal on tenants' rights held hearings in a field before a bar constructed of four log rails. An example of its "justice" was that shown to Justice of the Peace Samuel Peters, who was hauled before the "court" for taking evidence against

[74] Mark and Handlin, eds., "King v. Prendergast," 170; Beverly Robinson to James Duane, Highlands, Sept. 9, 1766, Duane Papers, NYHS. According to one contemporary, there were "upwards of three hundred" people on the Highland Patent in 1756 from a line three miles east of the Hudson to its eastern boundary. Though these people were often called tenants, testimony before the Council confirms that many were squatters or claimants under Indian leases. See "Timothy Shaw Affidavit," Mar. 6, 1767, and "Minute of Council on the Memorial of Roger Morris, Esq. and others," Feb. 6, 1765, Philipse-Gouverneur Land Titles, CU.

[75] Mark and Handlin, eds., "King v. Prendergast," 174, 176–80, 186, 188; Prendergast advised, however, that the farmers should "pay their Honest Debts" (177). Other leaders of the rebel farmers were Isaac Perry, Silas Washburn, Jacobus Gonsales, James Sicar (Secor), Micah Vail, Oliver A[u]stin, Simon Calkins, and John Cain. William Prendergast (1727–1811) was born in Waterford or Kilkenny, Ireland, and was married to Mehitabel Wing, a Quaker of Scotch descent whose family lived near Quaker Hill in Dutchess County. A. W. Anderson, *The Story of a Pioneer Family* (1936).

the rioters during one of their meetings. After threats of a mobbing, a whipping, and a kicking "for as long as they tho't proper," by the one to two hundred men gathered in the field to view the proceedings, Peters had to promise not to use his office against the rebels before he finally was released. As to the significance of such transactions, much would depend on the point of view. So absorbed with procedure did the New Englanders become at times that William Prendergast, a man of action, was heard to complain that the rebels "spent too much Time in Meetings" and not enough fighting the landlords.[76]

By the spring of 1766 the Dutchess County rebellion was beginning to spread to adjacent counties. Some tenants (if such they were) on the Manor of Cortlandt joined the agitators, though contrary to earlier assessments it does not appear that their number was large. Three Cortlandt Manor rebels had been arrested and placed in the New York City jail in April, and in accordance with their vow to free imprisoned comrades, Westchester and Dutchess County farmers joined forces at Kingsbridge preparatory to marching on the city jail. Estimates of the mob varied from five hundred to two thousand; it was sufficiently menacing in any case for Governor Moore to call out the militia. Even before the governor acted, however, it was becoming evident that the rebels had overreached themselves. Contrary to their expectations, the urban Stamp Act rioters did not rise to their aid and, as their momentum faltered, the show of force by Moore proved sufficient to disperse them.[77]

Back on their home ground, the rebels continued their hostilities against the landlords, and during May and June the rebellion spread to Albany County. On June 26, Albany Sheriff Harmanus Schuyler and a posse of 105 men clashed with a band of sixty settlers on Van Rensse-

[76] Mark and Handlin, eds., "King v. Prendergast," 170–71, 177, 179–81, 182–84, 193.

[77] Mark, *Agrarian Conflicts,* 137–38. Robert R. Livingston gives the number of farmers at Kingsbridge as "five or six hundred." Livingston to John Sargent, New York, May 2, 1766, Robert R. Livingston Papers, Bancroft Transcripts, NYPL. Both Mark and Handlin ("Eastern Frontier," 69) imply that the Westchester disorders were widespread, though this writer can find no evidence that any but the Manor of Cortlandt was affected. Kim even downgrades the significance of the riots there, showing that only the tenants of John Van Cortlandt were involved. The resident proprietor of the manor was Pierre Van Cortlandt (later a Whig Patriot and the first lieutenant governor of the State of New York), and he was generally well regarded by the manor residents. Kim, "Manor of Cortlandt," 230–31.

laer land in a fierce encounter which left four dead and many wounded. During the fray the sheriff's "Hat and Wig" were shot off, and Colonel Van Rensselaer's horse was killed under him. A mob of two hundred men at Livingston Manor threatened "to murthur the Lord of the Manor and level his house" unless he agreed to come to terms with the disgruntled farmers, and disagreeable doings may have been averted only by the timely arrival of the proprietor's son, Walter Livingston, and a contingent of forty armed men. Back in Dutchess County, several hundred armed rioters gathered at the Poughkeepsie jail and forced officials to release a farmer jailed for debt, while "companies" of farmers rampaged through the Highland Patent threatening loyal tenants with the destruction of their houses and fields. Thoroughly alarmed at the growing danger, the government determined to restore order. Proclamations for the arrest of the ringleaders had already been issued, and at the end of June Governor Moore dispatched the 28th Regiment to Dutchess County. After several sharp skirmishes in the northeastern section of the Highland Patent, Prendergast and a number of the other leaders were captured and taken to the Poughkeepsie jail. Rebel activity continued throughout the summer in Albany County, finally subsiding in the fall after detachments of the 46th Regiment, the 19th Infantry, and the 26th Regiment had been sent into the area.[78]

Of the more than sixty men indicted for riotous activities in Dutchess County alone, most pleaded guilty and "were variously punished with fines, imprisonment and pillories." But William Prendergast, the alleged leader of the Dutchess rebels, was not to get off so easily. He was to be made an example, and was indicted for "High Treason." After a showcase trial before a specially impaneled oyer and terminer commission, assisted by a jury of "respectable Freeholders," Prendergast was convicted and sentenced to death.[79] The judges, who

[78] New-York *Gazette; or The Weekly Post-Boy,* July 3, 1766; "The Montressor Journals," NYHS *Colls.,* XIV (1881), 375; Mark and Handlin, eds., "King v. Prendergast," 178, 184–85, 191; New-York *Gazette; and The Weekly Mercury,* May 5, 1766; *N.Y. Col. Docs.,* VII, 845–46; Mark, *Agrarian Conflicts,* 139–45. Montressor heard that there were 1,700 "Levellers" with "fire arms" at the Poughkeepsie jail. ("The Montressor Journals," 376.)

[79] Mark, *Agrarian Conflicts,* 145; Mark and Handlin, eds., "King v. Prendergast," 169 ff. Irving Mark believed it was the New York Supreme Court that tried the Prendergast case; for a correction of this, see Goebel and Naughton, *Law En-*

seem to have been more sympathetic toward the defendant than was the jury,[80] unanimously solicited a pardon from the King. Following a plea for clemency from Governor Moore, the pardon was granted by George III in December, 1766, and Prendergast became a free man. The comparative calm which prevailed following Prendergast's release confirmed the wisdom of the Earl of Shelburne, who believed that a show of leniency would "have a better effect in recalling these mistaken People to their Duty than the most rigorous punishment." [81]

7. Some Considerations

In the English colonies the principal fact with regard to land was its availability—in other colonies if not in New York, and for future if not immediate purchase. To some, the apparent benefits of short-term tenancy as a preparation for eventual purchase of their own farms were sufficient to drain off whatever discontent may have arisen from the restrictive aspects of tenant life. Moreover, the implication that high rent

---

forcement in Colonial New York, 87–89. The panel of judges was composed of Chief Justice Daniel Horsmanden, John Watts, William Walton, Oliver DeLancey, Joseph Reade, William Smith, Jr., Whitehead Hicks, and John Morin Scott. New-York *Gazette, and The Weekly Mercury*, Sept. 1, 1766. Mark's assertion that this court favored the landlords is questionable for, though no doubt all the members dabbled in land speculations, several of them were leading New York City merchants who within another year or two would emerge as political opponents of the landed men. Only two men on the panel were publicly known as members of the "landed interest," John Morin Scott and William Smith, Jr., and Smith tried to beg off from sitting on the ground of his "Wife's Connections with the Landlords" (he was married to Janet Livingston, daughter of James Livingston). *Smith's Historical Memoirs*, 2, 34.

[80] This was later disputed by the Tory historian Thomas Jones in a notation in the margin of the New-York Historical Society's copy of the New-York *Gazette; or, The Weekly Post-Boy* of Sept. 4, 1766. On the other hand William Smith, Jr., reports that popular opinion in New York City, where most of the judges lived, was opposed to a severe verdict for Prendergast in view of "the Tumultuousness of the Time. . . ." *Smith's Historical Memoirs*, 34.

[81] Earl of Shelburne to Gov. Moore, Whitehall, Dec. 11, 1766, *N.Y. Col. Docs.*, VII, 879; Shelburne definitely saw the small farmer troubles in the context of a border dispute, and recommended "concessions on both sides." The same was true with Chief Justice Horsmanden. New York *Gazette, and The Weekly Mercury*, Nov. 17, 1766; New York *Mercury*, Nov. 24, 1766.

was a genuine grievance seems not to be supported by the evidence. One of the few occasions that rents were even mentioned was at the time of the Philipse Highland Patent dispute when Beverly Robinson, puzzled by the rebels' criticism of "largeness of Rents," asked William Prendergast, "Did you ever pay any rent or was any ever demanded of you?"—and Prendergast had to reply, "No," but that he opposed the landlords "for the good of the Country." [82]

The real goal of the small farmers was not lower rents or even relief from the quarter-sale fee, though the latter was undoubtedly a genuine grievance among leaseholders. The real issue was title to the land; the farmers wanted to pay no rents at all but to own the land, either free and clear or under the longest-term "fee simple" leases possible. The landlords were never deceived by other charges trumped up to gain public sympathy. James Duane stated in emphatic terms that the rioters' "object was to intimidate the Proprietors to give them the fee of their farms"; and Robert Livingston, Jr., referred in similar words to the people who "take up little farms in my manor under pretence of Vacant Lands. . . . they are no objects of Charity, [but] on the Contrary mischievious wicked people in hopes to gitt my lands by this means." [83]

Perhaps the most persuasive element in the argument that title rather than terms was at the heart of the conflict is that of geography. For the fact remains that the rebellious activities of the small farmers were confined exclusively to those estates which shared a common border with Massachusetts and Connecticut. This was the case with Van Rensselaer lands, Livingston Manor, the Beekman Patent, the Oblong, the Highland Patent, and the Manor of Cortlandt. Had this indeed been a "tenant revolt," some manifestations of discontent might have been expected from tenants on the Manor of Philipsburgh, Schuyler's Saratoga Patent, or Sir William Johnson's Mohawk River lands, yet so far as has ever been determined no disturbances took place on those estates. Perhaps the most likely place for riots would have been the Manor of Philipsburgh, the heavily tenanted Hudson River domain of

---

[82] Mark and Handlin, eds., "King v. Prendergast," 181.

[83] James Duane to Capt. Abraham Duane, 1766, James Duane Papers Box 10, I, 57, NYHS, cited by Goebel and Naughton, *Law Enforcement in Colonial New York,* 87; Robert Livingston, Jr., to James Duane, Livingston Manor, Sept. 30, 1767, James Duane Papers, NYHS.

Colonel Frederick Philipse, the third proprietor, who apparently never sold an acre of land in the eighteenth century, who granted most of his leases "at will" rather than for a term of years, and who exacted his rents and quarter-sale fees with at least the same regularity as other New York landlords.[84] But there were no rioters at Philipsburgh. That estate stretched along the east shore of the Hudson River, comfortably within conceded New York boundaries, and was thus not subject to assaults by New England claimants. Rather than a contest between "lords" and "peasants," the New York disturbances grew out of a competition between landholders and would-be landholders for material advantage.

Though property rights were basic to the conflict, it would hardly do to claim that there were no social tensions at all. In a country without a legally protected aristocracy, where social rank "had always to be earned anew" by each generation, and where "social differences were considered to be incidental rather than essential to community order," [85] the anachronistic posturings of "manor lords" and "patroons" invited the irreverent scorn of ordinary folk. The "High Mightinesses" of the Hudson Valley, as one critic called them, were already something of an anomaly. There was no broader target for New England ridicule than Robert Livingston, Jr., who stormed about tearing down houses, destroying crops, and denouncing the squatters as "vile wicked animals." [86] That the small farmers could cast themselves as "poor Men" being hounded and harassed by "rich" and "monopolizing" landlords demonstrates perhaps as much as anything else what a thorough political preparation the American colonist had acquired by the 1760's.[87]

[84] Reubens, "Pre-Emptive Rights . . . Philipsburgh Manor, New York," 438–39; Halsey, ed., Tour of Four Rivers, 5. Philipsburgh had over 270 tenants in 1775. Reubens, "Pre-Emptive Rights. . . ," 438.

[85] J. R. Pole, Political Representation in England and the Origins of the American Republic (New York, 1966), 45; Bernard Bailyn, The Ideological Origins of the American Revolution (Cambridge, Mass., 1967), 319.

[86] New-York Gazette; or, The Weekly Post-Boy, Aug. 21, 1766; Robert Livingston, Jr., to Jacob Wendell, New York, May 26, 1753, Livingston Manor, Mar. 4, 1755, Livingston Papers, MCNY.

[87] Mark and Handlin, eds., "King v. Prendergast," 175; [Thomas Young], Some Reflections on the Disputes Between New York, New Hampshire, and Col. John Henry Lydius of Albany (New Haven, 1764), 15.

He knew how to arouse popular sympathy, and he had more than a glimmering notion of what public pressure might do to serve his interests.

The most compelling and persistent grievance against the landed elite concerned the power it exercised over the New York judiciary, a power so extensive that some deemed it unlikely that any opponent of the landed men could get a fair trial. When the Wappinger Indians sought legal redress in their dispute with the Philipse heirs over the Highland Patent, it was said that they could not get a New York lawyer to take their case, since all had been "previously Retained on the other Side. . . ." Colden believed that the 1766 rebellion would not have built to the proportions it did "had there not been a general Jealousy of a powerful Combination in the Courts of Justice, in favor of the extravagent Claims of the great landed Men." Another critic asserted that the farmers only turned to violence because "the law (the only channel thro' which people aggrieved can obtain redress) was absolutely barred against them. . . . the lawyers generally refusing to take their cause in hand. . . ." In view of the bond that existed between the landed families and the legal profession, the small farmers may well have had a valid complaint when they protested that there was "no Law for poor Men" in New York.[88]

Such class rhetoric thus represents a real part of the story, and the gulf between the wealth and power of the landed grandees and that of the small farmers was no illusion. But in reading over the record, with its many irreverences toward figures of authority, one is left with odd impressions. Throughout it all, those farmers really seemed to believe that time—to say nothing of the imperial government—was on their side. How long could elitist pretensions, if there was anything typical in this, be expected to survive in America? As Robert R. Palmer has remarked, "To be an aristocrat it is not enough to think of oneself as such, it is necessary to be thought so by others" as well.[89]

[88] Handlin and Mark, eds., "Chief Daniel Nimham v. Roger Morris et al.," 202; NYHS *Colls.*, X (1877), 456; Philanthropos, *A Few Observations on the Conduct of the General Assembly of New York, for some years past, addressed to the Freemen and Freeholders of the City and Province,* Feb. 9, 1768, Rare Book Room, NYPL; Mark and Handlin, eds., "King v. Prendergast," 191; Mark, *Agrarian Conflicts,* 134.

[89] Palmer, *Age of Democratic Revolution,* I, 235.

It remains, of course, to be explained how it was that such families as the Livingstons and the Van Rensselaers were able not only to hold on to their great estates during and after the Revolution, but to strengthen that hold to the point where it would take more violent upheavals as late as the 1840's to finally break it. Any answer to this seeming paradox must lie less in the social than in the political realm, and would be closely bound up with the events of 1776 and after. If there has been a tendency to overstate the social significance of New York's colonial land conflicts, there has been a corresponding tendency to underestimate their political implications, and this is one of the subjects that will be taken up in the following chapter.

VII

POLITICS, THE "UNIVERSAL TOPICK": 1765-1770

"Our Politicks are dirty and too low to stoop to," declared Robert Watts of New York in January, 1776: "They are such a compound of Malice, Dissimulation & Jealousy that my Soul abhors them." [1] Though Watts's Loyalist sentiments may have had something to do with this outburst, the frenzied quality of party conflict in the decade or so before the Revolution could hardly be questioned. The exceptional frequency of Assembly elections—three were held within eight years during the 1760's—was in itself a factor in the heightening of tensions. Another, of course, was the clamor raised, especially in New York City, against specific imperial measures. But over all this hung a kind of general irritability, an unspecified public apprehensiveness over what might come next. Crises now appeared with sufficient frequency that some sort of resolution between London and the provinces must have looked more and more imminent to ever-increasing numbers, and it was in this setting that "Politicks . . . [became] the Universal Topick for all Ranks of People." As political leaders tried to gain whatever advantage they could from each new disturbance, all the issues of past conflicts were revived. The merchants renewed their attacks on the landed gentry, the

[1] Robert Watts to Hon. John Watts, Esq., New York, Jan. 3, 1776, C05/40, micro., SHR.

upriver interest opposed the City, dissenters clashed with Anglicans, and the "court" confronted the "popular" party. Though this intensification of political activity was not restricted to one area ("This once Florising Continent," as Robert Morris put it, "is now become the Region of Party Dissention & politicks" [2]), probably in no place was it more acrimonious than in New York. Years of factious contention culminated in the election contests of the 1760's, which were in many ways the most bitter in the colony's history.

It might be supposed from the unstable fluctuations that characterized New York politics to the very end of the colonial era (men often changed sides, sometimes more than once), together with the willingness of local leaders to exploit imperial issues for party advantage, that New Yorkers shaped their politics mainly to promote private interests. And yet we know that something more than this was involved in the party battles of the 1760's. Decisions were made in the course of them that would start one group down the path to revolution; they drew in ever larger numbers of people; and they stimulated the development of a new set of leaders who would in time assist in the founding and governing of the State of New York.

1. The Parties Take Shape

Assembly elections were held in New York in 1761, 1768, and 1769. Many of the convolutions and intricacies of these contests can be understood only against the background of the previous decade, when James DeLancey was the dominant political figure in the province. Those years had seen a marked shift in the political center of gravity, as power tended to migrate from the Hudson Valley–Albany area to the New York City–seaboard region. A tentative effort in 1751 to lessen DeLancey's influence had failed, but by the late 1750's a number of minor controversies were making their effects felt. In the election of 1758 four members of the Livingston family had gained seats in the Assembly: Robert R. and Henry Livingston from Dutchess County, William Liv-

[2] Robert Morris to Mr. Duncan, Oct. 5, 1765, July 14, 1769, Morris MSS (Robert Morris Papers), Box 4, Rutgers.

ingston from the Manor, and Philip Livingston [II] from New York County.[3]

This sudden blossoming of Livingstons has led some New York historians to assume that a Livingston party came into being at that time, gaining and holding control of the Assembly until 1768.[4] Yet the evidence on this is conflicting. Of the contemporary observers, William Smith, Jr., does refer to a "Livingston Party," but adds that it "did not always proceed from motives approved of by that family." The Tory historian Thomas Jones says that a "republican faction," which included William Bayard and Abraham Ten Broeck as well as the four Livingstons, gained ascendancy in 1758. But perhaps the greatest difficulty is that one of the most dependable signs of party formation— voting regularity—was absent. Robert R. and William Livingston, both lawyers and closely tied to the landed interest, often voted on the same side. But Henry Livingston of Dutchess County frequently did not stand with the other two; while Philip, representing New York County, quickly developed a reputation as a moderate and judicious politician who, though descended from a landed family, fairly and fully represented the City mercantile interest—as indeed he had to do if he wanted to be reelected. Bayard and Ten Broeck were not elected until 1761. Bayard, a New York County representative, was usually found on the same side as Philip Livingston; Ten Broeck of Rensselaerswyck, though frequently absent, often voted with Robert R. Livingston.[5]

[3] Edgar A. Werner, *Civil List and Constitutional History of the Colony and State of New York* (Albany, 1888), 360. Philip [II] and William Livingston were brothers of Robert Livingston, Jr., the third proprietor of Livingston Manor; Robert R. Livingston, of the Clermont branch of the family, was their first cousin; and Henry Livingston, son of Gilbert, was another first cousin.

[4] Carl Becker, "Nominations in Colonial New York," *AHR*, VI (Jan., 1901), 274. It is Milton Klein's view that the Livingstons controlled the Assembly from 1758 to 1768. "The American Whig: William Livingston of New York," unpubl. Ph.D. diss. (Columbia University, 1954), 487–94. Roger Champagne dates the Livingston Assembly domination from 1761. "Family Politics versus Constitutional Principles: The New York Assembly Elections of 1768 and 1769," *WMQ*, 3rd Ser., XX (Jan., 1963), 59–60.

[5] William Smith, *The History of the Late Province of New York, From its Discovery to the Appointment of Governor Colden, in 1762* (New York, 1830), II, 333; Thomas Jones, *History of New York During the Revolutionary War* (New York, 1879), I, 17. For Philip Livingston [II] see *DAB*, XI, 316–18 (John A.

The question of whether the Livingstons controlled the Assembly in the 1758–1768 decade may be determined from the votes recorded in the Assembly Journal during that period. The Assembly elected in December, 1758, sat only until November, 1760. On the only three votes which might reflect party differences the Livingstons voted together and were on the losing side each time.[6] Following the death of George II a new election was held in March, 1761. Again, four Livingstons were elected, with Peter R. Livingston, son of Robert Livingston, Jr., replacing William as the Manor representative. During its seven-year span that Assembly recorded a total of forty-three divisions. In twenty-six of these the Livingstons were on the losing side, and in only five of them were all four Livingstons with the majority. In the remaining twelve instances their votes were split. Several of these votes involved obvious party issues, such as contested or fraudulent elections, and on these divisions the Livingstons voted together and were defeated each time.[7]

In view of this record it seems that if a Livingston party did exist, whether by that or any other name, it did not control the New York Assembly. In all likelihood what did happen was that after the sudden death of James DeLancey the Assembly was temporarily thrown into a state of uncertainty until new leaders emerged. That the 1761 election came too soon after DeLancey's death to reflect any marked party realignment is suggested in Colden's comment on the new Assembly. "A new set of Men want to take the Lead," he noted, "but the members as

Krout). For voting patterns see *Assembly Journal* (Gaine), II, Mar. 1, 1759 ff; *Assembly Journal* (Buel), Dec. 12, 1767 ff.

[6] *Assembly Journal* (Gaine), II, Mar. 2, 1759, Mar. 21, 22, 1760. Excluded from this analysis is a series of votes on Mar. 1, 1759 regarding militia quotas. In the majority of those divisions the more affluent assemblymen tended to vote together, offering a rare example of what may be a "class" cleavage, and possibly reflecting either the eighteenth-century custom which allowed the wealthy to buy their way out of militia service, or the fact that the wealthy assemblymen were often the colonels of the militia in their counties. *Assembly Journal* (Gaine), II, Mar. 1, 1759.

[7] *Assembly Journal* (Gaine), II, Sept. 10, Dec. 3, 4, 5, 16, 1761, Nov. 24, 26, Dec., 2, 7, 13, 14, 1763, Oct. 2, 6, 8, 12, 13, 1764, Dec. 19, 20, 1765. *Assembly Journal* (Buel), Dec. 12, 29, 30, 1767, Jan. 7, 8, 1768. For examples of clear partisan divisions, see votes of Mar. 22, 1760, and of September and December, 1761. There is no journal for the period from March, 1766, to June, 1767.

yet are so much unformed among themselves that it is extreamly difficult to manage them." [8]

But if the "new set of Men," consisting mainly of the upriver land
barons and New York City lawyers, had difficulty gaining the upper
hand in the Assembly they met with greater success elsewhere, for De-
Lancey's death had opened up numerous opportunities in administrative
offices. The main obstacle to increased power and patronage at that
level was Lieutenant Governor Cadwallader Colden, who was determined to remain aloof from all factional attachments that he might better serve the empire which had always been the primary object of his
loyalty. But if Colden was cool to provincial factional interests, the governors appointed during the 1760's were inclined to be more helpful. It
was Governor Robert Monckton (1761–1763) who appointed Robert R.
Livingston a judge of the Supreme Court in March, 1763. When Sir
Henry Moore became governor in 1765 the upriver-lawyer interest
gained a true friend at court. Moore recommended that Robert R. Livingston, whom he described as "well affected to His Majesty's person
and Government," be appointed to the Council, and though this choice
was not approved in London, Moore did succeed in appointing William
Smith, Jr., to a seat in 1767. Moreover, Philip Livingston, the son of
Peter V. B. Livingston, served as Governor Moore's private secretary,
and throughout his years in office Moore showed a clear preference for
the country grandees over the New York City–centered commercial
leaders. When the latter regained some of their former power in 1768,
they let it be known that one of their major goals was to "revenge the
Governors Neglect of them ever since he has been here. . . ." [9]

Another opportunity to redress the political balance arose during
the Stamp Act crisis of 1765–1766, when three New York City lawyers
with strong ties to the upriver interest, William Smith, William Livingston, and John Morin Scott, identified themselves with the New York

[8] Colden to John Pownall, Esq., New York, April 5, 1761, NYHS *Colls.*, IX
(1876), 81.

[9] William H. W. Sabine, ed., *Historical Memoirs of William Smith* (New York,
1956), 33, 38–40; Robert R. Livingston to Robert Livingston [of Clermont],
New York, Mar. 14, 1763, Robert R. Livingston Coll., Box I, NYHS; Gov.
Moore to Earl of Hillsborough, New York, Jan. 21, 1769, *N.Y. Col. Docs.*, VIII,
148–49.

City Sons of Liberty. At first the lawyer "triumvirate" probably was motivated less by factional interests than by a wish to hit at Acting Governor Colden, who had aroused their ire early in 1765 by challenging the finality of jury decisions and the independence of judges in the *Forsey* v. *Cunningham* appeal case. Indeed, by 1765 Colden seems to have been held in very low regard by a majority of New Yorkers, and his efforts to enforce the Stamp Act did little to improve his popularity. In any event, both the lawyers and a number of merchants became actively involved with the Sons of Liberty, though the lawyers' special talents as propagandists and organizers soon propelled them to the fore.[10] Taken altogether, these various signs boded well for the upriver-lawyer coalition, which had every reason to anticipate substantial gains at the next Assembly election.

It was at this critical juncture that the land riots of 1765–66 burst forth, upsetting all calculations and introducing an entirely new set of issues for the politicians to exploit. At about this same time, moreover, the lawyer triumvirate was discovering that the radicalism of the Sons of Liberty was threatening to outrun its leaders. Robert R. Livingston, a close observer of the Stamp Act excitements, reported on November 2, 1765, that "every man is wild with Politics & you hear nothing but the Stamp act talked of. Last night and the night before we had mobbing [;] there was such a one Last night as never was seen before in the City." At a public meeting attended by some 1200 people on November 26, the more radical element in the crowd urged that all legal and commercial business be resumed without stamps in open defiance of the law. The lawyers managed to modify these demands into a set of "instructions," apparently prepared by William Smith, Jr., to the Assembly members from New York County. They did so, however, at great cost

---

[10] *Smith's Historical Memoirs,* 27–28. Colden charged at the time of the New York Stamp Act riots that "the Lawyers of this Place are the Authors, Promoters, and Leaders of it." Colden to Conway, Nov. 9, 1765, *N.Y. Col. Docs.,* VII, 773. For confirming evidence see Gen. Gage to Sec. Conway, Dec. 21, 1765, in Clarence E. Carter, ed., *The Correspondence of General Thomas Gage with the Secretaries of State, 1763–1775* (New Haven, 1931–33), I, 78–79. See also Roger J. Champagne, "Liberty Boys and Mechanics of New York City, 1764–1774," *Labor History,* VIII (Spring, 1967), 116–17. For *Forsey* v. *Cunningham* consult Milton Klein, "Prelude to the Revolution in New York: Jury Trials and Judicial Tenure," *WMQ,* 3rd Ser., XVII (Oct., 1960), 439–62.

to their liberal credentials, for the subsequent disagreement over tactics caused the Sons of Liberty to split into two factions by the end of 1765. One group led by Alexander McDougall continued to support the lawyers, while a more extreme faction led by Isaac Sears, a ship-captain and small merchant, and John Lamb, a wine-merchant, were dissatisfied with the lawyers' moderate course.[11] Though acting as a damper on the hopes of the lawyer-upriver interest, neither the land conflicts nor the split in radical ranks would necessarily have proved fatal under other circumstances. But in a political setting as highly sensitive as that of New York, where contesting factions were experienced at picking out the weaknesses of the opposition, it was unlikely that such choice issues for exploitation would be overlooked. And to the further distress of the country interest, it was during the Stamp Act riots that the heir to the political leadership of former Lieutenant Governor James DeLancey, his son Captain James DeLancey, made a timely debut on the New York political stage.

It has been said of the younger James DeLancey that he could be "a very dangerous Enemy," and so far as narrow tactical matters were concerned this indeed proved to be the case. But it also appears from the rather scattered evidence that he lacked his father's subtlety and higher vision as well as his broad popularity. This eldest son of James and Anne Heathcote DeLancey was born in New York City in 1732 and received his education in England, where he first attended Eton and

[11] Robert R. Livingston to Robert Livingston [Clermont], Nov. 2 and Nov. 20, 1765, Robert R. Livingston Papers, Bancroft Transcripts, NYPL. For more details on this meeting, see Carl Becker, *The History of Political Parties in the Province of New York, 1760–1776* (Madison, Wis., 1909), 38; Champagne, "Liberty Boys and Mechanics," 118–21; L. Jesse Lemisch, "New York's Petitions and Resolves of December 1765: Liberals vs. Radicals," *New-York Historical Society Quarterly*, XLIX (Oct., 1965), 313–26; Klein, "The American Whig: William Livingston." The two factions of the Sons of Liberty held separate celebrations when the Stamp Act was repealed in 1766. Smith's draft of the instructions can be found in the William Smith, Jr., Papers, folder 197, NYPL. They were also printed in the New-York *Gazette; or, The Weekly Post-Boy,* on Nov. 28, 1765. Only two major demands were made, that there be no "internal Taxations," and that "Trial by Jury" be protected. For Sears see Robert Jay Christen, "King Sears: Politician and Patriot in a Decade of Revolution," unpubl. Ph.D. diss. (Columbia University, 1968), Chap. II; *DAB,* XVI, 539–40 (Clarence H. Vance). Isaac Q. Leake, *Memoir of the Life and Times of General John Lamb* (Albany, 1850), 9.

then went on in 1750 to his father's alma mater, Cambridge. He was admitted to Lincoln's Inn in 1753, though there is no evidence that he ever practiced law. Returning to New York shortly before the beginning of the French and Indian War, DeLancey was commissioned a captain in the British infantry and saw action in the campaigns around Lake George and Fort Niagara in 1758 and 1759. On receiving word of his father's death in July, 1760, DeLancey returned to New York City, where for the next few years he devoted himself to managing the family properties and to the pursuit of his favorite pastime, the breeding and racing of horses.[12] Though DeLancey sold his commission in the British army, he continued to be referred to as Captain DeLancey, and to distinguish him from his father he shall be so designated here.

Captain DeLancey's name was first connected with New York politics when he offered himself as a candidate for the Assembly in the election of 1761. He ran last in a field of six, perhaps because he had been back in the City only a short time, and despite his illustrious name was himself not well enough known. We next hear of him at the Stamp Act protest meeting of November 26, 1765, when he was among those placed on a committee to carry the moderate "instructions" to the Assembly chamber. How strong a stand to take in these resolutions was the question on which the Sons of Liberty split, and Captain DeLancey's political enemies later accused him of having exploited this division to curry favor with the radical leaders, Sears and Lamb, for his own political advancement. However this may be, it was observed by William Smith, Jr., in mid-1766 that "James DeLancey would probably get into the Assembly now as he was among the Sons of Liberty." At about that time, indeed, "Mr. I____c S____rs, in a knot of Sons of Liberty, at one of their meetings, mentioned him for a candidate" at the next election.[13] That next election would not take place until 1768, but it is apparent that the issues upon which the contest would turn began to take shape, and the sides began to mobilize, as early as 1765.

[12] *DAB*, V, 213–14 (Charles Worthen Spencer); Richard B. Morris, "James De-Lancey of New York," privately printed.

[13] New-York *Journal; or, The General Advertiser,* May 10, April 12, 1770; *Smith's Historical Memoirs,* 33. For results of the election of 1761, see *A Copy of the Poll List of the Election for Representatives for the City and County of New York . . . MDCCLXI* (New York, 1880).

2. On Party Labels

There has been a tendency, perhaps understandable, to simplify New York's political factions by dividing them into "Livingston" and "De-Lancey" family parties. It has already been noted that these designations have little significance for the period before mid-century. True, Livingstons and DeLanceys were prominent in New York politics in those years, but Morrises and Philipses were of equal if not greater importance, and there is no evidence that the Livingston and DeLancey names were used to designate parties. The unprecedented political power acquired by Chief Justice James DeLancey after 1745 did cause DeLancey's name to be used occasionally to identify his group of followers, but other labels, such as the "popular" or the "Assembly" party, were used as well. The Livingstons, who were less active politically in that period, not only did not regularly oppose DeLancey but were frequently aligned with him against Governor Clinton and Cadwallader Colden. In the years after 1765, and especially during the elections of 1768 and 1769, there is probably more evidence for casting the colony's politics in terms of Livingstons versus DeLanceys than at any other period. But even here, such categories are far from satisfactory.

The main evidence for a Livingston-DeLancey rivalry in the 1760's, or any other decade, comes from William Smith, Jr. Since Smith wrote more about the late colonial period than any other contemporary observer, his opinions have had a disproportionate influence. Smith's book of memoirs abounds with references to Livingston and DeLancey parties; he asserts in one oft-quoted passage that "the Province of New York is divided into two great Parties," and that "the Livingston Family" and "the DeLanceys" were their respective leaders. Most New Yorkers, however, saw the party contests as much more than family rivalries. Cadwallader Colden, for example, while noting that the parties sometimes "have taken their denominations from some distinguished Person or Family who have appeared at their Head," also asserted that they grew out of "the different political and religious Principles of the Inhabitants." Thomas Jones believed that the split in the late colonial years was between "republicans" and "Episcopalians." It is of interest that the most frequent use of family labels came from the Livingstons themselves. (Smith, of course, was married to a Livingston.) Since several members of that family were singled out as specific targets of opposition attacks, they may well have imagined that there was something provocative about being a Livingston. Peter R. Livingston in the heat of battle once described the opposition as "a party that has from the beginning of this Province opposed our famaly." And yet in that same letter he also said, "we have two partyes her [e] viz. Church & Discenters." [14] It thus would seem that the Livingston-DeLancey dichotomy is hardly adequate for dealing with the complexities of New York's party situation, even in the 1760's—or perhaps especially then. This somewhat cumbersome scheme has its disadvantages when one tries to fit it to the actual events of the 1760's. "Family," in short, has functioned as something of a red herring in the historiography of New York's colonial politics.

But though there is much confusion to be created in mistaking "genealogy for political history," [15] the problem of how the parties of the 1760's *should* be designated is still not easily solved. The terms "upriver" and "seaboard" might answer, inasmuch as that rivalry was certainly in evidence during this period. On the other hand the seaboard interest did make alliances with some Dutchess and Albany County politicians around 1768; moreover, though the lawyer triumvirate was indeed a part of the upriver interest, Smith, Livingston, and Scott all lived in New York City. Then there is the familiar landed-merchant rivalry, which was important in 1768 but not in 1769, while the Anglican-Dissenter division may have applied to 1769 but not to 1768. Since the clearest lines of division in the election of 1768 appear to have been laid down by the civil disturbances of 1765–1766, and since some of

---

[14] *Smith's Historical Memoirs,* 95; Colden to ?, New York, July 7, 1770, NYHS *Colls.,* X (1877), 223–24; Jones, *History of New York,* I, 18; Peter R. Livingston to Oliver Wendell, New York, Jan. 19, 1769, Livingston Papers, MCNY. In 1770 there was a printed exchange between "The Watchman" (probably William Livingston or William Smith, Jr.) and "Americanus" (a member of the opposition party, possibly Captain James DeLancey or Robert Watts) in which the matter of Livingston and DeLancey factions was discussed in some detail. See New-York *Journal; or, The General Advertiser,* April 5, 12, 19, 1770.

[15] J. H. Plumb, *The Origins of Political Stability: England 1675–1725* (Boston, 1967), xiv.

this tension carried over to the election of 1769, it might be helpful to think in terms of a kind of "radical-conservative" polarity. And yet even this may represent an undue weighting of emphasis. Implying too great an ideological distinction between the two parties at this point would be somewhat premature. Both considered themselves to have sound Whiggish views relative to London's efforts to tax and regulate the colonies. All in all, it may well be that the labels "popular Whigs" and "moderate Whigs" come closest to conveying at least the main rhetorical differences between the two factions which contended for power in the final two colonial elections.

3. The Election of 1768

The Assembly election of March, 1768, was the first to be held since 1761. Had Governor Henry Moore not been compelled by the New York septennial act to call a new election, he would no doubt have been content to keep the old Assembly in office, since it had steered a relatively moderate course considering the turbulence of the times. In its final weeks the Assembly had even agreed to provision the British troops stationed in the colony, as required by the Quartering Act. But by 1768 demands for a new election could be turned aside no longer. Rival politicians had been girding for battle since 1765, and the month-long campaign in February and March, 1768, proved to be one of the most intense and acrimonious in the province's history. The "Contagion of Politiks," according to one New Yorker, was so pervasive that "we . . . know Nothing Else nor Discourse upon Anything Else." The "Contagion" also spread to outlying areas, it being reported that "there are like to be warm Contests at the Election not only of your Matropolis [New York County] but of most of the other Countys." We know that there were two factions in Dutchess County, where Robert R. Livingston expected a "Warm Election." "I have sat up with John Carman," he wrote, "our Opponents are Dirk Brinkerhoff and Leonard Van Kleek." It was also reported that there would be "a great Contest" at Schenectady for the single township seat.[16] Electioneering

---

[16] Jonathan Landon to Robert Morris, Morrisania, Mar. 13, 1768, Robert Morris to Landon, Mar. 7, 1768, draft, Morris MSS (Robert Morris Papers), Box 4, Rut-

became so fierce in Orange County that riots ensued, while in the Borough of Westchester Lewis Morris [III] and John DeLancey (Peter DeLancey's son) revived the long-standing political rivalry between their families by entering the lists for the borough seat.[17]

Since there are few details of the rural elections, it is necessary to turn to that of New York County for information about the 1768 party battles. The compactness of the City facilitated electioneering, and its printing presses were kept busy turning out propaganda for the rival factions. Moreover, it was there that the stakes were highest, a rough system of proportional representation having given New York County four members in the Assembly.[18] Seven men competed for these four seats in 1768. They were Captain James DeLancey, Jacob Walton, James Jauncey, Philip Livingston [II], John Morin Scott, William Bayard, and Amos Dodge. Dodge, a carpenter by trade, lacked the sort of finish that was regarded in that day as more or less indispensable for holding high public office, and his candidacy seems not to have been taken very seriously by the others. In the final count Dodge finished last, even his fellow workingmen giving him no more than 12 per cent of their votes. William Bayard was a well-to-do merchant who had been in the Assembly since 1761. He seems not to have been very popular with the voters either, doing only a little better than Dodge in the election. Of the five other candidates, Philip Livingston [II], a popular incumbent, and James DeLancey, by now established as a leader of the

gers; [Robert R. Livingston] to Robert Livingston, Jr., Clermont, Feb. 21, 1768, Livingston-Redmond MSS, Reel 6; Abraham Ten Broeck to James Duane, Albany, Feb. 22, 1768, Duane Papers, 1766–71, NYHS. The best guide through the complex network of political issues in these years is Roger Champagne's "Family Politics versus Constitutional Principles."

[17] *Assembly Journal* (Buel), Oct. 29, Nov. 1, 1768. For the Westchester election see Jonathan Landon to Robert Morris, Morrisania, Mar. 13, 1768, Morris MSS (Robert Morris Papers), Box 4, Rutgers. Champagne asserts that these rural contests were an extension of the Livingston-DeLancey rivalry, but evidence for this is sparse ("Family Politics versus Constitutional Principles," 61). It seems more likely that they simply continued old local rivalries. Once the elected members met for the Assembly session in New York City, however, party patterns can be discerned.

[18] Albany County actually had a total of five representatives—two for the county at large, one for Livingston Manor, one for Rensselaerswyck and one for the Township of Schenectady. All other counties had two members, except Westchester which had four—two for the county at large, one for Cortlandt Manor, and one for the Borough of Westchester.

Sons of Liberty, were considered the favorites, and thus the main contest was to be among Walton, Jauncey, and Scott for the two remaining seats. Walton and Jauncey, both merchants, were allied with DeLancey, all three having announced their candidacies simultaneously in February. Apparently they shared DeLancey's popularity with the Sons of Liberty and New York City mechanics.[19] Because these three candidates assumed the more extreme position on imperial issues, they will be designated here as the popular Whigs.

It was plain from the tactics adopted by DeLancey, Jauncey, and Walton that they had decided to concede one Assembly seat to the well-liked Philip Livingston, who wisely managed to stay aloof from all factions in the 1768 campaign. This in turn allowed them to concentrate all their fire on the weaker candidate, John Morin Scott. Most of the popular Whig propaganda was directed toward tying Scott in with the lawyer-landed interest, which was depicted as having shown a reactionary and unpatriotic face during the critical days of 1765–1766. Their propaganda hit hardest at Scott's profession. Not only was Scott a lawyer rather than a merchant, and thus a questionable choice to represent a commercial city, but he was also closely connected to the great landed families as one of the colony's leading real property lawyers. He had represented the Philipse family against Nimham in 1767, had sat on the court that convicted Prendergast and other small farmers in the Dutchess County land cases in 1766, and had stood with the other two members of the lawyer triumvirate, William Livingston and William Smith, Jr., in opposing the more radical measures of the Sons of Liberty in 1765.[20]

In a score of campaign pamphlets and newspaper articles the anti-

---

[19] New-York *Gazette; or, The Weekly Post-Boy,* Feb. 13, 22, 1768. For information on Amos Dodge's candidacy, see Champagne, "Liberty Boys and Mechanics," 132.

[20] For Scott's connection with the landed interest, see Oscar Handlin and Irving Mark, eds., "Chief Daniel Nimham v. Roger Morris, Beverly Robinson, and Philip Philipse—An Indian Land Case in Colonial New York, 1765–1767," *Ethnohistory,* XI (Summer, 1964), 193–246; Handlin and Mark, eds., "Land Cases in Colonial New York, 1765–1767: The King v. William Prendergast," *New York University Law Quarterly Review,* IX (Jan., 1942), 165–94. Dutchess County landowner Beverly Robinson named Scott along with William Livingston and James Duane as having "always been our counsel" in land disputes. Robinson to John Thomas, Esq., Fredericksburg, May 8, 1772, Philipse-Gouverneur Land Titles, CU.

lawyer theme was sounded again and again. The essays of "Philanthropos" were representative. These charged the lawyers with having failed to defend colonial liberties at the time of the Stamp Act, accused John Morin Scott (though not by name) of opposing the Virginia Resolves, and pointed out that the lawyers did not approve of letting justices of the peace try cases of under £5 value, thus striking at a plan designed to "relieve the Poor." The lawyer "Gentry" had interests inimical to those of the city; it was the merchants who were "the properest Persons to represent us in the Assembly." "Philanthropos" further declared that the lawyers were responsible for the rupture between "the tenants and their lordly masters" in 1766 by refusing to take their cases and thereby driving them to "the disagreeable necessity" of violence. The landed assemblymen were accused of agreeing to quarter and provision British troops the more easily to put down small farmer dissidents; and it was suggested that galleries be provided in the Assembly hall so that people thereafter could "petition and remonstrate" against bad bills. No group of men that "fatten and grow rich upon the ruin of the people," as lawyers did, could ever in "Philanthropos' " view be proper representatives of the community. All popular Whig propaganda used this same tactic, that of identifying the lawyers with conservative and landed interests.[21]

The moderate Whig faction repelled these assaults as best it could. But the tone of the counter-argument was unmistakably defensive. "An Old Whig" tried to point out that in critical times it was a good thing to

[21] "A Few Observations on the Conduct of the General Assembly of New York, etc.," by "Philanthropos," Broadsides Coll., Rare Book Room, NYPL; "To the Freeholders and Freemen of the City and County of New-York," New-York *Journal; or, The General Advertiser,* Supplement, Feb. 25, 1768. In one article the author asked why the lawyers showed no concern when Robert Noble and his followers were dispossessed by the Albany County sheriff during the land riots of 1766. Letter of Johonas Von Dore Manadus in New-York *Journal; or, The General Advertiser,* Feb. 19, 1768. For other popular Whig propaganda see "The Occasionalist," "A Better Creed than the Last," "The Voter's New Catechism," "A Dialogue Between Two Respectable Personages," and A Collection of Political Cards, all dated 1768, Broadsides Coll., Rare Book Room, NYPL. James DeLancey was on a visit to England when the Assembly was dissolved for the new election, and had not yet returned home when the election took place in March, 1768. New-York *Gazette; or, The Weekly Post-Boy,* Feb. 13, 1768; The New-York *Journal; or The General Advertiser,* April 12, 1770; Ross J. S. Hoffman, *Edmund Burke, New York Agent* (Philadelphia, 1956), 87–88.

have "a Man skilled in the Law" sitting in the Assembly, while "The Querist" defended the lawyers' actions during the Stamp Act disturbances by insisting that they too had opposed internal taxes, but that to support all the radical demands "might have spread the Flame of *absolute Independency* throughout all the Colonies, to the total Ruin of the British Empire." As for the charge that the lawyers' private interests were contrary to the public good, "A Citizen" argued that the "Merchant," the "Farmer," and the "Churchman or Presbyterian" also had private interests, but this did not mean that men would "act upon such base and narrow principles" in the Assembly. Rather: "Because as those, who compose the legislature have various and opposite interests, so they are, and ever must be, a check upon each other: And therefore no one man, can, against the opinion of the rest, secure his own private interest, in a manner injurious to them and those they represent." [22]

By the final week of the campaign the pamphlet war reached its climax. The pro-Scott propaganda closely resembles the literary style of the *Independent Reflector,* and it is a fair assumption that William Livingston and William Smith, Jr., were working actively in Scott's behalf. That style, moreover, was well known in New York City, which no doubt gave added stimulus to the popular party's attacks on the legal profession. Nor were efforts to influence the electorate limited to propaganda. During the five days that the New York County polls were open

---

[22] New-York *Journal; or, The General Advertiser,* Mar. 3, 1768; "To the Freeholders and Freemen of the City and County of New York . . . in Answer to the Remarks on the 17 Queries," n.d., Broadsides Coll., Rare Book Room, NYPL; New-York *Gazette; or, The Weekly Post-Boy,* Feb. 29, 1768. For moderate Whig propaganda see such examples as "Political Creed for the Day" and others in the Broadsides Coll., Rare Book Room, NYPL; New-York *Gazette; or, The Weekly Post-Boy,* Mar. 7, 1768, and other newspapers in the three weeks or so prior to the elections.

The precocious balance-of-interests reasoning displayed by "A Citizen" crops up from time to time in New York political literature, especially in the writings of William Livingston, who well may have been the author in this case.

The nefarious connections between lawyers, the judiciary, and the landed interest, and the circulation of this propaganda in places like Dutchess County (where Supreme Court Judge and land magnate Robert R. Livingston was a candidate for reelection) could not have failed to undermine further the confidence, already shaky, in the benevolence of the local gentry. Though there were no rural newspapers at that time, the New York City papers as well as other printed election material were sent regularly to friends and relatives in the counties.

—March 7 through March 11—party managers bustled about the city rounding up votes. Isaac Sears and other Sons of Liberty urged the working people to support the popular faction's candidates, while gentlemen like Oliver DeLancey and Henry Cruger made themselves conspicuous at or near the polling place at City Hall. The treating of voters reached heroic proportions, if we may judge from the itemized bill presented to Captain DeLancey by tavernkeeper Benjamin Stout. DeLancey was charged for 248 "meals of victuals," 134 bottles of wine, 106½ "Double Bowls of punch," 117 "mugs of Beer & Seyder" and a variety of other beverages.[23] Scott's supporters were equally busy. It was later charged that Scott himself had attended a meeting of "Journey-man Carpenters Solliciting Votes and that he offered to give Money to their Box," and that he had threatened to sue a hatter if he did not vote the right way. These and other charges were flung back and forth when the election results were contested later in the Assembly, each side accusing the other of bribery, the conveying of fraudulent freeholds, and the judicious distribution or calling in of "loans" just before election day.[24]

The election results themselves, however, most clearly indicated the effectiveness of the popular Whig campaign. Philip Livingston [II] and Captain DeLancey headed the list with 1,320 and 1,204 votes respectively. Not far behind were the two other merchants, Jacob Walton with, 1,175 votes and James Jauncey with, 1,052. John Morin Scott came in a poor fifth with only 870 votes. Robert Morris, by no means unsympathetic to the moderate Whig faction, observed that "the Disappointed party deserve the treatment they have met with [.] It was presuming too much upon the favour of the Town to attempt to impose a

[23] "James DeLancey, Esq. to Benjamin Stout, For the Election," Mar. 7, 1768, DeLancey Papers, Box 1, NYHS; New-York *Journal; or, The General Advertiser,* April 12, 1770; Champagne, "Family Politics versus Constitutional Principles," 67–68; Champagne, "Liberty Boys and Mechanics," 131.

[24] "Brief of Mr. Jauncey's Defense against the Charge of Bribery and Corruption made against him by Mr. Scott," Nov., 1768, James Duane Papers, NYHS; *Assembly Journal* (Buel), Nov. 8, Dec. 14, 16, 1768. For more information on New York City election practices, see Patricia U. Bonomi, "Political Patterns in Colonial New York City: The General Assembly Election of 1768," *Political Science Quarterly,* LXXXI (Sept., 1966), 432–47.

man upon them that even his friends must allow was a very improper [person] to represent a trading city." [25]

In the Dutchess County election Robert R. Livingston, who was vulnerable to many of the same charges that had plagued Scott, was also defeated. If Cadwallader Colden's assessment is to be trusted, Livingston "had so far lost the esteem of the Freeholders in that County, that he gave up before half the Freeholders then present had given in their votes, tho' he had every thing in his favour, which power could give him." Colden's judgment in this case was probably fairly sound. As has been noted, an opposition to the Dutchess County landed proprietors had begun to gather as far back as the 1740's. In the 1761 Assembly election Robert R. and Henry Livingston had won reelection, but a piece of opposition doggerel, which accused them of offering "bounty" and using "deceit," had ended with the line, "Not a vote would you get if it wan't for your land." Though many farmers may have been intimidated by landlord power in 1761, the rural disturbances of 1765–1766 had sufficiently emboldened them by 1768 that they openly rejected the county's most illustrious citizen and his running-mate, electing Dirck Brinkerhoff and Leonard Van Kleeck from the Poughkeepsie area in their places.[26] The contest in the Borough of Westchester between Lewis Morris [III] and John DeLancey was so close that it was not finally decided until the new Assembly met in the fall of 1768. After throwing out the votes of several non-resident freemen, the House awarded the

[25] *A Copy of the Poll List of the Election for Representatives for the City and County of New York . . . MDCCLXVIII* (New York, 1880); Robert Morris to [?], n.d., draft, Morris MSS (Robert Morris Papers), Box 4, Rutgers. As for the other two candidates in the election, Bayard got 584 votes and Dodge got 255. For an interesting analysis of this vote, see Champagne, "Liberty Boys and Mechanics," 132.

[26] Colden to the Earl of Hillsborough, New York, April 25, 1768, *N.Y. Col. Docs.*, VIII, 61; *Yearbook* of the Dutchess County Historical Society, 1921, p. 36. They had to reject Livingston openly inasmuch as there was no secret ballot and Livingston and his relatives were probably listening as the votes were cast. Robert R. Livingston had requested Robert Livingston, Jr., and his son, Walter Livingston, to be present at the election after rounding up what votes they could on the Little Nine Partners Patent in the northern part of the county. [Robert R. Livingston] to Robert Livingston, Jr., Clermont, Feb. 21, 1768, Livingston-Redmond MSS, Reel 6.

election to John DeLancey by a margin of one.[27] The election results made it evident—and the party battles in the fall Assembly session would make it more so—that the popular Whigs were rapidly strengthening their position throughout the province.

4. Party Conflicts in the Assembly: 1768

The votes in the Assembly on contested elections offer the first positive evidence that colony-wide parties were forming. In those votes the most reliable members of the moderate Whig faction were Colonel Peter R. Livingston of the Manor, Abraham Ten Broeck of Rensselaerswyck, and a newcomer to the Assembly, Philip Schuyler of Albany County. These three, who shared an upriver-landed viewpoint, were soon joined by George Clinton and Charles DeWitt, new members from Ulster County, and sometimes by Pierre Van Cortlandt of the Manor of Cortlandt and Jacob Ten Eyck of Albany County. Philip Livingston, who was in a position to mediate between the two factions, having both landed and merchant connections, was elected Speaker. In most cases he did not vote in divisions, but on the four occasions when he did, he supported the moderate Whig side. The popular party nucleus of Captain James DeLancey, Jacob Walton, and James Jauncey was frequently augmented by John DeLancey, Frederick Philipse III, and John Thomas, all from Westchester, and by Dirck Brinkerhoff of Dutchess and Daniel Kissam of Queens. The rest of the members shifted back and forth, usually supporting the popular party on disputed election contests but standing with the moderates on issues affecting imperial relationships.[28]

[27] *Assembly Journal* (Buel), Nov. 17, 1768; Jonathan Landon to Robert Morris, Morrisania, Mar. 13, 1768, Morris MSS (Robert Morris Papers), Box 4, Rutgers.

[28] There were sixteen divisions in that session of the Assembly. *Assembly Journal* (Buel), Nov. 3 through Dec. 31, 1768. Schuyler, who had been urged to run for the Assembly seat by William Smith, Jr., had been supported by all the leading men in Albany County in one of the few uncontested elections of 1768. Abraham Ten Broeck to James Duane, Albany, Feb. 22, 1768, Duane Papers, NYHS; William Smith, Jr., to Schuyler, Jan. 18, 1768, Philip Schuyler Papers, Box 23, NYPL; Don R. Gerlach, *Philip Schuyler and the American Revolution in New York, 1733–1777* (Lincoln, Neb., 1964), 143–44. Pierre Van Cortlandt had defeated his brother-in-law, Philip Verplanck, who had represented the Manor for

The public support enjoyed by the New York City popular Whig leaders in the 1768 election cast them firmly in an opposition role in the Assembly, a role which they cultivated by mounting a strong campaign against imperial policies. They tried to withhold funds for government salaries and military provisions, and they proposed rejection of an address supporting the governor's handling of the city radicals. But the key debate of that session concerned what action should be taken on the Massachusetts Circular Letter protesting the Townshend Acts. The Earl of Hillsborough, secretary of state for the colonies, had already advised the governors that any Assembly endorsing the Circular Letter was to be dissolved at once. Though the moderate Whigs would have preferred to support Governor Moore's efforts to steady the ship, they also realized that if public pressure for endorsement of the Circular Letter was to make a dissolution inevitable, the popular faction should not be able to claim all credit for defending colonial liberties. The tactic they adopted was to stall for time, deferring consideration of the Circular Letter until other government business was completed.

The power of the public to bring pressure on the Assembly was strengthened by the urban surroundings in which it met, and the city radicals needed little prompting to intensify their demands for action. An article in one city newspaper questioned the Assembly's fitness to remain in office should it fail to answer the Circular Letter. On November 18, the city merchants marched "in a Body to attend the Assembly & ask what was become of the Boston letters. . . ." This was followed by a meeting of local activists who drew up a statement instructing their representatives to take up the question forthwith. Only the moderates' superior knowledge of parliamentary procedure enabled them to obtain a postponement, thereby heading off an immediate crisis with Governor Moore. But the issue had become too useful to the city radicals and too intertwined with party stratagems to permit of compromise. When it was finally taken up again on December 31, the Assembly voted to answer the Massachusetts Letter, whereupon Governor Moore dissolved it for new elections on January 2, 1769.[29]

---

thirty-four years, in the first contested election ever held in that district. Manor of Cortlandt Poll List, Mar. 10, 1768, Van Cortlandt MSS, SHR.

[29] New-York *Journal; or, The General Advertiser,* Nov. 17, Dec. 1, 1768; *Smith's Historical Memoirs,* 46–49. Roger Champagne discusses the Massachusetts Circu-

5. The Election of 1769

Councilman William Smith, Jr., a major force behind the scenes in all maneuvers of the moderate party, believed that the popular leaders had "lost Credit" with the people during the Assembly session and would not do as well in the forthcoming election as they had in that of the previous year. The popular faction saw it all quite differently. "I am not the least afraid," asserted one of them, "but we Shall Carry our Election All Hollow against the Miscreants—Notwithstanding all the Sly Endeavours of that Snake in the Grass—Will. Smith. . . ."[30]

As soon as it was evident that a new election would be called, the two parties began the by-then familiar scramble to develop exploitable issues. The skill with which the popular Whigs had reduced the 1768 campaign to the slogan "no lawyer in the Assembly" offered a lesson to the moderates, who now believed they had an issue of equal simplicity and emotional appeal for the impending campaign. This issue had begun to develop as early as March, 1768, and stemmed from the controversial proposal made in 1767 by John Ewer, Bishop of Landaff, recommending the establishment of an Anglican bishop in the colonies. The Reverend Thomas B. Chandler of Elizabeth, New Jersey, had written a pamphlet, *Appeal to the Public, in Behalf of the Church of England, in America,* at the behest of a number of northern Anglicans including Myles Cooper, President of King's College, strongly supporting the plan for a colonial bishop. Bishop Ewer's proposal and Chandler's *Appeal* had aroused the fears of New York dissenters who, like their brethren throughout the colonies, had always opposed any extension of Church authority in America. The issue had arisen too late to make

lar controversy in "Family Politics versus Constitutional Principles." Additional details are in Gerlach, *Philip Schuyler,* 150–73. A somewhat different interpretation of these events is offered by Bernard Friedman in "The New York Assembly Elections of 1768 and 1769: The Disruption of Family Politics," *New York History,* XLVI (Jan., 1965), 14.

[30] *Smith's Historical Memoirs,* 48; John Wetherhead to William Johnson, New York, Jan. 9, 1769, *The Papers of Sir William Johnson* (Albany, Univ. of the State of New York, 1921–1957), VI, 575. Wetherhead named Philip Schuyler, William Smith, Jr., William Livingston, and John Morin Scott as the main party leaders.

much of a stir in the 1768 election, though one moderate Whig writer did sound the alarm: "America is a Virgin as yet, undebauch'd by proud tyranical Ecclesiasticks . . . [and] the Man of Sin who always steals a Rape under a Priest's Garment. . . ." Constant vigilance was necessary, there being now "a Party who have a Project upon the Anvil, which if it ever succeeds will ruin the whole Continent.—Oh! the Appeal!—The Appeal!—OH! THE BISHOP!—THE BISHOP!" Following the election this issue had been pressed by William Livingston in the newspapers and in a pamphlet, *A Letter to the Right Reverend Father in God, John, Bishop of Landaff*. This in turn had brought a response from the Reverend Charles Inglis of Trinity Church, *A Vindication of the Bishop of Landaff's sermon*. And so it had gone all through the summer and fall of 1768.[31]

When the anti-Church agitation continued after the election of 1768, the popular party accused the moderates of trying to distract attention from their election defeat; religion, they claimed, was being made the "political Engine" of an "ambitious disappointed Faction." The reintroduction of it into the 1769 campaign shows that they were not wrong, though few could have forseen how ingeniously the moderate Whigs would manipulate the issue to challenge the liberal credentials of the New York County popular party leaders. Two factors helped determine their strategy. One was that the DeLanceys were prominent members of the Anglican Church, and few New Yorkers had forgotten that the late Lieutenant Governor James DeLancey had supported a plan to place King's College under Anglican auspices. Second, Captain

[31] Livingston signed himself "The American Whig" in articles in the New-York *Journal; or, The General Advertiser*, Mar. 3, 1768, and the New-York *Gazette; or, The Weekly Post-Boy*, Mar. 14, 1768. William Livingston, *A Letter to the Right Reverend Father in God, John, Bishop of Landaff*, Boston, 1768, Rare Book Room, NYPL; E. T. Corwin, ed., *Ecclesiastical Records*, State of New York (Albany, 1901–1916), VI, 4084. More details of this controversy can be found in the New-York *Gazette; or, The Weekly Post-Boy*, June 20, 1768; the New-York *Gazette; and The Weekly Mercury*, Oct. 10, 1768, July 3, 1769; and in Milton Klein's unpublished dissertation, "The American Whig, William Livingston of New York," Chap. XIV. This was not, of course, the first time an Anglican bishop had been proposed. For an interesting discussion of the unsuccessful efforts of some provincial Anglicans to obtain a bishop, and the connections between Anglicanism and Loyalism, consult William H. Nelson, *The American Tory* (New York, 1961), 14–17. The fullest study of Church influence in the colonies is Carl Bridenbaugh, *Mitre and Sceptre* (New York, 1962).

James DeLancey had made a trip to England in 1767–1768 and his political opponents had charged at the time that one of its main purposes
was to plead for an American bishop. Having identified the best known
popular leader as a member of the "Church interest," the moderate
Whigs next set out to expose the Church as a reactionary institution
that threatened the very civil and political liberties which the popular
Whigs pretended to defend. In a series of pamphlets and newspaper articles the moderate party writers raised the specter of "episcopal palaces
. . . pontifical revenues . . . spiritual courts, and all of the pomp, gran-
deur, luxury and regalia of an American Lambeth," all of which would
be sure to accompany the appointment of an American bishop.[32] They
also recalled the earlier conflict over Anglican control of King's College, and warned of another dire threat to religious freedom in the An-
glican-controlled Council's refusal to charter Lutheran and Presbyterian
churches in New York City, where the Church of England was established.[33]

This propaganda was designed to draw attention to the sinister
parallels between Church hierarchies and imperial hierarchies, between
Anglican oppression and governmental tyranny, at the same time emphasizing the liberty-loving values of the dissenting churches and their
members. The hope was that the dissenting churches in New York City

[32] New-York *Gazette; and the Weekly Mercury,* April 4, 1768; *A Political Creed,*
William Livingston, 1768, Rare Book Room, NYPL; New-York *Gazette; or, The
Weekly Post-Boy,* Mar. 14, 1768. On DeLancey's trip see above, n. 21.

[33] The Anglican Church was established in the four lower counties of New York.
The religious controversy kept New York's printing presses busy over a period of
many months. Articles by "The American Whig" (William Livingston) ran from
March 14, 1768 to July 24, 1769 in the New-York *Gazette; or, The Weekly
Post-Boy.* These were answered by "A Whip for the American Whig" by "Timothy Tickle, Esqr." in the New-York *Gazette; and the Weekly Mercury* from
April 4, 1768 to July 10, 1769. These in turn elicited "A Kick for the Whipper"
by "Sir Isaac Foot" in the New-York *Gazette; or, The Weekly Post-Boy* from May
23, 1768 to Jan. 29, 1770. Some representative pamphlets on both sides of the
question are *A Political Creed, Reasons for the present glorious Combination of
Dissenters, Answers to the Reasons Lately published by the Independants, in Support of their Malicious Combination, The Freeholder No. 1, A Continuation of
the Answers, to the Reasons, Freeholder, No. II, The Conclusion of the Answers,
to the Reasons, the Freeholder, No. III,* and *To the Dissenting Electors of All
Denominations.* All were printed in 1769 and are now in the Broadside Coll.,
Rare Book Room, NYPL.

might be encouraged to combine together to resist the proposal for an Anglican bishop—"this ecclesiastical stamp-act," as William Livingston labeled it. Had it been possible to exploit religious prejudices and to unite all dissenting church members against the Anglicans, the moderate Whigs would indeed have had a winning issue, for dissenters greatly outnumbered Anglicans in New York. But the moderate party writers —on this occasion anything but "moderate"—overstepped themselves. Their extravagant language and their blatant appeals to bigotry not only gave deep offense to the Anglicans but repelled some other sects as well. The large Dutch-Reformed congregations, for example, firmly refused to support the proposed association of dissenters.[34]

Before the religious issue had developed this far, some of the moderate Whigs had hoped to construct a coalition slate of two dissenters and two Anglicans. The popular Whigs would have none of this, determining instead to support "the Four old ones," [35] DeLancey, Jauncey, Walton, and Philip Livingston [II]. At this rebuff "Several hundred Dissenters met at Two in the Fields & unanimously named four vizt Philip [Livingston], P V B L [Peter Van Brugh Livingston, Philip and William's brother], Scott & Theod: Van Wyck." As William Smith, Jr., tells it, "Philip then refused to join the other Side & they took in John Cruger in his Stead—Now for it—Four against Four." Philip Livingston [II], obviously caught in the middle of this party wrangle, would have preferred a "peaceable Election" to these "most violent Heats and Animosities." But forced to choose one party or the other, he joined

---

[34] William Livingston to the Reverend Samuel Cooper, Mar. 28, 1768, cited in Corwin, ed., *Ecclesiastical Records*, VI, 4114; Peter R. Livingston to Robert Livingston, Jr., New York, June 15, 1769, Livingston-Redmond MSS, Reel 6. For the post-election formation of a Society of Dissenters in New York City, see Herbert L. Osgood, ed., "The Society of Dissenters founded at New York in 1769," *AHR*, VI (April, 1901), 498–507.

[35] "We Shall have a most contested Election here," wrote William Smith, Jr., to Robert R. Livingston. "Tuesday Evening upon a Talk that the four old members were to be Set up there was a Meeting of Delegates of all the Dissenting Churches—a Card was Sent to the other Party consenting that they may Set up two Churchmen & we two dissenters—They answered yesterday at Eleven that they could not comply & advertisements issued in Favor of the Four old ones." Smith to R. R. Livingston, New York, Jan. 5, 1769, Robert R. Livingston Coll., II, NYHS. See also "To the Freemen and Freeholders of the City and County of New-York, by John Cruger, James DeLancey, Jacob Walton and James Jauncey," New York, Jan. 9, 1769, Broadsides Coll., Rare Book Room, NYPL.

hands with the moderates. James Duane, his niece's husband, believed this decision cost him some important support. Philip, Duane said, was "at the Zenith of popular power" when courted by the DeLancey family to form a union with their party. "He rejected their offer and Joined the prespeterian party," which had agreed to keep out of public office any man "who professed the established Religion." Every "Churchman felt challenged by this combination & so opposed it." Others so disaffected were Philip's cousin, Judge Robert R. Livingston, and another nephew by marriage, John Jay. Both were Anglicans and both took offense at the injection of religion into the campaign. As Jay wrote to the judge, "Philip Livingston shakes—he is said to have played a double Game, appearances are against him, if true I hope he may lose his Election. —No Presbeterian has given Place to no Lawyer, and no Churchman is substituted in the Room of no Bishop." Robert R. Livingston, deeply alienated by the "unpardonable warmth & acrimony" of the dissenter propaganda, wrote a staunch defense of the Anglican church, which Jay promised to have printed at once.[36]

While all this was taking place, the popular party leaders had not failed to maintain their connections with the Sons of Liberty. These now provided, in the words of William Smith, Jr., "a Ladder to popular Preferment." This was very dramatically manifested in January, 1769, when Captain James DeLancey astonished Governor Moore by refusing a seat on the New York Council. Moore, in reporting this to London, said he would leave to DeLancey "the explanation of so singular a conduct." William Smith, Jr., had his own thoughts on that: the Council seat had been offered while DeLancey "was canvassing for Votes," and he "rejected the Kings Grace & preferred the Honors of the People." The timing, Smith observed, could not have been "more fortunate" for DeLancey's standing with the public. To enhance their radical connections, the popular leaders continued to remind their constituents of their

[36] William Smith, Jr., to Robert R. Livingston, New York, Jan. 5, 1769, John Jay to R. R. Livingston, Jan. 1769, R. R. Livingston draft statement on bishop controversy, n.d. [1769], Robert R. Livingston Coll., II, NYHS; James Duane to Robert Livingston, Jr., New York, June 3, 1769, Livingston-Redmond MSS, Reel 6. Philip Livingston's reasons for joining the "Presbyterian" party were stated in an open letter to the public, New-York Gazette; and The Weekly Mercury, Jan. 9, 1769. I know of no other New York County Assembly election where two full slates of candidates stood opposed.

strong defense of colonial rights in the 1768 Assembly. And once again they went over all of their opponents' transgressions, reaching back to the lawyers' equivocal position on the Stamp Act, and insisting as before on the importance of electing commercial men to represent a trading city. The Sons of Liberty responded as expected. Sears and Lamb scoured up votes for the popular Whigs, while Alexander McDougall, a firm Presbyterian, gave his all for the moderates.[37]

As the election approached, Peter R. Livingston, son of manor proprietor Robert Livingston, Jr., was busy with "management of the Votes" on behalf of the moderate Whigs. "I have been so immerged in Election Jobing," he confessed to a friend, "that I have had no time to write." "We are hott and pepper on both Sides. . . . I have two Uncles & two friends on our Side . . . so that you may thinck I am Employed with all my might. And by our Canvas thinck we stand Strong altho' it will be a tight match." Livingston thought there would be "a vast deal of Cross Voting [.] The two they all pitch on of our four are Philip & Scott which will put them in. . . . our people are in high Spirits and if there is not fair play shewn there will be blood shead as we have by far the best part of the Brusers on our side who are determined to use force if they use any foul play." [38] Yet whatever Peter Livingston's "Brusers" may have done, the "tight match" he predicted never materialized.

By the third day of the election it was obvious that the popular party had easily won all four Assembly seats. The winning total of the least successful popular party candidate, James Jauncey, was still over two hundred votes greater than that of the top moderate, Philip Livingston. The soundness of the moderates' defeat resulted at least partially from the poisonous effects of their anti-Church propaganda. The religious issue was in any case much more important than family names. "Believe me my dear Sir," wrote James Duane to his father-in-law, Robert Livingston, Jr., "Capt. DeLancey was not of Importance enough

---

[37] *Smith's Historical Memoirs,* 60; Gov. Moore to the Earl of Hillsborough, New York, Jan. 21, 1769, *N.Y. Col. Docs.,* VIII, 148; New-York *Journal; or, The General Advertiser,* Jan. 12, 19, 1769; Champagne, "Family Politics versus Constitutional Principles," 74–75.

[38] Peter R. Livingston to Oliver Wendell, New York, Jan. 19, 1769, Livingston Papers, MCNY: Peter R. Livingston to Philip Schuyler, New York, Jan. 16, 1769, Philip Schuyler Papers, Box 23, NYPL.

(tho a Gentleman of Some Weight) to decide in this Election. The pres-
bertereans put the Contest on a broader Basis. . . . The Consequences
fall heavy on our Family." John Watts declared that the "presbyterians
or Independants as the church writers call them" had issued "offensive"
publications, and were beaten by the votes of "the more substantial people." Peter R. Livingston saw the result in a somewhat different light.
"I have been very busy in our late Election," he wrote, "but have the
mortification to inform you that we lost it by the Church [party] having
too much power over our Common people." [39]

The very frequency with which the "Common people" were now
being referred to, and the growing prominence of the Sons of Liberty,
give more than a little reason to doubt that either church or family was
the decisive issue. Governor Moore believed that the Sons of Liberty,
with whom the Assembly candidates had been "courting popularity,"
had exerted "very great influence on the Elections of Members for this
City." A recent analysis of the 1769 election vote, moreover, shows
that the "mechanics," who made up slightly fewer than one-half of those
voting, gave from 61 to 63 per cent of their votes to what is here being
called the popular Whig party, and only 37 to 46 per cent to the moderate Whigs. Philip Livingston's percentage of the mechanic vote dropped
from a high of 66 per cent in 1768, when he won election despite a
strong popular Whig tide, to a low of 46 per cent in 1769, when he was
defeated.[40] This would suggest that it may indeed have been the "common people" who held the balance of power in these elections. Had the
patricians voted together as a "class," they probably would have prevailed. But this, in factious New York, was most unlikely.

Since the "mechanic" vote had become so important, it is little
wonder that political leaders should court and form alliances with the
lower ranks at election time. It was this evolution toward greater popu-

[39] *A Copy of the Poll List of the Election for Representatives for the City and
County of New York . . . MDCCLXIX* (New York, 1880); James Duane to
Robert Livingston, Jr., New York, June 3, 1769, Livingston-Redmond MSS, Reel
6; John Watts to Monckton, New York, Feb. 4, 1769, Chalmers Papers Relating
to New York, III, 19, NYPL; Peter R. Livingston to Oliver Wendell, New York,
Jan. 30, 1769, Livingston Papers, MCNY.

[40] Gov. Moore to Earl of Hillsborough, New York, June 3, 1769, *N.Y. Col.
Docs.,* VIII, 170; *Copy of the Poll List . . . MDCCLXIX;* Roger Champagne,
"Liberty Boys and Mechanics," 132.

lar involvement in, and influence upon, local politics that Carl Becker traced, and in this realm there is still no reason to doubt the soundness of Becker's findings. The present study has shown that such a development had long been under way in the province, but the new level of participation stimulated by the Stamp Act riots, meetings in the Fields, the instruction of Assemblymen, and the emergence of non-patrician popular leaders, appears, at least, to have captured the interest and energies of a whole new stratum of citizens. Whether this development—which revealed, among other things, sharp grievances of merchant seamen and pressures for popular reforms from various mechanics' committees—should be read as an incipient class movement or as a widening circle of special interest groups, is a question that may have to await the writing of a full history "from the bottom up." [41] But whatever remains to be learned, it is already apparent that politicians had for some time been aware of, and were making terms with, strong popular currents.

Though the evidence is scattered, it would appear that a number of the 1769 county elections were nearly as spirited as that of New York City. A contemporary comment on Suffolk County revealed that in that place "never before within memory of man was a poll Election [but] there is now like to be a Severe Controversy between Clerk Nicholls & Coll. Woodhull." In Dutchess County, where Robert R. Livingston again offered himself to the voters, this time in company with one of the Hoffmans from Rhinebeck, the victors were the incumbents Brinkerhoff and Van Kleeck. It was said that Livingston's defeat was "owing to all the Tenants of Beekman & R. G. Livingston's Voting against him. . . ." Moreover, James DeLancey injected himself into the election by sending up "a Certificate setting forth that our late Members [Brinkerhoff and Van Kleeck] opposed the Excise Bill . . . also that there was a Clause in the Bill he [DeLancey] proposed for paying the Quakers and Moravians [of whom there were many in Dutchess County] Fines. . . ." In Orange County the election was again so warmly contested—

[41] Jesse Lemisch, "Jack Tar in the Streets: Merchant Seamen in the Politics of Revolutionary America," *WMQ*, 3rd Ser., XXV (July, 1968), 371–407; "The American Revolution Seen From the Bottom Up," in Barton J. Bernstein, ed., *Towards A New Past: Dissenting Essays in American History* (New York, 1968), 3–45; Staughton Lynd, "The Mechanics in New York City Politics 1774–1788," *Labor History*, V (Fall, 1964), 225–46.

and interests presumably were so sharp—that it later occasioned a review before the Assembly.[42]

In the Borough of Westchester, that familiar battleground of the Morris and Peter DeLancey families, contention exceeded even that of the previous year as Lewis Morris [III] and John DeLancey once more fought it out between them. The vivid description by Jonathan Landon, a neighbor and friend of the Morris family, shows how fully each side realized the value of every vote. The DeLancey party, Landon wrote, "even sent above New Windsor [Connecticut] for a voter," and "every man in New York that was known to have Money at Interest in the Borough was applied to by Mr. [Peter] DeLancey for his Interest & Influence." On the morning of the election "the Old Devil of all i.e. P. D. L." approached "one *Woodcock* a Taylor & a Voter of ours—called him into his house & entreated him for his Vote." The tailor hesitated, since his customers were "all friends of Mr. Morris & therefore being himself a poor Man it was natural for him to go where his Interest was." DeLancey thereupon "plyd him well with Liquor, took out his hands full of Dollars & put them into the Hands of the poor fellow & swore he would lay them all with him, that he dare not Vote against Lewis Morris—the Bate took, he put the Dollars into his pocket and went up and voted for John." We are not told what Morris's supporters did to attract votes, but it appears that they were even more persuasive. Morris won the election by "a Majority of four Freeholders." [43]

Though this rivalry in the borough election was a local one between two leading families, its implications for the colony-wide division that had begun to develop in the 1768 Assembly session were probably lost on no one. To what extent Lewis Morris [III] was in communica-

---

[42] Robert Morris to Mr. Landon, Jan. 26, 1769, draft, Morris MSS (Robert Morris Papers), Box 4, Rutgers; Peter R. Livingston to Philip Schuyler, Feb. 29, 1769, Robert R. Livingston to Philip Schuyler, Clermont, Jan. 28, 1769, Philip Schuyler Papers, Box 23, NYPL; *Smith's Historical Memoirs,* 62–63. A potential controversy was avoided in Albany County when both William Johnson and Robert Livingston agreed to support the incumbents, Philip Schuyler and Jacob Ten Eyck. Peter R. Livingston wrote Schuyler, "I Beg you'll come again and not think of staying back." Livingston to Schuyler, New York, Jan. 23, 1769, Philip Schuyler Papers, Box 23, NYPL. For more information on the Albany County election, consult Gerlach, *Philip Schuyler,* 178–80.

[43] Landon to Robert Morris, Morrisania, Feb. 1, 1769, Morris MSS (Robert Morris Papers), Box 4, Rutgers.

tion with moderate Whigs elsewhere is not known, but we do know that William Smith, Jr., Peter R. Livingston, and Robert R. Livingston all corresponded with Philip Schuyler regarding election tactics in their respective counties, and that they considered it "agreeable News" that Morris had won in the Borough of Westchester. As for the popular party, William Smith, Jr., charged that the DeLanceys had "long preconcerted Matters [and] several Persons were brought in [to the Assembly] who were notoriously at their Devotion." [44]

6. Assembly Maneuvers: 1769

If the acrimony of this election carried party spirit to a new high in New York, it was shortly to be exceeded by the partisan tone of the new Assembly. "Both parties I believe," said Jonathan Landon, "have drawn the Sword and thrown away the Scabbard." Though the popular Whigs had now gained firm control of the Assembly, their party leaders proceeded at once to extend their dominion. A primary target was Philip Livingston [II]. Though the former Speaker had been defeated in the New York County election, the Livingston family had arranged to have him chosen representative from Livingston Manor. "They [the popular party] are Collecting their force as fast as they can to oppose Uncle Philip," reported Peter R. Livingston to his father at the Manor, "and to gitt Cruger in the Chair." [45] When the session opened, John Cruger of New York City was in fact elected Speaker. But this victory

[44] Peter R. Livingston to Philip Schuyler, New York, Jan. 23, 1769, Robert R. Livingston to Philip Schuyler, Clermont, Jan. 28, 1769, Philip Schuyler Papers, Box 23, NYPL. For further information on this point, see other correspondence in Box 23. Smith's comment on the DeLanceys is in *Historical Memoirs,* 60; it may have been written after the election and may have received even greater emphasis because of hindsight, for it is certainly true that once the Assembly met, new representatives like DeNoyelles and Gale of Orange County, and Billop of Richmond, were consistent supporters of the popular party.

[45] Landon to Robert Morris, Morrisania, Nov. 2, 1769, Morris MSS (Robert Morris Papers), Box 4, Rutgers; Peter R. Livingston to Robert Livingston, Jr., New York, April 3, 1769, Livingston-Redmond MSS, Reel 6. "The Delancey Interest prevails in the house greatly, & they have give the Livingston Interest prooff of it, by dismissing P. Livingston. . . ." Hugh Wallace to William Johnson, New York, May 15, 1769, *Johnson Papers,* VI, 758.

did not satiate the popular leaders. They next moved to expel Philip Livingston altogether by declaring him ineligible to represent the Manor on the ground that he did not actually reside there. The challenge was based on a clause in the election law of 1699 which prescribed that Assemblymen should be "Dwelling and Resident" within the counties, cities, and manors they were chosen to represent.[46]

The ensuing controversy called forth a review of the New York Assembly's position on the question of residency requirements throughout the previous seventy years of its history. Livingston's supporters contended that the 1699 law was based on an English statute that did not require "actual" residence of representatives within their districts. Sensitive to hints that they were advocating virtual representation, which they hastened to label a "pernicious doctrine," the partisans of Livingston stressed the latter's geographic tie to the Manor through his possession of a legal freehold within its boundaries. Thus the moderates, despite their disclaimers, took a clearly more conservative position in maintaining that possession of a freehold, rather than actual physical residence, should be the determinant of political privileges. Such a distinction by 1769 was an unpopular one, and it garnered no support for their cause.[47] On May 12, 1769, the popular Whig majority, who "carry

[46] Though this rule was followed in the vast majority of cases, there were a few exceptions. During times of factional stress, when rival groups stooped to any available means to exclude political opponents from the Assembly, the law was tightened or eased in accordance with the preferences of the majority party. Thus in 1701 three assemblymen were ousted for non-residency, as was another in 1745; in 1743, however, an assemblyman was permitted to continue as representative from Orange County despite common knowledge that he was a resident of New York City. In each of these cases the Assembly vote was guided by politics rather than by principle. *The Colonial Laws of New York from the Year 1664 to the Revolution* (Albany, 1894), I, 405; Smith, *History,* I, 160, II, 92–93; Hubert Phillips, *The Development of a Residential Qualification for Representatives in Colonial Legislatures* (Cincinnati, 1921), 110–13.

[47] *Assembly Journal* (Buel), April 14, 1769. To bolster their side of the case the Livingstons scoured the Assembly records, coming up with "twenty-one examples" of non-resident representation during the history of the New York General Assembly. This figure has been used by some students of New York history to suggest that non-resident representation was characteristic of New York, or that the practice was "one of the bastions of aristocratic privilege" in the colony. It is possible, however, to interpret this figure in quite another way. During the period canvassed by the Livingstons, 231 individuals sat as representatives in the New York Assembly. As only 21 of these were non-residents (and it is a fair assump-

all before them by Numbers," succeeded in having Philip Livingston dismissed from the House by a vote of seventeen to six.

Still not satisfied that the powerful Livingston family and its influence had been sufficiently eliminated from the legislature, the popular faction next offered a bill to exclude all Supreme Court justices from the House, a shaft obviously aimed at Judge Robert R. Livingston, who was to be proposed as Manor representative in place of his ousted cousin. Philip Schuyler attempted to expand this bill to encompass all Crown officials, but the effort was narrowly defeated by eleven votes to ten, and the bill excluding only Supreme Court judges then stood as passed.[48] The Livingstons, who did not intend to take these assaults passively, appealed the case to Whitehall. As it turned out, they were upheld; yet defiance of imperial orders had by now become something of a commonplace. When Judge Livingston asked the Council to press for Assembly compliance, he found that even the Council had "gone so far into Party" that the members pretended not to have heard of the order to repeal the exclusion bill. The Assembly majority thus continued to refuse Robert R. Livingston his seat, though in the succeeding

---

tion that the Livingstons had dug up every case), this means that 91 per cent of the assemblymen resided in the counties from which they were elected. It is true that when the issue of non-resident representation was raised, as it was only eight times in the colonial period, the rule was applied unevenly and according to political whim. However, this in no way detracts from the fact that in practice the overwhelming majority of New York assemblymen, including members of the DeLancey, Morris, Schuyler, Beekman, Van Cortlandt, and sometimes even the Livingston, families, resided among their constituents. *Assembly Journal* (Buel), May 12, 1769. Phillips, *Development of a Residential Qualification,* 128, 244; Lawrence H. Leder, "The New York Elections of 1769: An Assault on Privilege," *MVHR,* XLIX (March, 1963), 682. Leder suggests (677) that a law passed by the New York Assembly in 1769, which established a six-month residence requirement, was "the death knell of the English system of 'class' representation in colonial New York." This law was disallowed, however, in June, 1770, and the Assembly continued to bend residence rules to political purposes. *Laws,* IV, 1094; Robert R. Livingston to the Freeholders of Livingston Manor, n.d., Robert R. Livingston Coll., II, NYHS; Robert Livingston, Jr., to James Duane, Livingston Manor, March 9, 1772, Duane Papers, NYHS. On the other hand, it is true that non-resident representation was viewed by some colonials as a symbol of privilege, and as such was under attack in some quarters.

[48] Peter R. Livingston to Robert Livingston, Jr., New York, April 14, 1769, Livingston-Redmond MSS, Reel 6; *Assembly Journal* (Buel), April 12, May 12, May 17, 1769; *Smith's Historical Memoirs,* 62, 65.

four years he was elected representative of the Manor on five separate occasions.[49] This controversy raged on well into 1774, and was pursued by the popular Whigs with such grim partisan relish that even Speaker John Cruger at length conceded that there had been "too much of Party." [50] But with the opposition in control of both the Assembly and the Council, there was little the moderate party could do on behalf of Livingston or any of their other supporters. When Governor Moore died in the fall of 1769, the moderates lost their last powerful friend and advocate.

The exclusion of the two most politically astute members of the Livingston family from the Assembly after 1769 [51] further accelerated a political eclipse that had begun with the land riots of 1765–1766. During the four turbulent years that followed, the popular faction had given their most merciless attention to individual members of that family— especially Philip [II], Robert R., and William Livingston and their closest collaborators—and this was done with a clear strategic purpose. The Livingstons were a large and powerful clan whose vast estates and numerous public offices gave them extraordinary influence, particularly in the upriver region which often opposed policies favored by the commercially oriented seaboard counties. Moreover, the Livingstons' often conservative positions on questions relating to land policy, residence qualifications, and plural office-holding caused them to become identi-

[49] *Assembly Journal* (Buel), Dec. 9, 12, 13, 21, 1769; Peter R. Livingston to Robert Livingston, Jr., New York, May 15, 1769, Robert R. Livingston to Robert Livingston, Jr., Dec. 31, 1770, Livingston-Redmond MSS, Reel 6; Robert R. Livingston to Robert Livingston, Jr., Feb. 17, 1772, Robert R. Livingston to the Freeholders of the Manor of Livingston, Feb. 22, 1772, Robert R. Livingston Coll., II, NYHS; Robert Livingston, Jr., to James Duane, Livingston Manor, Feb. 17, 1772, Duane Papers, NYHS; *N.Y. Col. Docs.*, VIII, 207, 216, 265, 319, 443, 565; *Laws*, V, 73–74.

[50] Robert R. Livingston to Robert Livingston, Jr., Dec. 31, 1770, Livingston-Redmond MSS, Reel 6; Robert Livingston [Clermont] to Robert R. Livingston, Clermont, Mar. 5, 1772, Robert R. Livingston Coll., II, NYHS. Assemblyman George Clinton said after one of Livingston's dismissals that it was done "with a higher hand than at any Time heretofore and the Opposition by the Minority more Spirited." Clinton to Petrus Tappen, New York, Jan. 8, 1772, Misc. MSS, Clinton, NYHS.

[51] Peter R. Livingston was finally seated as the representative from Livingston Manor in 1774, but he never achieved the same stature as either Philip or Robert R. Livingston.

fied in the public mind with many of the evils of special privilege and defense of the status quo in a time of change and unrest. In the elections of 1768 and 1769, to be against the Livingstons was to take up symbolic opposition to the most tradition-bound and elitist segment of colonial society, and the popular party very shrewdly exploited the public's growing impatience with the old orthodoxies. That their offensive was directed more against a whole range of images than against the Livingstons as a family seems apparent in the way party labels were tailored to fit each new issue—from the lawyer party, to the landlord party, to the Presbyterian or dissenter party, to, occasionally, the "Livingston party." When that last label was used, as once in a while it was, it served mainly as a kind of shorthand for all the rest. In the upriver area it raised fairly specific images of landlord elitism; in New York City, it reminded the public of the lawyer triumvirate, with their opposition to strong measures during the Stamp Act demonstrations and their defense of landed interests. The DeLanceys, Crugers, and other patrician leaders of the popular faction were hardly less "elitist" in general outlook and preferences than were the Livingstons, Schuylers, and Morrises. But they had the wisdom to realize that election campaigns were not the occasions to let this show. The popular Whig leaders, moreover, were in most cases merchants. And trade did not have quite the connotations of privilege that had been associated through time with the landed gentry.

To the Livingstons it was only too obvious that the opposition was "stirring their utmost to make our family ridiculous and to keep them out of all Posts of Honor or Profit . . . which is too hard to bear." Robert Livingston, Jr., was convinced that the opposition's real goal was to "ruin me & my family with all their heats." After 1769 several members of the Livingston family were inclined to withdraw from politics altogether. Philip Livingston considered moving to Dutchess County, while William Livingston actually did leave New York in 1772, settling at his country retreat in New Jersey. He later re-entered politics in that state, serving as its first post-Revolutionary governor. Vowing "I am Serious," Robert Livingston, Jr., the Manor proprietor, threatened "to Sell all the Estate I have in this Province & move to one where . . . the Laws Govern & not the will of Tyrants." Judge Robert R. Livingston, the only member of the family with an important official position after the election of 1769, remained in New York City where he continued "to watch the Motions of the Enemy." Thus it was that the Livingstons' political fortunes reached their nadir in 1769.[52] Never since the first Livingston entered public life in the seventeenth century had that family been so shut out from influence in the circles of government.

Yet the Livingstons were not the only victims of the popular party. Lewis Morris [III], who had won a narrow victory in the Westchester election, had no sooner settled into his Assembly seat than the popular Whig majority began to agitate that he, too, be removed on the ground of non-residency. On April 20, by a vote of 12 to 11, they succeeded in doing it, and the seat was awarded to Morris's arch-rival John DeLancey. Continuing to chip away at the moderate Whigs' remaining power, the opposition later tried to exclude Abraham Ten Broeck of Rensselaerswyck on the same charge. That maneuver failed by a vote of fourteen to six. They also introduced a bill which would have required all manor, borough, and town representatives to submit their candidacies to the full county electorate; this plan was narrowly defeated in a clear upriver-seaboard split. Nonetheless, with the expulsion of the Livingstons and Morris, the popular faction had "so weeded the House," as

---

[52] Peter R. Livingston to Robert Livingston, Jr., New York, April 20, 1770, Philip Livingston to Robert Livingston, Jr., New York, Jan. 26, 1770, Robert R. Livingston to Robert Livingston, Jr., Dec. 31, 1770, Livingston-Redmond MSS, Reel 6: Robert Livingston, Jr., to James Duane, Livingston Manor, April 6, 1772, Misc. MSS, NYHS; Robert Livingston, Jr., to James Duane, Livingston Manor, Mar. 9, 1772, Duane Papers, NYHS. Milton Klein says William Livingston's move was motivated less by political disappointment than by the business depression and his wish to establish a rural seat, though Klein notes that the political defeats of 1768 and 1769 "undoubtedly hastened his decision." "William Livingston of New York," 679–83. Depressed economic conditions in New York City also had an influence on Philip Livingston; he finally chose to retain his residence on Brooklyn Heights.

By the end of the colonial era, however, the Livingstons' position began to improve dramatically, for every member of that family supported the Patriot cause. Their return to power and leadership in the new State of New York meant that the Livingstons and other Patriot landed families were able to reassert their influence over land policies. The continued maintenance of their huge estates and their harsh policies toward tenants led to further land upheavals in the nineteenth century. For that story see David M. Ellis, *Landlords and Farmers in the Hudson-Mohawk Region, 1790–1850* (Ithaca, N.Y., 1946).

William Smith, Jr., put it, that they were able on most issues to command a clear majority.[53]

But if the popular party expected to destroy all opposition they were to be disappointed, for with their experienced leaders barred from the Assembly, the moderates soon discovered fresh political talents in a new and younger set of men. Philip Schuyler of Albany County and George Clinton of Ulster were the two most prominent members of this group. Each had made his first appearance in province-wide politics with election to the Assembly in 1768. Philip Schuyler was thirty-five when he decided, following the footsteps of other members of his family, to expand his interests to include politics. Prior to that time he had devoted himself to the family mercantile business in Albany and to the development of his Saratoga estate. Tall, erect, and of sober and patrician mien, Schuyler adjusted himself quite naturally to the role of political leader. Though he had been trained in the arts of business and in military science, and, unlike many other sons of wealthy New Yorkers, had not had the benefits of a college education, Schuyler's membership in the colonial elite and his family's past involvement in public affairs had given him a wide understanding of the colony's politics. George Clinton's emergence as an Assembly leader was based less on family position than on his exceptional talents as an advocate and parliamentarian—skills which were of great advantage to anyone who possessed them in the tendentious debates of the 1769 Assembly session. He was the son of Charles Clinton, who had led a band of discontented Presbyterians from northern Ireland to New York in 1731, and had become a surveyor and moderately prosperous farmer of Ulster County. The younger Clinton, after a brief fling at privateering and a military career, had served an apprenticeship in the law office of William Smith, Jr., and from there had returned upriver to a country practice. He was but twenty-nine when elected to the Assembly in 1768. It was from the Assembly Chamber during 1769 that he wrote his love

---

[53] *Assembly Journal* (Buel), April 20, Dec. 29, 1769, Jan. 13, 26, 1770. On the bill to make manors, boroughs, and towns liable to county-wide elections, the popular party members from Westchester, Philipse, John DeLancey, and Thomas, voted with the upriver representatives. For Smith's comment see *Historical Memoirs,* 67.

letters to Cornelia Tappen, whom he married the following year, thereby connecting himself to a large Kingston family of middle-class circumstances.[54] These two men, Schuyler and Clinton, shared the leadership of the moderate Whigs in this final colonial Assembly.

One of their first acts in the spring session of 1769 was to propose that the "Doors of the House" be "thrown open" so the public could attend the debates. William Smith, Jr., described this as "one of the most popular Motions that could be made," and it was approved without a division.[55] Though the moderates no doubt hoped to identify themselves more closely with popular sentiment, they also believed that they could easily outshine their opponents in public debate. Within three weeks it was reported that the popular party was "heartily tired of having open doors but know not how to gitt them shut." As Peter R. Livingston described it, "They [the popular party] expose themselves most horribly [.] They have not one speaker in their whole party [.] Schuyler and Clinton cutt them all to pieces so that they have no Subterfuge except the Previous Question. . . . the People begins to have their Eyes open. . . ." During the debate over Philip Livingston's right to represent the manor, "the Number of Spectators," according to Peter Livingston, "was far greater than ever I saw since the House has been open. . . . the Inhabitants in general are very warm and find great fault with the whole proceedings. . . ."[56] Superior in debate, though fewer in numbers, the moderates continued to harass the majority leaders in the hope of exposing the shallowness of the latter's devotion to popular measures.

That the religious issue still had some life is apparent from the moderate Whigs' introduction of bills to exempt from church taxes the

[54] Gerlach, *Philip Schuyler,* 6–12; *DAB,* XVI, 477 (John A. Krout); Hugh Hastings, ed., *The Public Papers of George Clinton* (New York, 1899–1914), I, 18–19; Arthur Pound, "Charles Clinton, The First of the American Clintons," *Quarterly Journal of the New York State Historical Association,* XII (Oct., 1931), 375–89. Clinton's letters to Cornelia Tappen are in Misc. MSS, Clinton, NYHS.

[55] *Smith's Historical Memoirs,* 60–61. This measure had been proposed in 1768 by "Philanthropos," the popular Whig propagandist, in *A Few Observations on the Conduct of the General Assembly of New-York, etc.,* Broadsides Coll., Rare Book Room, NYPL. Schuyler's motion to open the doors had first been made on Nov. 3, 1768, but at that time the measure failed. *Assembly Journal* (Buel), Nov. 3, 1768.

[56] Peter R. Livingston to Robert Livingston, Jr., New York, April 24, May 6, 1769, Livingston-Redmond MSS, Reel 6.

dissenters in the four lower counties, where the Church of England was established. A measure to enable dissenting churches to hold the equivalent of a glebe in newly settled areas was also presented. About this same time a Society of Dissenters was organized in New York City "to inform the Different Congregations in the Province of everything that is carried on here [in the Assembly] in which their Religious or Civil Liberties are in any danger of Suffering." Peter R. Livingston, who was active in this movement, both inside and outside the Assembly, reported that letters had been sent "to all the Ministers and some of the leading Men in the Different Counties where we thought their Usefullness would best serve the Cause." The moderate party may have derived some benefit from these efforts, for Livingston said in June, 1769, that there was "vast discontent in the City with the Conduct of the . . . Heroes of the Last Sessions [.] They have lost the Interest of the Quakers to a man besides a number of the middling sort of People. . . ." [57] Yet, despite these few minor successes, the moderates remained hopelessly outnumbered, and the spring Assembly session closed with the popular majority still very much in command.

But with the death of Governor Moore in September, 1769, and the return of Cadwallader Colden as acting governor, the political kaleidoscope began to revolve once again, producing new political patterns. The most observable element in the new picture was the partial reconciliation that took place between members of the DeLancey family and Colden. Smith believed that the DeLanceys "were willing to venture the dangerous Association of Interests with a most unpopular Governor," in the hope of gaining new patronage and strengthening even further their Assembly majority, with which they then hoped to "manage" the next governor. Clearly, if the new governor found a compliant Assembly, he would be unlikely to dissolve it for new elections, and by avoiding elections the continuance of the popular Whig majority would be assured. In this sense the strategy was successful, for the 1769 Assembly election was the last that would be held in New York Colony. On re-

---

[57] *Assembly Journal* (Buel), April 6, 26, 1769; Peter R. Livingston to Robert Livingston, Jr., New York, June 15, 1769, Livingston-Redmond MSS, Reel 6. The minutes of the Society of Dissenters have been preserved and include the names of members and a draft copy of the circular letter. Osgood, "Society of Dissenters," 498–507.

turning to power, Colden moved at once to displace from office a number of supporters of the moderate faction. Philip Livingston, Jr., was removed as provincial secretary and the office was awarded to Colden's son David. James Livingston was replaced as sheriff of Dutchess County, and in Westchester, Lewis Graham, a relative and great supporter of the Morris family, was removed as sheriff and the post was given to John DeLancey. The New York City recorder was displaced by Thomas Jones, brother-in-law of Captain James DeLancey.[58]

Once the erstwhile popular Whigs could be fairly sure that there would be no dissolution to expose them to possible censure from the electorate, they were free to approve funds for the government and to support other measures which might have weakened their standing with the New York City populace. It is because of this that the labels "popular" and "moderate" lose their significance after the fall of 1769.

Predictably, the most sensitive issue facing the Assembly in the fall session was the government's request for £2,000 to provision the King's troops. Though the bill was sure to arouse popular heats, the majority managed to push it through by a vote of twelve to ten over the objections of a hardening opposition core which included Schuyler and Ten Broeck of Albany County, Clinton and DeWitt of Ulster, Woodhull of Suffolk, and Pierre Van Cortlandt of Westchester. Since the supply measure was coupled with another bill providing for the emission of £120,000 in paper currency, it is difficult to determine to what degree the vote reflects shifting attitudes toward larger imperial questions. There is every reason to believe that Schuyler, Clinton, and their supporters were still fundamentally loyal subjects of the Crown. But they were being squeezed inexorably to the "left" as the Assembly majority, which Colden now approvingly dubbed the "Friends of Government," took over much of their former territory.[59] Moreover, the personal pref-

[58] *Smith's Historical Memoirs,* 67–68, 95–97, 54–55; Jonathan Landon to Robert Morris, Morrisania, Nov. 2, 1769, Morris MSS (Robert Morris Papers), Box 4, Rutgers; Klein, "The American Whig: William Livingston of New York," 664. The city leaders did "manage" the next governor, John Murray, Earl of Dunmore, whom Smith describes as a "Blockhead" and "a Fool . . . in Leading strings" (*Historical Memoirs,* 100). His successor, Governor William Tryon, was not so easily manipulated, however, and apparently maintained a good deal of independence. *Ibid.,* 117–18, 143–44.

[59] *Assembly Journal* (Buel), Dec. 15, 20, 28, 29, 30, 1769. There was little doubt in Colden's mind that the Assembly minority opposed supplying the troops, but

erence of the Schuyler-Clinton group for moderation was not immune to the popular clamors which depicted the supply bill as a renewed threat to colonial liberties. All in all, they had little to lose in resisting it.

No sooner had the close vote on the supply bill become public than there appeared on the streets a broadside, "To the Betrayed Inhabitants of the City and Colony of New York," which accused the Assembly majority of the basest duplicity for its support of the King's troops. This paper was eventually traced to Alexander McDougall. It led to McDougall's arrest and imprisonment for seditious libel, and within a short time lifted him to fame, colony-wide and then continent-wide, as the "American Wilkes." The McDougall episode was colorful and exciting enough in itself, but considered in the full context of New York politics as they had evolved by the end of 1769, the case can be seen as a key element in the precipitation of new political alignments. And such were the multiple overtones which the episode took on that New Yorkers, still attached to local and provincial concerns, were jarred yet another step toward recognizing that issues of the widest significance between colonies and mother country impended.

7. Alexander McDougall and "the grand Cause of America"

The enemies of Alexander McDougall would try to depict him as an "insolent" and "obscure" demagogue of "humble Station." But though McDougall had been born to parents of plain circumstances, his personal history is a remarkable example of what wit, energy, and talent could do to start a man on the path to success in America. McDougall was six years old in 1738 when his parents arrived in New York from Scotland. Disappointed in his hopes for a piece of land on New York's northern frontier, McDougall's father settled in New York City where he made his living as a milkman. Young McDougall, having been raised in a port city, developed a fondness for the sea, and during the French and Indian War he became the commander of two privateers, the sloops

---

Schuyler's recent biographer says that both sides were more concerned with the paper money issue than with the supply bill. Colden to Earl of Hillsborough, New York, Jan. 6, 1770, *N.Y. Col. Docs.*, VIII, 199–201; Gerlach, *Philip Schuyler*, 199–203.

Tyger and *Barrington*. After the war he returned to New York City where he opened a merchandising business which quickly prospered; he became a prominent Presbyterian layman, serving as clerk of the First Presbyterian Church on Wall Street; and during the Stamp Act protests he emerged as one of the principal leaders of the Sons of Liberty. By the end of 1765 McDougall had drawn away from the more radical element led by Sears and Lamb, and in the elections of 1768 and 1769 he supported the lawyer-dissenter coalition, called here the moderate Whig party.[60]

Though McDougall's attack on the DeLancey-led Assembly majority could not fail to benefit the Schuyler-Clinton opposition, there is no evidence that McDougall was in league with any of the minority leaders. His first paper, "To the Betrayed Inhabitants," which he signed "A Son of Liberty," was published on December 17, 1769. Since the Massachusetts and South Carolina assemblies had refused to supply the King's troops stationed on their soil, McDougall insisted that the New York Assembly was guilty of "betraying the common cause of liberty" in failing to take a similar stand. "And what makes the Assembly's granting this money the more grievous," he declared, "is, that it goes to the support of troops kept here not to protect but to enslave us." Asserting that "this sacrifice of the public interest" was attributable "to some corrupt source," McDougall went on to name the "coalition" between the "DeLancey family" and "Mr. Colden" as the force behind the "abominable vote." "Is this a state to be rested in, when our all is at a stake?" "No, my countrymen, rouse!" Four specific steps should be taken "to prevent the accomplishment of the designs of tyrants." First, the people should "assemble in the fields . . . where your sense ought to be taken on this important point"; second, "go in a body to your members, and insist on their joining with the minority, to oppose the bill"; third, if they refuse, "appoint a committee to draw up a state of the whole matter, and send it to the speakers of the several houses of assembly on the continent, and to the friends of our cause in England";

---

[60] Sister Anna Madeleine Shannon, "General Alexander McDougall, Citizen and Soldier, 1732–1786," unpubl. Ph.D. diss. (Fordham University, 1957); Mary-Jo Kline, "The Emergence of the American Wilkes: The Early Career of Alexander McDougall," unpubl. M.A. thesis (Columbia University, 1963); *DAB*, XII, 21–22 (Daniel C. Haskell).

and fourth, "publish it in the newspapers, that the whole world may know your sentiments on this matter, in the only way your circumstances will admit." [61]

This was followed on the next day by a second paper, "To the Publick," signed "Legion," which called upon "every friend of his Country" to meet in the Fields to discuss "the late base inglorious Conduct of our General Assembly, who have in opposition to the loud and general Voice of their Constituents; the Dictates of sound Policy, the ties of Gratitude, and the glorious Struggle we have engaged in for our invaluable Birth Rights, dared to vote supplies to the Troops without the least Shadow of a prextext for their pernicious Grant." On December 19, 1769, the Assembly condemned both papers as "false, seditious and infamous" libels, and Colden approved a reward of £100 for information leading to discovery of the author. Schuyler objected to the wording of the Assembly resolution, but the final vote declaring the papers to be libelous was unanimous. They clearly constituted attacks on the government. The printer James Parker, subjected to great pressure from the Council, named Alexander McDougall as the author of the papers, and McDougall was then arrested and placed in jail on February 9, 1770.[62]

Rather than pay bail, McDougall chose to remain in prison as a martyr to the cause of liberty. He was thus consciously drawing parallels between his own case and that of John Wilkes, the English radical and popularly styled defender of constitutional freedom. Noting that he was the first American to be imprisoned in the struggle for colonial rights, McDougall declared, "The Cause for which I suffer is capable of converting Chains into Laurels, and transforming a Gaol into a Paradise." Nothing could have been more devastating to the Assembly majority's case, for by giving a focus to colonial grievances in his own person, McDougall helped to reactivate and reunite the Sons of Liberty, to stir new discontents, and to gain the support of political leaders opposed to the pro-government Assembly and Council majorities. Such was the general acclaim for McDougall's stand that the majority party

[61] McDougall's broadside is reprinted in *N.Y. Doc. Hist.*, III, 317–21.

[62] *N.Y. Doc. Hist.*, III, 322; *Assembly Journal* (Buel), Dec. 18, 19, 1769; *Smith's Historical Memoirs*, 71–76. For a discussion of this vote, see Gerlach, *Philip Schuyler*, 200–2.

at one point even offered to pay his bail, in the hope that his release from jail would reduce public interest in the case. Failing in this, they turned to ridicule and attacks on his character. The Newspaper articles charged that McDougall's broadsides, which tended to "Magnify his Abilities," had actually been written by anti-government party leaders, and that the New York Chamber of Commerce would not support its own brother merchant because the members thought him an "empty, insignificant, self-conceited" fellow. Cadwallader Colden scoffed at McDougall's pretensions in remaining in jail. "He is a person of some fortune, and could easily have found the Bail required of him, but he choose to go to Jail, and lyes there immitating Mr. Wilkes in every thing he can." James Duane described McDougall as "once a Seafaring man, but lately a warm petitioner. . . . [the] poor man thinks . . . he is a Wilkes Suffering for the good of his Country." [63]

The fullest discussion of the issues raised by the McDougall case was contained in a series of twelve essays titled "The Dougliad," and in the various responses elicited by those essays, which appeared in the New-York *Gazette; and The Weekly Mercury* from April 9 through June 25, 1770. The briefest survey of this lengthy and intricate exchange shows how many of the arguments that would fill the air five or six years later were foreshadowed here. The pro-administration authors of "The Dougliad" laid major stress on the responsibility of government to restrain licentiousness and anarchy. They frequently referred to the excesses of Cromwellian times, defined a republican as one who wanted to "depose his Prince," and defended the Church of England against the attacks of factious "Independents." In answer, McDougall and his friends called "The Dougliad" writers the "Tory Faction of New-York," and accused them of advocating "Star-Chamber Law" in the proceedings against him. They said that unlike the House of Hanover, the

---

[63] New-York *Journal; or, The General Advertiser,* Feb. 15, Mar. 29, April 12, 1770; Cadwallader Colden to Earl of Hillsborough, New York, Feb. 21, 1770, Alexander Colden to Anthony Todd, Esq., July 11, 1770, *N.Y. Col. Docs.,* VIII, 208, 220; James Duane to Robert Livingston, Jr., New York, July 19, 1770, Livingston-Redmond MSS, Reel 6; Jonathan Landon to Robert Morris, Mar. 24, 1770, Morris MSS (Robert Morris Papers), Box 4, Rutgers. For the relationship between the Wilkes case and the colonies, see Pauline Maier, "John Wilkes and American Disillusionment With Britain," *WMQ,* 3rd Ser., XX (July, 1963), 373–95.

Stuarts had been despotic kings, and declared that the purpose of their present opposition was to preserve the "Country from Slavery" and from "ministerial Jobbers." [64]

While the intellectual argument was being pursued in the newspapers, a more proletarian competition was taking place in the streets. The Sons of Liberty were particularly active in publicizing McDougall as the "American Wilkes." Seizing on the number forty-five, from Wilkes's allegedly libelous paper, *North Briton, 45,* the Sons marked the anniversary of the repeal of the Stamp Act by holding a dinner at which forty-five toasts were drunk—including salutes to McDougall, Wilkes, Chatham, Hampden, Sidney, "The LIBERTY of the PRESS," and "The Freedom of Elections." This was followed by what must have been a somewhat disorderly march to the jail, where McDougall addressed the crowd through the window-grating of his cell. McDougall received a number of such delegations during his confinement, including groups of gentlemen who dined with him in his prison room and a bevy of ladies from the Dutch church who serenaded him from the street. His critics made raucous use of the "Wilkes" and "number forty-five" symbolism in writing up these visits. One such account described a visit by "45 Gentlemen" who dined with the prisoner "on Forty-five Pounds of Beef Stakes, cut from a Bullock of forty-five Months old," and another told that McDougall had been serenaded by "45 Virgins," ungallantly reported as "45 years old." [65]

The real McDougall, however, bore no resemblance to any of these lampoons. He was a well-spoken man of considerable dignity and charm; he would in later years become a major general and close associate of George Washington, a member of both the First and Second Continental Congresses, and the first president of the Bank of New York. In 1770 he was described in a Pennsylvania newspaper as "decent in his manners," and "generally respected"; he "possesses great

[64] See especially the New-York *Gazette; and The Weekly Mercury,* April 9, 16, 23, 30, June 25, 1770; "To the Freeholders, Freemen, and Inhabitants of . . . New York," Alexander McDougall, New-York *Journal; or, The General Advertiser,* Feb. 15, 1770.

[65] New-York *Gazette; and The Weekly Mercury,* Feb. 19, 1770; New-York *Gazette; or, The Weekly Post-Boy,* Feb. 19, 1770; New-York *Journal; or, The General Advertiser,* Mar. 22, 29, 1770.

presence of mind, is methodical, and connected in the arrangement of his ideas," and "has great fire and vehemence without hurry and precipitation. . . ." [66]

"I spent one half Hour, almost alone with Capt. McDougall," wrote the substantial Jonathan Landon of Westchester on March 24, 1770, "and whatever may be reported of him as an insignificant and obscure man, I assure that from the Little Conversation that passed while we visited him he appeared to be as well read in History as any Person I ever conversed with, an extream distinct manner of conveying his Ideas, and his Language composed of as well Chosen Words as you would expect from an accomplished Speaker, in a Word I was charmed with the Man, and disposed to think much better of him than I ever should had not I been personally acquainted with him." Landon then turned to the broader significance of McDougall's protest. "His Cause gathers Partizans Daily from one End of the Continent to the Other— Many People of the First Figure in New York have taken the pains to send the Paper and all Proceedings which were antecedent to its Publication to several of the most noted Counsellors in the Neighbouring Provinces for impartial Opinions thereon & have received many Letters. . . . A standing Army must enevitable enslave the first and best principeld Government that ever was constituted by Man." After a discussion of the history of standing armies in England, Landon continued: "Many People I believe make a Meer Engine of McDougall [s] Cause to answer some selfish political Motives—But in my Opinion it is a Serious Matter and really I believe our Liberty is as much attacked now By the Mutiny Act & others Act of Trade as it was by the pestilent Last Act [the Stamp Act]—and therefore there ought to be a Stand made, and I rejoice that McDougall is imprisoned for the Cause as the like best way to bring things to a Crisis." Landon held up the recent Boston Massacre as "One of the Blessed Effects of a Standing Army in a Town in times of Peace," and added, "I fear there must be much Blood Spilt." Landon thus closed his long, thoughtful, and troubled letter: "The Behaviour of some people in power have carried things to such unwarrantable Lengths that our Freedom & Rights are invaded by Serpents & Harpies that We foster and Nourish in our Very Bowels— and there is no other Way that I can conceive but to keep up a steady

[66] *Pennsylvania Journal, and The Weekly Advertiser*, Mar. 22, 1770.

strenuous and persevering Opposition to git the Government rid of such, partial self interested, party spirited, and Iniquitous Rulers." [67]

William Smith, Jr., also believed that McDougall's imprisonment would advance "the grand Cause of America." As a member of the Council he did not feel free to say so publicly, but in an anonymous letter to a local newspaper Smith wrote: "Before this Alarm our Zeal for Liberty began to languish . . . we were all composing ourselves for a Nap of Security—There was a Necessity for fresh Oil to quicken that expiring Lamp. . . ." Through the press and private correspondence, news of the McDougall affair spread first to the hinterlands of New York and then to the other colonies. Dr. Benjamin Young Prime of New York City informed his friend Dr. Petrus Tappen at Esopus (Kingston) that "Capt. McDougal is indeed in Jail, & I hope if he is brought to tryal, he will come off with flying colours. . . . In case of a new Election I hope you will exert yourself . . . to procure the Election of such Members as you can believe will prove friends to their Country." [68] Peter R. Livingston, the rather impulsive son of Robert Livingston, Jr., and one of the first to embrace McDougall's cause, bent every effort to make certain that the other colonies were kept informed. Describing McDougall as "a Sensible Couragious fellow," Livingston wrote to his friend Oliver Wendell in Boston, "his Conduct is highly approved of here by a great Majority. . . . as he stands in the gap in the Cause of Liberty [.] Hope all the friends and Supporters of that Glorious Cause will support him with you." Livingston asked Wendell to have the New York newspaper reports about McDougall reprinted "in one of your best Papers." He repeated the request a few days later

[67] Jonathan Landon to Robert Morris, Mar. 24, 1770, Morris MSS (Robert Morris Papers), Box 4, Rutgers.

[68] New-York *Gazette; or, The Weekly Post-Boy*, Mar. 19, 1770. After publication Smith's letter was attributed to John Dickinson of Philadelphia, but the original draft is among the Smith papers in the NYPL; part of the letter is transcribed in *Smith's Historical Memoirs*, 75–76. Benjamin Young Prime to Dr. Petrus Tappen, New York, April 20, 1770, *New York City During the American Revolution . . . Manuscripts in the Possession of the Mercantile Library Association of New York City* (New York, 1861), 50–52. Dr. Prime noted that George Clinton, husband of Tappen's sister, though having voted McDougall's pamphlet a libel, was "a very good man." William Smith, Jr., wrote Philip Schuyler the news about McDougall. Smith to Schuyler, New York, April 29, 1770, Philip Schuyler Papers, Box 23, NYPL.

explaining, "We are indeavoring to make Capt. McDugalls Cause as popular as possible that in case he should be Convicted the fire may be light [ed], and the more we git the other Colonies to take the Alarm the greater the probability to git him Cleared." McDougall, Livingston insisted, "really is a Man of Worth and acts from a true Spirit of Liberty." He made similar efforts to have accounts of the case reprinted in the Philadelphia papers.[69] The campaign to spread the story of McDougall's martyrdom appears to have been a resounding success. Newspaper accounts appeared everywhere in the colonies; toasts were drunk to McDougall in Pennsylvania; South Carolina condemned the New York Assembly for its actions against him; and in a meeting at Faneuil Hall in Boston the hero was cheered as the "American Wilkes." [70]

McDougall remained in jail until April 28, 1770, when accompanied by an "immense Multitude" he appeared before the Grand Jury. "He spoke with vast Propriety," reported William Smith, Jr., "& awed and astonished Many who wish him ill & added I believe to the Number of his Friends." But despite his high standing with the people, McDougall was indicted for seditious libel and his trial was set for July. On this occasion McDougall paid his bail and was released from jail. Shortly before the court was to convene in July, the government's chief witness, James Parker, died, and thus the case never did go to trial. Not content to let the matter drop, the Assembly majority called McDougall before its bar in December, 1770. He refused to answer the charge of libeling the House on the grounds of what would today be called possible self-incrimination and double jeopardy. The Assembly thereupon accused him of being in contempt, and he was recommitted to jail for several more months. Only five members opposed this action. They were George Clinton, Pierre Van Cortlandt, Nathaniel Woodhull, Samuel Gale of Orange County, and Captain Seaman of Queens. Both Schuyler and DeWitt, who might well have voted with the minority,

[69] Peter R. Livingston to Oliver Wendell, New York, Feb. 15, 19, April 9, 1770, Livingston Papers, MCNY.

[70] A cursory check shows that the story was covered, often in considerable detail, in the Feb. 19, 26, Mar. 19, and May 3, 1770, issues of the Boston *Gazette;* the Feb. 22 and Mar. 1, 1770, issues of the Boston *Weekly News-Letter;* the Feb. 22, Mar. 8, 22, Apr. 12, 19, and 26, 1770, issues of the Pennsylvania *Journal and The Weekly Advertiser;* and the Feb. 22, Mar. 22, Apr. 5, 19, Aug. 2, 1770, the Jan. 17, Mar. 8 and Apr. 4, 1771, issues of the Virginia *Gazette* (Purdie and Dixon).

were absent during this part of the Assembly session. McDougall was finally released from jail in April, 1771, and the government's case was allowed to drop.[71]

It was the McDougall affair that created the greatest political excitement of the year 1770. There were, however, other issues, and it seems to have been the combined effect of them all at this critical point that coalesced those party alignments which were to persist into the revolutionary crisis of 1775–1776. As public opinion began to turn away from the old popular Whig Assembly majority, leaders like William Smith, Jr., William Livingston, John Morin Scott, and Peter R. Livingston set about to encourage this drift by identifying themselves and their party with the popular side of these new issues. We may, in conclusion, note a few examples. One that was already causing considerable stir when the McDougall affair first burst forth concerned an Assembly bill which called for all future New York elections to be by ballot. This question had arisen before, but it was only in the highly charged atmosphere of the 1769–1770 party rivalries that it gained the impetus it needed for a full hearing. Leading agitators for the balloting bill were John Morin Scott, Peter R. Livingston, and Sears, Lamb, and McDougall [72] for the Sons of Liberty. Even Judge Robert R. Livingston began inclining toward the measure. Its main opponents were the four New York County representatives, DeLancey, Jauncey, Walton, and Cruger, together with the public-spirited New York City merchant Isaac Low. The respective sides tried to mobilize popular support by holding public meetings in the Fields, and it was claimed by party managers that over 1500 citizens attended each rally. Whatever the true numbers, it is known that "One Thousand and Seven Freeholders and Freemen" signed anti-ballot petitions, and that pro-ballot petitions were circulated in Dutchess and Ulster as well as in New York County. The balloting bill was narrowly defeated on January 9, 1770, when the Speaker's negative vote broke a 12-12 tie.[73]

[71] *Smith's Historical Memoirs,* 81; *Assembly Journal* (Buel), Dec. 13, 1770; Dorothy R. Dillon, *The New York Triumvirate* (New York, 1949), 119–21.

[72] McDougall had not yet been arrested for his broadsides.

[73] *Assembly Journal* (Buel), Dec. 22, 1769, Jan. 9, 1770; Peter R. Livingston to Robert Livingston, Jr., New York, Dec. 23, 25, 1769, Feb. 5, 1770, Livingston-Redmond MSS, Reel 6; New-York *Gazette; and The Weekly Mercury,* Jan. 8, 15, 22, 29, 1770; New-York *Journal; or, The General Advertiser,* Jan. 4, 11, 18, 1770.

Another heated controversy was generated by a movement to erect a new liberty pole in place of one that had been cut down by British regulars after a fracas with the local Sons of Liberty. The New York City Common Council had refused permission by a vote of six to nine for a new pole to be erected in the Fields, and this had "Occasioned open doors in their assembly." Stepping in as the hero of the hour, Peter R. Livingston gave permission for the pole to be raised on a narrow strip of land he had bought at a sheriff's sale. On February 6, 1770, a large "Pitch Pine Mast. . . . was drawn through the Streets from the Ship-Yards, by 6 Horses, decorated with Ribbands, 3 Flags flying, with the Words Liberty and Property, and attended by several Thousands of the Inhabitants. It was raised without any Accident, while the French Horns played, God save the King. . . . and is in Height above the Ground, about 46 Feet; on the Top of it was raised a Topmast of 22 Feet, on which is fixed a Gilt Vane, with the Word LIBERTY." [74]

Shortly thereafter a new conflict broke out, this time over the question of enforcing non-importation against the Townshend Acts. Feeling was divided in New York, as elsewhere, over whether total non-importation should be replaced by a simple boycott of tea, the only item still carrying a duty after April, 1770. The reunited Sons of Liberty, led by Peter Livingston, Scott, Sears, McDougall and Lamb, opposed the re-opening of trade, while the New York County assemblymen and Isaac Low favored resumption. Guessing that currently depressed conditions had created sufficient hardship to turn public opinion against non-importation, the city-merchant faction shrewdly proposed that the question be decided by a house-to-house poll. Such a canvass was conducted during three days in July, 1770, and resulted in a "great majority" favoring the resumption of all imports except tea.[75] Radical activity thereupon

[74] Peter R. Livingston to Robert Livingston, Jr., New York, Feb. 5, 1770; New-York *Gazette; and The Weekly Mercury,* Feb. 12, 1770.

[75] Cadwallader Colden to Earl of Hillsborough, New York, July 10, 1770, Alexander Colden to Anthony Todd, Esq. July 11, 1770, *N.Y. Col. Docs.,* VIII, 218–21; New-York *Journal; or, The General Advertiser,* July 19, 1770; Becker, *Political Parties,* 85–94; Klein, "The American Whig, William Livingston," 676; Dillon, *New York Triumvirate,* 115–16. Carl Becker's treatment of this and succeeding disputes to 1776 remains the fullest account in print. For a recent study that includes new material on the Provincial Congress and constitutional convention of 1777, consult Bernard Mason, *The Road to Independence: The Revolutionary Movement in New York, 1773–1777* (Lexington, Ky., 1966).

subsided in New York, as it did in the other colonies, until about 1773. After that, fresh crises sent such agitation mounting once more, and so it continued until the final break.

The January, 1769, Assembly election was the last held in New York Colony, and thus it is difficult to find a measure for the impact that the issues raised during the 1769–1770 party battles may have had upon the voting public. But with the Assembly members the case is different. The votes recorded in the Assembly Journal reveal that beginning in the fall of 1768 two identifiable core-groups were forming in the House. One was composed of Philip Schuyler, Abraham Ten Broeck, and Peter R. Livingston of Albany County; George Clinton and Charles DeWitt of Ulster; and Pierre Van Cortlandt of Westchester. The other consisted of James DeLancey, Jacob Walton, and James Jauncey of New York County; John DeLancey and Frederick Philipse of Westchester; John Rapalje of Kings; Christopher Billop of Richmond; and John DeNoyelles of Orange. Though the DeLancey forces replaced the Schuyler-Clinton group as the pro-government party when Colden took charge after Governor Moore's death in the fall of 1769, the membership of the two cores remained the same. During 1770 the Schuyler-Clinton opposition party gradually added to its ranks such men as Nathaniel Woodhull of Suffolk County and Jacobus Myndertse of Schenectady, and gained occasional support from John Thomas of Westchester and Leonard Van Kleeck of Dutchess.[76]

It seems significant that in the great majority of cases this same alignment would carry over to the Loyalist-Patriot division of the Revolution. It is foreshadowed, for example, in the ballot issue of January, 1770; eleven of the twelve who voted in favor of it would later support the Revolution, and at least nine of the thirteen opposed—including, it might be noted, none other than Captain James DeLancey—would remain loyal to the Crown.[77] Such also would be the case with the street-

---

[76] *Assembly Journal* (Buel), Nov. 3, 7, 17, 23; Dec. 14, 16, 28, 31, 1768; April 11, 12, 14, 20, 26; May 9, 12, 17, 18; Nov. 24; Dec. 7, 12, 15, 19, 20, 21, 22, 28, 29, 30, 1769; Jan. 9, 10, 11, 13, 18, 23, 24, 25, 26, 1770.

[77] *Ibid.,* Jan. 9, 1770. Of those on the affirmative side Thomas, Van Cortlandt, Myndertse, Woodhull, Schuyler, Ten Broeck, DeWitt, Captain Seaman, Ten Eyck, Nicoli, and Clinton all supported the Revolution. It has not been possible to ascertain positively what stand Van Kleeck of Dutchess took. Of those voting against the ballot bill the two DeLanceys, Walton, Philipse, Rapalje, Billop, Kissam, Col. Seaman, and Jauncey all became Loyalists. DeNoyelles died in 1775;

corner coalitions that formed during the mass meetings and popular excitements of those years. Sears, Lamb, and McDougall all supported
independence, while Isaac Low—the leader of citizen support for the
Assembly majority—became a Loyalist. This is hardly to say that the
probable choice of most New Yorkers could have been predicted by
1770. A number of prominent provincials, notably the conservative
proprietor of Livingston Manor, Robert Livingston, Jr., and such prudent lawyers as John Jay, James Duane, and William Smith, Jr.,[78]
would suffer many self-doubts and false hopes before committing themselves. Many elements—principles, self-interest, patterns of life, and
habits of mind—would influence the choices. But for many New Yorkers the issues of the 1769–1770 period seem to have been of critical
significance. Such issues did, in any case, mean something special for
those men with whom this study has been particularly concerned, those
men most closely involved with the colony's politics. For them, in addition to everything else, it was politics itself—the very ongoing requirements, the very process of staking out separate political territory and
then of explaining and defending the positions taken—that had more
than a little to do with shaping and sharpening the final alternatives.

Speaker Cruger, though for a time on the Patriots' list of suspected persons, finally chose to support the Revolution. It has not been possible to determine the
positions of Gale and Boerum. Becker, *Political Parties*, 174–276; Alexander C.
Flick, *Loyalism in New York During the American Revolution* (New York, 1901);
Lorenzo Sabine, *The American Loyalists* (Boston, 1847).

[78] Livingston, Jay, and Duane all eventually chose independence; Smith found at
the last that he could not renounce the King. He went first to England and then
in 1786 to Canada, when he was appointed chief justice of Quebec.

VIII

~~~~~~

IDEOLOGY AND POLITICS: A CONCLUDING NOTE

THE RECENT RESURGENCE of interest in ideology that has been generated by the work of Bernard Bailyn, Gordon Wood, and others has added new and greatly broadened horizons to our understanding of the Revolutionary Era. This is an indispensable element, and fully worthy of the attention it has received. The reader will have noticed, however, that this ideological element has not been taken up in these pages except by occasional and indirect reference. There is a reason for this, and it is not owing to any lack of appreciation for the subject's vast importance.

By the time of the Revolution an ideological pattern had emerged which was more or less common to all the colonies. It had grown from both their local experience and their relations with the home government, and all things considered it varied little from one colony to another. Thus the expressed thoughts of an Adams in Massachusetts, a Jefferson in Virginia, and a very young Hamilton in New York are all variant versions of the Whig argument, and all show a remarkable internal consistency. Yet in examining the specific experience of any given colony—in this case, New York—over any extended period of time, one is confronted with a number of perplexities which impede the tracing of a consistent pattern of development on the level of ideology. Too many matters of an immediate, day-to-day, and seemingly fortuitous nature keep intervening to blur the clarity of such a pattern—matters such as personal and group interests, opportunism, place-seeking, and maneuverings within the governing elite. Even the Patriot-Loyalist division that existed on the eve of the Revolution is no sure guide, since that division could not have been predicted with much certainty along ideological lines more than a few years before the Revolution began. To be sure, when the final choice approached, the Patriots used one set of arguments and the Loyalists another. But this came relatively late. Before that time, the general political ideas which the colonials shared, and in which they were essentially united, probably constituted a far more coherent body of sentiment than did those that may have divided them. A decade before the Revolution, future Whigs and future Tories might have been heard uttering much the same fundamentally Whiggish slogans, and sometimes—as with the popular spokesman, but eventual Loyalist, Captain DeLancey—with exceptional zeal. Under these circumstances, looking for any pattern in terms of either pure opportunism or pure principle is obviously not satisfactory. One wants a mediating term, something to lay alongside the others, and the term that has been used here is politics.

It was once assumed that the colonists' first real political awakening occurred only in the years immediately preceding the American Revolution. There can be no doubt that an enormous intensification of political activity took place at that time. But the closer the historian looks at the earlier colonial years, the more convincing becomes the evidence for an evolutionary view of political development. This certainly appears to be the case in New York, where the Leislerian conflict and its twenty-year aftermath, the commercial-landed rivalry of the 1720's, the Morris-Cosby dispute, the court-Assembly struggle of the mid-century years, and the rancorous campaigns of the 1760's, exhibit a steadily rising intensity of competition among concerted factions for a share of the public authority. As one such contest followed another, New Yorkers refined and polished their skills as political partisans. They were forever drawing up petitions, writing political pamphlets, canvassing for votes, and organizing meetings in the Fields. Ever broader appeals went out to the people, and politics gradually permeated deeper and deeper into provincial life. What it all added up to, as this work has tried to emphasize, was an excessively "factious people."

If a case were to be made that the most distinctive feature of American provincial society was its political culture, and that talent in eighteenth-century America found its most satisfying outlet in politics, a number of factors might be appealed to in support of it. One would certainly be the suffrage, the comprehensiveness of which was not approached by any other society then in existence.[1] Even in an age of deferential politics, rival nabobs seemed to have a clear enough appreciation both of the liabilities of such a franchise and of the uses to which it could be put, and this was at least one of the bridges between an age of elite politics and a later one of mass politics. Another factor was the extraordinary number of public and private transactions that were subject to political acquaintance, political haggling, and political manipulation. Land grants, tax rates, religious dispensations, commercial policies, and appointments as well as elections to a multiplicity of offices were all strikingly political in character. The extent of this capacity of men both grand and not so grand to affect and be affected by their political community gave the American colonials a range of political competence that was elsewhere unknown.

A third feature of provincial politics, and perhaps in many ways the most distinctive, was the growth of "interest" representation—a fact, and eventually an idea, that would seriously subvert traditional concepts of the "public good." The society of New York, as has been seen, was notable for its pluralism, for the variety of its ethnic, religious, economic, and sectional subcultures. From these emerged groups, formal and informal, for whom the unifying element was self-interest, and who were more and more disposed to assume that such interests ought to have some sort of political counterpart. They included merchants, landlords, small farmers, mechanics, fur traders, merchant seamen, Anglicans, Presbyterians, Quakers, Moravians, Dutch, Germans, New Englanders, Huguenots, "East-Enders," "Yorkers," and Albany-

---

[1] In the colonies, electoral eligibility for adult white males ranged from 50 to about 80 per cent, and in some communities it may have reached nearly 100 per cent. The franchise in England, where it was the most liberal in Europe, may never have exceeded 15 per cent in the seventeenth and eighteenth centuries. Chilton Williamson, *American Suffrage: From Property to Democracy, 1760–1860* (Princeton, N.J., 1960), Chap. II; J. H. Plumb, "The Growth of the Electorate in England from 1600 to 1715," *Past & Present*, XLV (Nov., 1969), 111.

men. Examples of bloc voting, the petitioning or instructing of elected deputies, forming "parties" around particular issues, and even taking to the streets, are all to be found, as groups sought access to political power in their capacity as interests. The character of political representation should itself, they came to think, be some reflection of this principle. Over 90 per cent of the men elected to the Assembly throughout the colonial era were men who resided among their constituents, something that was by no means taken for granted in contemporary English practice. The non-resident deputy, the pocket borough, were for most intents and purposes unknown in America. Moreover, it had come to be assumed by the 1760's that New York City should be represented only by men of commerce; Dutchess County representatives were by mid-century acquiring a new responsiveness to Quakers and middling farmers; as early as the 1730's, Suffolk County assemblymen had assumed their role as defenders of "East End" concerns. The City interest fought for lower duties and controls on exports, Quakers for the right to affirm and practice their religion without harassment, "East-Enders" for their own customhouse and an end to regulation of the whaling industry— and so on.

The growing legitimacy, then, of self-interest as a public concept may well have been the sharpest single innovation of colonial politics. Not that it occurred easily. The coexistence of older values made for tensions that underlay political enterprise well into the national era. One side of the colonial mind could remain convinced that private interests, especially when they took political form as factions or parties, were destructive of the greater common good and of the higher public interest. New Yorkers might denounce "selfish factions" and deplore the evils of "party," while at the same time they built "Presbyterian," "Anglican," "merchant," or "anti-landlord" parties. They could honor the traditional formulations of the public interest, reserving the corollary that the overall public interest could not really be in good repair if a particular private interest—invariably their own—languished. They could piously agree that the most inspired of all arrangements for conserving and promoting the public good was the mixed government that blended monarchy, aristocracy, and commons, or the balanced government that harmonized executive and legislature. But they behaved as though in fact the whole public good resided in their own provincial assembly, and that it was embodied in men chosen by local communities and accountable to their particular self-interests. In any case, American self-interest was certainly one of the grounds on which the colonials defended themselves when it came to a break with Great Britain; and James Madison, a few years later, found the question of the regulation and balancing of "distinct interests" to be of sufficient importance that he made it the subject of the first *Federalist* paper he wrote.[2]

Not that any of the above should mean provincial politics was without ideological content; quite the contrary. Two major lines of influence established the overall context within which the colonists functioned politically and in which their political ideas evolved. On the one hand was a line of tradition and experience that included the English Constitution, the common law, the Civil War, and the Glorious Revolution. These created bonds that served to unite Englishmen on both sides of the Atlantic in a common heritage and common loyalties. On the other hand were the special conditions of life in the New World just noted, which made for special patterns of habit and a separate line of experience that was not so easily shared with Englishmen at home. It was from this, their experience as provincials, that the colonists' political notions took on so much of their tone and substance. Thus, to write a history of the development of ideology in New York Province, one would depend upon much the same materials that have been used in the present work for another purpose. For example, the capricious use of executive power during the twenty years or so following Leisler's Rebellion, or the weighting of it to favor one interest over another during the Hunter and Burnet administrations, led to unmistakable impulses to develop checks upon such power. The withholding of funds by the Assembly, and the legislative bargaining that took place between that body and the governor, were two very effective devices. Another was the resort to a London "interest," composed of friends, relatives, and business

---

[2] For a provocative discussion of the self-interest theme in New York during the Revolutionary and Constitutional eras, consult Bernard Friedman, "The Shaping of the Radical Consciousness in Provincial New York," *Journal of American History,* LVI (Mar., 1970), 781–801. Cecelia M. Kenyon has explored with great perception the subject of self-interest groups and their relation to Revolutionary political thought in "Republicanism and Radicalism in the American Revolution: An Old-Fashioned Interpretation," *WMQ,* 3rd Ser., XIX (April, 1962), 153–82. Madison's remarks on interest groups appear in Federalist Number Ten.

correspondents, to check the governor's patrons at home and to counter his particular version of events in the colony. A new element was added during the Morris-Cosby controversy of the 1730's when the Morris faction, recognizing the potential uses of popular pressure, employed the press to great effect and did much to stimulate petition campaigns and participation in elections.

The set of instructions that guided Lewis Morris in London was, among other things, a very comprehensive statement of New Yorkers' ideas about government at that early stage. It included demands for frequent elections, for a Council that would sit separate from the governor when acting as an upper house of the legislature, for a more independent judiciary, and for a more circumscribed executive power of appointment. And it was during that same period, with the first publication of Assembly divisions, "open doors" in the House, and the first agitations for a secret ballot, that representatives were in effect made more accountable to their constituencies. All such ideas, and the attitudes and impulses that accompanied them, were to become common currency, as may be seen in the New York election campaigns of 1768 and 1769, in which all factions reached for them with equal facility.

While all this was taking place, the colonials continued to be influenced by events at home and to draw many of their political attitudes from England. But their own special circumstances as provincials, remote from the seat of power, tended to make them highly selective, and led them to derive those attitudes from a very special sector of the English political community. They were peculiarly responsive to the opposition element in English public life, to the Commonwealthmen, the radical pamphleteers, the "country party" ideologues. Opposition writings on balanced government, frequent elections, responsible representation, separation of powers, and corruption in government seemed to embody the common sense of colonial circumstances. It was thus that the mentality of a fringe group of outsiders in England could be adopted throughout the colonies, where the entire community, not just a part of it, tended more and more to see themselves as outsiders in relation to the home government.

The colonists made a singular contribution to opposition thought —even though they did not always see it as such—by acting it out in their daily political practice. They thereby gave it a concreteness that it could never have acquired in the conjecturings of coffee-house theorists in England, who may have been geographically closer to the centers of power, but were in another sense far remoter from the actual exercise of it than were the provincials. For the latter, such "practice" had long been based on their closeness to institutions of representative government and on their competence, through widespread holding of property, to influence those institutions.

That a republican ideology was gradually being shaped by this experience—invoking as it would the principles of consent, direct representation, and legislative preeminence—is now obvious, though to the colonists themselves it was latent rather than manifest until the period of the final crisis. This, of course, was the "home rule" side of Carl Becker's famous equation. The other, the "who should rule at home" side, was really the obvious and manifest one. Another name for it is factious politics, something that had been going on all the time. During the years that have been examined in this study, these two lines of development seem somewhat separate. But at the onset of the Revolution they merge—or, at any rate, that is the point at which they are least separate. At that point, broadly speaking, a man either casts his lot with the Patriot Party and republicanism, or he remains loyal to the King and quits the country. Thus the Revolution acts, for a time at least, as a unifying force for the "interests" or "factions" that remain.

Still, the contentiousness of the people and the diversity of their interests were not to be subdued. Politics, for all ranks, had become a common idiom, and the factious habits they had fallen into carried them beyond ideology, and even beyond the culminating point of their colonial history, that of revolution.

It would be a long time, well into the republican era, before politics, as an activity in and of itself, would acquire any kind of independent standing and dignity in American life. But one of the first places where it did so was the State of New York, and one would prefer to think that there was something more in this than accident. The assumption here, at any rate, has been that it was a product of historical experience, reaching well back into the colonial era. A very great element in that experience was, of course, the Revolution. But that was by no means the only element. There was, in addition to all else, the day-to-day question, far antedating the Revolution, of "who should rule at home," a question which is of the very essence of politics. It was not, as Carl Becker once thought, so much a matter of which "class" should rule, but rather of which faction, and the time was eventually to come when factions themselves—or parties—would be accepted with equanimity in public life as part of a stable, continuing order. Faction was the instrument not simply of class, or interest, or ideology, but of all this and something more—of politics, which contained and absorbed everything else. New York's precocity in this sort of politics, generating as it did a dynamic of its own, promised a leading and innovative role to her political practitioners in the coming national era.

APPENDIXES

APPENDIX A: GENEALOGIES

DELANCEY *

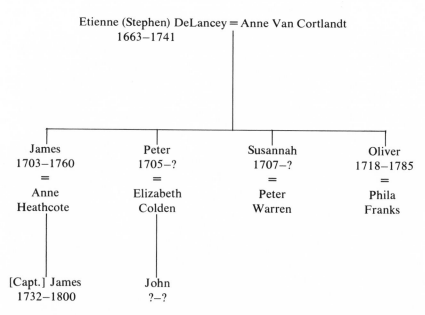

Etienne (Stephen) DeLancey = Anne Van Cortlandt
1663–1741

James	Peter	Susannah	Oliver
1703–1760	1705–?	1707–?	1718–1785
=	=	=	=
Anne	Elizabeth	Peter	Phila
Heathcote	Colden	Warren	Franks

[Capt.] James   John
1732–1800   ?–?

* D. A. Story, *The DeLancey's: A Romance of a Great Family* (London, 1931), 18, 173. The genealogies in this appendix show only those relationships discussed in the text. For full information consult the sources cited for each family.

LIVINGSTON *

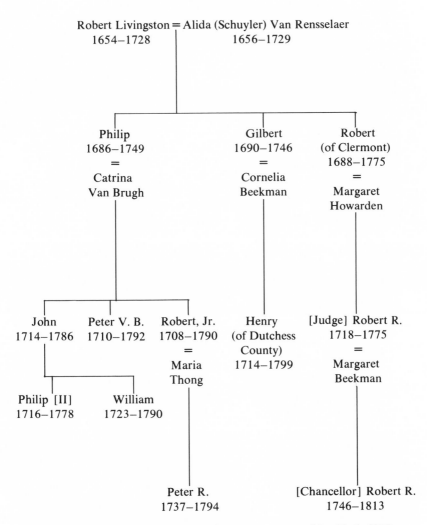

* Edwin B. Livingston, *The Livingstons of Livingston Manor* (New York, 1910).

MORRIS *

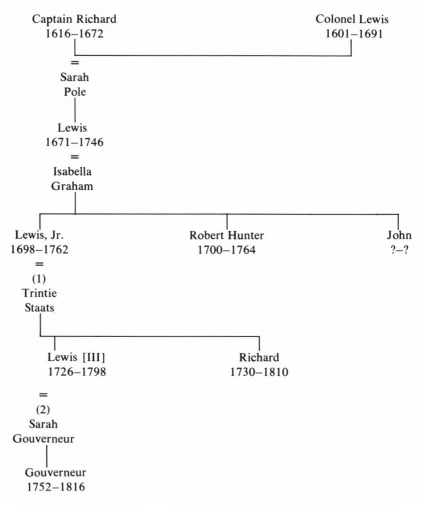

* John E. Stillwell, comp., *Historical and Genealogical Miscellany: Early Settlers of New Jersey and Their Descendants* (New York, 1903–1932), IV, 14–34.

PHILIPSE *

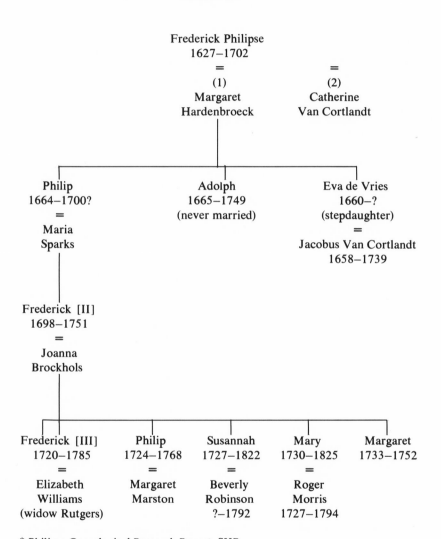

Frederick Philipse
1627–1702
=   =
(1)   (2)
Margaret   Catherine
Hardenbroeck   Van Cortlandt

Philip
1664–1700?
=
Maria
Sparks

Adolph
1665–1749
(never married)

Eva de Vries
1660–?
(stepdaughter)
=
Jacobus Van Cortlandt
1658–1739

Frederick [II]
1698–1751
=
Joanna
Brockhols

Frederick [III]   Philip   Susannah   Mary   Margaret
1720–1785   1724–1768   1727–1822   1730–1825   1733–1752
=   =   =   =
Elizabeth   Margaret   Beverly   Roger
Williams   Marston   Robinson   Morris
(widow Rutgers)   ?–1792   1727–1794

* Philipse Genealogical Research Report, SHR.

SCHUYLER *

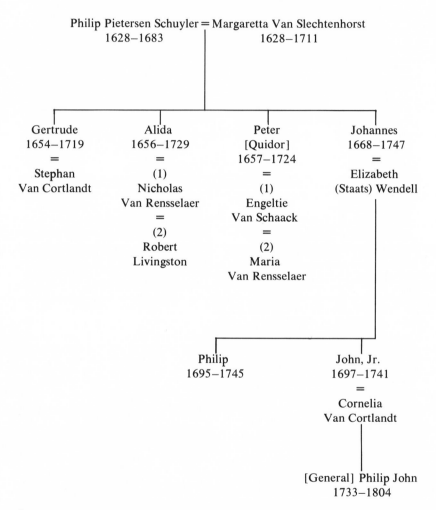

Philip Pietersen Schuyler = Margaretta Van Slechtenhorst
1628–1683   1628–1711

Gertrude   Alida   Peter   Johannes
1654–1719   1656–1729   [Quidor]   1668–1747
=   =   1657–1724   =
Stephan   (1)   =   Elizabeth
Van Cortlandt   Nicholas   (1)   (Staats) Wendell
                 Van Rensselaer   Engeltie
                     =   Van Schaack
                    (2)   =
                  Robert   (2)
                 Livingston   Maria
                                   Van Rensselaer

                 Philip   John, Jr.
               1695–1745   1697–1741
                                                    =
                                                 Cornelia
                                               Van Cortlandt

                                            [General] Philip John
                                                1733–1804

* Don R. Gerlach, *Philip Schuyler and the American Revolution in New York, 1733–1777* (Lincoln, Neb., 1964), Appendix A.

APPENDIX B: ENGLISH GOVERNORS OF NEW YORK*

GOVERNORS	APPOINTED
Richard Nicolls	Sept. 8, 1664
Colonel Francis Lovelace	Aug. 17, 1667
Major Edmund Andros	Nov. 10, 1674
Anthony Brockholles, Cmdr. in Chief	Nov. 16, 1677
Sir Edmund Andros, Knt.	Aug. 7, 1678
Anthony Brockholles, Cmdr. in Chief	Jan. 13, 1681
Colonel Thomas Dongan	Aug. 27, 1682
Sir Edmund Andros	Aug. 11, 1688
Francis Nicholson, Lt. Gov.	Oct. 9, 1688
Jacob Leisler [1]	June 3, 1689
Colonel Henry Sloughter	Mar. 19, 1691
Major Richard Ingoldesby, Cmdr. in Chief	July 26, 1691
Colonel Benjamin Fletcher	Aug. 30, 1692
Richard Coote, Earl of Bellomont	Apr. 13, 1698
John Nanfan, Lt. Gov.	May 17, 1699
Earl of Bellomont [2]	July 24, 1700
William Smith, as eldest Councillor present	Mar. 5, 1701

* Adapted from Edgar A. Werner, *Civil List and Constitutional History of the Colony and State of New York* (Albany, 1888), 165.

[1] Assumed title of Lt. Gov. Dec. 8, 1689; executed for high treason May 16, 1691.

[2] Died Mar. 5, 1701.

GOVERNORS	APPOINTED
John Nanfan, Lt. Gov.	May 19, 1701
Edward Hyde, Viscount Cornbury	May 3, 1702
John, Lord Lovelace	Dec. 18, 1708
Peter Schuyler, President of Council	May 6, 1709
Richard Ingoldesby, Lt. Gov.	May 9, 1709
Peter Schuyler, President of Council	May 25, 1709
Richard Ingoldesby, Lt. Gov.	June 1, 1709
Gerardus Beekman, President of Council	Apr. 10, 1710
Brigadier Robert Hunter	June 14, 1710
Peter Schuyler, President of Council	July 21, 1719
William Burnet	Sept. 17, 1720
John Montgomerie [3]	Apr. 15, 1728
Rip Van Dam, President of Council	July 1, 1731
Colonel William Cosby [4]	Aug. 1, 1732
George Clarke, President of Council [5]	Mar. 10, 1736
Admiral George Clinton	Sept. 2, 1743
Sir Danvers Osborne, Baronet [6]	Oct. 10, 1753
James DeLancey, Lt. Gov.	Oct. 12, 1753
Sir Charles Hardy, Knt.	Sept. 3, 1755
James DeLancey, Lt. Gov.	June 3, 1757
Cadwallader Colden, President of Council [7]	Aug. 4, 1760
Major-General Robert Monckton	Oct. 26, 1761
Cadwallader Colden, Lt. Gov.	Nov. 18, 1761
Major-General Robert Monckton	June 14, 1762
Cadwallader Colden, Lt. Gov.	June 28, 1763
Sir Henry Moore, Baronet	Nov. 13, 1765
Cadwallader Colden, Lt. Gov.	Sept. 12, 1769
John Murray, Earl of Dunmore	Oct. 19, 1770
William Tryon	July 9, 1771
Cadwallader Colden, Lt. Gov.	Apr. 7, 1774
William Tryon [8]	June 28, 1775

[3] Died July 1, 1731.   [4] Died Mar. 10, 1736.

[5] Commissioned Lt. Gov. July 30, 1736; sworn into office Oct. 30, 1736.

[6] Committed suicide Oct. 12, 1753.

[7] Commissioned Lt. Gov. Apr. 14, 1761; sworn into office Aug. 8, 1763.

[8] Sailed for England July 9, 1780.

APPENDIX C: REPRESENTATIVES IN THE COLONIAL ASSEMBLY

The information in Appendix C is based on Edgar A. Werner, *Civil List and Constitutional History of the Colony and State of New York* (Albany, 1888), 354–61, to which my own corrections have been added. Werner did not cite the sources of his information; my data has been drawn mainly from *Journal of the Votes and Proceedings of the General Assembly of the Colony of New York, 1691–1775*, 2 vols. (New York, Hugh Gaine, printer, 1764–1766) and *Journal of the Votes and Proceedings of the General Assembly of the Colony of New York, from 1766 to 1776 inclusive* (Albany, J. Buel, printer, 1820).

FIRST ASSEMBLY

1691—April 9 to May 18; September 11 to October 2.
1692—April 20 to April 29; August 17 to September 10.
Dissolved September 13, 1692.

Speaker—James Graham.
Clerk—John Clapp.

Sergeant-at-Arms—Benjamin Phipps.
Doorkeeper—William Welsh.

Albany.
Dirck Wessels,
Levinus Van Schaick.
Kings.
Nicolas Stillwell,
John Poland.
New York.
James Graham,
William Merrett,
Jacobus Van Cortlandt,
Johannis Kipp.

Queens.
John Bound,[1]
Nathaniel Pearsall,[1]
John Tredwell,[2,3]
Daniel Whitehead,[2]
John Robinson.[4]
Rensselaerwyck.
Killian Van Rensselaer.[5]
Richmond.
Ellias Duksberry,
John Dally,

Lambert Dorland.[6]
Suffolk.
Henry Pierson,
Matthew Howell.
Ulster and Dutchess.
Henricus Beekman,
Thomas Garton,[7]
William Demiere.[8]
Westchester.
John Pell.

SECOND ASSEMBLY

1692—October 26 to November 14.
1692-3—March 20 to April 10.
Dissolved July 27, 1693.

Officers same as before.

Albany.
Dirck Wessels,
Levinus Van Schaick.
Kings.
John Poland,
Coert Stuyvesant.
New York
James Graham,
William Merrett,
Jacobus Van Cortlandt,

Johannis Kipp.
Queens.
Daniel Whitehead,
John Robinson.
Rensselaerwyck.
Killian Van Rensselaer.
Richmond.
Thomas Morgan,
I. T. Van Pelt.

Suffolk.
Henry Pierson,
Matthew Howell.
Ulster and Dutchess.
Henricus Beekman,
Thomas Garton.
Westchester.
John Pell.

THIRD ASSEMBLY

1693—September 3 to September 22.
Dissolved November 16, 1693.

Officers same as before.

Albany.
Dirck Wessels,
Ryer Jacobs.
Kings.
Coert Stuyvesant,
Johannis Van Ecklen.
New York.
James Graham,
William Merrett,
Jacobus Van Cortlandt,

Johannis Kipp.
Queens.
Daniel Whitehead,
John Jackson.
Rensselaerwyck.
Killian Van Rensselaer.
Richmond.
Thomas Stillwell,
John Shadwell,[9]
John Teunisen.[10]

Suffolk.
Henry Pierson,
John Tuthill.
Ulster and Dutchess.
Thomas Garton,
Jacob Rutsen.
Westchester.
John Pell,
Joseph Theale.

FOURTH ASSEMBLY

1693–4—March 1 to March 26.
1694—September 25 to October 23.
1694–5—March 21 to April 13.
Dissolved April 20, 1695.

Speaker—Henry Pierson.
Other officers the same as before.

Albany.
Dirck Wessels,
Ryer Jacobs.
Kings.
Henry Filkin,
Johannis Van Ecklen.
New York.
Peter DeLanoy,
Samuel Staats,
John Spratt,

Robert Blackwell.
Queens.
Daniel Whitehead,
John Jackson.
Rensselaerwyck.
Killian Van Rensselaer.
Richmond.
Thomas Stillwell,
John Teunisen.

Suffolk.
Henry Pierson,
Matthew Howell.
Ulster and Dutchess.
Jacob Rutsen,
Thomas Garton.
Westchester.
John Pell,
Humphrey Underhill.

FIFTH ASSEMBLY

1695—June 20 to July 4; October 1–26.
1696—March 25 to April 24; October 15
  to November 3.
1697—March 25 to April 22.
Dissolved April 2, 1698.

Speaker—James Graham.
Sergeant-at-Arms (1697)—Richard
  Stoakes.
Other officers same.

Albany.
John Abeel,
Dirck Wessels.
Kings.
John Van Ecklen,
Cornelius Sebring.
New York.
James Graham,
Brandt Schuyler,
Lawrence Reade,
Tunis DeKay.

Queens.
Daniel Whitehead,
John Jackson.
Rensselaerwyck.
Killian Van Rensselaer.
Richmond.
Thomas Stillwell,
Elias Duksberry.
Suffolk.
Matthew Howell,
John Tuthill.

Ulster.
Henry Beekman,
William Demiere.
Westchester.
Humphrey Underhill,[11]
Joseph Purdy,
Joseph Theal.[12]

[1] Refused to take the oath, being Quakers, and were dismissed.

[2] Admitted April 14, 1691.

[3] Arrested on a "scandalous" charge and expelled April 16, 1691.

[4] Elected in place of Tredwell.   [5] Admitted May 1, 1691.

[6] Admitted September 17, 1691, in place of Dally, deceased.

[7] Resigned April 10, 1691.   [8] Admitted April 25, 1691, in place of Garton.

[9] Declined to take the oath and was dismissed.

[10] Admitted September 21, in place of Shadwell.

[11] Excluded April 1, 1697, for refusing to attend "before he had his money."

[12] Admitted April 12, 1697, in place of Underhill.

SIXTH ASSEMBLY

1698—May 19 to June 14.
Dissolved June 14, 1698.

Speaker—Philip French.
Clerk—Benjamin Jackson.
Sergeant-at-Arms—Richard Stoakes.
Doorkeeper—Richard Plaisted.

Albany.
Jan Jansen Bleker,[1]
Ryer Schermerhorn.[1]
Kings.
Meyndert Coerten,[2]
Gerardus Beekman,[2]
Cornelius Van Brunt,[1,3]
Cornelius Sebring.[1,3]
New York.
Philip French,
Jacobus Van Cortlandt,

Thomas Wenham,
Johannis Kipp.
Queens.
John Jackson,
Daniel Whitehead.
Rensselaerwyck.
Killian Van Rensselaer.
Richmond.
John Teunisen,[4]
Thomas Morgan,[1]
John Woglom.[1,5]

Suffolk.
Henry Pierson,
Matthew Howell.
Ulster.
Abraham Haasbrook,
Thomas Garton.
Westchester.
John Drake,
Joseph Purdy.

SEVENTH ASSEMBLY

1699—March 2 to May 16.
1700—July 25 to Aug 9; October 2 to
   November 2.
1701—April 2 to April 19.
Dissolved June 1, 1701.

Speakers—James Graham (March 21,
   1699), Abraham Gouverneur (May 15,
   1699).
Clerk—Gabriel Ludlow.
Sergeant-at-Arms—Richard Stoakes.
Doorkeeper (1700)—Gabriel Thompson.

Albany.
Hendrick Hansen,
Jan Jansen Bleker,
Ryer Schermerhorn.
Kings and Orange.
Abraham Gouverneur,
Cornelius Sebring,
Cornelius Van Brunt.
New York.
James Graham,
Johannis De Peyster,

John Kerfbyl,[6]
David Provoost,[7]
Leonard Lewis.
Queens.
John Jackson,[8]
Daniel Whitehead.[8]
Rensselaerwyck.
Killian Van Rensselaer.[8]
Richmond.
Thomas Morgan,
Garrat Veghte.

Suffolk.
Henry Pierson,[8]
Matthew Howell.[8]
Ulster.
Jacob Rutsen,
Abraham Haasbrook.
Westchester.
John Drake,
John Hunt.

EIGHTH ASSEMBLY

1701—August 19 to October, 18.
1702—April 21 to May 2.
Dissolved May 3, 1702.

Speaker—Abraham Gouverneur.[9]
Other officers the same.

Albany.
Dirck Wessels,[10,11]
Ryer Schermerhorn,[11]
Meyndert Schuyler,[12]
John Abeel,[12]
Johannis Bleker,[13]
Hendrick Hansen.[13]
Kings.
Cornelius Sebring,
Cornelius Van Brunt.
New York.
Isaac De Riemer,
Abraham Gouverneur,
Johannis De Peyster,
David Provoost.

Orange.
Peter Haring.
Queens.
John Jackson,[12]
Daniel Whitehead,[12]
Thomas Willet,[14]
John Tallman,[14]
Thomas Hicks,[20]
Jonathan Smith.[20]
Rensselaerwyck.
Killian Van Rensselaer,[12]
Andries Coejemans.[13]
Richmond.
Garret Veghte,
Thomas Morgan.[15]

Suffolk.
William Nicoll,[10,16]
Matthew Howell.[12]
Ulster.
Jacob Rutsen,
Adrien Garretsen.
Westchester.
John Drake,[12]
Joseph Purdy,[17]
Henry Fowler,[17]
William Willet,[14]
Caleb Heathcote.[20]

NINTH ASSEMBLY

1702—October 20 to November 27.
1703—April 13 to June 19; Oct. 14–23.
1704—April 13 to June 27; Oct. 6 to
Nov. 6.
Dissolved November 6.

Speaker—William Nicoll.
Clerk—Gabriel Ludlow.
Sergeant-at-Arms—Edward Cole.[18]
Doorkeeper—Gabriel Luff.

Albany.
John Abeel,
Myndert Schuyler,
Evert Banker.
Kings.
Cornelius Sebring,

Cornelius Van Brunt.
New York.
Stephen De Lancey,
Thomas Coddrington,
Philip French,
Jacobus Van Cortlandt.

Orange.
Floris Crum.
Queens.
John Jackson,
Daniel Whitehead,
Jonathan Whitehead.[19]

[1] Announced their withdrawal, in a petition presented to the Governor and Council June 9. This petition was delivered to the Assembly by the Governor, who held it to be "not cognizable by him," and advised its signers to return, which they formally did June 11, saying: "but cannot sit and act as members at present —but desire further time for consideration."

[2] Declared "not qualified according to law," May 28.   [3] Admitted June 6.

[4] Declared "not qualified according to law," May 27.   [5] Admitted June 7.

[6] Died before the meeting of the Assembly.   [7] In place of Kerfbyl, deceased.

[8] The Earl of Bellomont, Governor, being dead, and the Lieutenant-Governor absent, the Council and General Assembly concurred in the opinion that the administration of the Government devolved on the Council. This was disputed by Colonel William Smith, president of the Council, who claimed that the government [was] vested in him. These gentlemen then signed a paper in opposition to the position of the Council and Assembly, whereupon the latter adopted a resolution declaring that the subscribers had "offered the greatest scandal to the Whole House of Representatives" and were "liable to the severest rebukes of this House for their disloyalty and insolence, and that Major Matthew Howell, being the writer and deliverer in of the said paper, be forthwith expelled this House." Howell was expelled on April 17, 1701, and was not replaced in that session.

[9] Abraham Gouverneur received 10 votes; William Nicoll, 9; not voting, 2.

[10] Declared disqualified for non-residence, and "ordered to withdraw," August 19.

[11] Wessels dismissed, and Schermerhorn, the candidate with the next highest number of votes, admitted August 20.

[12] Withdrew with Wessels and Nicoll August 20, "not withstanding the speaker often commanded them, in the name of the House, to stay and attend the service of this House." [*Assembly Journal.*] Expelled for non-attendance August 26, and new elections ordered.

[13] Admitted September 18, in place of Schuyler, Abeel and Van Rensselaer, respectively.

[14] Admitted September 12, in place of Jackson, Whitehead and Drake, respectively. Expelled September 22, for having presented a paper "writ in barbarous English," representing that the organization of the House is illegal, and Gouverneur an alien; and for refusing to recognize a summons to appear and answer with regard thereto. The succeeding assembly (November 11, 1702), adjudged Gouverneur an alien, and adopted a resolution that acts passed under the speakership of an alien are "not binding upon the citizen."

[15] Died in the interval between the two sessions, and new election ordered.

[16] Dismissed for non-residence August 22.

[17] Purdy withdrew with the other seceders, August 20. Fowler contested Purdy's seat and was admitted August 26. The House then consisted of 12, including Schermerhorn and Fowler, one more than a quorum.

[18] Appointed October 29, 1702.

[19] Admitted October 26, 1704, in place of Daniel Whitehead, deceased.

[20] Admitted October 13, 1701.

NINTH ASSEMBLY (CONT.)

Rensselaerwyck.
Killian Van Rensselaer,
Andries Dow.[1]
Richmond.
John Stillwell,
Abraham Lakerman.

Suffolk.
Matthew Howell,
William Nicoll.
Ulster.
Henry Beekman,
Thomas Garton.

Westchester.
William Willet,
Joseph Purdy,
Josiah Hunt.[2]

TENTH ASSEMBLY

1705—June 9 to August 4; September 26 to October 13.
1706—May 29 to June 27; September 27 to October 21.
Dissolved May 15, 1707.[3]

Officers same as preceding session.

Albany.
Myndert Schuyler,
Johannis Cuyler,
Peter Van Bruggen.
Kings.
Cornelius Sebring,
Cornelius Van Brunt.
New York.
Stephen De Lancey,
Thomas Coddrington,
Jacobus Van Cortlandt,
Philip French.

Orange.
Floris Crum.
Queens.
John Jackson,
Jonathan Whitehead.
Rensselaerwyck.
Hendrick Van Rensselaer.
Richmond.
Abraham Lakerman,
John Stillwell.

Suffolk.
William Nicoll,
Samuel Mulford.
Ulster.
Henry Beekman,
Thomas Garton.
Westchester.
William Willet,
Edmund Ward,
Josiah Hunt.[2]

ELEVENTH ASSEMBLY

1708—August 18 to November 27.
Dissolved January 5, 1709.

Speaker—William Nicoll.
Clerk—Gabriel Ludlow.

Sergeant-at-Arms ———.
Doorkeeper—William Churchill.

Albany.
Johannis Cuyler,
Hendrick Hansen,
Myndert Schuyler.
Kings.
Cornelius Sebring,
Cornelius Van Brunt.
New York.
Stephen De Lancey,
Jacobus Van Cortlandt.
Lawrence Reade,
Thomas Coddrington.

Orange.
Michael Hawdin.
Queens.
Jonathan Whitehead,
John Jackson.
Rensselaerwyck.
Hendrick Van Rensselaer.
Richmond.
John Stillwell,
Abraham Lakerman.

Suffolk.
William Nicoll,
Samuel Mulford.
Ulster.
Henry Beekman,
Thomas Garton.
Westchester.
William Willet,
Edmund Ward,
Josiah Hunt.[2]

TWELFTH ASSEMBLY

1709—April 6 to July 5; September 7 to November 12.

Officers same as before.

Albany.
Myndert Schuyler,
Johannis Cuyler,
Robert Livingston.
Kings.
Cornelius Sebring,
Cornelius Van Brunt.

New York.
Captain ——— Wilson,
Johannis Jansen,
John Van Horn,
Johannis Hardenbrook.
Orange.
Peter Haring.

Queens.
John Talman,
John Townsend.
Renesselaerwyck.
Henry Van Rensselaer.
Richmond.
Abraham Lakerman,
John Stillwell.

TWELFTH ASSEMBLY (CONT.)

Suffolk.	Ulster.	Westchester.
William Nicoll,	Henry Beekman,	Joseph Purdy,
Samuel Mulford.	Thomas Garton.	John Drake,
		Josiah Hunt.[2]

THIRTEENTH ASSEMBLY

1710—September 1 to November 25.   *Speaker*—William Nicoll.
1711—April 12–20.   *Clerk*—Gabriel Ludlow.
Dissolved April 20.   *Sergeant-at-Arms.* ———.
    Doorkeeper—Cornelius Post.

Albany.	Johannis Jansen.	*Suffolk.*
Johannis Cuyler,	*Orange.*	William Nicoll,
Johannis Schuyler,	Hendrick Ten Eyck.	Samuel Mulford.
Robert Livingston.	*Queens.*	*Ulster.*
Kings.	Thomas Willet,	Henry Beekman,
Cornelius Sebring,	John Jackson.	Thomas Garton.
Cornelius Van Brunt.	*Renesselaerwyck.*	*Westchester.*
New York.	Henry Van Rensselaer.	Lewis Morris,[5]
Lawrence Reade,	*Richmond.*	William Willet,
Jacobus Van Cortlandt,	John Stillwell,	Edmund Ward,
Stephen DeLancey,	Abraham Lakerman.	Josiah Hunt.[2]

FOURTEENTH ASSEMBLY [7]

1711—July 2 to August 4; October 2 to November 24.
1712—April 30 to June 26; August 25 to December 10.
Dissolved March 3, 1712–13.

Officers same as preceding Assembly.

Albany.	David Provoost.	*Suffolk.*
Robert Livingston, Jr.,[6]	*Orange.*	William Nicoll,
Johannis Cuyler,	Hendrick Ten Eyck.	Samuel Mulford.
Johannis Schuyler.	*Queens.*	*Ulster.*
Kings.	Thomas Willet,	Henry Beekman,
Cornelius Sebring,	John Jackson.	Thomas Garton.
Cornelius Van Brunt.	*Renesselaerwyck.*	*Westchester.*
New York.	Henry Van Rensselaer.	William Willet,
Jacobus Van Cortlandt,	*Richmond.*	Edmund Ward,
Lawrence Reade,	Abraham Lakerman,	John Hoite,[4]
Stephen DeLancey,	John Stillwell.	Lewis Morris.[2]

[1] Admitted October 14, 1703, in place of Van Rensselaer, appointed to Council.

[2] Representative of the Borough.

[3] According to the Assembly Journal, dissolved by proclamation dated at Burlington. According to the Council Minutes, dissolved by order in Council, at executive session, July 9, 1708.

[4] Elected under writs issued May 15, 1712, in place of Ward, deceased.

[5] Expelled on November 9, 1710, when "falsely and scandalously vilified the Integrity and Honesty" of the House.

[6] This Robert Livingston, Jr. (1688–1775) is the first Livingston Manor proprietor's third son, who became Robert of Clermont.

[7] This Assembly may have been dissolved sometime between August 4, 1711 and September 10, 1711, though this cannot definitely be ascertained. Such a dissolution would throw off Werner's numbering of the sessions, but because these were arbitrary designations in the first place they will be left unchanged.

FIFTEENTH ASSEMBLY

1713—May 27 to July 7; October 15 to November 4.
1713–14—March 24 to September 4.
Dissolved by the death of Queen Anne.

Speaker—William Nicoll.
Clerk—Gabriel Ludlow.
Sergeant-at-Arms—Robert Crannel.
Doorkeeper—Cornelius Post.

Albany.
Robert Livingston, Jr.,
[of Clermont]
Myndert Schuyler,
Peter Van Brugh.
Dutchess.
Leonard Lewis.
Kings.
Cornelius Sebring,
Cornelius Van Brunt.
New York.
Jacobus Van Cortlandt,

Stephen De Lancey,
Lawrence Reade,
Samuel Bayard.
Orange.
Cornelius Haring.
Queens.
Thomas Willet,
John Jackson.
Rensselaerwyck.
Henry Van Rensselaer.
Richmond.
John Stillwell,

Abraham Lakerman.
Suffolk.
William Nicoll,
Samuel Mulford.
Ulster.
Henry Beekman,
Jacob Rutsen.
Westchester.
William Willet,
Joseph Drake,
Lewis Morris.[1]

SIXTEENTH ASSEMBLY

1715—May 3 to July 21.
Dissolved August 11, 1715.

Speaker—William Nicoll.

Albany.
Johannis Cuyler,
Hendrick Hansen,
Karel Hansen.
Dutchess.
Leonard Lewis,
Baltus Van Kleeck.
Kings.
Cornelius Sebring,
Cornelius Van Brunt.
New York.
Jacobus Van Cortlandt,

Stephen De Lancey,
Samuel Bayard,
John Reade.
Orange.
Cornelius Haring.
Queens.
Thomas Willet,
John Jackson.
Rensselaerwyck.
Andries Coejemans.
Richmond.
John Stillwell,

Abraham Lakerman.
Suffolk.
William Nicoll,
Samuel Mulford.[2]
Ulster.
Henry Beekman,
Jacob Rutsen.
Westchester.
Josiah Hunt,
Jonathan Odall,
Lewis Morris.[1]

SEVENTEENTH ASSEMBLY

1716—June 5–30; August 7 to Sept. 1.
1717—April 9 to May 28; Aug. 27 to Dec. 23.
1718—May 21 to July 3; Sept. 24 to Oct. 16.
1719—April 28 to June 25.
1720—October 13 to November 19.

1721—May 16 to July 27.
1722—May 30 to July 7; Oct. 3 to Nov. 1.
1723—May 8 to July 6.
1724—May 12 to July 24.
1725—August 31 to November 10.
1726—April 6 to June 17.
Dissolved August 10, 1726.

Speakers—William Nicoll,[3] Robert Livingston,[4] Adolph Philipse.[5]
Clerk—Gabriel Ludlow.
Sergeant-at-Arms—Robert Crannel.
Doorkeepers—Cornelius Post, Thomas Brasier,[6] Derrick Egbertsen.[7]

Albany.
John Cuyler,
Hendrick Hansen,
Karel Hansen,
Myndert Schuyler.[8]
Dutchess.
Leonard Lewis,
Baltus Van Kleeck,
Johannis Terbosch,[9]
Henry Beekman.[10]

Kings.
Cornelius Sebring,
Samuel Garretsen,
Joseph Hegeman,[11]
Richard Stillwell.[12]
Livingston.[13]
Robert Livingston.
New York.
David Provoost,
John Jansen,

Jacobus Kipp,
Garret Van Horne,
Stephen De Lancey.[23]
Orange.
Peter Haring,
Cornelius Cuyler.
Queens.
Isaac Hicks,
Thomas Willet,
Benjamin Hicks.[14]
Rensselaerwyck.
Andries Coejemans.

Richmond.
John Stillwell,
Abraham Lakerman,
Richard Merrill.[24]
Suffolk.
William Nicoll,[15]
Samuel Mulford,[16]

Samuel Hutchinson,[17]
Epenetus Platt.[18]
Ulster.
Jacob Rutsen,
Henry Beekman,
Abraham Gaasbeck
Chambers.[19]

Westchester.
William Willet,
Joseph Budd,
Adolph Philipse,[20]
Lewis Morris.[1]

EIGHTEENTH ASSEMBLY

1726—September 27 to November 11.
Dissolved August 21, 1727, in consequence of the death of George I.

Officers same as before.

Albany.
Myndert Schuyler,
Ryer Garretsen.
Dutchess.
Henry Beekman,
Johannis Van Kleeck.
Kings.
Richard Stillwell,
Samuel Garretsen.
Livingston.[13]
Robert Livingston, Jr.
[of Clermont]
New York.
Stephen DeLancey

Adolph Philipse,
Garret Van Horne,
Anthony Rutgers.
Orange.
Lancaster Symes,
Cornelius Haring.
Queens.
Isaac Hicks,
Benjamin Hicks.
Rensselaerwyck.
Jeremiah Van Rensselaer.
Richmond.
Richard Merrill,
John Le Count.

Schenectady.[21]
Jacob Glen.
Suffolk.
Samuel Hutchinson,
Epenetus Platt.
Ulster.
Abraham Gaasbeck,
Albert Pawling.
Westchester.
William Willet,
Frederick Philipse,[25]
Lewis Morris.[22]

---

[1] Representative of the Borough.

[2] Expelled June 2, 1715, "for printing speech formerly made to the General Assembly, without leave of the House, in which are many false and scandalous reflections upon the Governor of this province."

[3] Resigned on account of ill health.   [4] Elected May 27, 1718.

[5] Elected August 31, 1725.   [6] Appointed December 23, 1717.

[7] Appointed in 1722.

[8] Admitted June 16, 1724, in place of Hansen, deceased.

[9] Admitted May 4, 1717, in place of Van Kleeck, deceased.

[10] Admitted August 31, 1725, in place of Terbosch, deceased.

[11] Admitted July 5, 1721, in place of Sebring, deceased.

[12] Admitted November 1, 1725, in place of Hegeman, deceased.

[13] Manor.

[14] Admitted September 13, 1725, in place of Willet, deceased.

[15] Death announced to the House, May 8, 1723.

[16] Declined to act with the House on the ground of illegality, October 26, 1720, and expelled.

[17] Admitted May 17, 1721, in place of Mulford, expelled.

[18] Admitted June 11, 1723.

[19] Admitted May 16, 1717, in place of Beekman, deceased.

[20] Admitted June 26, 1722, in place of Budd, deceased.

[21] Township.   [22] Borough.

[23] Admitted on September 21, 1725, in place of Provoost, deceased.

[24] Admitted on September 13, 1725, in place of Stillwell, deceased.

[25] This Frederick Philipse (1698–1751) served in the Assembly until his death in 1751.

NINETEENTH ASSEMBLY

1727—September 30 to November 25.   Officers same as before.
Dissolved November 25, 1727.

Albany.
Johannis Cuyler,
Peter Van Brugh.
Dutchess.
Henry Beekman,
Johannis Van Kleeck.
Kings.
Samuel Garretsen,
Johannis Lott.
Livingston.[1]
Robert Livingston, Jr.
[of Clermont]
New York.
Stephen De Lancey,

Adolph Philipse,
Garret Van Horne,
Anthony Rutgers.
Orange.
Lancaster Syms,
Cornelius Haring.
Queens.
Isaac Hicks,
Benjamin Hicks.
Rensselaerwyck.
Jeremiah Van Rensselaer.
Richmond.
Richard Merrill,
John Le Count.

Schenectady.[2]
Nicholas Schuyler.
Suffolk.
Samuel Hutchinson,
Epenetus Platt.
Ulster.
Abraham Gaasbeck,
Albert Pawling.
Westchester.
William Willet,
Frederick Philipse,
Lewis Morris.[3]

TWENTIETH ASSEMBLY

1728—July 23 to September 21.
1729—May 14 to July 12.
1730—August 26 to October 29.
1731—August 25 to September 30.
1732—August 10 to October 14.
1733—October 16 to November 1.

1734—April 25 to June 22; October 2
to Nov. 28.
1735—October 16 to November 8.
1736—October 14 to November 10.
1737—April 5 to May 3.
Dissolved May 3, 1737.

Officers same as before, except—
Sergeant-at-Arms—Alexander Lamb, appointed October 15, 1732, in place of
Derrick Egbertsen.

Albany.
Philip Schuyler,
Myndert Schuyler,
Cortlandt.[1]
Philip Verplanck.[4]
Dutchess.
Henry Beekman,
Johannis Van Kleeck.
Kings.
Samuel Garretsen,
Johannis Lott.
Livingston.[1]
Gilbert Livingston.
New York
Stephen De Lancey,

Adolph Philipse,
Garret Van Horne,
Anthony Rutgers.
Orange.
Lancaster Syms,
Cornelius Haring,
Vincent Matthews.[11]
Queens.
Isaac Hicks,
Benjamin Hicks.
Rensselaerwyck.
Jeremiah Van Rensselaer.
Richmond.
Richard Merrill,
John Le Count.

Schenectady.
Jacob Glen.[5]
Suffolk.
Samuel Hutchinson,
Epenetus Platt.
Ulster.
Abraham Gaasbeck
Chambers,
Albert Pawling.
Westchester.
William Willet,
Frederick Philipse,
Gilbert Willet,[3]
Lewis Morris, Jr.,[6]
Lewis Morris.[7]

TWENTY-FIRST ASSEMBLY

1737—June 15–16; September 1 to
December 16.
1738—September 4 to October 20.
Dissolved October 20, 1738.

Speaker—Lewis Morris, Jr.
Clerk—Gabriel Ludlow.
Sergeant-at-Arms—James Crannel.[1]
Doorkeeper—Alexander Lamb.

Albany.
Philip Schuyler,
Peter Winne.
Cortlandt.[1]
Philip Verplanck.

Dutchess.
Henry Beekman,
Jacobus Ter Boss.
Kings.
Johannis Lott,
Abraham Lott.

Livingston.[1]
Robert Livingston, Jr.[12]
New York.
Garret Van Horne,
James Alexander,
John Walter,

Simon Johnson,
Adolph Philipse.[8]
Orange.
Vincent Matthews,
Cornelius Kuyper.
Queens.
Isaac Hicks,
David Jones.

Rensselaerwyck.
Jeremiah Van Rensselaer.
Richmond.
John Le Count,
Adam Mott.
Schenectady.[2]
Arent Bradt.
Suffolk.
Epenetus Platt,
David Pierson.

Ulster.
Abraham G. Chambers,
John Hardenburgh.
Westchester.
Frederick Philipse,
Lewis Morris,[9]
William Willet,[10]
Lewis Morris, Jr.,[3]

TWENTY-SECOND ASSEMBLY

1739—March 27 to April 14; August 28 to October 3; October 9 to November 17.
1740—June 30 to July 12; September 9 to Nov. 3.
1741—April 14 to June 13; Sept. 15 to March 16.
1742—April 20 to Sept. 29; Oct. 12 to Oct. 29.
1743—April 19 to September 27.
Dissolved September 27.

Speaker—Adolph Philipse.
Clerk—George Duncan.

Sergeant-at-Arms—James Crannel.
Doorkeeper—Alexander Lamb.

Albany.
Philip Schuyler,
Peter Winne.
Cortlandt.[1]
Philip Verplanck.
Dutchess.
Henry Beekman,
Jacobus Ter Boss.
Kings.
Abraham Lott,
Johannis Lott.
Livingston.[1]
Robert Livingston, Jr.[12]
New York.
Adolph Philipse,

John Moore,
David Clarkson,
William Roome.
Orange.
Gabriel Ludlow,
Thomas Gale.
Queens.
David Jones,
Thomas Cornell.
Rensselaerwyck.
Jeremiah Van Rensselaer.
Richmond.
John Le Count,
Richard Stillwell.

Schenectady.[2]
Arent Bradt.
Suffolk.
David Pierson,
William Nicoll.
Ulster.
John Hardenburgh,
Abraham Haasbrook.
Westchester
Frederick Philipse,
Daniel Purdy,
Lewis Morris, Jr.[3]

[1] Manor.   [2] Township.   [3] Borough.

[4] Right and seat recognized June 11, 1734; admitted June 22.

[5] Township. Seat declared vacant July 25, 1728, Glen and Wouter Vrooman having received an equal number of votes. At a subsequent election, Glen was elected and was admitted August 12.

[6] Admitted from the Borough of Westchester, August 17, 1732.

[7] Admitted from the County of Westchester November 1, 1733, in place of William Willet, deceased.

[8] Elected in place of Van Horne, deceased, September, 1737; admitted on decision of contest brought by Cornelius Van Horne, and decided October 12, 1737.

[9] Resigned September 5, 1738.

[10] Elected in place of Morris, admitted October 6, 1738.

[11] Admitted June 14, 1729.

[12] This Robert Livingston, Jr. (1708–1790) is the grandson of Robert Livingston the founder, and was the third proprietor of Livingston Manor. He was continuously elected to the Manor seat through 1758.

TWENTY-THIRD ASSEMBLY

1743—November 8 to December 17.
1744—April 17 to May 19; July 17 to September 21.
1744–5—March 12 to May 14.
Dissolved May 14, 1745.

Officers same as before.

Albany.
Philip Schuyler,
Peter Winne.
  Cortlandt.
Philip Verplanck.
  Dutchess.
Henry Beekman,
Johannis Tappen.
  Kings.
Abraham Lott,
Johannis Lott.
  Livingston.[1]
Robert Livingston, Jr.
  New York.
Adolph Philipse,

John Moore,
Paul Richards,
Cornelius Van Horne,
David Clarkson.[2]
  Orange.
Gabriel Ludlow,
Thomas Gale.
  Queens.
David Jones,
Thomas Cornell.
  Rensselaerwyck.[1]
John Baptist
  Van Rensselaer.
  Richmond.
John Le Count,
Richard Stillwell.

Schenectady.[3]
Abraham Glen.
  Suffolk.
David Pierson,
William Nicoll.
  Ulster.
Wm. Gaasbeck Chambers,
Abraham Haasbrook.
  Westchester.
Frederick Philipse,
John Thomas,
Lewis Morris, Jr.[3]

TWENTY-FOURTH ASSEMBLY

1745–6—June 25 to February 27.
1746—March 4 to May 3; June 3 to
  December 6.

1747—March 24 to September 22;
  September 29 to November 25.
Dissolved November 25, 1747.

Speaker—David Jones.
Clerk—George Duncan.

Sergeant-at-Arms—John Meyer.[5]
Doorkeeper—Alexander Lamb.

Albany.
Philip Schuyler,
Peter Winne.
  Cortlandt.[1]
Philip Verplanck.
  Dutchess.
Henry Beekman,
Johannis Tappen.
  Kings.
Abraham Lott,
Johannis Lott.
  Livingston.[1]
Robert Livingston, Jr.
  New York.
David Clarkson,

Cornelius Van Horne,
Paul Richards,
Henry Cruger.
  Orange.
Thomas Gale,
Abraham Haring.
  Queens.
David Jones,
Thomas Cornell.
  Rensselaerwyck.[1]
John Baptist
  Van Rensselaer.
  Richmond.
John Le Count,
Richard Stillwell.

Schenectady.[2]
Arent Bradt.
  Suffolk.
David Pierson,
William Nicoll.
  Ulster.
Albert Pawling,
John Hardenburgh,
Wm. Gaasbeck
  Chambers.[11]
  Westchester.
Frederick Philipse,
John Thomas,
Lewis Morris, Jr.[3]

TWENTY-FIFTH ASSEMBLY

1747–8—February 12 to August 30; September 20 to November 12.
1749—June 27 to August 4.
Dissolved July 21, 1750.

Officers same as before.

Albany.
Coenradt Ten Eyck,
Peter Douw.

Cortlandt.[1]
Philip Verplanck.

Dutchess.
Henry Beekman,
Johannis Tappen.

TWENTY-FIFTH ASSEMBLY (CONT.)

Kings.
Abraham Lott,
Johannis Lott.
Livingston.[1]
Robert Livingston, Jr.
New York.
David Clarkson,
Cornelius Van Horne,
Paul Richards,
Henry Cruger.
Orange.
Thomas Gale,
Theodorus Snediker.

Queens.
David Jones,
Thomas Cornell.
Rensselaerwyck.
J. Bapt't Van Rensselaer.
Richmond.
John Le Count,
Richard Stillwell,
Paul Micheaux.[6]
Schenectady.[3]
Jacob Glen.

Suffolk.
William Nicoll,
Eleazer Miller.
Ulster.
Abraham Haasbrook,
Johannis Jansen.
Westchester.
Frederick Philipse,
John Thomas,
Lewis Morris, Jr.[4]

TWENTY-SIXTH ASSEMBLY

1750—September 4 to November 24.
1751—May 30 to June 6; Oct. 1 to
Nov. 25.
Dissolved November 25, 1751.

Officers same as before, except—
Clerk—Abraham Lott, Jr.[7]

Albany.
Philip Schuyler,
Hans Hansen.
Cortlandt.[1]
Philip Verplanck.
Dutchess.
Henry Beekman,
Johannis Tappen,[12]
Henry Filkin.[13]
Kings.
Johannis Lott,
Dominicus Vander Vier.
Livingston.[1]
Robert Livingston, Jr.
New York.
David Clarkson,

Cornelius Van Horne,
Paul Richards,
Henry Cruger,
William Walton.[8]
Orange.
Theodorus Snediker,
Samuel Gale.
Queens.
David Jones,
Thomas Cornell.
Rensselaerwyck.[1]
J. Bapt't Van Rensselaer.
Richmond.
John Le Count,
Paul Micheaux,
William T. Walton.[9]

Schenectady.[3]
Jacob Van Slyck.
Suffolk.
William Nicoll,
Eleazer Miller.
Ulster.
John Hardenburgh,
Johannis Jansen.
Westchester.
Col. Frederick Philipse,
John Thomas,
Frederick Philipse,[10]
Peter De Lancey.[4]

[1] Manor.
[2] Admitted April 2, 1745, in place of Moore, appointed member of the Council.
[3] Township.   [4] Borough.   [5] Appointed 1746.
[6] Admitted June 23, 1748, in place of Stillwell, deceased.
[7] Appointed October 8, 1751.
[8] Admitted October 9, 1751, in place of Clarkson, deceased.
[9] Admitted October 25, 1751, in place of Micheaux, deceased.
[10] Admitted October 24, 1751, in place of Col. Philipse, deceased. This Frederick Philipse (1720–1785), son of Col. Frederick Philipse, served through the final Assembly of the colonial period.
[11] Admitted November 12, 1745, in place of Pawling, deceased.
[12] Dismissed from the Assembly October 23, 1751, having left the province.
[13] Admitted November 12, 1751, in place of Tappen.

TWENTY-SEVENTH ASSEMBLY

1752—October 24 to November 11.
1753—May 30 to July 4; October 31 to
December 12.
1754—April 9 to May 1; May 2 to May 4.
1754–5—August 20, 1754 to September
11, 1755.

1755–6—December 2 to July 9.
1756—September 21 to December 1.
1757–8—February 15 to February 26;
August 31 to December 16.

Officers same as before.

Albany.
Peter Winne,
Petrus Douw.
Cortlandt.[1]
Philip Verplanck.
Dutchess.
Henry Beekman,
Henry Filkin.
Kings.
Johannis Lott,
Dominicus Vander Vier.
Livingston.[1]
Robert Livingston, Jr.
New York.
Paul Richards,

Henry Cruger,
William Walton,
Cornelius Van Horne,
John Watts.[2]
Orange.
Theodorus Snediker,
Samuel Gale,
Vincent Matthews.[5]
Queens.
David Jones,
Thomas Cornell.
Rensselaerwyck.
J. Bapt't Van Rensselaer.
Richmond.
John Le Count,

William Walton.
Schenectady.[3]
Jacobus Myndertse.
Suffolk.
Eleazer Miller,
William Nicoll.
Ulster.
Johannis Jansen,
Moses De Pue, Jr.
Westchester.
John Thomas,
Frederick Philipse,
Peter De Lancey.[4]

TWENTY-EIGHTH ASSEMBLY

1759—January 31 to July 3; December 4–24.
1760—March 11 to June 10; October 21 to November 8.
Dissolved March 2, 1761, in consequence of the death of George II.

Speaker—William Nicoll.

Other officers unchanged.

Albany.
Peter Winne,
Jacob H. Ten Eyck,
Volkert P. Douw.[6]
Cortlandt.[1]
Philip Verplanck.
Dutchess.
Robert R. Livingston,
Henry Livingston.
Kings.
Johannis Lott,
Abraham Schenck.
Livingston.[1]
William Livingston.

New York.
Oliver De Lancey,
John Cruger,
Philip Livingston,
Leonard Lispenard.[14]
Orange.
Abraham Haring,
Henry Wisner.
Queens.
Thomas Hicks,
Zebulon Seaman.
Rensselaerwyck.[1]
J. Bapt't Van Rensselaer.
Richmond.
William Walton,

Benjamin Seaman.
Schenectady.[3]
Isaac Vrooman.
Suffolk.
William Nicoll,
Eleazer Miller.
Ulster.
Abraham Haasbrook,
Jacobus Bruyn.
Westchester.
John Thomas,
Frederick Philipse,
Peter De Lancey.[4]

TWENTY-NINTH ASSEMBLY

1761—March 10 to May 19; Sept. 2–11.
1761–2—November 24 to January 8.
1762—March 2 to May 22; November
10 to December 11.
1763—November 8 to December 20.
1764—April 18–21; Sept. 4 to Oct. 20.

1765—November 12 to December 23.
1766—June 11 to July 3; November 10
to December 19.
1767—May 27 to June 6.
1767–8—November 17 to February 6.
Dissolved February 6, 1768.

Officers same as before.

Albany.
Jacob H. Ten Eyck,
Volkert P. Douw.
Cortlandt.[1]
Philip Verplanck.
Dutchess.
Robert R. Livingston,
Henry Livingston.
Kings.
Abraham Schenck,
Simon Boerum.
Livingston.
Peter R. Livingston.
New York.
John Cruger,

Philip Livingston,
Leonard Lispenard,
William Bayard.
Orange.
Abraham Haring,
Henry Wisner.
Queens.
David Jones,[7,8]
Zebulon Seaman,[8,9]
Thomas Cornell,[7,9]
Daniel Kissam.[10]
Rensselaerwyck.
Abraham Ten Broeck.
Richmond.
Benjamin Seaman,

Henry Holland.
Schenectady.[3]
Ryer Schermerhorn,[11]
Nicholas Groot.[12]
Suffolk.
William Nicoll,
Eleazer Miller.
Ulster.
Abraham Haasbrook,
Jacobus Bruyn.
Westchester.
John Thomas,
Frederick Philipse,
Peter De Lancey.[4]

THIRTIETH ASSEMBLY

1768–9—October 27 to January 2.
Dissolved January 2, 1769.

Speaker—Philip Livingston.
Clerk—Edmund Seaman.[13]
Other officers same as before.

Albany.
Jacob H. Ten Eyck,
Philip Schuyler.
Cortlandt.[1]
Pierre Van Cortlandt.
Dutchess.
Leonard Van Kleeck,
Dirck Brinckerhoff.
Kings.
Simon Boerum,
John Rapalje.
Livingston.[1]
Peter R. Livingston.
New York.
Philip Livingston,

James De Lancey,
Jacob Walton,
James Jauncey.
Orange.
Henry Wisner,
Selah Strong.
Queens.
Zebulon Seaman,
Daniel Kissam.
Rensselaerwyck.[1]
Abraham Ten Broeck.
Richmond.
Henry Holland,
Benjamin Seaman.

Schenectady.[3]
Jacobus Myndertse.
Suffolk.
William Nicoll,
Eleazer Miller.
Ulster.
Charles De Witt,
George Clinton.
Westchester.
John Thomas,
Frederick Philipse,
John De Lancey.[4]

[1] Manor.

[2] Admitted November 8, 1752, in place of Van Horne, deceased.

[3] Township.   [4] Borough.

[5] September 1, 1757, in place of Gale, deceased.

[6] Admitted October 17, 1759, in place of Winne, deceased.

[7] Declared illegally returned April 3, 1761, and new election ordered, which was held April 20 and 21.

[8] At the new election, Sheriff submitted two returns, one certifying to the election of Jones and Cornell and the other to the election of Seaman and Cornell. A scrutiny was ordered by the House and Seaman seated December 9, 1761.

[9] Elected at the new election.

[10] September 5, 1764, in place of Cornell, deceased.

[11] Election declared void September 10, 1761.

[12] Admitted on contest, in place of Schermerhorn, Sept. 10, 1761.

[13] Appointed in 1767.

[14] This Philip Livingston (1716–1778), son of the second proprietor of the Manor, served in the Assembly until May 12, 1769, when he was dismissed.

1769—April 4 to May 20.
1769–70—November 21 to January 27.
1770–71—December 11 to March 4.
1772—January 7 to March 24.
1773—January 5 to March 8.
1774—January 6 to March 19.
1775—January 10 to April 3.

Adjourned to May 3, 1775.
Prorogued (May 1) to June 7, 1775.
Prorogued (June 3) to July 5, 1775.
Prorogued to August 9, 1775.
Prorogued (July 31) to September 6, 1775.
Prorogued (September 4) to October 4, 1775.
Prorogued (September 29) to November 1, 1775.
Prorogued (October 31) to December 6, 1775.
Prorogued (December 1) to January 1, 1776.
Prorogued (December 23) to February 1, 1776.

1775, December 26—At an Executive Council on board the ship *Dutchess of Gordon,* the Governor was advised that, inasmuch as the limitation of seven years for the continuance of an Assembly was about expired, that the Assembly be dissolved, and writs for a new election issued.

1776, January 29—Governor advised by council to prorogue the Assembly until March 14. Writ approved February 14.

1776, March 11—Assembly prorogued until April 17, 1776.
The last session of the General Assembly was April 3, 1775.

Speaker—John Cruger.
Clerk—Edmund Seaman.
Sergeant-at Arms—William Scott.
Doorkeeper—Alexander Lamb.[2]

Albany.	*New York.*	*Schenectady.*
Jacob H. Ten Eyck,	John Cruger,	Jacobus Myndertse.
Philip Schuyler.	James De Lancey,	*Suffolk.*
Cortlandt.[3]	Jacob Walton,	William Nicoll,
Pierre Van Cortlandt.	James Jauncey.	Nathaniel Woodhull.
Cumberland.	*Orange.*	*Tryon.*[9]
Samuel Wells,[4]	John De Noyelles,	Hendrick Frey,
Crean Brush.[4]	Samuel Gale,	Guy Johnson.
Dutchess.	John Coe.[8]	*Ulster.*
Leonard Van Kleeck,	*Queens.*	Charles De Witt,
Dirck Brinckerhoff.	Zebulon Seaman,	George Clinton.
Kings.	Daniel Kissam.	*Westchester.*
Simon Boerum,	*Rensselaerwyck.*[3]	John Thomas,
John Rapalje.	Abraham Ten Broeck.	Frederick Philipse,
Livingston.[3]	*Richmond.*	Lewis Morris [III] [1,10]
Philip Livingston,[5]	Benjamin Seaman,	John De Lancey, [1,11]
Robert R. Livingston,[6]	Christopher Billop.	Isaac Wilkins.[1,12]
Peter R. Livingston.[7]		

[1] Borough.

[2] John Johnson was appointed Doorkeeper in 1775.

[3] Manor.   [4] Admitted February 2, 1773.

[5] Dismissed for non-residence May 12, 1769.

[6] Elected in place of P. Livingston; declared disqualified by reason of being a Judge of the Supreme Court November 24, 1769. Again elected December 6, and again declared disqualified, December 21. Three elections followed, and the same decision was made, January 25, 1771, February 5, 1772, and January 26, 1774.

[7] Admitted February 21, 1774.

[8] Admitted February 17, 1775, in place of De Noyelles, deceased.

[9] Admitted January 11, 1773.

[10] Declared disqualified for non-residence April 20, 1769.

[11] Contested seat of Morris and admitted May 18, 1769; declared disqualified by reason of non-residence January 16, 1772.

[12] Admitted February 5, 1772.

APPENDIX D: COUNCIL OF THE COLONY OF NEW YORK*

YEARS	COUNCILLORS	YEARS	COUNCILLORS
1665	Thomas Topping	1676–80	William Darvall
1665–67	Robert Needham	1680–88	Stephen Van Cortlandt
1665–72	Thomas Willet	1683	John Youngs
1667–73	Thomas Delaval	1683–86	John Spragge
1667–80	Mathias Nicolls	1683–86	Lucas Santen
1668–69	Ralph Whitefield	1683–88	Anthony Brockholles
1669–73	Cornelius Van Ruyven	1684–85	Lewis Morris
1670–73	Cornelis Steenwyck	1684–85	John Palmer
1671–73	Thomas Lovelace	1685	Nicholas Bayard
1672–79	John Laurence	1685	James Graham
1674–79	Anthony Brockholles	1685–88	Jervas Baxter
1674–81	William Dyre	1686–88	John Youngs
1675–88	Frederick Philipse	1687–88	Nicholas Bayard

* Adapted from Edgar A. Werner, *Civil List and Constitutional History of the Colony and State of New York* (Albany, 1888), 317–18.

YEARS	COUNCILLORS	YEARS	COUNCILLORS
1687–88	James Graham [1]	1690	William Laurence
1687–88	John Palmer	1690	Jacob Milborne
1688	John Allen	1690	Samuel Staats
1688	Walter Clarke	1690	Johannis Vermillye
1688	Joseph Dudley	1690	Thomas Williams
1688	Robert Mason	1691	William Pinhorne [3]
1688	Walter Newberry	1691–92	Joseph Dudley
1688	Edward Randolph	1691–97	Thomas Willet
1688	Richard Smith	1691–98	Nicholas Bayard
1688	John Usher	1691–98	Chidley Brooke
1688	John Walley	1691–98	Gabriel Monvielle
1688	John Winthrop	1691–98	William Nicoll
1688	John Youngs	1691–98	Frederick Philipse
1689	Richard Panton [2]	1691–1700	Stephen Van Cortlandt
1689	Theunis Roelofsen [2]	1691–1704	William Smith [4]
1689	Jan Demarest [2]	1692	Thomas Johnson
1689	Daniel De Klercke [2]	1692–97	Caleb Heathcote [5]
1689	Johannis Vermillye [2]	1692–98	John Laurence
1689	Samuel Edsall [2]	1692–98	Richard Townley [6]
1689	Peter De La Noy [2]	1692–98	John Youngs
1690	Gerardus Beekman	1692–1720	Peter Schuyler
1690	Peter De La Noy	1693–98	William Pinhorne
1690	Samuel Edsall		
1690	Hendrick Jansen (van Feurden)		

[1] In place of Youngs.

[2] Committee of Safety appointed by inhabitants. This Committee organized the Leisler Government and designated a Council December 11, 1689, which is next above given.

[3] Dismissed September 1, 1692, for non-residency. Reinstated June 10, 1693, after moving to New York.

[4] Died in 1704. This Smith is not related to William Smith, Jr., the eighteenth-century historian.

[5] In place of Dudley.

[6] Refused to sit, being a resident of East Jersey.

YEARS	COUNCILLORS	YEARS	COUNCILLORS
1698	Robert Livingston [1]	1725–50	Philip Livingston [28]
1698–1702	Abraham De Peyster [2,6]	1726–61	Archibald Kennedy [29]
1698–1702	Samuel Staats [3,6]	1729–53	James De Lancey [30]
1698–1702	Robert Walters [4,6]	1730–48	Philip Van Cortlandt [31]
1699–1700	James Graham	1733–44	Henry Lane [32]
1701	Robert Livingston	1733–47	Daniel Horsmanden [33]
1701–2	Thomas Weaver [5,6]	1738–54	George Clarke, Jr.[34]
1701–2	William Atwood [6]	1744–58	Joseph Murray [35]
1702–3	John Bridges [7]	1745	Sir Peter Warren [36]
1702–4	Sampson Shelton	1745–46	Jeremiah Van Rensselaer [36]
	Broughton [8]	1745–49	John Moore [37]
1702–6	William Laurence	1745–58	John Rutherfurd [38]
1702–8	Wolfgang William	1746–47	Stephen Bayard [39]
	Romer	1748–56	Edward Holland [40]
1702–20	Caleb Heathcote [7]	1750–56	James Alexander [41]
1702–23	Gerardus Beekman	1751–74	Sir William Johnson [42]
1702–35	Rip Van Dam [9]	1752–63	John Chambers [43]
1703–4	Matthew Ling [10]	1753–67	William Smith [44]
1703–9	Thomas Wenham [11]	1755–60	James De Lancey [45]
1704–19	Killian Van	1755–69	George Clarke, Jr.
	Rensselaer [12]	1755–76	Daniel Horsmanden
1705–15	Roger Mompesson [13,14]	1758–68	William Walton [46]
1705–21	Adolph Philipse [13]	1758–76	John Watts [47]
1705–28	John Barbarie [13,15]	1759–62	Josiah Martin [48]
1708	Abraham De Peyster [16]	1760–76	Oliver De Lancey [49]
1708–9	William Peartree	1762–63	Benjamin Pratt [50]
1708–11	David Provoost	1762–68	William Alexander [51]
1710–16	Samuel Staats [17]	1764–71	Joseph Reade [52]
1710–22	Abraham De Peyster	1764–76	Charles Ward
1710–31	Robert Walters [18]		Apthorpe [53]
1711–25	Thomas Byerly [19]	1764–76	Roger Morris [54]
1716–22	John Johnston [20]	1767–72	Henry Cruger [55]
1716–36	George Clarke [21]	1767–76	William Smith, Jr.[56]
1720–35	Francis Harison [22]	1769	James De Lancey [57]
1721–29	Lewis Morris, Jr.[23]	1769–76	Hugh Wallace [58]
1721–37	James Alexander [24]	1769–76	Henry White
1721–76	Cadwallader Colden [25]	1771–76	William Axtell [59]
1723–32	William Provoost [26]	1773–76	John Harris Cruger [60]
1723–41	Abraham Van Horne [27]	1775–76	James Jauncey [61]

[1] Appointed September 28, 1698, in place of Monville.

[2] Appointed September 28, 1698, in place of Bayard.

[3] Appointed September 28, 1698, in place of Laurence.

[4] Appointed September 28, 1698, in place of Philipse. Died in 1704.

[5] In place of Graham, deceased.   [6] Suspended June 9, 1702.

[7] Appointed June 15, 1702.   [8] Died in 1704.   [9] Suspended November 24, 1735.

[10] Died in 1704.   [11] Died September, 1709.   [12] Appointed October 27, 1704.

[13] Appointed February, 1705.   [14] Died in 1716.   [15] Died in 1728.

[16] Declined to act.   [17] Died in 1716.   [18] Died in June, 1731.

[19] In place of Provoost.   [20] In place of Staats, deceased.

[21] In place of Mompesson, deceased. Appointed Lieutenant-Governor in October, 1736.

[22] Left the province in April, 1735.   [23] In place of Heathcote.

[24] In place of Philipse. Elected to the Assembly in June, 1737.

[25] In place of Schuyler. Lieutenant-Governor, August 4, 1760, to October 26, 1761; November 18, 1761, to June 14, 1762; June 28, 1763, to November 13, 1765; September 12, 1769, to October 19, 1770; April 7, 1774, to June 28, 1775. Died in September, 1776.

[26] In place of Johnston.   [27] In place of De Peyster. Died in 1741.

[28] In place of Beekman. Died in 1750.

[29] In place of Byerly. Resigned in November, 1761.

[30] In place of Barbarie, deceased. Lieutenant-Governor, October 12, 1753, to September 3, 1755; and June 3, 1757, to July 30, 1760.

[31] In place of Morris. Died in 1746.

[32] In place of Walters, deceased. Died in 1744.

[33] In place of Provoost. Suspended September, 1747.

[34] In place of Harison. Never qualified.   [35] In place of Lane. Died in 1758.

[36] Did not qualify.   [37] In place of Van Horne. Died in 1749.   [38] Died in 1758.

[39] Suspended in September, 1747.   [40] In place of Van Cortlandt. Died in 1756.

[41] In place of Moore. Died in 1756.

[42] In place of Livingston. Died in November, 1774.

[43] In place of Bayard. Died in 1763.   [44] Resigned in 1767.

[45] Died in July, 1760.   [46] In place of Holland. Died in 1768.

[47] In place of Alexander.

[48] In place of Murray. Went to West Indies in May, 1762.

[49] In place of Rutherfurd.   [50] Died in 1763.

[51] Claimed to be Earl of Stirling. Resigned in 1768.

[52] In place of Martin. Died in 1771.   [53] In place of Pratt.

[54] In place of Chambers.   [55] Resigned in 1772.

[56] In place of William Smith, Sr.

[57] In place of William Alexander, Earl of Stirling. Declined the appointment.

[58] In place of Walton.   [59] In place of Reade, deceased.

[60] In place of Henry Cruger, resigned.

[61] In place of Sir William Johnson, deceased.

BIBLIOGRAPHY

A number of books concerning particular aspects of New York's colonial history have been published in the past thirty-five years. These include Stanley N. Katz, *Newcastle's New York: Anglo-American Politics, 1732–1753* (Cambridge, Mass., 1968); Lawrence H. Leder, *Robert Livingston, 1654–1728, and the Politics of Colonial New York* (Chapel Hill, 1961); L. F. S. Upton, *The Loyal Whig, William Smith of New York & Quebec* (Toronto, 1969); Don R. Gerlach, *Philip Schuyler and the American Revolution in New York, 1733–1777* (Lincoln, Neb., 1964); Dorothy R. Dillon, *The New York Triumvirate: A Study of the Legal and Political Careers of William Livingston, John Morin Scott, and William Smith, Jr.* (New York, 1949); Philip L. White, *The Beekmans of New York in Politics and Commerce, 1647–1877* (New York, 1956); Dixon Ryan Fox, *Yankees and Yorkers* (New York, 1940); Irving Mark, *Agrarian Conflicts in Colonial New York, 1711–1775* (New York, 1940); Samuel McKee, Jr., *Labor in Colonial New York, 1664–1776* (New York, 1935); and Virginia D. Harrington, *The New York Merchant on the Eve of the Revolution* (New York, 1935).

Other studies of importance are at present available only as unpublished doctoral dissertations. Outstanding among these are Milton M. Klein, "The American Whig: William Livingston of New York," unpubl. Ph.D. diss. (Columbia University, 1954); Nicholas Varga, "New York Government and Politics During the Mid-Eighteenth Century," unpubl. Ph.D. diss. (Fordham University, 1960); Roger James Champagne, "The Sons of Liberty and the Aristocracy in New York Politics, 1765–1790," unpubl. Ph.D. diss. (University of Wisconsin, 1960); David Arthur Armour, "The Merchants of Albany, New York: 1686–1760," unpubl. Ph.D. diss. (Northwestern University, 1965). The only study which attempts a comprehensive analysis of the colony's political history is Beverly McAnear, "Politics in Provincial New York, 1689–1761," unpubl. Ph.D. diss. (Stanford University, 1935). Though somewhat restricted in viewpoint by today's standards, it nonetheless contains much valuable information.

With the exception of the first chapter of Carl Becker's *History of Political Parties in the Province of New York, 1760–1776* (Madison, Wis., 1909), few efforts have been made to draw together the various strands of New York's early life. The closest approximation to a convenient summary is David M. Ellis, James A. Frost, Harold C. Syrett, and Harry F. Carman, *A Short History of*

New York State (Ithaca, N.Y., 1957), which devotes the first nine of forty-two chapters to the colonial period. Herbert L. Osgood's *The American Colonies in the Seventeenth Century,* 3 vols. (New York, 1904–7), and *The American Colonies in the Eighteenth Century,* 4 vols. (New York, 1924–25), as well as Charles M. Andrews's *Colonial Period of American History,* 4 vols. (1936–38), and Lawrence H. Gipson's *The British Empire before the American Revolution,* 13 vols. (New York, 1936–67), all have excellent chapters on New York Colony, but of necessity these are widely separated and scattered throughout several volumes. There is also the ten-volume *History of the State of New York,* edited by Alexander C. Flick (New York, 1933–37), of which the first three are devoted to the colonial era. However, because each chapter was written by a different historian, there is no central theme or unity to these volumes, though as individual studies many of the chapters are still valuable.

Manuscripts

New-York Historical Society (New York City)
  Alexander Papers
  Henry Beekman Manuscripts
  Cadwallader Colden Manuscripts (not in published volumes)
  DeLancey Papers
  James Duane Papers
  John Jay Papers
  Livingston Papers
  Robert R. Livingston Collection
  Alexander McDougall Papers
  Miscellaneous Manuscripts: George Clinton (colonial governor),
    George Clinton (state governor), Van Cortlandt family.
  Rutherfurd Collection
New York Public Library (New York City)
  Broadsides Collection
  Bancroft Transcripts
    Robert R. Livingston Papers
  Chalmers Papers Relating to New York
  Philip Schuyler Papers
  William Smith Papers
Museum of the City of New York (New York City)
  DeLancey Family Papers
  Livingston Papers
Sleepy Hollow Restorations (Irvington, New York)
  Philipse Family Papers
  Van Cortlandt Family Papers
Franklin Delano Roosevelt Library (Hyde Park, New York)
  Livingston-Redmond Manuscripts (microfilms used)
Rutgers University Library (New Brunswick, New Jersey)
  Morris Papers
New Jersey Historical Society (Newark, New Jersey)
  Robert Hunter Morris Papers

Columbia University Libraries (New York City)
  Philipse-Gouverneur Land Titles
New York State Library (Albany, New York)
  Miscellaneous colonial manuscripts
Municipal Archives and Record Center (New York City)
  Petitions Collection
Houghton Library, Harvard University (Cambridge, Mass.)
  Jared Sparks Collection
    Governor Francis Bernard's Official Papers

Official Documents and Records

An Account of Her Majesty's Revenue in the Province of New York, 1701–09; The Customs Records of Early Colonial New York. Julius M. Block, Leo Hershkowitz, Kenneth Scott, and Constance D. Sherman, eds. Ridgewood, N.J.: The Gregg Press, 1966.

The Annals of Albany. 10 vols. Albany: J. Munsell, 1854–1871.

"Calendar of Council Minutes, 1668–1783," New York State Library, *Bulletin,* 58 (March, 1902), Berthold Fernow, ed.

Calendar of Historical Manuscripts in the Office of the Secretary of State, Albany, N.Y. E. B. O'Callaghan, ed., 2 vols. Albany: Weed, Parsons & Co., 1866.

Calendar of New York Colonial Commissions. E. B. O'Callaghan, comp. New York: 1929.

Calendar of New York Colonial Manuscripts Indorsed Land Papers; in the Office of the Secretary of State of New York, 1643–1803. Albany: Weed, Parsons & Co., 1864.

Calendar of State Papers, Colonial Series, America and West Indies. W. N. Sainsbury, J. W. Fortescue, and Cecil Headlam, eds. 42 vols. London: 1860–1953.

Colonial Charters, Patents and Grants to the Communities Comprising the City of New York. Jerrold Seymann, comp. New York: The Board of Statutory Consolidation of the City of New York, 1939.

A Copy of the Poll List of the Election for Representatives for the City and County of New York . . . MDCCLXI, and . . . MDCCLXVIII, and . . . MDCCLXIX. New York: New-York Historical Society, 1880.

The Documentary History of the State of New York. Edmund B. O'Callaghan, ed. 4 vols. Albany: 1849–1851.

Documents Relative to the Colonial History of the State of New York. Edmund B. O'Callaghan and Berthold Fernow, eds. 15 vols. Albany: Weed, Parsons & Co., 1853–1887.

Ecclesiastical Records of the State of New York. E. T. Corwin, ed. 7 vols. Albany: 1901–1916.

Journal of the Commissioners for Trade and Plantations, 1704–1782. 14 vols. London: 1920–1938.

Journal of the Legislative Council of the Colony of New York, 1691–1775. 2 vols. Albany: Weed, Parsons & Co., 1861.

Journal of the Votes and Proceedings of the General Assembly of the Colony of New York, 1691–1765. 2 vols. New York: Hugh Gaine, printer, 1764–1766.

Journal of the Votes and Proceedings of the General Assembly of the Colony of New York, from 1766 to 1776 inclusive. Albany: J. Buel, printer, 1820.

The Colonial Laws of New York from the Year 1664 to the Revolution. 5 vols. Albany: James B. Lyon, 1894.

Minutes of the Common Council of the City of New York, 1675–1776. 8 vols. New York: 1905.

Historical Records Survey. *Minutes of the Board of Supervisors of Ulster County, New York, 1710/1 to 1730/1.* Albany: 1939.

——*Town Minutes of Newtown, New York, 1653–1734.* 2 vols. New York: 1941.

——*Minutes of the Town Courts of Newtown, New York, 1656–1690.* New York: 1940.

Newspapers

New York *Gazette* (Bradford)
New-York *Weekly Journal* (Zenger)
New-York *Gazette; or, The Weekly Post-Boy* (Parker-Weyman)
New-York *Journal; or, The General Advertiser* (Holt)
New-York *Gazette; and The Weekly Mercury* (Gaine)

Memoirs, Letters, and Public Papers

Alexander, James. *A Brief 'Narrative of the Case and Trial of John Peter Zenger . . . by James Alexander.* Stanley Nider Katz, ed. Cambridge, Mass.: Harvard University Press, 1963.

Burke, Edmund. *Edmund Burke, New York Agent with His letters to the New York Assembly and Intimate Correspondence with Charles O'Hara, 1761–1776.* Ross J. S. Hoffman. Philadelphia: The American Philosophical Society, 1956.

"Chief Daniel Nimham v. Roger Morris, Beverly Robinson, and Philip Philipse —An Indian Land Case in Colonial New York, 1765–1767." Oscar Handlin and Irving Mark, eds. *Ethnohistory,* XI (Summer, 1964), 193–246.

Clinton, George. *The Public Papers of George Clinton,* Hugh Hastings, ed. 10 vols. New York: 1899–1914.

Colden, Cadwallader. "The Colden Letters on Smith's History," New-York Historical Society, *Collections,* I, 1868, pp. 181–235.

——"The Colden Letter Books, 1760–1775," New-York Historical Society, *Collections,* IX–X, 1876–1877, New York: 1877–1878.

——"The Letters and Papers of Cadwallader Colden," New-York Historical Society, *Collections,* L–LVI, LXVII–LXVIII, 1917–1923, 1934–1935, New York: 1918–1937.

——"History of Gov. William Cosby's Administration and of Lt. Gov. George Clarke's Administration through 1737," New-York Historical Society, *Collections,* LXVIII, 1935, pp. 283–355.

——*The History of the Five Indian Nations.* 2 vols. New York: 1902.

Crèvecoeur, St. John de. *Letters from an American Farmer.* New York: E. P. Dutton & Co., Inc., 1912.

Denton, Daniel. *A Brief Description of New York*. New York: Columbia University Press, 1937.

Family Record and Events, Compiled Originally from the Original MSS in the Rutherfurd Collection. Livingston Rutherfurd. New York: 1894.

The Lee Max "Friedman Collection of American Jewish Colonial Correspondence": Letters of the Franks Family (1733–1748). Studies in American Jewish History, 5. Leo Hershkowitz and Isidore S. Meyer, eds. Waltham, Mass.: American Jewish Historical Society, 1968.

Gage, Thomas. *The Correspondence of General Thomas Gage with the Secretaries of State, 1763–1775*. Clarence E. Carter, ed. 2 vols. New Haven: Yale University Press, 1931.

The Glorious Revolution in America, Documents on the Colonial Crisis of 1689. Michael G. Hall, Lawrence H. Leder, and Michael G. Kammen, eds. Chapel Hill: University of North Carolina Press, 1964.

Gordon, Lord Adam. "The Journal of Lord Adam Gordon," in *Travels in the American Colonies*. Newton D. Mereness, ed. New York: Antiquarian Press, Ltd., 1961.

Grant, Anne. *Memoirs of an American Lady*. 2 vols. New York: Dodd, Mead and Co., 1901.

The Independent Reflector, or Weekly Essays on Sundry Important Subjects More particularly adapted to the Province of New-York, by William Livingston and Others. Milton M. Klein, ed. Cambridge, Mass.: Harvard University Press, 1963.

Johnson, Sir William. *The Papers of Sir William Johnson*. James Sullivan and Alexander C. Flick, eds. 14 vols. Albany: University of the State of New York, 1921–1965.

Jones, Thomas. *History of New York During the Revolutionary War*, 2 vols. New York: New-York Historical Society, 1879.

Kalm, Peter. *Travels in North America*. Adolph B. Benson, ed. 2 vols. New York: Dover Publications, Inc., 1966.

"Land Cases in Colonial New York, 1765–1767: The King v. William Prendergast," *New York University Law Quarterly Review*, IX (January, 1942), 165–194.

[Livingston, William]. *A Review of the Military Operations in North-America, from the Commencement of the French Hostilities on the Frontiers of Virginia in 1753, to the Surrender of Oswego, on the 14th of August, 1756; in a Letter to a Nobleman,"* Massachusetts Historical Society, *Collections*, 1st Series, VII–VIII (1801–1856), 67–163.

Montressor, James and John. *The Montressor Journals*. New-York Historical Society, *Collections*, XIV, 1881. G. D. Scull, ed. New York: 1882.

Morris, Lewis. *The Papers of Lewis Morris, Governor of the Province of New Jersey from 1738 to 1746*. New Jersey Historical Society *Collections*, IV, 1852. Newark, New Jersey: 1852.

"R. H. Morris: An American in London, 1735–1736," Beverly McAnear, ed., *Pennsylvania Magazine of History*, LXIV (1940), 164–217, 356–406.

New York City during the American Revolution, Being a Collection of Original Papers (now first published) from the Manuscripts in the Possession of the Mercantile Library Association of New York City. New York: 1861.

"A Packet of Old Letters," *Yearbook* of the Dutchess County Historical Society, 1921.

Smith, Richard, *A Tour of Four Great Rivers, The Hudson, Mohawk, Susquehanna and Delaware in 1769, Being the Journal of Richard Smith.* Francis W. Halsey, ed. Port Washington, N.Y.: Ira J. Friedman, Inc., 1964.

Smith, William. *Historical Memoirs of William Smith.* William H. W. Sabine, ed. 2 vols. New York: Colburn & Tegg, 1956.

——*The History of the Late Province of New-York, From its Discovery, to the Appointment of Governor Colden, in 1762.* New York: New-York Historical Society, 1830.

"The Society of Dissenters founded at New York in 1769," Herbert L. Osgood, ed. *American Historical Review*, VI (April, 1901), 498–507.

"The Town Book of the Manor of Philipsburgh," *The New York Genealogical and Bibliographical Record*, LIX (July, 1928), 203–213.

Van Rensselaer Bowier Manuscripts. A. J. F. van Laer, ed. Albany: University of the State of New York, 1908.

Wraxall, Peter, *An Abridgment of the Indian Affairs . . . in the Colony of New York . . . 1678 to . . . 1751.* Charles H. McIlwain, ed. Cambridge, Mass.: Harvard University Press, 1915.

Monographs, Biographies, Articles, and Dissertations

"American Council of Learned Societies Report of Committee on Linguistic and National Stocks in the Population of the United States," *Annual Report* of the American Historical Association for the Year 1931, Vol. I, pp. 107–125.

A. W. Andersen. *The Story of a Pioneer Family.* 1936.

Andrews, Charles M. *The Colonial Background of the American Revolution.* New Haven: Yale University Press, 1924.

——*The Colonial Period of American History.* 4 vols. New Haven: Yale University Press, 1934–1938.

Armour, David Arthur. "The Merchants of Albany, New York: 1686–1760." Unpublished Ph.D. dissertation, Northwestern University, 1965.

Bailyn, Bernard. *The Ideological Origins of the American Revolution.* Cambridge, Mass.: Harvard University Press, 1967.

——*The Origins of American Politics.* New York: Alfred A. Knopf, 1968.

Barrow, Thomas C. *Trade and Empire: The British Customs Service in Colonial America, 1660–1775.* Cambridge, Mass.: Harvard University Press, 1967.

Becker, Carl. "Growth of Revolutionary Parties and Methods in New York Province, 1765–1774," *American Historical Review*, VII (October, 1901), 56–76.

——*The History of Political Parties in the Province of New York, 1760–1776.* Madison, Wis.: University of Wisconsin Press, 1909, 1960.

——"Nominations in Colonial New York," *American Historical Review*, VI (January, 1901), 260–275.

Becker, E. Marie. "The 801 Westchester County Freeholders of 1763 and the Cortlandt Manor Land-Case Which Occasioned Their Listing," *New-York Historical Society Quarterly*, XXXV (July, 1951), 283–321.

Bidwell, Percy W., and Falconer, John I. *History of Agriculture in the Northern*

United States, 1620–1860. Washington, D.C.: Carnegie Institution of Washington, 1925.

Bishop, Cortlandt F. *History of Elections in the American Colonies*. "Columbia University Studies in History, Economics and Public Law," Vol. III. New York: Columbia University Press, 1893.

Bolton, Robert. *The History of the Several Towns, Manors, and Patents of the County of Westchester from Its First Settlement to the Present Time*. 2 vols. New York: Charles F. Roper, 1881.

Bonomi, Patricia U. "Political Patterns in Colonial New York City: The General Assembly Election of 1768," *Political Science Quarterly*, LXXXI (September, 1966), 432–47.

Bridenbaugh, Carl. *Cities in Revolt: Urban Life in America, 1743–1776*. New York: Alfred A. Knopf, 1955.

——*Cities in the Wilderness: The First Century of Urban Life in America, 1625–1742*. New York: The Ronald Press, 1938.

——*Myths and Realities: Societies of the Colonial South*. Louisiana State University Press, 1952.

Brigham, Clarence S. *History and Bibliography of American Newspapers, 1690–1820*. Worcester, Mass.: American Antiquarian Society, 1947.

Brodhead, John Romeyn. *History of the State of New York*. 2 vols. New York: Harper and Brothers, 1853–1871.

Buffinton, Arthur H. "The Canada Expedition of 1746: Its Relation to British Politics," *American Historical Review*, XLV (October, 1940), 552–580.

——"The Policy of Albany and English Westward Expansion," *Mississippi Valley Historical Review*, VIII (March, 1922), 327–366.

Buranelli, Vincent. "Peter Zenger's Editor," *American Quarterly*, VII (Summer, 1955), 174–181.

Champagne, Roger. "Family Politics versus Constitutional Principles: The New York Assembly Elections of 1768 and 1769," *William and Mary Quarterly*, 3rd Ser. XX (January, 1963), 57–79.

——"Liberty Boys and Mechanics of New York City, 1764–1774," *Labor History*, VIII (Spring, 1967), 115–135.

——"New York's Radicals and the Coming of Independence," *Journal of American History*, LI (June, 1964), 21–40.

——"The Sons of Liberty and the Aristocracy in New York Politics, 1765–1790." Unpublished Ph.D. dissertation, University of Wisconsin, 1960.

Christen, Robert Jay. "King Sears: Politician and Patriot in a Decade of Revolution." Unpublished Ph.D. dissertation, Columbia University, 1968.

Colbourn, H. Trevor. *The Lamp of Experience: Whig History and the Intellectual Origins of the American Revolution*. Chapel Hill: University of North Carolina Press, 1965.

Condon, Thomas J. *New York Beginnings: The Commercial Origins of New Netherland*. New York: New York University Press, 1968.

Dangerfield, George. *Chancellor Robert R. Livingston of New York, 1746–1813*. New York: Harcourt, Brace and Co., 1960.

Dawson, Henry B. *The Park and Its Vicinity*. Morrisania, New York, 1867.

DeLancey, Edward F. "Memoir of the Hon. James DeLancey: Lieutenant-Governor of the Province of New York," *Documentary History of the State of New York,* IV, 627–639.

DePauw, Linda Grant. *The Eleventh Pillar: New York State and the Federal Constitution.* Ithaca, New York: Cornell University Press, 1966.

Dillon, Dorothy R. *The New York Triumvirate: A Study of the Legal and Political Careers of William Livingston, John Morin Scott, and William Smith, Jr.* New York: Columbia University Press, 1949.

D'Innocenzo, Michael N., Jr. "Voting in Colonial New York." Unpublished masters essay, Columbia University, 1959.

Duncombe, Frances R. *Katonah: The History of a New York Village and Its People.* Katonah, New York: Katonah Village Improvement Society, 1961.

Eager, Samuel W. *An Outline History of Orange County with an Enumeration of the Names of Its Towns, Villages, Rivers, Creeks, etc. etc.* Newburgh, New York: S. T. Callahan, 1846–1847.

Edwards, George William, and Peterson, A. E. *New York as an Eighteenth Century Municipality, 1731–1776.* "Columbia University Studies in History, Economics and Public Law," Vol. LXXV. New York: Columbia University Press, 1917.

Ellis, David M.; Frost, James A.; Syrett, Harold C.; and Carman, Harry J. *A Short History of New York State.* Ithaca, New York: Cornell University Press, 1957.

Fairlie, John A. *Local Government in Counties, Towns and Villages.* New York: The Century Co., 1906.

Flexner, James Thomas. *Mohawk Baronet: Sir William Johnson of New York.* New York: Harper and Brothers, 1959.

Flick, Alexander C., ed. *History of the State of New York.* 10 vols. New York: Columbia University Press, 1933–1937.

——*Loyalism in New York During the American Revolution.* New York: Columbia University Press, 1901.

Fowler, Robert Ludlow. *History of the Law of Real Property in New York.* New York: Baker, Voorhis and Co., 1895.

Fox, Dixon Ryan. *Caleb Heathcote, Gentleman Colonist: The Story of a Career in the Province of New York, 1692–1721.* New York: Charles Scribner's Sons, 1926.

——*The Decline of Aristocracy in the Politics of New York.* New York: Columbia University Press. 1919.

——*Yankees and Yorkers.* New York: New York University Press, 1940.

Fox, Edith M. *Land Speculation in the Mohawk Country.* Cornell Studies in American History, Literature and Folklore, III. Ithaca, New York: Cornell University Press, 1949.

Friedman, Bernard. "The New York Assembly Elections of 1768 and 1769: The Disruption of Family Politics," *New York History,* XLVI (January, 1965), 3–24.

——"The Shaping of the Radical Consciousness in Provincial New York," *Journal of American History,* LVI (March, 1970), 781–801.

Friis, Herman R. "A Series of Population Maps of the Colonies and the United States, 1625–1790," *Geographical Review,* XXX (July, 1940), 463–470.

Gerlach, Don R. *Philip Schuyler and the American Revolution in New York, 1733–1777*. Lincoln, Neb.: University of Nebraska Press, 1964.

Goebel, Julius, Jr., and Naughton, T. Raymond. *Law Enforcement in Colonial New York: A Study in Criminal Procedure, 1664–1776*. New York: The Commonwealth Fund, 1944.

Goebel, Julius, Jr. "Some Legal and Political Aspects of Manors in New York," Order of Colonial Lords of Manors in America, New York Branch, *Publications*, no. 19 (1928).

Gordon, Joan. "The Livingstons of New York 1675–1860: Kinship and Class." Unpublished Ph.D. dissertation. Columbia University, 1959.

Greene, Evarts B., and Harrington, Virginia D. *American Population before the Federal Census of 1790*. New York: Columbia University Press, 1932.

Greene, Jack P. *The Quest for Power: The Lower Houses of Assembly in the Southern Royal Colonies, 1689–1776*. Chapel Hill: University of North Carolina Press, 1963.

Hall, Edward H. *Philipse Manor Hall at Yonkers, New York*. New York: 1912.

Handlin, Oscar. "The Eastern Frontier of New York," *New York History*, XVIII (January, 1937), 50–75.

Harrington, Virginia D. *The New York Merchant on the Eve of the Revolution*. New York: Columbia University Press, 1935.

Headley, Russel, ed. *The History of Orange County, New York*. Middletown, New York: Van Deusen and Elms, 1908.

Higgins, Ruth L. *Expansion in New York with Especial Reference to the Eighteenth Century*. Columbus: Ohio State University Press, 1931.

Howell, George R., ed. *History of the County of Albany, New York from 1609 to 1886*. New York: W. W. Munsell & Co., 1886.

Huntting, Isaac. *History of Little Nine Partners (of N. E. Precinct, and Pine Plains, N.Y. Dutchess County)*. Amenia, New York: Charles Walsh & Co., 1897.

"Interpretive Paper of the Restoration of Van Cortlandt Manor." Prepared by the Architects Office of Colonial Williamsburg. Williamsburg, Va.: May 1, 1959.

Kammen, Michael G. "The Colonial Agents, English Politics and the American Revolution," *William and Mary Quarterly*, 3rd Ser., XXII (April, 1965), 244–263.

Kantrowitz, Nathan. "Ethnic and Racial Segregation in the New York Metropolis, 1960," *American Journal of Sociology*, LXXIV (May, 1969), 685–695.

Katz, Stanley N. "An Easie Access: Anglo-American Politics in New York, 1732–1753." Unpublished Ph.D. dissertation, Harvard University, 1961.

——*Newcastle's New York: Anglo-American Politics, 1732–1753*. Cambridge, Mass.: Harvard University Press, 1968.

Kemmerer, Donald L. *Path to Freedom: The Struggle for Self-Government in Colonial New Jersey, 1703–1776*. Princeton: Princeton University Press, 1940.

Kenney, Alice P. "Dutch Patricians in Colonial Albany," *New York History*, XLIX (July, 1968), 249–283.

——"The Gansevoorts of Albany and Anglo-Dutch Relations in the Upper Hudson Valley, 1664–1790." Unpublished Ph.D. dissertation, Columbia University Press, 1961.

Kenyon, Cecelia M. "Republicanism and Radicalism in the American Revolution: An Old-Fashioned Interpretation," *William and Mary Quarterly,* 3rd Ser., XIX (April, 1962), 153–182.

Keys, Alice Mapelsden. *Cadwallader Colden, A Representative Eighteenth-Century Official.* New York: 1906.

Kim, Sung Bok. "The Manor of Cortlandt and Its Tenants, 1697–1783." Unpublished Ph.D. dissertation, Michigan State University, 1966.

——"A New Look at the Great Landlords of Eighteenth-Century New York," *William and Mary Quarterly,* 3rd Ser., XXVII (October, 1970), 581–614.

Klein, Milton M. "The American Whig: William Livingston of New York." Unpublished Ph.D. dissertation, Columbia University, 1954.

——"Democracy and Politics in Colonial New York," *New York History,* XL (July, 1959), 221–246.

"Politics and Personalities in Colonial New York," *New York History,* XLVII (January, 1966), 2–15.

——"Prelude to Revolution in New York: Jury Trials and Judicial Tenure," *William and Mary Quarterly,* 3rd Ser., XVII (October, 1960), 439–462.

Kline, Mary-Jo. "The Emergence of the American Wilkes: The Early Career of Alexander McDougall," Unpublished masters thesis, Columbia University, 1963.

Knittle, Walter Allen. *The Early Eighteenth Century Palatine Emigration.* Philadelphia: 1936.

Kramnick, Isaac. *Bolingbroke and His Circle: The Politics of Nostalgia in the Age of Walpole.* Cambridge, Mass.: Harvard University Press, 1968.

Leake, Isaac Q. *Memoir of the Life and Times of General John Lamb.* Albany, New York: Joel Munsell, 1850.

Leder, Lawrence H. "The New York Elections of 1769: An Assault on Privilege," *Mississippi Valley Historical Review,* XLIX (March, 1963), 675–682.

——"The Politics of Upheaval in New York, 1689–1709," *New-York Historical Society Quarterly,* XLIV (October, 1960), 413–427.

——*Robert Livingston, 1654–1728, and the Politics of Colonial New York.* Chapel Hill: University of North Carolina Press, 1961.

LeFevre, Ralph. *History of New Paltz, New York.* Albany: Ft. Orange Press, 1903.

Lemisch, Jesse. "New York's Petitions and Resolves of December 1765: Liberals vs. Radicals," *New-York Historical Society Quarterly,* XLIX (October, 1965), 313–326.

——"Jack Tar in the Streets: Merchant Seamen in the Politics of Revolutionary America," *William and Mary Quarterly,* 3rd Ser., XXV (July, 1968), 371–407.

Levy, Leonard W. "Did the Zenger Case Really Matter? Freedom of the Press in Colonial New York," *William and Mary Quarterly,* 3rd Ser., XVII (January, 1960), 35–50.

Livingston, Edwin Brockholst. *The Livingstons of Livingston Manor,* New York: 1910.

Lovejoy, David S. "Equality and Empire: The New York Charter of Libertyes, 1683," *William and Mary Quarterly,* 3rd Ser., XXI (October, 1964), 493–515.

Lunn, Jean. "The Illegal Fur Trade Out of New France, 1713–60," Canadian Historical Association, *Report,* 1939, pp. 61–76.

Lynd, Staughton. *Anti-Federalism in Dutchess County, New York*. Chicago: Loyola University Press, 1962.

——"The Mechanics in New York City Politics, 1774–1788," *Labor History*, V (Fall, 1964), 225–46.

——"Who Should Rule at Home? Dutchess County, New York, in the American Revolution," *William and Mary Quarterly*, 3rd Ser., XVIII (July, 1961), 330–359.

McAnear, Beverly, ed. "Mr. Robert R. Livingston's Reasons Against a Land Tax," *Journal of Political Economy*, XLVIII (1940), 63–90.

——"Politics in Provincial New York, 1689–1761." Unpublished Ph.D. dissertation, Stanford University, 1935.

McCracken, Henry Noble. *Old Dutchess Forever! The Story of an American County*. New York: Hastings House, 1956.

McKee, Samuel, Jr. *Labor in Colonial New York, 1664–1776*. New York: Columbia University Press, 1935.

McKinley, Albert E. "The English and Dutch Towns of New Netherland," *American Historical Review*, VI (October, 1900), 1–18.

——"The Transition from Dutch to English Rule in New York," *American Historical Review*, VI (July, 1901), 693–724.

Main, Jackson Turner. "Government by the People: The American Revolution and the Democratization of the Legislatures," *William and Mary Quarterly*, 3rd Ser., XXIII (July, 1966), 391–407.

——*The Social Structure of Revolutionary America*. Princeton: Princeton University Press, 1965.

Mark, Irving. *Agrarian Conflicts in Colonial New York, 1711–1775*. New York: Columbia University Press, 1940; Port Washington, New York: Ira J. Friedman, Inc., 1965.

Mason, Bernard. *The Road to Independence: The Revolutionary Movement in New York, 1773–1777*. Lexington, Ky.: University of Kentucky Press, 1966.

Melick, Harry C. W. *The Manor of Fordham and Its Founder*. New York: Fordham University Press, 1950.

Morgan, Edmund S. "The American Revolution: Revisions in Need of Revising," *William and Mary Quarterly*, 3rd Ser., XIV (January, 1957), 3–15.

——The Puritan Ethic and the American Revolution," *William and Mary Quarterly*, 3rd Ser., XXIV (January, 1967), 3–43.

Morris, Richard B. *Government and Labor in Early America*. New York: Columbia University Press, 1946.

——*James DeLancey of New York*, Privately printed.

——, ed., *Select Cases of the Mayor's Court of New York City, 1674–1784*. Washington: 1935.

Nammack, Georgiana C. *Fraud, Politics, and the Dispossession of the Indians: The Iroquois Land Frontier in the Colonial Period*. Norman: University of Oklahoma Press, 1969.

Naylor, Rex M. "The Royal Prerogative in New York, 1691–1775," New York State Historical Association, *Quarterly Journal*, V (July, 1924), 221–255.

Nettels, Curtis P. *The Money Supply of the American Colonies Before 1720*. University of Wisconsin Series in Social Sciences and History, XX, Madison, Wis.: 1934. Reprints of Economic Classics, New York: 1964.

Newbold, Robert C. *The Albany Congress and Plan of Union.* New York: Vantage Press, 1955.

Nissenson, Samuel G. *The Patroon's Domain.* New York: Columbia University Press, 1937.

O'Callaghan, Edmund B. *Origin of Legislative Assemblies.* Albany: Weed, Parsons & Co., 1861.

Order of Colonial Lords of Manors in America, New York Branch, *Publications,* nos. 1–14, 17, 20–21, 23, 25–26. (1914–1935).

Osgood, Herbert L. *The American Colonies in the Seventeenth Century.* 3 vols. New York: 1904–1907.

——*The American Colonies in the Eighteenth Century.* 4 vols. New York: Columbia University Press, 1924–1925.

Palmer, R. R. *The Age of Democratic Revolution.* Vol. I. Princeton: Princeton University Press, 1959.

Pearson, Jonathan. *A History of the Schenectady Patent in the Dutch and English Times.* Albany: J. W. MacMurray, 1883.

Pelletreau, William S. *History of Putnam County, New York, with Biographical Sketches of Its Prominent Men.* Philadelphia: 1886.

Phillips, Hubert. *The Development of a Residential Qualification for Representatives in Colonial Legislatures.* Cincinnati: The Abingdon Press, 1921.

Pole, J. R. *Political Representation in England and the Origins of the American Republic.* New York: St. Martins Press, 1966.

Pope, Franklin L. *The Western Boundary of Massachusetts, A Study of Indian and Colonial History.* Pittsfield, Mass.: 1886.

Pound, Arthur. *Johnson of the Mohawks.* New York: The Macmillan Co., 1930.

Pyrke, Berne A. "The Dutch Fur Traders of Fort Orange and Albany," The Dutch Settlers Society of Albany, *Yearbook,* 1942–1944, XVIII–XIX, 5–19.

Rainbolt, John C. "A 'great and usefull designe': Bellomont's Proposal for New York, 1698–1701," *New-York Historical Society Quarterly,* LIII (October, 1969), 333–351.

Reich, Jerome R. *Leisler's Rebellion, A Study of Democracy in New York, 1664–1720.* Chicago: University of Chicago Press, 1953.

Reubens, Beatrice G. "Pre-Emptive Rights in the Disposition of a Confiscated Estate—Philipsburgh Manor, New York," *William and Mary Quarterly,* 3rd Ser., XXII (July, 1965), 435–456.

Robbins, Caroline. *The Eighteenth-Century Commonwealthman, Studies in the Transmission, Development and Circumstance of English Liberal Thought from the Restoration of Charles II until the War with the Thirteen Colonies.* Cambridge, Mass.: Harvard University Press, 1961.

Rolland, Siegfried B. "Cadwallader Colden, Colonial Politician and Imperial Statesman, 1718–1760." Unpublished Ph.D. Dissertation, University of Wisconsin, 1952.

Runcie, John D. "The Problem of Anglo-American Politics in Bellomont's New York," *William and Mary Quarterly,* 3rd Ser., XXVI (April, 1969), 191–217.

Sabine, Lorenzo. *The American Loyalists, or Biographical Sketches of Adherents to the British Crown in the War of the Revolution.* Boston: Little, Brown Co., 1847.

Scharf, J. Thomas, ed. *History of Westchester County, New York.* 2 vols. Philadelphia: L. E. Preston & Co., 1886.

Schlesinger, Arthur Meier. *The Colonial Merchants and the American Revolution, 1763–1776.* New York: Columbia University Press. 1918.

Schoonmaker, Marius. *The History of Kingston, New York.* New York: Burr Printing House, 1888.

Schutz, John A. *William Shirley, King's Governor of Massachusetts.* Chapel Hill: University of North Carolina Press, 1961.

Schuyler, George W. *Colonial New York.* 2 vols. New York: Charles Scribner's Sons, 1885.

Schwab, John C. *History of the New York Property Tax.* Baltimore: American Economic Association, 1890.

Seligman, Edwin R. A. "The Income Tax in the American Colonies and States," *Political Science Quarterly,* X (June, 1895), 221–247.

Shannon, Sister Anna Madeleine. "General Alexander McDougall, Citizen and Soldier, 1732–1786." Unpublished Ph.D. dissertation, Fordham University, 1957.

Smith, James H. *History of Duchess County, New York with Illustrations and Biographical Sketches of Some of Its Prominent Men and Pioneers.* Syracuse, New York: D. Mason & Co., 1882.

Spaulding, E. Wilder, *New York in the Critical Period, 1783–1789.* New York: Columbia University Press, 1932.

Spencer, Charles Worthen. "The Land System of Colonial New York," *Proceedings* of The New York State Historical Association, XVI (1917), 150–164.

——*Phases of Royal Government in New York, 1691–1719.* Columbus, Ohio: 1905.

——"Sectional Aspects of New York Provincial Politics," *Political Science Quarterly,* XXX (September, 1915), 397–424.

Stevens, John Austin, Jr. *Colonial Records of the New York Chamber of Commerce, 1768–1784, with Historical and Biographical Sketches.* New York: John F. Trow & Co., 1867.

Stiles, Henry R. *The Civil, Political, Professional and Ecclesiastical History and Commercial Record of the County of Kings and the City of Brooklyn, N.Y. from 1683 to 1884.* 2 vols. New York: W. W. Munsell & Co., 1884.

Still, Bayrd. *Mirror for Gotham: New York as Seen by Contemporaries from Dutch Days to the Present.* New York: New York University Press, 1956.

Sutherland, Stella H. *Population Distribution in Colonial America.* New York: Columbia University Press, 1936.

Sydnor, Charles S. *Gentlemen Freeholders.* Chapel Hill: University of North Carolina Press, 1952.

Sylvester, Nathaniel Bartlett. *History of Ulster County, New York, with Illustrations and Biographical Sketches of Its Prominent Men and Pioneers.* Philadelphia: Everts & Peck, 1880.

Thompson, Benjamin F. *History of Long Island.* 3 vols. New York: Robert H. Dodd, 1918.

Trelease, Allen W. *Indian Affairs in Colonial New York: The Seventeenth Century,* Ithaca, New York: Cornell University Press, 1960.

——"The Iroquois and the Western Fur Trade: A Problem in Interpretation,"
Mississippi Valley Historical Review, XLIX (June, 1962), 32–51.

Upton, L. F. S. *The Loyal Whig, William Smith of New York & Quebec.* Toronto, Canada: University of Toronto Press, 1969.

Van Wyck, Frederick. *Select Patents of New York Towns,* Boston: A. A. Beauchamp, 1938.

——*Select Patents of Towns and Manors.* Boston: A. A. Beauchamp, 1938.

Varga, Nicholas. "Election Procedures and Practices in Colonial New York,"
New York History, XLI (1960), 249–277.

——"New York Government and Politics During the Mid-Eighteenth Century."
Unpublished Ph.D. dissertation, Fordham University, 1960.

Vlekke, Bernard H. M. *Evolution of the Dutch Nation.* New York: Roy Publish-
ers, 1945.

Waller, G. M. *Samuel Vetch, Colonial Enterpriser.* Chapel Hill: University of
North Carolina Press, 1960.

Werner, Edgar A. *Civil List and Constitutional History of the Colony and State
of New York.* Albany: Weed, Parsons & Co., 1888.

White, Philip L. *The Beekmans of New York in Politics and Commerce,
1647–1877.* New York: New-York Historical Society, 1956.

——*The Beekman Mercantile Papers, 1746–1799.* 3 vols. New York: New-York
Historical Society, 1956.

Williamson, Chilton. *American Suffrage, from Property to Democracy,
1760–1860.* Princeton: Princeton University Press, 1960.

Wood, Gordon S. *The Creation of the American Republic, 1776–1787.* Chapel
Hill: University of North Carolina Press, 1969.

——"Rhetoric and Reality in the American Revolution," *William and Mary
Quarterly,* 3rd Ser., XXIII (January, 1966), 3–32.

Young, Alfred F. *The Democratic Republicans of New York, The Origins,
1763–1797.* Chapel Hill: University of North Carolina Press, 1967.

INDEX